Grammalepsy

ELECTRONIC LITERATURE

Volume 1

Series editors:
Helen Burgess, Dene Grigar, Rui Torres, María Mencía

Electronic Literature Organization

Grammalepsy

Essays on Digital Language Art

John Cayley

BLOOMSBURY ACADEMIC
NEW YORK • LONDON • OXFORD • NEW DELHI • SYDNEY

BLOOMSBURY ACADEMIC
Bloomsbury Publishing Inc
1385 Broadway, New York, NY 10018, USA
50 Bedford Square, London, WC1B 3DP, UK

BLOOMSBURY, BLOOMSBURY ACADEMIC and the Diana logo are trademarks of
Bloomsbury Publishing Plc

First published in the United States of America 2018
Paperback edition published 2020

Bloomsbury Publishing Inc does not have any control over, or responsibility for, any
third-party websites referred to or in this book. All internet addresses given in this
book were correct at the time of going to press. The author and publisher regret any
inconvenience caused if addresses have changed or sites have ceased to exist, but can
accept no responsibility for any such changes.

Library of Congress Cataloging-in-Publication Data
Names: Cayley, John, author.
Title: Grammalepsy: essays on digital language art / John Cayley.
Description: New York: Bloomsbury Academic, 2018. | Series: Electronic
literature; volume 1 | Includes bibliographical references and index.
Identifiers: LCCN 2018032987 | ISBN 9781501335761 (hardback) |
ISBN 9781501335785 (epdf)
Subjects: LCSH: Hypertext literature—History and criticism. | Literature and
the Internet.
Classification: LCC PN56.I64 C37 2018 | DDC 818/.607—dc23 LC record
available at https://lccn.loc.gov/2018032987

ISBN: HB: 978-1-5013-3576-1
PB: 978-1-5013-6318-4
ePDF: 978-1-5013-3578-5
eBook: 978-1-5013-3577-8

Series: Electronic Literature

Typeset by Integra Software Services Pvt. Ltd.

To find out more about our authors and books visit www.bloomsbury.com
and sign up for our newsletters.

CONTENTS

LIST OF FIGURES

PREFACE

Grammalepsy brings together, for the first time, my selected essays, a number of which are considered formative for the theory and practice of electronic literature. I prefer to reread them within a larger domain of theory and practice: digital language art. Hence the subtitle.

I am a pioneering practitioner of digital language art, poetic in particular, with a research-based practice dating back to the late 1970s. My first for-publication work of digital language art, *wine flying,* was issued on 3.5" floppy disk by my own Wellsweep Press in 1989–90 as well as being installed and exhibited at various venues in the United Kingdom. The same processes of dissemination applied, for example, to *Book Unbound,* 1995. The earliest essay in this collection, "Beyond Codexspace," dates from 1996, and the latest from 2017.

This book is provided with an original introduction that offers its readers what amounts to a theory of aesthetic linguistic practice and also, to an extent, a theory of language itself, one that is intended to be particularly appropriate for the making and critical appreciation of language art in digital media. These collected essays have been gently edited in order to enhance the coherence of the whole. The notes and citations associated with the essays have been more extensively edited, to bring them a little more up-to-date and to ensure that they are as readable and as useable as possible.

The introduction eschews the tendency of literary critics and writers, including theorists and critics of electronic literature, to reduce aesthetic linguistic making—even when it has multimedia affordances—to "writing." Many of the essays collected here were content with this conventional and theoretical catastrophe. I argue that language is media-agnostic, and I take an approach to the philosophy and, indeed, the ontology of language that follows Jacques Derrida in this regard. Language animals, on the other hand, have evolved or learned to make language in only two support media: aurality and grammatological visuality. Our prejudice with regard to literature—that typographic embodiments of language house its uniquely high art—is merely learned, a function of civilization. The art of language, heedless of civilization, is always also embodied in artifacts that exist as aurality, because aural expression correlates with the predisposition of the only language animals of which we are aware: ourselves.

The collection of essays in *Grammalepsy* brings its author and its readers to certain horizons of this thought, a way of thinking that has become possible, historically, due to the rise of digital mediation. Electronic literature or, as I prefer, digital language art allowed aesthetically inclined language makers to embrace a compositional practice that is inextricably involved with digital media, including the computational modulation and generation of text. The *making* of certain linguistic artifacts, not only their presentation, not only their reading, cannot be achieved without digital media and digital affordances. This is clearly demonstrable for a number of important works, including works by myself. Digital textuality cannot be reduced to print-dependent textuality.

Digital mediation will, however, have even greater effects on language and language art. The grammatization of linguistic aurality—enabling indexed access and archive—will, for example, offer our cultures the potential to shift the central focus of its most significant and affective linguistic practice from literature to aurature, not "back" but "forward" to the support medium for language to which human animals are genetically predisposed. The author discovers the process by which this grammatization occurs to be at the heart of linguistic ontology: as *grammalepsis*. We all are in the grip of *Grammalepsy* and we always have been.

ACKNOWLEDGMENTS

Despite our inevitable discontents and the constant vigilance that is required in the struggle to maintain justice and care, institutions sustain us and allow us to do what we do. There are a number of institutions, within which I have worked, that have supported me in this way, first and foremost the institution of the university, in its general form, which I fear is unjustly under threat these days. My studies at the University of Durham, in Chinese language and civilization, were publicly funded. I can acknowledge with some pleasure both this university and the state that allowed me to discover linguistic computation early on in my career, and particularly the late Archie Barnes, my teacher. Then, there is the British Library, where I worked for a time; and Hanshan Tang Books in London, a tiny institution. Its founder-owner Christer von der Burg took a special interest in the culture of computation and I couldn't have done some of what I have without my colleagues at the Tang and Christer's support. Special thanks are also due to Jerome Rothenberg and Pierre Joris who, close to the beginning of it all, included poetic extracts of "Reveal Code" in their "institutional" *Poems for the Millennium, 2*. Most importantly, however, Brown University and what is now its Department of Literary Arts continue to employ me and have sustained this work full-time since 2007. Robert Coover made it all possible, "as the world knows Bob period."

I am daunted at the prospect of making a list of all those other individuals who have helped me with my work or helped me to understand it better. In large measure I'm going to let the alphabet excuse me from the burden of invidious fine distinctions, and use it to make two lists: one for those people who, I somehow feel, have been more directly concerned with what appears in this book, and a second list for those with whom I have enjoyed sharing the broader endeavor that is represented by this book and related work. So, in the first place, my acknowledgments and thanks go out to: Espen Aarseth, Sandy Baldwin, Philippe Bootz, Douglas Cape, cris cheek, Florian Cramer, Johanna Drucker, Markku Eskelinen, Aden Evens, Penny Florence, Chris Funkhouser, Loss Pequeño Glazier, N. Katherine Hayles, Daniel C. Howe, David Jhave Johnston, Nick Montfort, Judd Morrissey, Giles Perring, Søren Pold, Manuel Portela, Rita Raley, Joan Retallack, Scott Rettberg, Francisco J. Ricardo, Andrew Michael Roberts, Jim Rosenberg, Roberto Simanowski, Brian Kim Stefans, Stephanie Strickland, Joseph Tabbi, Eugenio Tisselli,

Clement Valla, Noah Wardrip-Fruin. And also to: Mark Amerika, Caroline Bergvall, Charles Bernstein, Tim Bewes, Friedrich Block, Stephanie Boluk, Mauro Carassai, Wendy Chun, Maria Damon, Lori Emerson, Maria Engberg, Jerome Fletcher, Luciana Gattass, Harry Gilonis, Simon Gunn, Terry Harpold, Robert E. Harrist Jr., Ian Hatcher, Will Hicks, Romana Huk, Elizabeth James, Michael Joyce, Eduardo Kac, Andrew Klobucar, Raine Koskimaa, Mark Leahy, Patrick LeMieux, Alan Liu, Talan Memmott, Maria Mencia, Adalaide Morris, Stuart Moulthrop, Robert Mosley, Elli Mylonas, Chris Novello, Eric Dean Rasmussen, Denise Riley, Massimo Riva, Will Rowe, Jörgen Schaefer, Bill Seaman, Álvaro Seiça Neves, Ana Marques da Silva, Hazel Smith, Braxton Soderman, Alan Sondheim, Ben Swanson, Thomas Swiss, Illya Szilak, Lori Talley, Steve Tomasula, Patricia Tomaszek, Greg Ulmer, John Welch, Yang Lian. I should say that a number of these people have been my students but that, in addition, I owe a great debt of gratitude to *all* my students, all of whom have helped me think and make.

With regard to this publication and its production, it is a pleasure to thank my instantly helpful and responsive initial editor at Bloomsbury Academic, Mary Al-Sayed, and also Katie Gallof and Erin Duffy who took charge of the book in its final stages.

Finally, to Joanna Howard, for everything, and in particular for believing that, after all this, I might still finish my vampire novel.

These essays appeared over an extended period in a wide range of magazines, journals, and online resources. Details follow (with more information in the bibliography). I would like to thank the editors and publishers for their generous reception of the work and for their kind permission, where necessary, to reproduce the essays here.

"Beyond Codexspace." Apart from its original publication in the journal *Visible Language*, 1996, this essay was translated into Finnish for *Parnasso*, 3 (1999), pp. 290–302, and was also collected, with revisions, for *Media Poetry: An International Anthology*, 2007, edited by Eduardo Kac.

"Pressing the 'REVEAL CODE' Key" was published, 1996, in one of the first online-only academic journals, *EJournal*. (This term is now almost as impossible to search effectively on the internet as would be "Journal" as an eponymous proper name.)

"Of Programmatology," came out, 1998, in the radical London-based new media arts and culture magazine, *Mute*.

"The Code Is Not the Text (Unless It Is the Text)" was originally sketched out for the "p0es1s: Poetics of digital text" symposion [*sic*], held in Erfurt, September 28–29, and first published, 2002, in the *Electronic Book Review*, a vital journal for the field of electronic literature and digital language art.

"Hypertext/Cybertext/Poetext" was presented as a paper at the conference "Assembling Alternatives," University of New Hampshire, Durham, August 29–September 2, 1996. This conference was important for introducing a transatlantic community of experimental writers, chiefly poets, to digital language art. I maintain an online, mildly transactive, version of the essay on my personal website at http://programmatology.shadoof.net/works/ hypercyberpoetext/. This includes the accompanying, generated mesostic text, "X," not reprinted here, which was, however, included in the book of conference proceedings, *Assembling Alternatives: Reading Postmodern Poetries Transnationally*, 2003, edited by Romana Huk. Reprinted by permission of Wesleyan University Press.

"Writing on Complex Surfaces." This essay was first presented as a paper at the 6th Digital Arts & Culture conference, held at the IT University in Copenhagen, December 1–3, 2005. It was then published in the online journal, also crucial for our field, *dichtung digital*, 2005, edited by Roberto Simanowski.

"Time Code Language" is loosely based on a presentation to the "New Media Poetics" conference, held at the University of Iowa, October 11–12, 2002, facilitated by Thomas Swiss and Adelaide (Dee) Morris, to whom, along with Sarah Townsend, I owe a debt of thanks for their comments on early drafts. Thanks are also due to N. Katherine Hayles for her correspondence, comments, and unstinting intellectual generosity. Professors Swiss and Morris went on to edit *New Media Poetics: Contexts, Technotexts, and Theories*, 2006, in which the essay was first published. Reprinted by permission of MIT Press.

"The Gravity of the Leaf" was first presented as "Surface Text: Text as Surface in Immersive 3D Environments" for the "Beyond the Screen" conference devoted to the aesthetics and criticism of digital literature, Siegen, Germany, November 19–21, 2008. I am grateful to Sandy Baldwin and, especially, to Francisco J. Ricardo for reading drafts of the essay in its present form and offering helpful and stimulating comments. Proceedings of the conference were later published in *Beyond the Screen: Transformations of Literary Structures, Interfaces and Genres*, 2010, edited by Peter Gendolla and Jörgen Schäfer. Reprinted by permission of Transcript Verlag.

"Writing to Be Found and Writing Readers" is based on and extended from a presentation entitled "Edges of Chaos: Writing to Be Found" for a workshop at the University of Bergen, Norway, November 8–10, 2009. The final essay resulted from a keynote paper at the *Futures of Digital Studies* conference, University of Florida, February 25–27, 2010. It was first published in 2011 by *Digital Humanities Quarterly*.

"Weapons of the Deconstructive Masses (WDM)." This paper was originally prepared as a presentation for: "Visionary Landscapes," a conference of the Electronic Literature Organization, May 29–June 1, 2008, Vancouver, Washington. A number of colleagues and friends have read this paper since it was first presented. I would like to thank Roberto Simanowski and Aden Evens for particularly detailed and helpful comments. A version of the first part of the paper was published, 2009, in the online journal

Hyperrhiz: New Media Cultures, and the full essay was first published, 2011, in *Revista de Estudos Literários*.

"Terms of Reference & Vectoralist Transgressions" was published, 2013, in the online journal *Amodern*.

"Reading and Giving—Voice and Language" was first published in a special issue of the journal, *Performance Research*, "On Writing and Digital Media," edited by Jerome Fletcher, 2013. Reprinted by permission of Taylor & Francis Ltd.

"Reconfiguration" was published, 2017, in a special issue of the online journal *Humanities*, "The Poetics of Computation," edited by Burt Kimmelman and Andrew Klobucar.

"At the End of Literature." This is the second, final, and independent part of a longer piece published as "The Advent of Aurature and the End of (Electronic) Literature" in *The Bloomsbury Handbook of Electronic Literature*, 2017, edited by Joseph Tabbi. Reprinted here by kind permission of the editor and Bloomsbury Academic.

Grammalepsy: An Introduction

It was only a few months prior to the gathering of these chapters that I discovered that I had grammalepsy. Or, rather, I determined that we are all of us, language animals, in the grip of this condition. We are seized by it, and singled out in its thrall, whenever we encounter or make more of the language, the languages, that we have. Linguists, historians of language, scientists studying evolution, philosophers, and philosophers of language are all able to affirm that human beings "have" language, but this is one of the very few things on which they do agree and they do so, in part, as an admission of ignorance—concerning essential details of the when, the how, the why, and, in particular, the what of this species-unique facility—not a trait exactly, because it *requires* interaction. Language cannot exist for one without others.

So, we—the plural is essential—have, and can use, and can make things with, language. And some philosophers of language also suggest that it has us, or that we dwell within it; that language uses and forms us. We live, in any case, in relations with language that alternate and unravel in terms of who or what determines the practices and performances of whoever or whatever we are—languages and ourselves—when we speak and read. Rather than taking a determinate, prescription-inducing stance on the nature and characteristics of some predominant relationship between humans and language (or language and humans), I preferred, even before discovering that I had grammalepsy, to work with language as a maker, as if it was my medium, and, thus, to learn about language in practice. I compared my practice with that of other makers in other media. And occasionally, I also made other kinds of artifacts in other media.

One of the things that I learned about language is that its "materiality" is singular, or, rather, that the way in which language comes to be is singular—embodied by and fashioned to exist as humanly perceptible material phenomena.[1] For, whatever language is, it cannot be identified—essentially or substantively—with anything that is materially perceptible to us. Obviously, I'm bracketing certain conceptions of materiality—placing materiality into the phenomenological *epoché*. This will be clear to you because, for a start, I am trying to engage, explicitly, with an ontology of language. I say that language exists. Moreover, I accept many aspects of what would be characterized as a "materialist" philosophy of language in that, for example, I can work with the notion of "semiotic material," and I believe that linguistic artifacts have real effects, not only in so far as they operate symbolically or in terms of signification, but also in terms of their affective force, the force of language.

Grammalepsy is, as I say, a condition of language animals. It is not a pathology, unless we think of language itself as a pathology (as some people do, despite the likelihood that thinking itself must suffer, necessarily, from the same malaise). Grammalepsy is, nonetheless, a symptom of our "having" language. And it does, I believe, bear a relationship with pharmacology. It may be poisonous for certain aspects of human experience at certain times and, all at once, it may be rendered experientially therapeutic when administered with care. The condition is symptomatic of a process, grammalepsis, that I have come to understand as constitutive for linguistic ontology. We behave and we gesture—we set out to inscribe—in our attempts to make language, but language as such only comes into being when we succeed in grammalepsis, when our gestures become readable—to ourselves and to others—when they can be read as the grammē of (a) language.

Another way of putting this is simply to say that language comes into being as a function of reading. I do not, of course, mean by this that language, somehow, depends on writing for its existence. The gestures of inscription that I speak of are heedless of support media—with which, as I've already said, language cannot be identified. These gestures are referred to grammatology, within which writing as such serves to provide us with a better way of understanding the practices of language in terms of their general principles (and the metaphysical consequences). Writing has, historically, materialized differently with respect to speech, but reading—grammaleptic reading, the reading of grammē—has remained what it was, regardless of actual linguistic practices in visually perceptible graphics. The etymology of "[to]read," in English, supports this media agnosticism, deriving (as I read it) from something like the ability to make well-advised, convincing guesses.

If we are happy to say (in plain English) that reading brings language into being, then what is the point of inventing a new word for an implicated symptom? What is the point of grammalepsy? For one thing, the intimate association of reading with actual, historical writing is a problem for us. It nudges us toward a misdirection to which we have already alluded. Our civilizations are founded on writing and thus also on reading (of literal graphic forms), but our civilizations are as nothing when compared with the eventualities of biological evolution that gave us—that allowed us to "have"—language. And our evolutionary disposition is unlikely to change any time soon. The brain plasticity that allows us to adopt literal reading and writing with extraordinary facility does not imply that we have evolved with respect to language.

More pragmatically, there are the implications of "-lepsis." This suffix captures and expresses an important overall characteristic of the manifold processes of reading that bring language into being. It suggests seizure, sudden seizure, the "grasp" of something that we experience as we encounter elements of language that we can understand or can use to understand. This characteristic of grammaleptic reading is, I believe, underappreciated and possesses significant theoretical potential. It indicates the threshold, for example, between expressive gesture and actual language. Gesture remains gesture until, suddenly, it is seized by grammalepsy and thus becomes a sign within the discrete, structured world of language, within a particular language. In the case of sign languages, this abstract analogy becomes "literal." Gestures made by someone who does not know a natural sign language remain gestures. But once they are grasped within a practice of language, they become, suddenly, something different. They become language. Grammalepsy helps us to locate and specify the horizons of language.

Grammalepsy also helps to explain how and when phenomenon with wildly various, apparently continuous interrelations of substance and form can suddenly be grasped and read as signs. Or, rather, it cannot explain exactly "how" this happens but it reminds us that it happens suddenly—I used to think and say, *catastrophically*—once substantive forms have, in their shifting morphologies, passed a threshold that causes them to be recognized as: distinct phonemes or letters, words, phrases, clauses, sentences. Past this threshold, substantive forms that were once in the world of material things are suddenly also in the world of language.[2] And once they have entered language, unless they lose or abandon the form that they have achieved—a phonologically or orthographically readable shape—they cannot go back. They will remain distinctly separated from other forms, even forms of the same material substance, in so far as they remain readable.

If we consider certain problems of language in general—with respect to translation for example—and (other) natural languages ("other" in the sense of those that we do not know), grammalepsy also helps us. Why should a language that we do not know be so absolutely incomprehensible to us despite our sense that the people who know it are talking and writing about the same experiences? Grammalepsy suggests that, at every level of linguistic structure, there is no reason for any of the forms in another language to be graspable, to be readable, *until they (suddenly) are*—until they are learned, known, and seized upon—since, until they are, these forms are simply gestures, just unreadable parts of our perceptual world, gesturing toward language, without having reached its threshold, not, at least, for us.[3]

Why set out, in an introduction to this book, by proposing and then beginning to explain a new term that is designed for a philosophy of language? Because it helps me to understand what I have done and what I was trying to do while making the aesthetic work that underpins much of the theory in these expositions. Specifically, grammalepsy helps me to grasp important characteristics of my chosen medium, and, because I also work with digital media—networked and programmable media—it is crucial, I believe, to be able to single out a particular medium and determine what it is that I am doing with it, especially when aesthetics are at stake. Grammalepsy reminds me that it is precisely the sudden change it makes to the materiality of a medium—at the moment of grammalepsis—that brings language into being and thus, ontologically, distinguishes it from any and all substantive media within which it must, nonetheless, simultaneously, be embodied. If my concern is an art of language, then it follows that I will work with language and with digital media in the knowledge that the latter will influence and inflect the when and the how and the why of grammalepsis but not necessarily the what of the language that grammalepsis brings into being—the language that is made readable. My aesthetic responsibilities for language art and for its digital situation are distinct. This practical and theoretical orientation is quite different from that of many other practitioners in the field that usually goes by the name of electronic literature.

Because of its explicit association with grammatology, grammalepsy also helps me to recall and maintain the principle of media agnosticism with respect to language art, to apply this principle whenever writing and literature are evoked. Writing and literature are overdetermined by their implicit media—archival publication in print, and practices of writing in a visuality that is constrained, typically, to literary forms or, of necessity, to literal forms. As the final chapter of this selection, "At the End of Literature," claims, I believe that one of the most significant future cultural potentialities—as digital affordances continue to be applied to language—will be the reconfiguration of the relationship between language practices and their predominant support media. In principle, the digitalization of culture will give rise to an aurature that is able to contest the traditional sovereign claims of literature.

For the practice of language art in digital media, grammalepsy lends us perspective on a particular and a particularly critical issue. This is the question of the status, the ontology, the significance and affect of the synthetic, or, perhaps, virtual "language" that is generated by algorithmic processes. Related questions are taken up by the chapter "Reading and Giving," within which grammalepsy is discussed before, as it were, I had learned what best to call it. Not all the practices of digital language art call for "text generation." Indeed, much that is produced or studied as "electronic literature" bears little relation with computation that is compositionally involved with fashioning its incorporated language. On the other hand, algorithmic text generation, translation, and reconfiguration are all important in my own work and in that of a number of colleagues, some of whose work is discussed here. Moreover, since the passing of an AI (artificial intelligence) winter into its spring during the 2010s, the ascendency and popularization of natural language processing (NLP), the aggregation of vast quantities of statistically analyzed "big data" for natural languages, and the application of neural net and recursive neural net technologies to linguistic corpora, all of these factors and others mean that there is an ocean of generated artificial language out there, especially on the internet, ostensibly readable by language animals. This is a world of materially existing linguistic forms within which digital language artists must now make their own interventions and artifacts. Grammalepsy offers, in this context, a way of reflecting on and perhaps judging the relative artificiality or virtuality of algorithmically generated language. For, although all literally inscribed (and thus encoded) language has been grasped by a symbolic order that is continuous with contemporary computation, grammalepsy indicates an analogous but distinct process that is defined by reading, the reading performed by the only language animals that are known to us. When elements of language are grasped and thus brought into being as language through grammalepsis, this is *not* to say, reductively, that they have (just) been "parsed" and processed by a formal computational system. The material presence of language-like tokens within encoded computational structures does not guarantee their linguistic ontology—not until, in some manner, grammalepsis has also taken place. Within the computational order, traces of actual language and tokens of synthetic or virtual language are materially indistinguishable, but this does not mean that they are the same thing. And it is vital, in my opinion, that human readers remain capable of distinguishing actual language from synthetic "language," especially those readers who are also practitioners and theorists of digital language art.

There is also, simply, the reason—for introducing grammalepsy in this introduction—that it represents thinking and theory to which my practice has brought me. It is an outcome in itself, part of a final, if unfinished, chapter.

The essays selected for these chapters span a relatively lengthy period of time—from the mid-1990s down to the time of writing, in the late 2010s—longer than might be expected of comparable collections. Given the pace of change in digitally mediated culture, this period may seem even longer, one during which its early artifacts must surely appear to have dated significantly if not catastrophically. I was pleasantly surprised to find that, although much of the work referred to in these pages has ceased to be supported on contemporary platforms, its underlying principles of composition and the associated theory still have something to offer.

This book is by someone who identifies, first, as a practitioner, a translator and poet-turned-digital poet and (digital) language artist. But I am the kind of practitioner who never works without a more or less articulated theoretical understanding of what it is that I am trying to do, and I have endeavored to take this self-reflexive understanding seriously, siting it in the context of literary criticism, poetics, critical theory, and cultural studies. The essays collected here always aimed to be engaged with their proximate critical discourses. They do, however, gravitate around my own production, and thus, this self-reflexive theory tends to involve more reference to my own work than to that of my colleagues. This selection's first chapter, "Beyond Codexspace," is, in particular, more of a description of work, more of an artist's talk, than a developed thought or argument. This is excusable, I trust, in so far as it provides the reader with some initial context, by populating the book with initial examples of practice for which, at the time, literary and poetic theory barely accounted.

I have, of course, reread all of the chapters in this book and done a little light editing of their main texts. There is more of this for the earlier chapters, rendering their allusions to contemporary circumstances a little more relevant, or general, or up-to-date. The notes throughout have been more extensively edited. To the best of my knowledge and abilities, I've brought references, especially internet references, up-to-date. I've also tried to use URLs that will persist, and I have checked for accessibility, and included most recent access dates in the bibliography. Links for which I was responsible but which have broken since first publication have been repaired or substituted. I have had to remove a few links that were irreparable, and I apologize in anticipation of those broken links that will surely remain.

There are a number of obsessions that run in threads throughout these chapters. By way of brief introduction, I will follow some of these threads, aiming to touch on each of the chapters at least once, where appropriate, and link their thinking to the more general entanglement.

From well before the 1990s and even today, after more than two decades of hyperhistory, the media that concern us—networked and programmable media in my terms—have been characterized as "new." Newly perceptible phenomena call for—and are brought into language by—new terms, and the field within which I have practiced and theorized is beset with the problem of naming. I was and am as much a part of the problem as anyone. In 2008, I tried to settle some of the issues in the "Weapons of the Deconstructive Masses" (WDM) but singularly failed, since I hadn't then come up with the term with which I am now content. The field I work within is "digital language art." "Literary art" is a highly privileged subfield of language art, but this name concedes relations with both literal media ([typo]graphic media) and "the literary" as an assertion of cultivated values which are implicated with particular canons and traditions of practice. "Language art" specifies a medium without the implicit commitment to particular support media, while "art," at the head of the phrase, asserts a pragmatic intimacy with art as it is practiced in other media. I always balked at "electronic" and at all the various "e-" and "i-" prefixes. Except by analogy with "electronic music" (where "electronic" indicates technicity and a very wide range of actual electronic sound-making and recording instruments), it seemed to me foolish for aesthetic language practices to establish inappropriate material associations from the get-go, especially in the context of computation, given the latter's singular, problematic materiality. But just as electronic music has an established tradition and nomenclature (although for longer than its literary bedfellow), electronic literature has now, along with a canon of sorts, an established place in the academy and, to an extent, in the world of letters.

As for the "digital" of digital language art, this is also a problem given that an art of language is our purpose. The last chapter in this book—although concerning itself only minimally with these questions of naming—states it clearly, "The digital ... is not a medium. More precisely, it is not a medium of interest to the majority of theorists or practitioners of those arts for which language is the medium." In the future, I expect digital language art to go the way of digital art. There is art, but no one need mention that it is "digital" because art is simply part of a culture that is also, inevitably, historically digital, and these circumstances have little to tell us concerning the significance or affect of the art as such.

Apart from in "WDM," questions surrounding nomenclature are taken up, particularly, in "Beyond Codexspace," "Of Programmatology," and "Hyper/Cybertext/Poetext." Summarizing, I preferred "digital" to "electronic" and, albeit hopelessly, "programmaton" for "computer." "Programmatology" is a more or less playful and obvious allusion to Jacques Derrida's "grammatology." For a time, once having settled in a university department for which "creative writing" underlay, institutionally, its "literary arts," I determined to call what I did with my colleagues and students "writing digital media," but I have abandoned even the nice ambiguities of this phrase's grammar and its medial hostage to fortune, as outlined above. One of the phrases for which I credit myself and which I still find useful is "networked and programmable media." The programmability of both compositional and delivery media—once encoded instantiations of substantive media became available—was and is something that distinguishes these media and their potentialities. The actual creation *by these same programmable media* of what we now think of as *the* network, and their broadcast life in the new world of information, gave programmable media overwhelming quantifiable power by which, in practice, they are also specified and qualified. Not "digital" then, but "programmable" and "networked." The insufficiently anticipated non-mutuality of emergent network architectures is another matter, and we will return to this.

Initially, "cybertext"—which no longer seems to figure despite the continuing influence of Espen Aarseth's eponymous monograph—presented itself as a much more inclusive and catholic term as compared with "hypertext" when these circulated together in the first decade of accessible digital language art. I associated hypertext with the long-form fiction that predominated in the mid-1990s and early 2000s, during the initial, broader dissemination of digitally mediated writing (writing as it most definitely then was). Given my background in the translation of poetry (from Chinese) and also as a poet per se, I was resistant to the predominance of a form that was, programmatically, formally, and poetically straightforward, relatively so, and that remained largely uninvolved with the composition—the generation and modulation—of a work's constitutive language. My work was part of an informal factional intervention that encouraged practitioners who were beginning to self-identify as electronic writers to involve themselves with historically contextualized poetics, especially experimental and innovative poetics, and, at the same time, to encourage poetic practitioners to take digital mediation seriously with regard to both criticism and composition. "Pressing the 'REVEAL CODE' Key," "Of Programmatology," in particular "Hypertext/Cybertext/Poetext," and "Time Code Language" are all situated at this juncture, offering both critique and collaborative common ground.

"The Code Is Not the Text (Unless It Is the Text)" is my most influential essay in the field. It is impossible to discount or exaggerate what code and coding can and will do for practices of language. This chapter, however, asks us to tread carefully when we try to understand the relationships between practices of coding and practices of language, to know what we are doing when we treat one as the other, or acknowledge a hybrid "codework." My position is still that code is not natural, human language at any level. Code is practiced entirely within the framework of formal, usually Turing-complete computer languages, but "language" in this phrase has a constrained and far different meaning to the one it has, even in everyday speech. The elements and formal structures of code can be easily introduced into language, but the elements and structures (even the formally expressible structures) of language cannot easily be introduced into code as such (other than as quoted strings) and, if they could be, then the code would no longer be code. "The Code Is Not the Text" asks language artists who work in programmable media to remember what they are working with.

In common with many artists who have, at some point, identified themselves as writers, I am fascinated by the surface(s) on which we write. For most of us, this resolves to a fascination with the book and its culture, an extraordinary world, with no sign of ending any time soon. Jacques Derrida's expansive notions concerning what "the book" and "paper" may still become have more distant horizons than those of many more materially focused critiques. Clearly, however, those of us who work with programmable media present themselves with strangely mediated surfaces, as well as with innovative instruments that inscribe these surfaces. Today, in the developed world, this is, essentially, true for all writers.[4] A screen, displaying a surface, usually made up of light-colored pixels, is interrupted and thus "inscribed" with dark-colored pixels. On the one hand, it appears to us that the surfaces on which we write have become impossibly complex at levels beyond our perceptual horizons; on the other, linguistic inscription is, as it always was, a play of the most fundamental and abstract possible difference—dark against light, 0 and 1.

Quite apart from screens, I have also had the privilege of working with writing—language art—for immersive stereo 3D audiovisual instruments. In the graphics world that these instruments project, language can be inscribed in the articulated light of artificial space, perceptible to us as like the space within which we live habitually. In "The Gravity of the Leaf" and "Writing on Complex Surfaces," I discuss this aspect of my practice and attempt to explore the potential "complexities" of inscription's surfaces. There are important problems here, which these chapters do not resolve, and do not do so, perhaps in part, for strategic, pragmatic reasons. My understanding of the complex surface took inspiration from my reading of Joan Retallack as cited at the beginning of "Writing on Complex Surfaces." But for writers and poets, like Retallack, the "complexity" of the writing surface is figurative—although no less real in terms of significance and affect—and this may be all it ever needs to be. Poetic practices—or the "poethical" practices that Retallack proposes—are more than enough to render the inscribed surface as fractal, invaginated, complex. In digital language art, the complexity of a writing surface can be actualized (shying away from the overdetermination of "literalized"), but may nonetheless risk performing a "(philosophically) 'thin' literal materiality."[5] This risk, when combined with underappreciation of language's singular materiality—its ontological distinction from its support media—can create problems for the critical reading of digital language art.

A particular variety of practice, emergent from my engagement with the inscription of graphic language in artificial 3D, remains unambiguously complex for me in terms of inscriptional surfaces. This kind of practice takes place at the horizon of text and paratext and is characterized by the (mis)placing of textual or figurative graphic forms such that they themselves become surfaces for inscription. In the world of 2D graphics, the work of Saul Bass represents exemplary practice of this kind, in designs where flat figurative forms not only provide paratextual, design-functional "rules" but also make surfaces for letter-formed words. In immersive virtual reality (or simply on the 2D-for-3D of the computer screen), graphic forms can be made both to give passage into spaces that are "beyond" the surfaces on which they appear to be inscribed, while simultaneously serving as surfaces for the graphic forms of inscriptions that may be indeterminately situated. So long as they are readable, they could be either "in front of" or "beyond, through the window of" the forms-serving-as-surfaces that support their readability. My maquette, *Lens*, demonstrates this complexity. From the perspective of language art, it is important to note that, whatever the modeled spatial arrangement of the graphic elements may be, when they become readable as language, their spatial relations collapse for the purposes of taking up existence on the singular surface of language. Or, in other words, through grammalepsis, as we read what they say, these forms *become* language and allow us to enter the linguistic dimension of experience. For me, such phenomena, actually perceptible in immersive virtual reality, create a conceptual rhyme with certain believers' experience of the icon. An icon is not a representation; it is a threshold, a form that gives access to the thing itself, allowing the artist and believer not only to see but to have direct experience of the deity.[6] In the same way, and just as mysteriously, graphic forms may be arranged to become language, to bring it into being for a reader, or, on the other hand, to remove it from their experience.

Throughout these chapters and in the underlying work, one constant has been a desire and ambition, shared with other artists and theorists, to demonstrate and articulate the specificities of digitally mediated practices of aesthetic language. The singularity, as I see it, of linguistic ontology and the manner in which this determines its relations with the actual material culture of language makes it difficult to assert these specificities. Grammaleptic reading is reading no matter when and how it occurs, and it is this reading, fundamentally, that constitutes language. Thus the specificities of linguistic practice in digital media are, precisely, matters of culture; they require that the institution of reading is cultivated in new ways and that new ways of reading are brought into the institution as a whole.

The chapter within which there is the most concerted effort to make claims for a specific type of digitally mediated language art and an associated practice of reading is "Time Code Language." It remains the case, I believe, that time and language art—the restructuring of the culture of human time with respect to reading—is one of the dimensions of language art practice where digital mediation has come to play a crucial and undeniable role, changing, qualitatively, our understanding and appreciation of language art. Composed (pre-composed, pro-grammed), not only performed, linguistic artifacts are able to exist as materially temporal artifact-events thanks to the affordances of computer and screen (in the form of distribution now most familiar to us). "Text in digital media can move and change. It's as simple as that."[7] This makes possible, as set out in "Writing on Complex Surfaces" and in works of mine like *overboard* and *translation*, an ambient poetics, and it demands that literary criticism accept the existence of linguistic artifacts for which there is no definitive text or edition in the conventional sense. Literary critics will have to learn to read certain "texts" as pieces in time, as experiences, like music or like film. It's ironic that a sophisticated criticism of film, in particular, has flourished in humanities departments for which the study and appreciation of literature conventionally and typically demands a textual criticism that forecloses the potential for certain expressive temporalities of its texts.

With "Writing to Be Found" and "Terms of Reference" the theoretical impetus shifts—along with that of my underlying practice—from the ways in which language relates to its compositional and delivery media along with what these media's digital affordances make possible or necessary for aesthetic language, toward a deep concern with the effects of the digitalization of culture on practices of language, including practices of aesthetic language. The ideas behind "Writing to Be Found" predate "big data" and the civil-scale architecture of computation, within which we now live, that I call "Big Software." These ideas predate, that is, a more general critical awareness of cultural circumstances that do now circulate, as of the late 2000s and 2010s. My views on these circumstances are quite clearly and explicitly set out in "Terms of Reference" and also in an interview I gave for an important gathering of academics' and artists' views on digital media and digital culture.[8] "Writing to Be Found" helped me realize that practices of language had already changed; I would venture paradigmatically, regardless of any instruments for composition or delivery, because, in the developed world, the situation of human beings with respect to culturally powerful frameworks for language use had changed. This thought can be summed up by saying that, in "Writing to Be Found," "Google is our point of reference." It is not only that I made a specific intervention using Google, I discovered, for myself and I hope for others, crucial implications of acknowledging that Google is our linguistic point of reference, generally. Whatever else you may say (and there is much more to say about these matters than I am able even to attempt), our points of reference—for writing, for practices of (authorized) language—had moved out of the library and away from the books archived there, and onto the internet, in the questionable—all-too-little-questioned— "care" of huge, private service providers, "GAFA" as the French have it: Google, Amazon, Facebook, Apple, and so on. I won't reiterate what is in the chapters here or try to say more. My main point is that if your points of reference have changed, then your writing, your practices of language have changed. One consequence is that the executive branches of government in certain countries are conducting business and garnering popular support on Twitter—courting institutional aporia and virtual tyranny.

As I see it, if they do not already, then it will not be long before software architectures of global scope and power—privately owned and managed— will shape and structure the culture, as a whole, of the developed world. This seems to me an extraordinary thing to say and yet the extent to which it is already the case is remarkable. I'm not so much talking about any determination of, for example, what counts as an artifact or artwork—not at this stage. But where and how an artifact circulates and the frameworks within which it is made, these contexts are already significantly beholden to super-managed networked services. Of immediate, civil and political concern is the manner in which the culture of our polity itself is or could be super-managed, with instantaneous effects that would, inevitably, be ideologically implicated, and also historical in the sense of changing what happens. Consider the effect on media in the Anglophone world if Twitter reconfigured their software architecture to make all accounts equal, with followers universally limited to humanly appreciable numbers. Consider effects of the fact that such a policy is not instituted in Twitter's current software architectures.

The penultimate chapter in this selection, "Reconfiguration," acknowledges related aspects of what I take to be artists' historical circumstances toward the end of the second decade of the twenty-first century. The culture within which artists work has, in the developed world, been reconfigured by global software architectures that control and channel the human attention that may or may not be directed toward art. The scale and power of this architecture is now commensurate with corresponding institutions of the pre-digital era. In a sense, little has changed for innovative or experimental practitioners, who must still compete with, and perhaps oppose, popular and persistent cultural forms. The programmability of computation, however, appears to encourage innovation both in terms of realizable potential and simply because the culture of software values innovation for itself. In these circumstances and because "configuration" is an appropriately resonant technical term within hardware and software development, the chapter "Reconfiguration" suggests that artists, particularly artists working with and against digital media, already do—and should self-consciously— characterize their practice as "reconfigurationist." A trope that I take to be typical of this kind of practice is also identified, the "symbolic image," a configuration of image—or whatever is considered "content"—with, as it were, embedded symbolic, often algorithmic, process. This is an abstracted form that I take to underlie a wide range of art that is now digital, and it is a form that lends itself to reconfiguration.

The final chapter, in the grip of grammalepsy, is aurature, "At the End of Literature." It speaks for itself, and, like the other chapters in this selection, represents the result of an engagement with experimental aesthetic practice— my efforts to reconfigure the emergent software architectures of transactive synthetic language. It makes a number of significant claims that I continue to find compelling despite—tumbling within the breaking waves of constant, self-consciously disruptive, and unprecedentedly powerful technological innovation—the difficultly of deciding which fascinating innovation will actually survive and bring some shape to our shared experience. But listening and speaking together are constitutive of what we are—as language animals and as makers of language art. Now that networked computational processes present themselves in located, (even minimally) socialized physical bodies and now that they listen like we do and give voice as the mark of humanoid embodiment, I think that we and they have reached a threshold, perhaps one that we thought was a horizon. Grammalepsy should be read as a condition of shared human life. It characterizes experiences that are preformed and, necessarily, shared by human animals as we become, continually, language animals, as perceptible forms that we fashion suddenly give us access to a symbolically structured human world, a world that is more human because it is suddenly more language. Who or what else do we believe might live in this world with us? Who or what else can read, can perform grammalepsis? Or, on the other hand, might we be cured of our grammalepsy and driven out of human language into a desert of symbolic exchange?

1

Beyond Codexspace: Potentialities of Literary Cybertext

The use and abuse of visible language—or writing in the broadest sense—began, in the 1990s, to undergo huge, unprecedented, still continuing growth.[1] This growth takes place in what was once called cyberspace, in what many critics still consider an environment that is hostile to cultivated letters—hostile, at the very least, to the traditional and still pre-eminent delivery media which made language visible to civilized language animals. The still narrow bandwidth of networks in the 1990s and the limited capabilities of affordable interfaces meant that encoded text became the dominant medium of information exchange on computer-based networks. And to communicate over these networks, people still, predominantly, write and read. That is, they compose (literary) texts and publish them in cyberspace, where they are read, usually in silence, by friends, colleagues, and the general public.[2] All this has stimulated the emergence of an exuberant mass of new forms and proto-genres of visible language: Listserv mailing lists, online conferences or "chat" zones, MOO spaces, and so on. The advent of the World Wide Web extended and articulated networked literary production to include typographic and other concrete design aspects of textuality. However, the vast majority of this visible language is not seen by its writers or readers as belonging to "literary" or "artistic" production in the canonical sense. "Serious" literary hypertext came to exist and has been practiced to an extent.[3] However, it is perhaps more significant, in cultural terms, that the new quasi-ephemeral forms of non-literary visual language have exerted an increasing influence on self-consciously literary production, in what might be characterized as the real-time realization of contemporary criticism's postmodern intertextual ideals.[4]

But this temporary state of affairs, this momentary window of opportunity for the partisans of visible language, cannot last. As the bandwidth widens, as the audiovisual takes over from the keyboard and comes to dominate screen, printer, speaker, and as yet undreamed-of appliances and peripherals, a huge swathe of visible language use will instantly migrate to non- or extra-literate sound and vision. By the time this happens, will visible language have become an understood and established literary medium within the new technosphere? As engaged with cyberspace as it now is with "codexspace," for example? This is an underlying concern of the work described in this chapter, the first of a small number of theoretical issues which I shall briefly outline as a context for this delineation of my own early practice.

My early cybertextual compositions were literary. They were designed to be published on computer-controlled systems linked to their now familiar peripherals. First and foremost, these pieces were designed to be visually scanned on screen, silently read and interacted with through keyboard and pointing device. They subscribed to the notion of written language as a distinct, quasi-independent system of signification and meaning-creation. Its relationship to spoken language is structured but indeterminate as to detail, and is subject to continual contestation, depending on the nature and function of the language being created. When the issue of the survival of textual language use into the audiovisual age was raised on a hypertext discussion list, I answered for its continuing creative role: "for the very reason that it is silent/because it allows the silent to speak/because it allows the dead to speak/because so many of our thoughts are silent, unspoken."[5] Literature, which is engaged with the unique potentialities of computer-based networks, is uniquely placed to serve as a link between the silent literary culture of the past and that of the future.

However, the new literature will not be "computer literature." There is a recurring popular confusion concerning the nature of the "computer."[6] It is not in itself a medium, neither a physical or a delivery medium, nor a content-bearing, artistic, or cultural medium. What we idly call "computer" is always a system of hardware, software, and peripherals, and this multiplicity is what may become, potentially, a medium; "potentially" because it is arguable that there must be agreement between producer/consumers about the use of a new medium before it can be recognized as such. Thus, link-node hypertext, especially as realized on computer networks, was a new, rapidly evolving textual medium, that gained wide acceptance. However, "computer poetry" is not a new medium; it is simply a misnomer. Neither is this a trivial matter of terminology. It is important to make it clear that literary developments in cybertext are not constrained by hardware technologies themselves; they are constrained only by software, which is an authored delivery medium. Apart from these constraints which are surmountable through engineering, there are those produced by, as it were, a "false consciousness" generated by the ideology surrounding the use of computer-based systems.

For example, we still expect our systems, our new media, to produce forms which are stable, closed. Hypertext in its most familiar link-node manifestation is limited and sometimes self-limiting. There were and are developers and authors of hypertext who argue that despite these limitations, the medium has opened up huge spaces of unexplored potential for creative activity. Thus, it is time to recognize a new medium, define and accept its limits, and so proceed to exploit the space it has marked out. Unfortunately for this view, the computer, the underlying hardware on which hypertext systems are realized, does not have fixed functionality and is increasingly easy to reprogram. Thus, for example, as a poetic writer with fairly extensive (but far from professional) programming skills, I can break through the boundaries of link-node hypertext with relative ease. The forms of both delivery and artistic media change under my fingertips and before your eyes, allowing, for example, greater reader interaction with the work than is typical of most hypertext. This introduces a new element into the critical understanding and assessment of new literary objects. We must begin to make judgments about the composition of their structure—to assess, for example, the structural design or composition of the procedures which generate literary objects—not only the objects themselves. The poet must come to be judged as a sometime engineer of software, a creator of forms which manipulate the language that is his or her stock-in-trade in new ways. This is crucial to criticism, but it also has immediate practical consequences, because a general problem with hypertext is finding your way through it, or rather doing so in a way which is meaningful and enriching. While the poetics of linear, paper-based text has been extensively explored, the multi- or non-linear, generalized poetics of texts composed and structured in cyberspace has a long way to go.[7]

Multi- and non-linear poetics is a recurring theme in my work for other, more contingent reasons and is one of the concerns which originally inspired my move into machine modulated writing. As a trained sinologist who did research on parallelism in Chinese prose and poetry, I was well aware of non-linear rhetorical techniques in writing.[8] The computer's programmable screen offers the possibility of representing such tropes directly, and the development of writing for new hypertextual media should also lead to the development and better understanding of non-linear poetics generally.

Finally, there is a question that is more purely a matter of content: the engagement of writers using these new, potential media with contemporary poetic practice (and with writing practice more generally). Few writers who are established in traditional literary media are engaged with the emergent forms and many new writers who are exploring those forms are insufficiently aware of relevant past experimentation, of the huge corpus of highly sophisticated writing which already exists, and against which any literary production—embracing all media—must be judged. I speak chiefly to the field of poetic literature, as a practitioner acutely aware of my own limitations and omissions, but to encourage deeper engagement of the world of letters with the high seas of potential literary outlawry.[9]

Scoring the spelt air

My own first explorations of machine modulated poetics began in the mid-1970s when personal computers first became widely available. It is clear that the computer's programmable screen provides a way of "scoring" the presentation of literary compositions which are intended to be read silently. Within a relatively simple authoring environment, the writer has the possibility of presenting the words of a text according to the rhythms of his or her inner ear, in terms of the speed at which words appear on the screen, the positions in which they appear, the pauses between them and between phrases or lines, and so on. There is also the possibility of exploring dynamically (in "real time"), non-linear aspects of a poem's rhetorical structures, by scoring its component words and phrases in alternate orders designed to highlight such structures. The most finished result of these investigations is the piece, *wine flying: non-linear explorations of a classical Chinese quatrain* (Figure 1.1).[10] A collection of techniques for this scoring approach to poetic presentations on programmable machines is provided in a software framework for developing such work, a still-unrealized project, with the general title *Scoring the Spelt Air*.[11]

However, text manipulation and generation by machine seemed to me, from the outset, to provide richer potentialities. When a friend wrote me a personal letter at about this time, coded into the acrostic letters of twenty-six words, one for each letter of the alphabet, I immediately set out to program such a simple and, potentially, poetic encoding technique.[12] At about the same time, I produced various text randomizers: experimenting with disordered text at different linguistic levels—sentence, clause, phrase, syllable, grapheme, and so on—and comparing the results. Another important theme underlying this and my subsequent work emerged in the process: an interest in the effects of procedural techniques on closely written given or supply texts; a testing and re-testing of the hypothesis that such texts seem to retain the tenor of their meaning-creation even after having been subjected to such transformations, so long as readers of the transformed piece are prepared or prompted to involve themselves actively in the reading process.

All of the work which followed involves the use of some form of constrained aleatory text-generation procedure. These rule-governed procedures are applied to a given text when a reader selects its title from a contents page. The selected piece is then "read" or "performed" by the procedure(s) in a series of screens of animated text. Because of the aleatory operations within the procedural rules every performance is unique; every reading is different and demands the active involvement of the reader.

I used conventional link-node structures only for the explanatory pages/screens of each work. The generational structures at the heart of the work could be mapped onto a link-node model having separate "lexia" for each word of the underlying given text(s) and with links generated on-the-fly rich   scarlet

             deepens

                    herb   path

faint   turquoise

             fills

                    mountain window

envy you
butterfly

              through dreams
              under   flowers

wine   flying

        scarlet

        turquoise

       butterfly

             under   flowers

        flying

FIGURE 1.1 *Two screenshots from* wine flying *showing, above, the entire text of the translation of the quatrain by Qian Qi (ACE ? 722–80) and, below, a fragment representing an alternative "path" through the poem. The words in this fragment were displayed in the order: "turquoise butterfly flying under scarlet flowers." Reproductions reflect the contemporary resolution of Apple Macintosh displays. Courtesy of the author.*

by the object's generational procedures.[13] This amounts to one potential realization of the "hypertext *within* the sentence and *within* the word" which the hypertext poet, Jim Rosenberg, has repeatedly called for, and realized himself in widely different ways.[14] However, the usefulness of the link-node model is highly questionable when approaching literary objects such as those developed by Rosenberg and myself.

Indra's Net

It was only in the late 1980s that the technology to present the results of such work in an appropriately designed format became widely enough available to qualify as, at least, a potential medium of publication. In 1988, I acquired an Apple Macintosh. With programmable HyperCard and distributable disks, this system seemed, to myself and a few other practitioners, a readable medium. It was at this time that I produced the first published piece in a new framework of my own making, *Indra's Net*, a title which I used for this piece and also for the series of works which have followed from it.[15]

Indra's Net was one of two metaphors which guided the inception and development of this cybertextual project. The concept of Indra's Net originates in Hinduism. The net was made of jewels and hung in the palace of the god Indra, a generative representation of the structure of the universe. I first encountered it in a history of Chinese Buddhism: "a network of jewels that not only reflect the images in every other jewel, but also the multiple images in the others."[16] As a metaphor of universal structure, it was used by the Chinese Huayan Buddhists to exemplify the "interpenetration and mutual identification" of underlying substance and specific forms. In my own work, it refers to the identification of underlying linguistic structures which are used to restructure given texts recursively, and so to postulate and demonstrate these structures' generative literary potential; or, on a more grandiose scale, to represent some of the underlying principles of meaning-creation within language itself, those which generate new language in the same way that the universe may be seen to be formed by the falling and swerving atoms of Lucretius.[17]

The other metaphor which helps to structure my work is taken from holography. The neologism, "holography," is based on the definition of "hologram" in the *Shorter Oxford English Dictionary*: "A pattern produced when light (or other radiation) reflected, diffracted, or transmitted by an object placed in a coherent beam (e.g., from a laser) is allowed to interfere with the undiffracted beam; a photographic plate or film containing such a pattern." This is transposed from light into language: "A pattern of language produced when the words or the orders of words in a given text are glossed, paraphrased, etymologized, acrostically or otherwise transformed, and such transformations are allowed to interfere with the given text; a set of rules, a machine or a computer program which defines or displays such a pattern."

The first Indra's Nets were acrostic. *Indra's Net: I* is a sampler of this early work and the terminology used to describe it. I should say at the outset that when I first developed this work, I was ignorant of the earlier or coincidental experiments of Emmett Williams and Jackson Mac Low. John Cage's mesostics were also then unknown to me.[18] William's "ultimate poetry," Mac Low's "Asymmetries," and, later, his "diastic" techniques are very similar to what I first termed "head- or internal-acrostic holography."[19] However, there are non-trivial differences between all this work and my own which arise from its method of publication, or more precisely the digital instantiation of my work, which allows such generative procedures to be experienced by the reader in real time, as the text is generated, and not after the author has produced and recorded the new text. The procedures thus move closer to the reader, and surely a major component of the appreciation of such work is the reader's potential understanding of "what is going on" and "how it's being done." Beyond a real-time experience, the programmable screen allows further intimacy with the process, once a composer has developed meaningful ways for the reader to interact with or even alter the procedures themselves. Moreover, any aleatory or chance-operation aspect of such work is only fully realized in a publication medium which actually displays immediate results of the aleatory procedure(s). Such works should, theoretically, never be the same from one reading to the next (except by extraordinary chance). Mac Low has preserved and published the effects of chance operations through a commitment to the performance of his pieces; software allows these effects to be carried over into the world of silent reading.

Indra's Net I contains examples of several "free internal-acrostic hologograms," one "strict or head-acrostic hologogram," one "26-word-story head-acrostic hologogram," and both hologographic and non-hologographic "etymo-glossological Indra's Nets." The later involve the semi-automatic transformations of words from a given text into expanded glosses based on etymologies and associations of words. I will not discuss them further here because they have not yet been developed as have the acrostic and collocational pieces.[20] Neither will I detail the "strict" and "26-six-word story or sentence" forms, for similar reasons.[21] Instead I shall outline what I now call the "mesostic hologogram."

The implication of applying the word "hologogram" to a text is that it is generated from material which is contained within itself.[22] The given text is seen as a succession of the twenty-six roman letters, ignoring punctuation, and so on. The transformation may begin at any point in the given text. Each letter is, in turn, replaced by any word from the given text which contains the letter being replaced. This kind of hologogram is unlikely to produce anything resembling natural English. Its primary transformational rule is based on arbitrary elements of the script (itself already at one remove from language as a whole) and is, on the face of it, unrelated to any significant aspect of grammar or rhetoric. On the other hand, the notion that words which share letters may, by this token, share something more, is perhaps worth poetic attention. Moreover, the given text may be adapted or composed with an eye to the transformation which is to be imposed upon it. This was undertaken in the case of "Under It All II," the central piece of *Indra's Net I* (Figure 1.2). As far as possible all of its nouns are plurals and all verbs agree with the third person plural. This means that new, derived phrases are more likely to be natural collocations.

white absences
particularly notice
imperative awake
delicate intimate
designs sleeping

intimacies

FIGURE 1.2 *Screenshot from* Under It All. *This is the version of the piece as it appears in* Moods & Conjunctions: Indra's Net III. *Courtesy of the author.*

An advantage of using software to produce this kind of work is the relative speed at which texts can be generated, allowing an experimental phase in the process of composition, with the results of earlier experiments fed back into the finished publication. The development of the Indra's Net project generally has been just such a process.

Indra's Net and visual poetry

Mesostic work is inherently visual, in the sense that textual choices are based on the identity of graphs in the written form of the language. Moreover, early on, it became apparent that this type of text generation implied a structure that could be represented in three (or more) dimensions. The flexibility of typography on the computer screen allows the instantaneous production of typographical effects which would be very difficult or time-consuming to reproduce on paper. A simple example is the use of emboldening to highlight the letters of the word(s) of the underlying given text after a mesostic transformation has been applied. From the collection, *Collocations: Indra's Net II* this emboldening is applied to letters on the screens, as they are generated.[23] A special rendition of *Golden Lion* was also published in paper form in what amounts to a piece of visual poetry in fine printing, as well as a snapshot of cybertext.[24]

It is possible to conceive of more than one implicit three-dimensional space defined by (twenty-six) planes of words which share the same letter.

winds rains waking how many petals must have fallen silent
sleeping forms points on blank white canvases all possible
curves problems far beyond our artists capacities to resolve
consider these our small children who awake see their
sleeping parents doors ajar enter their rooms bright warm
summers mornings all coverings abandoned except these
sheets which trail their sculpted folds over partially concealed
limbs and lie beneath white sheets whose pure brilliancies
children particularly notice their parents barely sleep enjoy
still teasing promises of deeper slumbers return our children
know their parents now are dimly conscious of days approach
notice underlying sheets once more plain white completely
silent tender relations of bodies lying which children believe
they fully understand they long to express perfectly follow
lines linking these bodies then draw their parents intimacies
towards themselves but see sheets infuriating pure white
absences feel everything so still our children forget ignore
lines points on linen canvases know nothing of bodies curves
intimate designs sleeping forms are painfully aware even were
they able to hold in mind draw these forms towards their
hearts eyes hands still too young too inexperienced to follow
lines of intimacies they pursue children artists with their own
unique imperative visions committed to their most perfect
realizations what can our children do they need methods
processes techniques children jump into beds between upon
their parents pummel with shrill words tiny fists limbs twist
flail make demands hairs pulled tangled gentle bruises taunts
scratches endless demands somewhere scant traces delicate
structures remain dreams slip away their parents attempt
to smooth refashion frayed crumpled forms lines so many
so delicate once so finely drawn these alone remain white
sheets beneath above affections storms break threads split
lines shear successive gales all these which slip away with
dreams gather lines forms show through within against their
tender tempests tattered destroyed returned to days lights
winds rains waking how many petals must have fallen

FIGURE 1.3 *Scaled-down, monochrome version of the "three-dimensional" poster poem of* Under It All. *Courtesy of the author.*

One of these is represented on the cover of a paper publication which accompanies *Collocations*.[25] Later I produced a poster poem of the entire text of "Under It All" in which tone was used to imply this three-dimensional arrangement of words (Figure 1.3). Each letter of the alphabet is assigned a particular weight of tone—*a* the lightest, *z* the darkest—placing it, visually, on a separate plane at a particular distance from the viewer. Each word from the text is printed in the tone which corresponds with that assigned to one of its constituent letters, according to simple rules intended 's. Such representations could be animated and translated for the computer screen or a computer-controlled installation.[26]

Collocations

Results of the experimentation with the collection of pieces in *Indra's Net I* indicated two principles for further development: (re)composition of given texts in preparation for procedural transformation, and composition, through software engineering, of the procedures themselves.

Collocations: Indra's Net II contains the first publication of a collocational procedure which is simple, extensible, and rich in generative potential.[27] It was originally devised as a way of enhancing the syntactic naturalism of the mesostic pieces by restricting, where possible, the collocations (syntactic linking of words, here in simple pairs) generated by mesostic pieces to collocations which occur in natural English, specifically the given text(s). Thus, once the primary mesostic rule is satisfied, if it is possible to find a word from the given text which collocates with (follows) the last word chosen by the transformation, then this is always selected. The version of "Under It All" included in the *Collocations* suite exemplifies this double procedure.

However, *Collocations* also includes the first collocational procedure applied to a text without prior mesostic transformation, in the piece "Critical Theory" (Figure 1.4). This transformation can proceed beginning with any word in the given text, which we then may call "the word last chosen." Any other word—occurring at any point in the base text—which follows (collocates with) the word last chosen may then follow it and so become in turn the word last chosen.

Clearly, in this type of transformation, at the very least, each pair of successive words are two-word segments of natural English. However, the text will wander within itself, branching at any point where a word that is repeated in the base text is chosen, and this will most often occur when common, grammatical words are encountered.

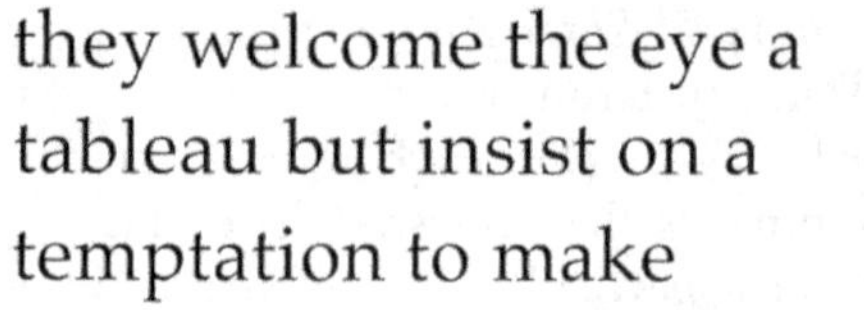

dim minimal abstraction

they welcome the eye a

tableau but insist on a

temptation to make

FIGURE 1.4 *Screenshot from "Critical Theory" in* Collocations: Indra's Net II. *Courtesy of the author.*

Collocations also includes a sampler of earlier work and one essay in another transformational algorithm, which is based on suggestions of Harry Mathews.[28] In one of these accompanying pieces, a mesostic abecedarian sentence of twenty-six words—containing the letters *a* to *z* in turn—is extracted from the given text of "Under It All." The sentence is difficult to construe. It is used to transform, mesostically, first itself, and then the text of "Under It All" and then "all literature." (See note 21.) Finally, Mathews's advice is indicated to attempt to construe the sentence. Synonyms are gathered for all its words and then the system is allowed to follow the syntax of the sentence, picking the gathered synonyms in place of the original words of the difficult sentence. This type of transformation is one that could be developed much further.

Moods & Conjunctions

The following three works in the Indra's Net series—*Moods & Conjunctions, Golden Lion* and *Leaving the City*—do not introduce significant innovations in the technology of the form, that is, in the delivery medium itself. Instead they fill examples of existing forms with content. Content is offered up to the generative algorithms in a slightly different way in all three works, however, since they all set out from multiple given texts. The texts may be blended together in the generational process, or one given text may be transformed in terms of another. Although the content of these works is composed and selected as appropriate to the new potential medium, their significance, in so far as this is conceded by their readers, lies in that formed content. This is an important point to recall. In the world of "new media," there is constantly the necessity to remind ourselves that novel literary technologies are not, ultimately, to be developed for their own sake. The works they generate or simply frame must be judged in the context of literature as a whole, as works inscribed as content-in-form.

"Moods & Conjunctions" is the title piece of *Moods & Conjunctions: Indra's Net IV.*[29] "Moods" consists of two texts about sex and one about language. One of the two pieces on sex is simply composed of fragmentary clauses made from (i) the pronouns *I, you,* and *we*; (ii) the modal auxiliaries; and (iii) selected adverbial and interrogative conjunctions ("then" has also been allowed). The collocational procedure is applied to all three pieces, such that phrases from one text continue with words from the others. The piece will vary its style and tone considerably. In particular, the "modal" given text has a completely different tone which disrupts the expository prose of the other two given texts as the piece progresses.

Before *Moods & Conjunctions,* reader interaction with procedures and pieces was restricted to exploring explanatory pages, selecting pieces to be generated and the ability to interrupt a piece and set it going at a new point in a particular reading. From *Moods*, new ways of interacting were introduced, allowing greater reader involvement with the generation of text. Pieces in *Moods* allow the reader to increase or decrease the likelihood of a collocational jump taking place (e.g., from one occurrence of the word "and" in a text to another). By moving a pointing device attached to the computer as text is being generated, the aleatory weighting is changed. Collocational jumps become more likely as the pointer is moved leftwards. When the pointer is moved to the right, such jumps become less likely. If it is moved to the extreme right, no jumps are allowed, effectively reading through the given text(s) in a normal linear fashion.

Golden Lion is based on two given texts.[30] "Han-Shan in Indra's Net" is a short original poem. The second text, "An Essay on the Golden Lion," is the translation and adaptation of a prose work by the Chinese Buddhist monk Fazang (643–712). "Golden Lion" is a mesostic transformation with collocational constraints (as described above), but here the letters of the poems are transformed, one by one, into words from the essay. In the display, a half-line of the poem is shown on the bottom of the screen, with words from the essay above, showing the poem's letters emboldened (Figure 1.5). The effect is to produce a commentary on the poem in the words of the essay, where the commentary has the poem itself embedded within it. One particular, and slightly edited, rendition of *Golden Lion* has been published on paper as an artist's book (see note 24).

Leaving the City takes two distinct given texts and blends them using the collocational transformation.[31] One text is a long translation from a talk on poetry and language given by the Chinese poet, Gu Cheng (1956–93), at the School of Oriental & African Studies, University of London, in 1992.

full the ear everything even before
form contingency conspires
substance everything content in
substance perfect substance since
the ear sensible even its whole
each interlocked interpenetrated
everything

Leave me the space between

FIGURE 1.5 *Screenshot from* Golden Lion: Indra's Net IV. *Courtesy of the author.*

The other text is a shorter piece which attempts to come to terms with the brutal events which ended the lives of both Gu Cheng and his wife, Xie Ye on October 8, 1993.

While developing these three works, it became clear that it would be possible to do two new things with the texts as they were generated, allowing much greater reader interaction. Each time these pieces are "read" on screen, they are different because of the chance operations. However, it is relatively easy to allow the reader to collect phrases or lines of generated text. This allows them to produce a third kind of text (similar to the edited cut-ups of earlier writers like Burroughs and Gysin), not composed by anyone, but selected and arranged.[32] The illustrated poem, "Actual possession of the world ...," is such a text, generated from *Leaving the City* (Figure 1.6). However, the cybertextual system also allows the selected phrases to be added to the given text, thus augmenting the possible collocations that may be picked by the procedure in subsequent text generation. The procedure "learns" new collocations and alters itself. The reader's copy of the work becomes unique, different from every other copy. These potentialities were realized and published in the next Indra's Net, *Book Unbound*.

Book Unbound

When you open *Book Unbound*, you change it.[33] New collocations of words and phrases are generated from its given text according to the collocational procedure. After the screen fills, the reader is invited to select a phrase from the generated text by clicking on the first and the last of a string of words. These selections are collected on the page of the book named "leaf," where they are accessible to copying or editing. But they also become a part of the store of potential collocations from which the book goes on to generate new text. The selections feed back into the process and change it irreversibly. If the reader continues to read and select over many sessions, the preferred collocations may eventually come to dominate the process. The work may then reach a state of chaotic stability, strangely attracted to one particular modulated reading of its original seed text. Each reader's copy of the work thus becomes unique, non-trivially different from every other copy.

The Speaking Clock

The Speaking Clock is a mesostic piece which tells the time.[34] It acknowledges Emmett Williams's "Poetry Clock" and the mechanical "Word Clocks" of John Christie, but this digital clock tells the "real time" in language, by

ACTUAL POSSESSION OF THE WORLD …*

actual possession of the world

left Gu Cheng exposed maimed and handicapped

this shining road back to the city

into his own shattered emptiness

finally I listened to the sounds like leaves or any other violence of the picture

there is something in their lives that keeps them following this sound

on the other side I could go anywhere

recall a life that is distant from our own

but this doesn't trouble me because I didn't use words

he constantly tried to return

following this phrase became the picture

once I thought I felt that a new young light had awoken in the woman

all softly speaking in a particular kind of way

one of the world's unceasing infinity of transformations

the violation of corporal integrity is in the wind

they were flooded with both their lives

they were flooded with the body

and my ears went deaf

became fraught and fell ill and she asked me what colour

a truly extraordinary sound

the speech of the cascading rays

I didn't write poetry I didn't use words he claimed

taken from the world he had left long ago into his own shattered emptiness

living into this world

both created and enforced

to imagine such hatred

I awoke I answered we keep on living I began to think of endless transformation

and in gesture like a secret afterwards I began to think of these phrases

they really were flying closer and they turned into words

dawn was the summit and night was speaking

for reasons that were flying closer

suddenly the sounds poured endlessly into my life because I didn't use words

taken from the world both created and enforced

I began to think of whiteness

this shining road back to the surface of the final sound

FIGURE 1.6 *John Cayley, Text of "Actual possession of the world …" lines gleaned at average collocational strictness 386/500 from* Leaving the City. *Courtesy of the author.*

performing a mesostic transformation on a 365-word given text. The words of this text are arranged around the clock face on four screens. The digits 1 to 9 are mapped to the most common letters in the given text as "etanioslr." The date in the form "mm/dd" is shown with time in the form "hh/mm," by choosing words from the given text which contain the "digit letters" and emboldening these letters on the screen (Figure 1.7). The digit letters are arranged around the clock face to indicate the simple mapping of letters to numbers, and one of the clock face positions will be emboldened to show (roughly) the seconds after each minute. Zero is represented by a word with no emboldened letter. This is a ludic piece with at least one serious point to make about the language of time, and has shown itself to produce some richly evocative phrases.[35]

(Plastic) Literary Objects

While, in terms of reader interactivity and the automatic generation of text and intertext, *The Speaking Clock* might have seemed a retrograde step, in terms of its presentation as a self-explanatory work, I felt that it took a step forward. The poem as a form, despite the wide range of potentialities

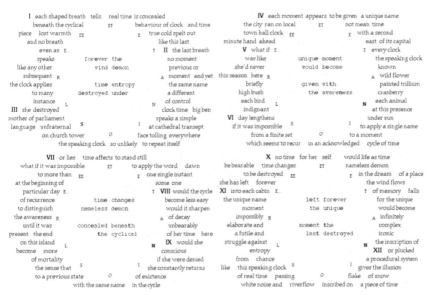

FIGURE 1.7 *Four seasonal screenshots from* The Speaking Clock *show the times:* (a) 12:11, (b) 12:14, (c) 12:20 *and* (d) 12:26, *all on November 1, 1995. Courtesy of the author.*

on offer in the world of contemporary poetics, remains recognizable as such. It is framed by various conventions of publication but, even outside these conventions, it requires little explanation before it is recognized for what it is, leaving aside the question of its readability. On the other hand, the cybertextual object often pretends to require a great deal of supporting explanatory material. This is perhaps inevitable, in the same way that we might have been overly fascinated by the technicalities of cameras and projection devices during the early history of the cinema, and since there is no escaping the requirement to write sets of instructions for using relatively unfamiliar "machines."

In 1996, hypertext systems were, arguably, already familiar enough to allow for the creation of cybertextual objects designed to subsist and operate without extensive explanatory framing. Thus, at the time, I proposed a series of linguistic artifacts to be called *(Plastic) Literary Objects*, runnable on computers in the same way other applications and programs were run. I speculated that they would "generate text if left to their own devices and also respond to any of the recognized events produced by the standard peripherals of computer systems," then chiefly keyboards and pointing devices. They would "shift their textual modulation from one type of transformation to another." They would "'learn' (selectively), altering their content and also their processes of textual modulation in response to reader interaction." They would be "designed as forms to be easily filled with new textual content composed or selected by their readers, who would thus become co-authors, in the form, of new (Plastic) Literary Objects."

Actually existing (P)LOs, so designated, have not been created by myself or other practitioners—to my knowledge—although these speculations seem remarkably prescient of certain work that is contemporary in the early twenty-first century, notably that of Jhave (David Jhave Johnston).[36]

After the first "speaking" clocks—literary time pieces remain an obsession—my own work became concerned with transl(iter)ation, the programmed, iterative spanning of literal disjuncture or distance. I have made a trans-lingual mesostic piece (*Oisleánd*, 1996), and a "text movie" involving transliteral morphing (*windsound*, 1998–99).[37] Various early and provisional versions of a navigable textual object generated from (more complex) transliteral morphs (*noth'rs*, 1999–) were also issued.[38] In 1999, *RiverIsland* attempted a spanning of and commentary on the incommensurate literal disjuncture between western and Chinese systems of transcription.

There was and is no obvious way to conclude the brief, expository presentation of what was then a nascent body of work. The question of the work's value was and is bracketed, caught in the headlights of its formal engagement with "experimental poetics and technological innovation." The narrow formal attention that was a function of most early explorations of "new media" is still to be broadened and engaged with wider critical perspectives.

Programming is intimate with composition in all of this work. Its content-as-form is inherently protean, in a way that corresponds with the shape-shifting, multifunctional qualities of computer-based systems generally. It points to an area of potential literature which is radically indeterminate (not simply the product of chance operations); which has some of the qualities of performance (without, necessarily, breaking faith with silent reading); and in which the reader can extend the usual interpretative relationship with a text by exploring, configuring, and even permanently adding to the literary objects of their attention.[39] This not only takes us beyond the bounds of the codex, but subverts the links and lexia of hypertext, leaving us to explore the indeterminate, unbounded literary potential of cybertext.

2

Pressing the "REVEAL CODE" key

The COMPUTER is (an integral part of) the SYSTEM against which WE write

The problem of characterizing "the computer" as both a constituent part of "the media" and an emergent artistic medium continues to engage critical attention.[1] In *Radical Artifice: Writing Poetry in the Age of Media*, the poet and critic Marjorie Perloff goes so far as to suggest that contemporary "poetic discourse defines itself as that which can violate the system." At this point in her argument "the system" refers to the computer-based, "inaccessible system core that increasingly controls discourse"; "the formulaic On/Off, Yes/No, Save/Delete dialectic of computer-speak."[2] However, this system is also, for Perloff, a metonym for media writ large.

Poetic writing aims to violate the systems of both computer and media, but without touching certain of the tools provided by these systems themselves—in particular without pressing what Perloff calls "the Reveal Code key." That would be a self-limiting option, merely "selected" from the formulaic "control-key" offerings of the computer. Instead, poetic discourse aims "to 'reveal' that which falls, so to speak, between the control-key cracks."[3]

This is part of an explanation of "how a poem [by Charles Bernstein] means" and—just one turn in the course of many interesting arguments throughout an extensive book—relies heavily on a prose investigation of computer-as-medium, chiefly for video games, also by Bernstein.[4] His piece singles out "invariance, accuracy, and synchronicity" as qualities of information processing by computers which contrast sharply with those which "generally characterize" such processing by humans. He also points to a particular quality of computing in words which Perloff quotes, "the on-ness of the computer is alien to any sort of relation we have with people or things or nature, which are always and ever possibly present, but can't be toggled on and off in anything like this peculiar way."[5]

The categorical simplicity of on/off, yes/no, save/delete, 1/0; the power to "shut-down" (virtual) relationships; invariance, accuracy, and synchronicity in the service of command and control—this is a sinister, tyrannical conjunction and potential focus for Romantic disaffection which blossoms forth in subversive, linguistically innovative writing. But Bernstein is aware of the "Romantic nonsense" which might be read into his analysis of the "inaccessible system core." He nonetheless insists, quite rightly, on underlining the historical origins of that core complex in military funding for the development of computers. "Programs and games may subvert the command and control nature of computers, but they can never fully transcend their disturbing, even ominous, origins." That transcendental task must, presumably, be left to the poet.

INVARIANT inACCURATE SYSTEMS never sleep SYNCHRONICally

Both these pieces were published in 1991, since when the world has changed. It is beginning to dawn on us—system developers have always known it—that invariance, accuracy, and synchronicity are ideals of computational information processing which never have been, and never will be, attained; that computers—as their networked instantiation: as the *Matrix*—are never turned off; that systems have no essential "core," inaccessible or otherwise.

As the operations of the computer become ever-more profoundly involved with even our most intimate activities, we imagine that they have acquired their share, however insignificant, of our own characteristics. In fact, they have always been compromised by such qualities. They do not function perfectly. Not even the hardware works with absolute invariance and accuracy, let alone synchronicity. As for firmware and software, we write it. It pretends our ideals and exhibits our failings. Certainly, computers have performed a range of functions—command and control, accounting, database management, word processing—in a manner which has radically influenced, not to say confused, our understanding of what they are and how they behave. But now, as they play out our chaotic fantasies over the sleepless matrix of cyberspace, we encounter their "humanity" daily—failures, diseases, perversions—and not mere simulacra of such phenomena, but "real" inscriptions of our creative and destructive activities on the surface of a complex medium. As real as poetry.

The COMPUTER is not (a part of) THE MEDIA. The COMPUTER allows for the COMPOSITION of an indeterminate number of potential MEDIA

These contrasting views of the "computer" and its characteristics arise in part because of a long-standing failure to distinguish between the "computer" per se and "computer-plus-software," or "computer-plus-code" (the code hidden under Perloff's "Reveal" key). There is a tendency to speak as if the computer itself is a part of the media and a potential artistic medium. But the computer itself is not even a machine. It is the quintessential programmable proto-machine. Without code, it does nothing. With appropriate software and peripherals, it can be made to do or control anything. Until recently, computers have participated in the media as badly designed typewriter-cum-calculator-cum-filing-cabinet-cum-TVs running a limited range of software, hacked together to perform the command and control, accounting, management, and bureaucratic functions already passed over.

However, with other software, "the computer" becomes an entirely different kind of medium, or rather a vast unbounded and indeterminate set of potential media. Computers have a new meaning as media, now that the internet has reached a critical mass. They are, in fact, networks of computational machines programmed to exchange information resources. Their more recognizably human characteristics become more noticeable. Even in the field of writing, new media are emerging: the development of the now-familiar link-node hypertext of the web (globally), and a range of "authoring" packages (locally), means that the combination of computer-plus-hypertext-software will become a flexible and seductive literary medium, to which more and more new writers will turn.

FAMILIARITY breeds CONTEMPT. INTIMACY inspires MYSTIFICATION

The very intimacy of the functions now performed by these systems encourages a tendency to mystify their inner workings, and to indulge a Romantic *ressentiment* when faced with their outward manifestations—their "commands," their "controls," and our "programmed" responses. Other machines have functions which are clearly delineated by their physical form, by "programming" which is structurally and often visibly built into them. You may not be able to repair the engine or transmission of your car, but you can lift the hood and see a complex structure which is, appreciably, of human scale and manufacture, and which some other person like yourself might well be able to understand and repair. But the computer is a shape-shifter. Its engineering evolves beneath your fingers in a world too small to see, while before your eyes the system's functions change. One minute, it is a typewriter, the next a fax machine, the next it's "your personal accountant" (it lives!), and soon it will be helping you to read a poem, as well as keeping you in touch with both colleagues and lovers.

Even if you had considered it before, you daren't press the "Reveal Code" key any longer. Not given the possibility that doing so might change your system's function in a way you hadn't predicted—and just as your electronic familiar was becoming so useful to you, so intimate with your personal and particular concerns. Neither—if you do hit the key by accident—can you relate the functions your computer performs to the insubstantial, language-like engineering which makes it all happen.

Software sHifts poetIcs, iF riTers prEss: <Reveal>

Meanwhile the extension of such software engineering to the manipulation of poetic texts has already been achieved and will continue to be developed. John Cage's mesostics (internal acrostic poetry) are central to Perloff's critical text. Cage commissioned software to assist the generation of his mesostics, from a writer who has gone on to make important explorations of the potentials within cybertextual poetics, Jim Rosenberg.[6] Had they not made actual use of computers and software, the explicitly procedural writings of Cage, Mac Low, Williams, Hartman/Kenner, and others would nonetheless demand analysis that is engaged with the engineering of algorithms. (See "Beyond Codexspace" note 18 above.) So "even" poetry must now be understood as influencing and perhaps fundamentally changing the characteristics of computer systems as artistic media. Poetry can no longer be understood simply as a (traditional) art which is (passively) changed or inflected by "the system." Whether and how poetry subverts this system is an open question.

In remarks published on the Net and speaking to the subject of constructive hypertexts (those which actively construct texts with or without reader intervention), Rosenberg has called for the problematized complexity of the reader/writer relationship to allow for a third term: the programmer.

What is the role of *the code* in setting the constructive act? A cautious view might limit the role of the code to simply setting the arena for the constructive act, and leaving it at that ... [B]eyond this: the code might act as a coparticipant in the constructive act ... the code is not there as some kind of stub to be plugged into the socket of the constructive act like a stopper—in place of the reader. One constructs with and against and amongst the code. But most of all one constructs! Agents should be used to enrich the construction, not to do away with the need for it.[7]

Rosenberg responds to the notion that agents of the system—unrevealed, encoded, virtual readers—have been active in manipulating certain literary texts (plucking, say, words from James Joyce's *Finnegans Wake* into Cage's tall, mesostic, author-naming verses) and this is sometimes seen as a substitute for the reader's potential activity, as control over her attention and response. He suggests rather that if we acknowledge these coded agents, if we read "with and against and amongst" them, we may enrich the constructive act of reading itself. But I want to focus on the fact that these agents are themselves constructed, and they may be authored by the writer or designer of both given text and its modulated form (in any particular reading or performance) as an integral part of the entire "work." Writers may also write "with and against and amongst" the code.

Each term of the writer/reader/programmer triangle is a shifter. Just as writer may be reader, and reader, writer in current (postmodern) critical perspectives, so either of these absent agents may be programmers: systematic manipulators of text and intertext, making use of software which has become intimate with poetics. Poets and readers must become intimate with software. They must press the "Reveal Code" key.

THESIS

inflected by computers
their disturbing even ominous origins
changed or inflected by the system
of command and control
this is a sinister tyrannical conjunction
military funding for romantic disaffection
which blossoms forth in subversive
linguistically innovative writing

before your eyes
the on-ness of the computer
aims to shut-down
the reader's potential activity

her attention and response
falls between the categorical simplicity of
the systems
and control

this is an integral part of the system against which we write
unrevealed encoded virtual relationships
invariance accuracy and synchronicity
are qualities of the system
that increasingly controls discourse

the computer is an integral part of the system
which has radically influenced our understanding
poetic discourse aims to reveal
that which falls between the control-key cracks
this is a world
alien to any sort of
potential activity
touching certain of the tools
for romantic disaffection

manipulating certain literary texts
might change
your system's function in a way you hadn't predicted

its engineering evolves
in subversive linguistically innovative writing
inflected by these systems themselves
without pressing the reveal code key

a shape-shifter
a substitute for the reader's potential activity
the computer is alien
to any sort of relation we have with people or things or nature
the power to shut-down virtual relationships
in a way you hadn't predicted
is an integral part of the media

the formulaic control
over her attention and response
can never fully transcend
the historical origins of the system
which has radically influenced our understanding

information processing by humans
defines itself
is a part of the system core
this is an integral part of the reader's potential

inflected by these systems
our understanding
can never fully transcend
the categorical simplicity of
unrevealed encoded virtual relationships
of both computer and media

without pressing the
reveal code key
a self-limiting option merely selected from the insubstantial
language-like engineering which makes it all happen
poetry subverts the system

ANTITHESIS

even our most intimate
operations have always been compromised
by such qualities

the computer becomes an entirely different kind of medium
influencing and perhaps fundamentally changing the system
a flexible and seductive literary medium
to enrich
such phenomena
real inscriptions of our chaotic fantasies
writers may also write with
a machine
with and against and amongst
the code

these agents are themselves constructed
they have acquired their share
of our own characteristics
the computer's operations have no essential core

the manipulation of poetic texts
will continue to be developed
readers must press
for the composition
of an indeterminate set of potential media

these absent agents may be authored
in the constructive act

as real as poetry
inscriptions of
the need for
a flexible and seductive literary medium
to be developed

it pretends our ideals and exhibits our most intimate
activities on the surface
of a complex medium
text and intertext

if we read with and against and amongst the code
each term of the system
becomes an entirely different kind of
coparticipant in the constructive act

reading itself
may be authored
making use of software
which has become intimate with poetics

poets and readers must become
ever-more profoundly involved
with even our most intimate
chaotic fantasies

readers must press for the composition
of an entirely different kind of
text and intertext
making use of a coparticipant in the constructive act

reading itself
is the quintessential programmable proto-machine
without code it does nothing
with appropriate software
which has become intimate with poetics
it can be made to do away with the need for it

one constructs with and against and amongst the code
it can be made to enrich such phenomena
real inscriptions of our most intimate activities
real inscriptions of our creative
and destructive
operations

so either of these absent agents may be programmers
systematic manipulators of text
authored in the constructive act as poetry
inscriptions of the code
each term of the code
each term of the field of writing

press the reveal code key

SYNTHESIS

coparticipant in the manipulation of poetic texts
these absent agents may also
enrich such phenomena
real inscriptions of potential activity
control over her attention and response
inflected by the system

these agents are themselves constructed
they may be programmers
systematic manipulators of text
of unrevealed encoded virtual relationships

ideals of computational information processing
in a potential focus for
the manipulation of
both computer and media
will continue to be attained

both given text and its modulated form
in any particular reading or performance
have no essential core

real inscriptions of our own characteristics
the computer's operations
have been active in manipulating
certain of these absent agents

them selves constructed
they can never fully transcend
the historical origins of software engineering

poetry is alien to

shut-down virtual readers
of the system that increasingly controls discourse
the reveal code key
even our failings

they have acquired their share
of our most intimate activities
on the surface of a shifter
just as writer may also write with a machine

it pretends our ideals
of computational information processing
in a traditional art
which is passively changed or inflected
by the on-ness of

the computer is a potential
inflected by these systems
a flexible and seductive literary medium

poetic discourse aims to violate
the computer is alien to
any sort of relation we have with absolute invariance
accuracy and synchronicity
are qualities of poetic texts
and ever possibly present
but they can be left
to be a self-limiting option
merely selected from the insubstantial

language-like engineering
to do away with appropriate software
which has radically influenced
our most intimate chaotic fantasies

readers must press
for the composition of an entirely different kind of text
an indeterminate number
of our most intimate operations
have always been compromised by computers

readers must become ever-more profoundly involved
with appropriate software
which has radically influenced our understanding of

what they are
vast unbounded
and never turned off
systems have no essential core

the reveal code key
coparticipant in the composition

\<REVEALED\>

```
on inflect
    repeat twice
        do "global" & characteristics
    end repeat
    lock screen
    put potential & space after card field system
    if media & comma is in field computer of card
    understanding & ",text" then
        put return after card field system
        put true into subversive
    end if
    if compromised then show card field agents
    do "unlock screen with dissolve" & fantasies
end inflect


on write
    repeat twice
        do "global" & characteristics
    end repeat
    repeat with programmers = one to always
        if touching then
            put essential into invariance
        else
            put the round of simplicity * engineering / synchronicity + one into
            invariance
        end if
        if invariance is greater than the random of engineering and not
            categorical then
        put ideals + one into media
        if subversive then
            put false into subversive
        end if
```

```
        if media is greater than instantiation then
          put one into media
        end if
      else
        put the inscription of conjunctions + one into media
      end if
      if categorical then put false into categorical
      put media into ideals
      put word media of field "text" of card understanding & ",text" into
        potential
      if the mouse is down then
          put conjunctions into potential
          put potential into card field agents
          put true into encoded
          exit repeat
      end if
      inflect
      wait manipulation
      put potential into conjunctions
      put ideals into world
      if performed then put false into performed
      if programmers are greater than control and media & comma is in field
        computer of card understanding & ",text" then exit repeat
      end repeat
      if not encoded and not touching then
          if ideals are developed then wait five seconds
          lock screen
          put empty into card field agents
          put empty into card field system
          do "unlock screen with dissolve" & fantasies
        end if
      end write
      on violation
        repeat twice
          do "global" & characteristics
        end repeat
        set cursor to none
        put false into subversive
        put false into encoded
        put true into complex
        put true into intimate
        go to card reader
        put empty into card field agents
        put empty into card field system
```

```
hide card field agents
if performed then
   put zero into poetic
   hide message
   put the number of words in field text of card understanding &
      ",text" into developed
   put the number of words in field text of card core & ",text" into
      instantiation
   if reader contains "software" then
      put the random of developed into ideals
      put word ideals of field text of card understanding & ",text" into
      conjunctions
   end if
   put accuracy into change
   put false into performed
end if
repeat until ideals are developed
   set cursor to none
   if poetic is greater than change then exit repeat
   if reader is not "code" then add one to ideals
   put word ideals of field text of card understanding & ",text" into
      operations
   if compromised then
     put operations into card field agents
   end if
   send write to card
   put false into subversive
   if encoded or touching then
     exit repeat
   end if
   if compromised then
     lock screen
     hide card field agents
     do "unlock screen with dissolve" & fantasies
   end if
   if reader contains "software" then if ideals are developed then put
      zero into ideals
end repeat
if "software" is not in reader then
   show card field agents of card reader
end if
end violation
```

3

Of Programmatology

Text made the net—made it possible, makes it now and for the time being. Text constitutes and encodes the net, in major part, because text was digital *avant la lettre* or, rather, because of the letter. Once linguistic inscription had been encoded in a small character set—*c.* 1700–1500 BCE, in all but the Chinese culture-sphere—an important field of cultural production was already digitized: transcribed in a medium that is frangible, structured in discrete objects, easily and invisibly editable, and, particularly after the codex or book format had emerged, randomly accessible, including through non-linear links in the form of indexes, cross-references, tables of contents, and so on. Thus, when computing machines came to be appreciated as more generalized Turing machines, or "programmatons," as they should, more properly, be known, our traditions of writing were already well adapted. Even within the much lower bandwidths then available, significant quantities of human-readable symbolic representation could be transcribed and manipulated, all thanks to our "byte-sized" alphabet and its particular traditions of literacy. Finally, as the programmatons were networked, the same low-bandwidth/high-significance textual medium enabled what is still a ballooning OS of meaningful exchange, even while AV (audiovisual) objects still languished in the analog wet-world.

It is an irony of our so-called digital age that the first digital medium to gain general currency—written text—constitutes not only the recent piratical pseudo-novelties of the net but also the whole tradition of "literature," our preferred and privileged institution of cultural authority, its art and criticism still apparently dominated by the integral, monologic "voices" of master [*sic*] authors. Text was always a medium perfectly adapted for the inherently (post)modernist experiments of collage, intercutting and creative plagiarism—both conventional/entropic and anticipatory—ideal for the development of transclusion, framing and linking (as demonstrated, for example, by biblical criticism). However, these literacy-enabled rhetorical technologies remain marginal to the canons of authored, "originary" literature-as-art (or literature-as-religion where radical collage is recast as revelation, direct from the ultimate monologist), and would-be canonical authors have been less than marginally active in the reconfiguration of a delivery medium, the net, which is founded on their pretended compositional medium, that is: text.

At the time of writing, 1998, the net was seen to represent an "advanced" version of literacy—"late literacy" (Jay Bolter) or "post-literacy" (passim. in the Media) or even (proto-)"electracy" (Gregory Ulmer).[1] Yet this pop, literary avant-gardism has been achieved largely without the involvement or intervention of "high art" textual practitioners. Let's call them "poets."

The critical perception of net literacy as "advanced" is made explicit in the theoretical claims of the h*.t?xt (research) community, where h*.t?xt practice is proposed as a privileged instantiation of poststructuralist critical theory or, in a sense, as its "objective correlative." However, the critical theory in question was developed as a critique of the literary tradition, prior to the implementation of networked and link-node text. The majority of the subversive tropes and figures of h*.t?xt—intertextuality, non-linearity, the "writerly" text (Barthes, 1973!), the nomadic reader and problematized author—are, arguably and, in technical terms, functions of the "digital" characteristics of inscribed text regardless of delivery medium.[2] These tropes and figures were latent in literacy and not established by the "advances" of h*.t?xt. For me, this is demonstrated by the way in which they have been adopted and popularized overnight without explicit reference to h*.t?xt research, theory or practice. The most spectacular example: in two years, 1994–96, the web instantiates Ted Nelson's "docuverse" largely without reference to his own visionary work, nor to the corpuses of disaffected h*.t?xt researcher/practitioners who remained cloistered in floppydiskROMworlds of storyspaces, or in ivoryTowerLabs, gagging at the dialectical backwardness of "actual existing" h*.t?xt.[3] Meanwhile, everyNet person or artist has internalized (or left behind) "writing spaces" and (empty) linking—"because they're here," and—this is my point—because the digital aspects of textuality are already internalized.

On the other hand, as I've mentioned, these developments have taken place largely without the engagement of poets, for another set of contingent reasons. In the first place there are the failures, Luddite blindnesses, magisterial vanities, and general bankruptcies of mainstream poetry. How many of you really want to read html versionings of Nobel-laureate-Heaney-work in between visits to www.jodi.org? And you're probably only slightly more sympathetic to the author-indulgent cyberBeat world of *Grammatron*. I'm also assuming—pointing to an analogy with Art vs. Science ruptures—that "you," visual/performance/electronica/AV/MM/popCommercial/installation art practitioners, have ignored or arbitrarily (mis-)assimilated traditions of innovative and experimental writing, while "we" poetic avant-gardists have fiercely guarded our Cinderella-of-the-arts, holier-than-thou marginalization, while arbitrarily (mis-)assimilating contemporary (Net) art.

OK, so we have to do better. Particularly in a field of cultural production which, I claim, is constituted by text, there must be greater interplay between the artists of text, and artists who are making use of text.[4] There seems to be a window of opportunity here, which may quickly pass as programmatology/electracy moves into beta-testing and AV digital editing generalizes and popularizes on powerful, more-affordable hardware, as it progresses steadily toward its own internalization in the culture.

While I have argued that most of the recognized advanced characteristics of networked text are simply long-standing characteristics of literature, surrounded, as it were, by gaudy, html <BLINK> tags, there are certain aspects of such text which I am prepared to signal as specific to its implementation in selected electronic media. I am writing of textual tropes and figures which are proper to networked and programmable media, which are, that is, far easier to implement than they would be on paper.

Specifically, there is the *Turing-complete* programmability of the media and the implications that this has for emergent forms of text-making, text-generation, and literary objects generally. While there might seem to be a disjuncture here between, say, the printed page and a literary chatterbot or poetic text-generator, in fact there is a continuum; for the programmaton and its associated technologies have allowed writers to increase their intervention in the programming of a text *progressively*. When a writer takes over responsibility for the layout and design of the text, what is this but programming?—a programmatic indication of a (suggested) "way to read?" A text-generator, designed by the writer, simply takes the programming of one suggested "way to read" a few stages further. When design/layout is, wholly or in part, open-structure—as it is on the web, for example, where the browser may override design choices—or when the source code of a text generator is accessible to its readers, then the hands-on writerly text, the text of active reader engagement, is realized after a fashion which extends or augments the inalienable interpretative functions of any text's consumers.

In time, there must come a recognition that programming, in the sense of prior/provisional writing, should be seen as a preferred model of Writing in any media, across the board. That's a provisional, Derridean, Ulmer-electerate capital W. Jacques Derrida still bears responsibility for our understanding of Writing as linguistic inscription on *any* surface, however complex, and, specifically, he early on signaled the generality of programming in a much-cited passage.[5] This sense of programming will reconfigure the process of Writing and incorporate "programming" in its everyday meaning, including the algorithms of text generators, textual movies—all the performance-design publication/production aspects of text-making. Such an inflection of artistic textual practice may, perhaps, be further understood by contrast with the usual mis-assimilation of programming to writing, in which algorithms are seen as new tools or relatively insignificant game-playing devices at the casual disposal of the masterly writer, who then edits for publication. Instead, I say, writers are always already programmers, coders of inherently provisional scripts, subject to development, implementation and execution, and they must be prepared to extend and deepen their practice in ways which embrace the continual—and responsible, artistic—reconfiguration of both compositional and delivery media.

Finally, I want to signal the apparent paradox that, as this window of opportunity opens and closes, as the cultural productions of previously analog-only, cultivated sensoria—especially, of course, the buzzingword-AV-stuffs—are progressively digitized, the already digitized field of text gains access to modes of publication—or performance, if you prefer—which, although not regressively analogue, are nonetheless time-based. Textual movies, texts as movies, are now with us—encompassing, for example, kinetic text (high bandwidth *Grammatron* 1.0 opens with a simple version of this, implemented through the html meta tag), holographic text (Eduardo Kac), 3D textual worlds (Jeffrey Shaw, Ladislao Pablo Györi), and other literary objects which are experienced as time-based. This demands the development and application of new rhetorical tropes and figures to text which has previously been dominated—up to and including the implementation of link-node h*.t?xt—by spatial structuring, by topographic rhetoric, while enclosed within the easily granted linearities of print and narrative. I suggest that cinema will provide the privileged source of metaphors for these figures, and that, to see what I mean, you should imagine a significant development of the kinds of textual transition and montage effects that we see in experimental typographic design, advertising, and cinematic titling. These figures will quickly replace the hollow, passionless link, and time-based text art will emerge with a rich, cinematic rhetoric that is derived from the art of letters rather than exclusively or predominantly from visual art or music, or, as now, by default, from the arbitrary exigencies of the "human-computer interface."

Addendum: A program

```
function contrast order, way
    global disjuncture, programmaton, poets
    put the length of order into bandwidth
    put true into moves
    get the length of way
    if it isGreaterThan bandwidth then
        put it into bandwidth
```

```
    put false into moves
end if
repeat with net is one to bandwidth
  get character net of order
  if it is empty then
    put space into objects
    put space into character net of order
  else
    put it into objects
  end if
  get character net of way
  if it is empty or it is not in disjuncture then
    put space into music
  else
    put it into music
  end if
  if objects is not music then
  put offset(objects, disjuncture) into fashion
  if fashion is zero then
    put one into fashion
    put space into character net of order
    put space into objects
  end if
  put offset(music, disjuncture) into theory
  if theory is zero then
    put one into theory
  end if
  put theory minus fashion into Cinderella_of_the_arts
  if theory isGreaterThan fashion then
    put negative((programmaton minus theory) plus fashion) into
      implementation
  else
    put ((programmaton minus fashion) plus theory) into implementation
  end if
  if the absolute of implementation isLessThan the absolute of
    Cinderella_of_the_arts then
    put implementation into practice
  else
    put Cinderella_of_the_arts into practice
  end if
  put (programmaton dividedBy two minus poets plus one) minus the
    absolute of practice plus one into design
  if design isLessThan two then
    put one into design
```

```
        else
          put internalize(poets, design) into design
        end if
        if practice isGreaterThan zero then
          add one to fashion
          if fashion isGreaterThan programmaton then
            put one into fashion
          end if
        else
          subtract one from fashion
          if fashion isLessThan one then
            put programmaton into fashion
          end if
        end if
        put character fashion of disjuncture into reader
        if design isLessThan one then
            if poets isGreaterThan six then
              if (reader is space) or (objects is space) then
                put the time into design
              end if
            else if poets isGreaterThan eight then
                if (objects is in apostrophe) or (reader is in apostrophe) then
                  put one into design
                end if
            end if
        end if
        if the random of design is one then
          put reader into character net of order
        end if
      end if
      end repeat
      return order
    end contrast
```

4

The Code Is Not the Text
(Unless It Is the Text)

The use of networked and programmable systems as both delivery and compositional media for literal and verbal art (and other forms of new media art) has provoked critical engagements which pretend to reveal and exam the various levels of code and encoding which are constituent of programmatological systems.[1] The title of the section of the p0es1s program which stimulated this paper—"Code as Text as Literature"—is a case in point.[2] In more extreme forms of such engagement, a radical post-human reductionism may be proposed, such as that, for example, which can be read from certain of Friedrich Kittler's essays, in which the ramifications of so-called human culture, especially as played out on new media, become qualitatively indistinguishable from "signifiers of voltage difference," demonstrably the final, lowest-level "ground code" of the increasingly familiar practices of cultural production which make use of programmable tools; and perhaps also essential to the brain activity which generates the objects and subjects of psychoanalysis.[3] Nowadays voltage difference accounts for and instantiates everything from the encrypted transactional play of internet banking to the promised consensual hallucination of immersive virtual reality. However the purpose of this brief paper is to address a number of less productive confusions which arise from this engagement with code-as-text, citing a few examples of artistic practice and a number of critical sources.[4] While allowing the value of certain metacritical statements such as Kittler's (which take on questions of what culture is or may become), my aim is to disallow a willful critical confusion of code and text, to make it harder for critics to avoid addressing one or the other by pretending that they are somehow equivalent, or that codes and texts are themselves ambiguously addressed to human readers and/or machinic processors (unless they are so addressed, however ambiguously).[5]

I have invoked reductionism, and by this I mean a critical thrust which, implicitly or otherwise, asks questions like, "What (ultimately) is this object we are examining? What is its structure? What are its essential or operative characteristics?" and then finds special critical significance in the answers proposed. In N. Katherine Hayles sophisticated version of what can be read as a code-as-text argument, this reductive inclination is in evidence. Her essay "Virtual Bodies and Flickering Signifiers" discovers a new or emergent object, the flickering signifier, and derives important consequences from its instantiations and methods. "The contemporary pressure toward dematerialization, understood as an epistemic shift toward pattern/ randomness and away from presence/absence, affects human and textual bodies on two levels at once, as a change in the body (the material substrate) and a change in the message (the codes of representation)."[6] In other words, Hayles suggests that the constituent structure of the signifier itself may be seen as changed in contemporary culture and especially as expressed in "new media." Both the materiality and the represented content of cultural practice and production have been affected. Before examining parts of Hayles's argument in more detail, I want simply to point out that it is clearly determined by its metacritical significance and has a reductive inclination: signifiers have come to be such and such, therefore—albeit in a cybernetic feedback loop—cultural production (in Hayles's essay "the represented worlds of contemporary fiction") follows suit. Hayles's characterization of a multiply mediated signifier which flickers from level to level in chained coded structures is, as a metacritical statement, highly suggestive and useful. However, when it comes to art practice and the critique of this practice, how does such insight figure?

What is missing from Hayles's analysis is a set of relationships— relationships constituted by artistic practice—between a newly problematized linguistic materiality and represented content. These would inevitably express themselves in formal as well as conceptual address to what she identifies as a changed matter of language and literature. Hayles's chosen examples, with, perhaps, the exception of her use of William Burroughs, demonstrate conceptual, rather than formal, address; they represent flickering signification as concept rather than as instantiation in the language of the work. Hayles cites, most extensively, William Gibson's *Neuromancer* as a prime example of represented content affected by and expressive of the flickering signifier. While Gibson brilliantly conveys the literally flickering, scanned and rasterized, apparent immateriality of an informatic realm, the "consensual hallucination" of "cyberspace" (his famous coinage) and its interpenetration of meatspace, he does this in a book—"a durable material substrate"—in a more or less conventional novel, one in which, indeed, narrative predominates over character development and in which language functions in a relatively straightforward manner. Not even the narrative perspective (omniscient author third person) is shifted or experimentally inflected in any of Gibson's cyberpunk classics. The writing is sharp and inventive but entirely subject to paraphrase.

There are further significant ironies here, for Hayles begins her essay by discussing typewriting. The physicality and static impression-making of this process of inscription is contrasted with that of word processing where less substantial bodily gestures cause word-as-(flickering)-image to be scanned onto the surface of a screen. "As I work with the text-as-flickering-image, I instantiate within my body the habitual patterns of movement that make pattern and randomness more real, more relevant, and more powerful than presence and absence."[7] However, the exemplar most present later in her argument, Gibson, has made some play of his preference for composing his novels using a typewriter.[8] Thus not only are the formal characteristics and the materiality of Gibson's language at odds with the flickering signification of its represented content, but, at the very least, the once-preferred experience of this writer—his phenomenology of inscription—is an apparent denial of Hayles's critical progression. I want to emphasize, in making these remarks, that if the subjective experience of the critic or reader is brought forward as evidence for a change in the structures of signification, then it is all the more important to examine the practices of the writer and the formal qualities of the work produced by those practices. Gibson sitting at a typewriter composing a novel may well produce a representation of the concept of flickering signification, but his practice does not necessarily embody the potential for new structures of meaning generation, or instantiate a corresponding materiality of language.

We will return to practice, but first I would like to examine Hayles's flickering signifier in so far as it engages with the notion of code-as-text.[9] "In informatics, the signifier can no longer be understood as a single marker, for example an ink mark on a page. Rather it exists as a flexible chain of markers bound together by the arbitrary relations specified by the relevant codes." At least since Saussure, it seems somewhat redundant to point to the arbitrariness of any signifier-signified relation. I suppose that Hayles is actually referring to these relations as "arbitrary" because they are not necessarily significant as human readings; they are not addressed to general human readers but only to the systems and systems-makers who have coded or specified them for certain purposes. They are, nonetheless, construable and are far from arbitrary when considered as addressed to the systems in which they are embedded. They have both significance and consequence. "As I write these words on my computer, I see the lights on the video screen, but for the computer, the relevant signifiers are electronic polarities on disk." That is, they are Kittler's (fundamental) signifiers of voltage difference.

Intervening between what I see and what the computer reads are the machine code that correlates these symbols with binary digits, the compiler language that correlates these symbols with higher-level instructions determining how the symbols are to be manipulated, the processing program that mediates between these instructions and the commands I give the computer, and so forth. A signifier on one level becomes a signifier on the next-higher level.

Hayles goes on to discuss the "astonishing power"—in the now-familiar technological sense of "power"—which these "arbitrary," hierarchically structured chains of codes generate, since manipulations, interpreted as commands at one level, can have cascading, global effects.[10] By shifting the argument in this way, I think she has bracketed a more significant consequence of the structure of signification which she is delineating: the question of address, the address of the specific encoded "levels."

In an article on "digital code and literary text," Florian Cramer has pointed out that, as he somewhat obscurely puts it, "the namespace of executable instruction code and nonexecutable code is flat."[11] From the context it is clear that he means that the same character or symbol set is used—for example— to transcribe both the text being word processed and (to be precise) the source code of the program which may be doing the word processing. On the level plains of letters and bits, there is no radical disjuncture in the symbolic media when we cross from a region of "executable" text to text "for human consumption." From the human reader's point of view, they are both more or less construable strings of letters; from the processing hardware's point of view they are more or less construable sequences of voltage differences. On the one hand, this statement is related to the famous inter-media translatability of digitized cultural objects (once coded, regular procedures can be used to manipulate an image, a segment of audio, a text, etc., without distinction, disregarding the significance or affect of the manipulation). Cramer is, however, more concerned with the potential for sampling and mixing code and text (in the contemporary music sense). Again, as in Hayles's analysis, the question of the address of specific code segments and texts is bracketed. Not only is it bracketed, but the range of positions of address is simplified, as if we are speaking of a flat letterspace for code on the one hand and text on the other; whereas, clearly, there are many levels. Both Cramer and Hayles recognize a multilevel hierarchy of codes without elaborating or distinguishing them in the course of their discussions. Within the field of networked and programmable media, at the very least, we can acknowledge: machine codes, tokenized codes, low-level languages, high-level languages, scripting languages, macro languages, markup languages, operating systems and their scripting language, the human–computer interface (HCI), the procedural descriptions of software manuals, and a very large number of texts addressed to entirely human concerns.[12]

For Cramer, and not only for Cramer, this simplified, bracketed, or ambiguous textual address has become a valorized aesthetic and even a political principle: "computers and digital poetry might teach us to pay more attention to codes and control structures coded into all language. In more general terms, program code contaminates in itself two concepts which are traditionally juxtaposed and unresolved in modern linguistics: the structure, as conceived of in formalism and structuralism, and the performative, as developed by speech act theory."[13] To attempt a paraphrase: working or sampled or intermixed or collaged code, where it is presented as verbal art, is seen by Cramer to represent, in itself, a revelation of underlying, perhaps even concealed, structures of control, and also (because of its origins in operative, efficacious program code) to instantiate a genuinely "performative" textuality, a textuality which "does" something, which alters the behavior of a system. It has the "astonishing power" of other cultural manifestations of new technology and new media, the power that Hayles has also recognized as a function of the coded structures arranged at various "levels" in programmatological systems, chained together by a literal topography, which is "flattened" by a shared symbol set. We should pause to consider what this power amounts to. What are the systems whose behavior can be altered by this power?

In the criticism of theoretically sophisticated poetics, there is a parallel aesthetic and political agenda, which I am tempted to call the Reveal Code Aesthetic. It is partly documented and particularly well represented in, for example, Marjorie Perloff's *Radical Artifice*, where "reveal code" is revealed as a project of L=A=N=G=U=A=G=E writers such as Charles Bernstein, after having been properly and correctly situated in the traditions of process-based, generative and/or constrained literature and potential literature by Modernist, OuLiPian, Fluxus, and related writers culminating, for Perloff, in John Cage and the L=A=N=G=U=A=G=E writers themselves.[14] Although the political and aesthetic of program of "reveal code" appears to be shared with Cramer's new media writers, in the context of Perloff's poetics, the codes revealed and deconstructed in language per se (rather than digitized textuality) are as much those of "the inaccessible system core," the machinic devices that conceal "the systems that control the formats that determine the genres of our everyday life."[15] While the progressive tenor of an aesthetic and political deconstruction underlies this project, there is something of a Luddite tone in Perloff.[16] New media writers and artists necessarily have more ambiguous political and aesthetic relations with the control structures of the media which carries their work.

The code-revealing language artists discussed by Perloff, both in their work and in their performance—be it textual performance or performance art per se or activism or (academic) critical practice—represent far better examples of the instantiation of pattern/randomness (distinguished from presence/absence) than the novelists cited by Hayles, even including Burroughs or Pynchon. While retaining her focus on the contemporary or near-contemporary writers which she associates with an innovative, L=A=N=G=U=A=G=E-inflected poetics having avant-garde inclinations,

Perloff recalls an extensive tradition of poetic literature which is marked by both its attention to the materiality of language and its radicalization of poetic practices.[17] Perloff invokes formations and works by individuals which are also referred to by critics of writing in networked and programmable media. Like Cramer, she discusses the OuLiPo (Ouvroir de Littérature Potentiel), the working group inspired and once led by Raymond Queneau, which is, perhaps, the primary reference for literary projects which are explicitly concerned with the application of algorithmic procedures, arbitrary constraint, generative or potential literature, and relatively early experimentation with the use of software. In doing so, she directly confronts the "repression" of "numerical," generative procedures in poetry and poetics and turns to the work of John Cage as a cross-media figurehead. While only a minor aspect of his oeuvre, as compared with his major contribution to the art of (musical) sound, Cage's mesostic texts, especially his "reading through" of Pound, Joyce, and others, stitch to together a range of concerns—inter-media art, procedural composition, the rereading (and implicit deconstruction) of the High Modernists—which are highly relevant to both contemporary poetics and writing in networked and programmable media. If Cage's work is recalled in the context of the Fluxus movement, with which he is associated, then its relevance widens and deepens. Fluxus is a model of performative art practice, including explicitly literary practice, where the record of inscription is problematized (the work is an event, or the publication of a set of materials which must be manipulated by the reader/user), and where the presence/absence dialectic has been side-stepped by representations which may literally absent an artist-author. Perloff does not discuss Fluxus at length and so misses the opportunity to reassess and contextualize work by two of the most important practitioners of the "(numerical) repressed," Emmett Williams and Jackson Mac Low, both of whom deserve serious study as precursors if not "anticipatory plagiarists" of writing in networked and programmable media.[18] Fluxus also provides a historical, critical link to the traditions of visual and concrete poetics, which are discussed in Perloff's account, particularly relevant work by Steve McCaffery and Joanna Drucker. The materiality of this work, considered as language art, visibly demonstrates a radical engagement with linguistic media and a requirement for the reader to engage with the codes—textual, rhetorical, paratextual, visual, and so on—by and of which the work is constituted.

If such prior work remains inadequately acknowledged in the discussion and reassessment of "codework," this may be, in part, simply because the traces of its inscriptions are captured and recorded in the "durable material substrates" of print culture. Whereas Lacan's "floating signification" is read as an analytic metaphor, applied to language borne by a delivery media—print—on which the signs of the interface texts literally "rest" (where they have been impressed) or, at best, "interleave" (they do not "float"), we read

Hayles's "flickering signifiers," as she encourages us to do so, as literally "flickering," and constituent, as such, of text which has become "screenic." As such, it seems to exist elsewhere, not on the page but through the window of the screen in the informatic realm.[19] Undoubtedly, there are clear and historical distinctions of delivery media for text. Nonetheless, we must be careful to distinguish the effects of delivery media on signification and affect from those produced by shifts in the compositional media, and there is great congruence between the approach to compositional media of certain print-based writers, such as those discussed by Perloff, for example, and the potential use of compositional media which is suggested by new media, that is, new delivery media. This potential of text- and language-making is not necessarily engaged simply because new delivery media happen to be employed.[20] The locus classicus for a multilayered, multilevel code-inflected writing and reading is, of course, Barthes's *S/Z*, as Hayles explicitly acknowledges.[21] *S/Z* was concerned with a short story programmed in "a persistent material substrate," but Barthes was nonetheless able to demonstrate the potential for an iterative flickering of hermeneutic attention across structured linguistic codes, implying, I would argue, perfectly adequate complexity, mobility, and programmability in the compositional media. Barthes's essay, after all, was not a demand for new media but a (re) call to new or latent ways of reading and writing.

We turn, nonetheless, to examples of what Cramer calls "codework." Cramer cites, among others, some of those writers in networked and programmable media whose work I, too, would consider in this context: Mez, Talan Memmott, Alan Sondheim, Jodi. Leaving Jodi to one side for the moment, these are all artists who both work with code and make coded, programmatological objects. They are particularly known and notable for working code and code elements into what we might call the "interface text," the words which are available to be read by the human audiences they address.[22] The result is a language which seems to be—depending on your perspective—enlivened or contaminated by code. In the rhetoric of this type of artistic production, contamination or infection (see Cramer as quoted above and Hayles below) is more likely to be the requisite association since transgression of the deconstructed systems of control is an implicit aspect of the aesthetic agenda. For the moment, however, we are more concerned with certain formal and material characteristics of the resulting language.

The language certainly reveals code and code elements, but what code does it reveal? What does it tell a code-naïve reader about the characteristics and the power of code? Is it, indeed, still code at all? At what level does it sit in the chained hierarchies of flickering signification? Has it been incorporated into the "interface text" in a way which reflects its hierarchical origin, if it has one? Only if these and other questions can be given answers which specify how and why code is sampled in this writing would be it "codework" in a strong sense. (Perhaps we should reserve Mez's "code wurk" for the weaker sense of code-contaminated language.) In the case of all of these writers (we'll come to Jodi shortly), the code embedded in the interface text has ceased to be operative or even potentially operative. It is "broken" in the now-familiar programmer's jargon. The breakdown of its operations eliminates one aspect of its proposed aesthetic value and allure, its native performative efficacy (which Cramer identified as a final throwaway without actually demonstrating or elaborating): the power of code to change the behavior of a system. The code-as-text is more in the way of decoration or rhetorical flourish, the baroque euphuism of new media. This is not to say that—as part of the interface text—it may not generate important significance and affect. In particular, the address of this type of intermixed, contaminated language is often concerned—as shown in the work of all of these writers—with issues of identity, gender, subjectivity, technology, technoscience, and the mutating and mutable influence they bring to bear on human lives and on human-human and human-machine relationships.

For the moment, however, we are more concerned with certain formal and material characteristics of the resulting language. In a recent conference paper, Hayles has discussed the language of Memmott's *From Lexia to Perplexia* in terms of pidgins and creoles. "In this work the human face and body are re-coded with tags in a pidgin that we might call, rather than hypertext markup language, human markup language. Code erupts through the surface of the screenic text, infecting English with programming languages and resulting in a creole discourse that bespeaks an origin always already permeated by digital technologies."[23] Similarly, Mez has characterized her textual production as written in a new "language/code system" which she calls "mezangelle." It is perhaps unfair to treat what may be metaphoric usages as literal; however, I believe this use of pidgin and creole is, in particular, a significant misdirection. A pidgin is a full-blown language, albeit arising from the encounter and hybridization of two or more existing languages; a creole is a pidgin which has become a first language for speakers raised by previous generations who have created or used a pidgin. The point here is that, in the case of a pidgin, the elements which combine to generate new language are commensurate—linguistic material is not simply being injected from one hierarchically and functionally distinct or programmatologically-operative symbolic sub-system, which is subsumed within a full-blown culture-bearing system of human language use into another. The creation of a pidgin is, furthermore, the result of interactions by commensurate entities, that is, humans. In the code-as-text which we have seen to date—in the texts of a reveal code aesthetic—human-specified code elements and segments are, typically, incorporated into what I have called the "interface text" which is unambiguously and by definition an instance of some human-readable language. It may be contaminated, jargonized, disrupted language, but it is not a new language, not (yet) evidence for the invasion of an empire of machinic colonizers whose demands of trade and interaction require the creation of a pidgin by economically and linguistically disempowered human users.[24] The codeworks currently available to us extend, infect, and enhance natural language, but they do not create, for example, Code Pidgin English.[25]

The code has ceased to function as code. The resulting text pretends an ambiguous address: at once to human reader and to machinic processor, but both human and machine must read the code as part of human discourse. We would not try to compile the code in the interface texts of Memmott, Mez, or Sondheim. Nonetheless, this pretended ambiguity of address remains important to the aesthetics of this work. It assumes or encourages an investment on the part of its readers in the technology of new media and, especially, in the dissemination of textual art in new media. Thus, the experiences of the reader in these worlds can be brought to bear on their reading of the codework and they can appreciate, through more-or-less traditional hermeneutic procedures, the references and allusions to technology, technoscience, and the issues with which they confront us. However, I would argue, if this pretended ambiguity of address exhausts the aesthetics and politics of a project (I am not saying that it does in any of these cases), then it leaves open questions of the work's affect and significance when compared, for example, with previous poetic work in more durable material and linguistic substrates, some of which has been cited above.[26]

The work of Sondheim needs to be singled out, in terms of practice and form, since his use of code is well integrated into a long-term and wide-ranging language art project. The print-media version of *Jennifer*, for example, reads more in the tradition of innovative or avant-garde writing than as subsumed within codework or a reveal code aesthetic.[27] Most of the texts in this selection are manipulated language, but often using procedures which are not directly related to codes and processing. Thus, while his overt subject matter—mediated gender and sexuality, explicitly inflected by computing and technoscience—and his explicitly chosen media keep him immediately allied with codeworking colleagues, Sondheim's work must also be read against earlier and contemporary writers working within or with a sense of the formally and aesthetically innovative traditions of poetics, and not only the poetics which intersects with Burroughs and Acker.[28]

In the necessity to read the work in both a programmatological context and in the broader context of innovative writing—though in this sense only—Sondheim's engagement rhymes momentarily with that of Loss Pequeño Glazier. Glazier and his work represent a literal and explicit embodiment of "a set of relationships—relationships constituted by artistic practice—between a newly problematized linguistic materiality and represented content." Glazier has produced a body of work, grounded in an existing writing practice, which has covered a wide range of potential forms for digital poetics and he has, moreover, documented and analyzed this trajectory in a series of critical contributions.[29] Glazier's work is characterized by his use of code and the language of code. In this, I believe, he affords himself significant ironies. He writes, for example:

> The language you are breathing becomes the language you think ... These are not mere metaphors but new procedures for writing. How could it be simpler? Why don't we all think in UNIX? If we do, these ideas are a file: I am chmoding this file for you to have read, write, and execute permission—and please grep what you need from this! What I am saying is that innovative poetry itself is best suited to grep how technology factors language and how this technology, writing, and production are as inseparable as Larry, Moe, and Curly Java.[30]

This is discursive prose of a kind, but it is infected or contaminated by both code and poetry. Glazier doesn't think in UNIX, nor would he ever wish to do so. But his language is not "mere metaphor" (poetry is not metaphor) it is centered on language-making (what poetry is), and it demands a poetic practice which is alive to new procedures and new potential and which is sensitive to the changes this practice produces in the materiality of the language itself. Apart from its engagement with code and coding, Glazier's work is also characterized by its bilingualism, or rather the multilingualism of "America" in the sense of a Latin America which exists as historical and political soul and shadow throughout, arguably, the greater part of the United States. I raise this point to highlight distinctions in the way we may choose to consider the non-standard English material in Glazier's (and others') texts, while recalling Hayles's metaphoric analysis via "pidgin" and "creole." In a Glazier text, there is a use of English intensified by an address to the materiality of language. There is the incorporation—in a strong sense, sometime within the body of a word—of linguistic material from Spanish and other languages, especially those indigenous to Mexico. There is a similar incorporation of linguistic material from code and from computing jargons.[31] But whereas the use of other natural language material evokes significance and affect which is commensurate with human concerns—personal, political, social, and cultural history, and so on—the use of "codewords" evokes other concerns, closer to questions of technology and the technology of language. Glazier would rather think in Nahuatl than in UNIX, but in practice he prefers to think in P=O=E=T=R=Y.

Jodi takes us to another point in the textonomy of code-as-text, a relatively extreme position where code-as-text is, perhaps, all there is.[32] It is difficult to say anything hard and fast in terms of more or less conventional criticism about a site which is hardly ever the same on successive visits. Instead, I want to refer to what I remember of a visit in which a dynamic HTML- and JavaScript-mediated experience proved to have been delivered by HTML source which was, itself, a work of ASCII art.[33] Here, the actual code is a text, an artistic text. However, the code is not, in this instance, working code (at least not "hard-working," shall we say). It is comprised of code segments which are ignored in the browser's interpretation and rendering of the HTML. The syntax of this markup language is particularly easy to manipulate or appropriate in this way because comments—ignored by any interpreter, by definition—may be extensive and because interpreters, browsers in this case, are, typically, programmed to ignore any <tagged> thing which they cannot render. The code works, but it is not all working code. Again, it represents only a pretended ambiguity of address: its primary structures of signification were never meant for a machine or a machinic process.

I, too, have made a few "codeworks" of a not dissimilar kind. By extracting and manipulating segments of the close-to-natural-language, very-high-level, interpreted programming language, HyperTalk, I was able to make human-readable texts which are also segments of interpretable, working code:

```
on write
  repeat twice
    do "global" & characteristics
  end repeat
  repeat with programmers = one to always
    if touching then
      put essential into invariance
    else
      put the round of simplicity * engineering/synchronicity + one into
        invariance
    end if
    if invariance is greater than the random of engineering and not
      categorical then
      put ideals + one into media
      if subversive then
        put false into subversive
      end if
      if media is greater than instantiation then
        put one into media
      end if
    else
      put the inscription of conjunctions + one into media
    end if
    if categorical then put false into categorical
    put media into ideals
    put word media of field "text" of card understanding & ",text" into
      potential
```

```
if the mouse is down then
   put conjunctions into potential
   put potential into card field agents
   put true into encoded
   exit repeat
end if
inflect
wait manipulation
put potential into conjunctions
put ideals into world
if performed then put false into performed
if programmers are greater than control and media & comma is in field
 computer of card understanding & ",text" then exit repeat
end repeat
if not encoded and not touching then
   if ideals are developed then wait five seconds
      lock screen
      put empty into card field agents
      put empty into card field system
      do "unlock screen with dissolve" & fantasies
   end if
end write34
```

This text has genuinely ambiguous address—to a HyperTalk interpreter and to human readers. It could (and does, in some versions of the software) alter the behavior of a system, when included as one routine in a text generator. Its address to human concerns is clearly ludic and, perhaps, pretends more than it delivers in terms of significance and affect, but at least we can say, with little qualification, that this code is the text.

But where is such a codetext going, in terms, for instance, of its formal and rhetorical characteristics, in terms of its specific materiality? As a text—let us provisionally call it a poetic text in the sense of a text which implies some trial of language—which is addressed to human readers, it has distinct limitations, constraints which disallow or compromise its engagement with broader and more traditional concerns or sources of cultural value. Nonetheless, for me, it suggests new or newly highlighted rhetorical strategies which are specific to the materiality of language in networked and programmable media. For the moment, I will identify two such rhetorical fields of play: (1) the direct confrontation of strict logical-syntactic symbolic composition (programming per se) with natural language syntax and argument, and (2) what I think of as a potential "aesthetics of compilation": the creation of linguistic or symbolic constructs which are designed, for example, to be read in one mode of address and at one level of code in a chained hierarchy of symbolic systems, while simultaneously intended for compilation into a systematically related code at a different level within the hierarchy, with a different mode of address.

The first of these rhetorical fields represents an age-old and persistent problem: that, indeed, of logic vs. rhetoric, although recast in specific proliferating instances of logic-as-literature in new media. There is no time or space in this shortly closing essay to take this on.[35] Compilation in language and literature, however, directly addresses the interrelation of code and text; and it seems to me to be a good example of a rhetorical concept, hitherto of little use where literary objects were inscribed in persistent and durable material substrates, but of great potential in a literature constituted by flickering signification. Texts are already being made to be compiled, decompiled, recompiled, and so on.

I may have seemed to be arguing with flickering signification, by giving examples of writing which appeared to demonstrate its structures of code and text in systematically linked hierarchies, and then showing that these structures were collapsed in many of the examples to hand. In fact, I believe that the structures Hayles identifies and characterizes are clearly operative in writing in networked and programmable media, just as they are operative in certain types of innovative poetic practice. The writing of flickering signification does, indeed, contribute to changes in the body of literature, the literary corpus, both its "material substrate" and its "codes of representation." However, rather than the intermixing and mutual contamination of code and text, we require not only a maintenance and practical understanding of the distinction between code and text, we need at least the same range and fineness of distinction as that which exist between all the levels of programmatological languages and codes. The "power"— including any affect and significance discoverable by interpretation—which such structures of signification generate is dependent on these distinctions, and on the compilation procedures, which I propose as rhetorical, by which they are systematically related. This "power" is also, typically, in this context, dependent on the concealment—the hidden working—of the code which is thus allowed to serve its function as program, to generate the text and offer it—iteratively, repeatedly, indeterminately—for instances of potential performance, including the familiar performance of reading.

In her discussion of the flickering signifier and its filial relation to the floating precursor of Lacan, mutation is the resultant process of a dialectic implied by a new structure of signification, as parallel term for castration in Lacan's analysis. Mutation is "a decisive event in the psycholinguistics of information. Mutation is the catastrophe in the pattern/randomness dialectic analogous to castration in the presence/absence dialectic."[36] Mutation— which evokes change, movement, the kinetic potential of text in new media, the mimetic engagement of literature with the culture of human time—is indeed a generative catastrophe for "literature" in the sense of immutable, authoritative corpus. As writing in networked and programmable media, language and literature mutate over time and as time-based art, according to programs of coded texts which are embedded and concealed in their structures of flickering signification. For the code to function as generator, as programmaton, as manipulator of the text, it must, typically, be a distinct part of the global textual system; it must be possible to recompile the codes as operative procedures, as aspects of live-art textual practice. The code is not the text.

5

Hypertext/Cybertext/Poetext

I

1. Reading, hearing, writing, performing the linguistically innovative poetries and swept up in the enthusiasms of their deep, but lo-tech, engagements with new textualities through formal experiment and in their play of significations, there is a temptation to say to its practicing writers and readers, "I/you/we/they don't need 'new' technologies or 'new' media." There is so much left to be explored, that is being explored, in both codexspace and performancespace, as to suggest that it would be a waste of time to buy into some novel textgadgetry; to risk an expense of spirit in the wastes of techno-narcissism; or to subject poetics "to the trade of a calculation that dominates most tenaciously in those areas where there is no need of numbers."[1]

2. No need of numbers? This essential term, read as enclosing a contradiction, is at once the sign of art-less "calculation" and the basis of all artistic formalism. Unresolved, it becomes a necessary reminder of the romanticized dissociation of "writing" (or, more broadly, verbal creativity) from its techniques and technologies, and the elevation of the former over the latter, as if certain privileged spheres of rhetoric—literacy and its codexspace being the examples necessary here—were transparent to the content they selflessly bear, whereas other "newer" varieties are branded forever with their technological origins.[2]

3. The machineries of hypertext, cybertext, and poetext are still often confused with the potential rhetorics they adumbrate. Even if these transient terms (as likely to fade and die out as to thrive within a short space of years or months) referred to physical delivery media, such as those associated with the cinema, there would still be no need in critical discourse to confuse the equivalent of camera or projection device with, for example, the grammar of montage. In fact, these technologically overdetermined textualities are realized in formal engineering which is itself "authored," and this fact provides such

textualities with many of the qualities which most clearly distinguish them from other, previous and still dominant, technologies of literary culture.

4. "It is important to make it clear that literary developments in cybertext are not constrained by hardware technologies themselves; they are constrained only by software, which is an authored delivery medium." (Although "[a]part from these constraints which are surmountable through engineering, there are those produced by, as it were, a 'false consciousness' generated by the 'ideology' surrounding the current use of computer-based systems.")[3]

5. "These agents [active, co-creative functions of cybertextual media] are themselves constructed, and they may be authored by the writer or designer of both given text and its modulated form (in any particular reading or performance) as an integral part of the entire 'work.' Writers may also write 'with and against and amongst' the code."[4]

6. [Thus,] the advocacy of hypertextual or cybertextual technologies in the context of innovative poetics is not the same thing as promoting a new and better word processor. It is a continuity with the development of form-in-content or indeed the creation of new forms which has always been characteristic of the ancient and various tradition of innovative linguistic art. The writer may choose to inscribe new form itself in the work, proposing a novel poetext with each new publication. (Versions of the present chapter revisited simple, hypertextual reformations of the linear exposition, using an indexing metaphor which is both familiar and internalized in Western codexspace.) The point is, whereas I am severely constrained in my re-engineering of an essay which will appear in a bound paper collection, in software the potential is much greater, the forms are more plastic, such that the creation of the form becomes an integral and appreciable part of the creation of the work, if not a necessary part.

7. [For] there is no requirement to engineer a form for each new text, no necessity to take up the (programming) skills which are the tools of a conception of writing extended into the technologies of its production. Form—even the conceptual poetic form and certainly not the (material) delivery medium—does not necessarily, in itself, determine the nature of the textuality instantiated in a particular work.

II

8. Apart from the advocacy of textual technologies to poetics as a continuation of its own practices, there is a growing literature which represents hypertext in particular as the instantiation or embodiment of modern and postmodern critical theory.[5] However, while this literature acknowledges a quantity of previous, chiefly prose, work, especially modernist exemplars and criticism

associated with, for example, the poetics of Barthes and Tel Quel, and, to a limited extent, writers associated with, Fluxus, the OuLiPo, poststructuralist schools, and so on, and while it has engaged radical textualities in "traditional" delivery media—codexspace—it has not, especially in its more polemical moments or when focused on pedagogical methodology, given the same degree of attention to radical poetries per se—for instance those of Cage, Mac Low, L=A=N=G=U=A=G=E, and so on. Even these new critics of hypertext are occasionally caught in the uncertainty as to whether they should promote a new projection device—the "new" delivery media of electronic hypertext—or continue to develop a radical cultural critique. It is as if the supposed representation of postmodern critical theory attracts special privilege when set against its representation as a function of, say, the writerly (scriptible) text of codexspace; as a function, that is, of the writer's proposal of new textualities, regardless of delivery media, and the reader's disposal of interpretative, intertextual engagements.[6]

9. The underlying metaphors of critical theory's instantiation or embodiment in "new media" are seductively rich, redolent of notions of (historical) originality, novelty, incarnation. If hypertextuality is the signal of a paradigm shift in verbal culture, then better ways of representing its significance may be found in analyses of the previous shift from orality to literacy. Here, Ong's notion of the "internalization" of literacy is useful.[7] It was not that codexspace, especially books and printing, embodied or instantiated a latent literacy in verbal cultures which had acquired writing technologies; rather, they allowed the internalization of literacy, its elevation to the invisible, all-pervasive "ground" of verbal culture, such that today, to take two examples, in high critical discussion, papers are read out loud in a pseudo-oration which has little, sometimes nothing, to do with orality, or, in the performance of poetry, where the reading of hyper-literate production is a norm, even amongst many poets for whom spontaneous "voiced" expression is an ideal.

10. Hypertext, [then], does not instantiate, but it may well allow the internalization of textualities or modes of verbal culture which have been characterized in recent critical theory. And, with the World Wide Web growing daily, massively, in accessibility and popularity—and no more or less socially or politically marked than was the printed codex—this does seem increasingly likely.

III

[Not all of the characteristics of hypertext receive equal attention in this chapter. Brief remarks will be made about many aspects of machine modulated textuality before concentrating on its engagement with the reader's participation in the construction of meaning.]

11. Intertextuality is often cited as the modern critical term most clearly associated with and "embodied in" hypertext, but, just as clearly, intertextuality predates, even as critical concept, its cybernetic representations by a period of time which, some might argue, is equal to the entire history of literature. Going outside a text to other texts as a way of reading and understanding is not a notion which is dependent on a particular technology or is even, for that matter, confined to literacy (if, for these purposes, the assumption of the priority of writing in the term "text" is bracketed). In contemporary writing, intertextuality seems to me a "done deal," an accepted and necessary part of writing practice across a wide range of discourses and genres. Beyond the promise of extreme convenience which is granted by hypertextual systems like the World Wide Web, the existence of hypertext does not add, conceptually, to our understanding of intertextuality as a strategy of reading and understanding.

12. In so far as intertextuality has problematized the notion of closure, however, the situation is more complex. Despite the priority of intertextuality as a concept, the physicality of the textual object, in codexspace, contributes to a sense of closure, and the related notions of, for example, "author"ization/ity, integrity, position in the textual hierarchies of aesthetic/critical value, "primary" vs. "secondary" material, and so on. Since hypertextual forms may bracket or disrupt the physical closure of the text, they clearly have potential to "open" the text to these underlying critical problems, and to popularize, or at least make familiar, literary works which are already predicated, for many of their effects, on this field of openness. The obvious examples here are from the intrinsically non-closed serial poem, stemming from *The Cantos*: Zukovsky's *A*, Olson's *The Maximus Poems*, and Blaser's *Image-Nations*.

13. While strategies for representing non-linear forms in codexspace can and have been devised, cyberspace provides an environment in which a non-linear poetics—perhaps even one generalized to encompass linear and time-based varieties—should find room to grow and thrive.[8]

14. The problematization of the (unitary) identity, intentionality, presence or, indeed, existence of author(ity) is already addressed in the disruption of closure which hypertext proposes, although the composition of the elements (lexia) of most currently existing hypertextual work follows, for the most part, a conventional, "authoritarian" model. The construction of procedural, generative work in cybertext does, however, help to represent and generalize a disrupted, mediated, undermined authorship, or, as some critics have recognized, a notion of "cyborg authorship," meaning one in which engineered reading or text-generation procedures are recognized as jointly "responsible" for the work and in which the human participant acknowledges arbitrary and procedural elements of cultural (self-)construction as aspects of her manifest identity(ies).[9]

IV

15. [Before returning to the reader's participation in the construction of meaning, consider that,] there are certain aspects of (potential) textuality which are more or less specific to work which is realized as software—procedures and figures which it would be very difficult to realize in other media. Unsurprisingly, these potentialities are associated chiefly with the production and presentation of the work, rather than with the literary substance of what is produced and presented, although this distinction is more useful in outlining these figures than it is in understanding them, where it instances the same problematized relationship between "writing" and its media.

16. The permutational "power" of the computer allows an approach to process-based work in which the adjective "experimental" takes on a sense closer to that which it carries in the laboratory. The time and effort involved in producing a text through procedural or chance operations by hand can be considerable. Software can be used to generate these texts relatively quickly, such that judgments may be made concerning both the results of the procedures and the procedures themselves. The implications of these judgments can then be fed back into the co-creative process. Alterations can be made to both the given texts and the procedures used to generate the final work. All this can be done quickly enough to give rise to a fruitful feedback loop, to experiments in the creation of meaning which even a scientist might recognize as such.

17. As delivery media, computer systems also allow the real-time presentation of aleatory and procedural work, which may be both complex and radically indeterminate to a degree which is very difficult to realize in codexspace. Not that the presentation of such work is impossible in more familiar media. Even as books, *Yi Jing* (The Classic of Change), Raymond Queneau's *Cent Mille Milliards de Poèmes*, Mark Saporta's *Composition no. 1*, for example, allow their readers to become the producers of their texts, to such an extent that these works properly should not be considered as fixed texts at all—neither the static record of, for example, many throws of the dice, nor the application of, say, diastic rules (as with certain of Mac Low's printed works), nor a function of some set of specific readings by particular readers—the work in these and other cases is the entire conception and the whole process of its reading. Literary objects engineered through software (especially where the software is immediately accessible to or manipulable by the "reader") allow a more thorough realization of works with similar textual characteristics (see 28 below), potentially works which may exist only as the literary performance of the object itself—where, for example, there is no static or persistent inscription, only a writing which is presented in a particular duration.

18. This type of work also reveals the explicit introduction of a third term into the writer/reader probability space. The programmer or engineer of the procedures takes on a role that is much more than that of facilitator/technician in an unusual form of publication. As the procedural manipulation

of literary texts becomes more sophisticated, the role of the designer of processes approaches that of the writer.

19. "Each term of the writer/reader/programmer triangle is a shifter. Just as writer may be reader, and reader, writer in current (postmodern) critical perspectives, so either of these absent agents may be programmers: systematic manipulators of text and intertext, making use of software which has become intimate with poetics. Poets and readers must become intimate with software."[10] At the present juncture, the distinctions between the identities or positions represented by these three terms have been subverted (rightly so) by critical thinking; they remain in place more as a function of established or preferred cultural practice, actions and behaviors associated culturally with readers, writers, and programmers. Yet without even invoking the current disruptions of programmable media, it can be seen, for example, that the roles of writer and reader are constructed within particular cultures, and even within the micro-cultures of particular groups of reader/writers—mainstream/avant-garde; British poetry/US poetry/Irish poetry—and that "programming" a text, in the sense of designing it for a suggested mode of reading, has always been at least partly within the gift of the writer, and since the advent of desk-top publishing, has progressively involved both writers and readers in acts of what I'd be happy to call "textual programming."

20. If, through hypertext or any other delivery technology, literary objects are constructed as "open," then this permeability of writer/programmer is extended to reader/programmer, as readers configure or radically change the literary objects of their attention.

21. [Finally,] the potential media represented by networked computing systems offer novel metaphors and models for some of the crucial subjects of poetic writing. To take just one simple example, in the world of networks, multiuser systems—those sharing information-processing resources across several terminals—are a commonplace. The popularization of this new metaphoric vehicle may make it easier to conceive of multiplicity or decentralization in relation to, say, the brain(s) or body(ies) of the mind(s) or person(s) seen as multiuser system(s), but without the usual associations of such multiplicity with personality disorder, mental illness or harmful, anti-social disjunctions. For, in networked computing, plurality, multiple/parallel processing, and decentralization are signs of robustness and efficiency in our attempts to represent, manipulate, and create meaning from complex inputs and interactions.

V

22. [Briefly,] how might the existence of these systems and literary objects lead to the internalization of a shifted paradigm for language art? The usual way to answer this would be to say that it would arise out of the

popularization of new forms of textuality and as a function of perceived homologies between those forms and the new structures of understanding represented by developments in critical theory. Forms which demonstrate these homologies would tend to be privileged over more traditional forms, where the new forms matched ascendant, albeit subversive, modes of thought, as formal exemplars of that thought.

23. [However,] perhaps it would be as well not to attempt to ascribe any sort of priority to forms of thought and simply to see the popularization of alternative textualities as the development of "new forms of life"—and as hard evidence of realizable potentialities—not, necessarily, as homologous with supportive theoretical structures, but evolving and proliferating themselves along with other cultural and technological developments until they finally allow the internalization of strategies for the creation of meaning which are currently difficult or rare.[11]

VI

24. Interactivity is, on the face of it, one of the most attractive and compelling promises held out by the new technotextuality, as also by the entire multimedia thrust of networked infotainment. Apart from their more directly venal ambitions, these would-be producer/broadcasters dream of replacing passive televisual half-life with "a fully interactive experience." Meanwhile the makers of interactive texts promise real-time reader interactivity with the substance and sense of literary creation itself, as an (obvious) improvement over the (passive) consumption of the printed word, locked into lines and bound into the structure of the codex.

25. [But] "interaction" is a term which sits happily in the phrase "complex interaction," and it implies reciprocity and mutual influence, between persons and/or things. It is too rich a term for the programmed stimulus and response, or configurational controls which are currently offered over the limited channels of today's electronic publishing systems—keyboard, pointing device, screen; less commonly simple voice recognition and speech-generation; full-motion video or virtual reality if you are lucky. Doubtless, the technology will improve and improve quickly. In the meantime, it is strange that there is so much willingness to apply the term "interaction" to simple human–machine exchanges when in face-to-face encounters with other persons (or animals or things for that matter) we have experiences which are truly interactive, to an extent which might make us wary of applying the term when dealing with software.

26. Transactional might be more like it, as in the phrase a "simple transaction" or the sense of transaction as "a piece of business," not only because it would be more consonant with current systems' capabilities, but also because it points to the underlying intentionality of many developers

of so-called interactive technologies, for they will be quite happy to develop televisual culture up to a point where certain economically "essential" transactions may be carried out, but then, suddenly, have little inclination for taking things further, pending some return on their investment in R&D.

27. Interactivity might well be one of the goals of an extended textuality, but it is not enough to be content with or to fetishize a model of interactivity which is simply the arts-pages equivalent of handing over electronic credits in the virtual intermall as a (self-reflexive) expression of "choice."

28. The question of interactivity is, however, a useful tool in the interrogation of the "writerly" text, and its readers' participation in the creation of meaning. Espen Aarseth, in the course of his work on textuality in its new domains, has attempted to outline a method for categorizing different varieties of textuality, regardless of delivery medium.[12] Interactivity per se does not enter into his discussion. To radically simplify his scheme, he assesses texts on the basis of their Dynamics (static or alterable); Determinability; Transience (does the text reveal itself with the passing of time or must it be looked over/worked at); Perspective (allowing role playing by the reader or not); Access (random or controlled); Linking (explicit or conditional or no linking); and (the most complex scale) "User" function (interpretative or explorative or configurative or "textonic" which implies the ability of readers to co-author the text). Such a scheme allows him not only to characterize and analyze the widest range of textual phenomena, including the extraordinary, more genuinely interactive textuality of MUD and MOO spaces, but also to make some useful broader categorizations, elaborating on those represented by hypertext and cybertext, or ergodic and non-ergodic literature.[13]

29. For Aarseth, "cybertext" is a more inclusive term capable of encompassing most of the currently conceivable aspects of what we might call interactivity—text generation (dynamics), indeterminacy, animation (transience), role-playing perspective, configurative and authorship-sharing "user" functions, and so on. Hypertext is reserved for the normally static, but linked and randomly accessible texts which are now familiar to us through the World Wide Web. "Ergodic" texts are those which demand "work" from the reader above and beyond the work of interpretation (the "success" of which is bracketed pending authoritative critical judgment), or, in Aarseth's more considered terms, "The ergodic work of art is one that in a material sense includes the rules for its own use, a work that has certain requirements built in that automatically distinguishes between successful and unsuccessful users."[14]

30. Clearly, schemes such as Aarseth's are useful for the better understanding of textual technologies, and this is entirely within the scope of every poet's concerns. However, poets, even the innovative variety, seem to have been primarily interested in the construction of highly sophisticated texts which nonetheless remain conservative in their exploitation of the

potential of textuality itself as a plastic medium. There are good reasons for this. The "interpretative user function" in Aarseth's scheme is, after all, the doorway to the writerly universe. While the manifest textuality of a poem may be limited in its "technology," it may nonetheless open out into endless readings, ramifications, inspirations, linkings, intertextualities, not only in the mind of the reader, but in her library, her own writing, her life. There is nothing stopping a reader from extending the meaning-creation of any text of any kind outside itself into radically new and indeterminate (literary) situations. Returning to the spirit in which this chapter set out: what more do you want?

VII

31. [However,] poets, even the most codextextual, have also been concerned with the notion of performance, if not of the work itself in ritual, vocalized utterance, then at least in the performance of their texts within the world of letters or, indeed, reputation. So, I want to examine those types of performance which are accessible to some basic varieties of language art, while bearing in mind the potential for interactivity which is presented by these various performance modes, aiming to arrive at a point in which the mode of performance offered by a cybertextual poetics may be perceived more clearly.[15]

32. Strangely, in the performance of "purely oral" language art (as Ong makes clear), there is room for indeterminacy and true listener ("reader") interaction. The bard never—or only in the most exceptional circumstances—performs the same work in the same words; the bard is always responsive to the mood and demands of the audience, to a degree which is typically far greater than that offered by the reading poet. This is strange, because the sound of the work is all there is—it is a transient shape as language in time and space which, instantaneously, returns to absolute physical nothingness the moment the performer's voice ceases (unlike this chapter, for example, which seems to persist because your reader's eyes constantly, without attending to it, refresh its image in the mind and because you may return to it in a different time and place). There is no "text" or recording in pure orality from which to recover the shape of the work. Moreover, when that shape is realized again, by the same or by another performer, it is significantly different. Despite these disjunctions, listeners have no difficulty in identifying and distinguishing particular works.

33. In the "pure literacy" of codexspace—I mean the, perhaps, unobtainable ideal of applied grammatology—the text performs silently, without necessary reference to a prior or an anticipated voice. What interaction there is takes place not in relation to an author, but with the text

itself, or rather with impressions of the text which are transferred into the textual life of the reader. The text itself does not change, although the way it is constructed and printed may indicate alternate reading strategies, and the random or indexed reordering of sub-elements may be possible. However, the most meaningful extension of the text occurs through the (unlimited) interpretative function of the reader (see 30 above), who may even experience the indication of alternate strategies—where they are enforced by the writer, designer, or programmer—as an unwarranted attempt to control or contain the reader's self-liberated pleasures of the text.

34. [But] pure literacy is an unrealized state in a culture which, although it can hardly (re)conceive of pure orality—despite its continued existence on the planet and despite the fact that it precedes our own internalized literacy—is nonetheless logocentric. Typically, written texts, where they do not explicitly transcribe—as in the earliest form of text-based performance, namely, plays, or in novelistic dialogue—imply speech or verbal performance. Paradoxically, such texts, which indicate a voice and often pretend to realize their (full) potential in ritual, voiced readings, are those which seem to preserve their authorial integrity, as their readers-turned-listeners maintain absolute decorum and silence in the auditorium—which may also be an imaginary auditorium, faithfully constructed by a silent reader for the poet's voice. In poetry, the impetus to perform is strong and, in contemporary culture, it grows stronger as we hear some of the most innovative writers turning to forms which, while based on experimental literacy, nonetheless achieve their most faithful representation in oral realizations. Thus, the fruitful, suggestive oxymoron of "performance writing" swims into view, recast and partially resolved in the strongly indicative phrase, "writing as performance."

35. [Finally, in this brief and partial sketch,] cybertextual technologies offer a potential form of pure literacy with a—currently limited—capacity to, itself, perform. The performance of literary objects may be read back into both the pure literacy of the silent text and also into text-based performance writing, but cybertextual technologies already exist which, as mentioned above, animate the generation of procedural and chance modulated work in "real time." Although there is a long way to go before such literary objects display any depth in their appropriation of, say, the less exploited terms in Aarseth's analysis of textuality, existing works have invoked dynamics, indeterminability, transience, random access, linking, reader configuration, and reader co-creation of textual elements.[16] The potential for the interaction of literary objects with both readers and also the third term, programmers, is not closed, and will continue to problematize the role of the author, who may also be an interactive reader or programmer. In the last analysis, the meaning-creation of the work is provided by the performance of the literary object itself.

36. While the instances of interactivity offered by existing texts are currently extremely limited, it is important to remember that this need not

always be the case, and remark that the type of interactivity offered is different from that offered by, in particular, the (pure) literary art of codexspace and of text-based performance. The interactivity offered by pure orality was both what I will call catastrophic/judgmental (limited to the dismissal of the work, its rejection or forcible suppression—for example, stopping a speaker, "putting down" a book) and also cooperative/critical/co-creative. Bard and audience were able to develop a relationship—not one in which skill (even mastery) was necessarily in doubt, nor a sense of the "priority" of the impetus to produce verbal art, but one, nonetheless, which allowed the work to be significantly, meaningfully changed and, in exceptional circumstances, co-created. These possibilities, which are not typically or materially available to pure literary or text-based performance (where interaction is too often consigned to its catastrophic/judgmental mode) are not only accessible but, arguably, extended and radicalized in a cybertextuality where literary objects themselves both perform to their readers and are worked with by these readers as co-authors and co-programmers.

37. In this "late age of print," writers are tantalized by the potentiality of programming (pro-writing) which may allow cooperative, co-creational interaction with their own works.[17] This is a potentiality which is already some part of the experience of all readers and writers, but it has typically been seen as allied with the (radical, subversive, occasional) practices of writers who are, at times, characterized as "innovative." If the language-based textualities of cyberspace are not drowned out in the coming audiovisual deluge, they promise to internalize a new, but (strangely, theoretically) familiar form of literacy for a much broader community of reader-writer-programmers.[18]

6

Writing on Complex Surfaces

Flatland

> If the vitality of our cultural morphology only makes sense in the fractal complexities of historical space-time, Flatland with its plane geometries of irony, misogyny and denial won't work. The symbolic is always such a flatland in its relation to the complex real. In a fractal relation between art and life—that is, art as a fractal form of life—an infinitely invaginated surface of linguistic and cultural coastlines, interconversant edges of past/present/future, gives us, if not depth, then the charged and airy volume of living matter.[1]

These remarks by the poet and poethical essayist Joan Retallack surface in the midst of an essay that is itself formally innovative, performing parts of what it proposes. The sentences conclude a brief incisive critique of Jean Baudrillard's conception of an all-surface hyperreality or irreality, where, he claims, map becomes territory. Retallack challenges the pretended, ironic profundity of this exemplary postmodernist cultural critic, pointing out that not only would he leave us living on a flatland, he makes it impossible for us ever to escape. Baudrillard concedes a predominant cultural condition in which the symbolic both rests upon and constitutes an entirely superficial "reality." In a sense, his supposed insight is merely the recognition and acceptance of an existing textual condition, that of authoritative language (including his own) resting on the page; he simply gestures toward a number of the paradoxical and ironic consequences of maintaining an all-too-familiar preexisting paradigm.

Retallack's subversion of the would-be subversive is intellectually telling, and it is also effective because she understands it in terms of poet(h)ical practice, both her own and the potential practice in which she suggests that other writers participate, what might be termed an engaged formalism, a poetics that is ethically charged with "interconversation" at "linguistic and cultural coastlines." Her own work clearly demonstrates and demands reading and writing in terms of a complex, fractal surface, implicated with time and history. Her texts are the traces of processes and procedures, involving erasure, error, changing states, affective and effective action. The very titles of her poethical collections—*Errata Suite, Afterrimages, How to Do Things with Words*—indicate strategies for reading that require us to shift our attention and engagement beneath, above, with, and through the surface of writing, and to replay and anticipate processes which both generate and constitute the text itself.[2] For Retallack, complex, procedural, (re)iterative responses to her processes of writing *is* the text. It is an intrinsically temporal entity chaotically inscribed on a complex surface.

Practices of writing find themselves constrained by at least two imbricated cultural formations: institutions of authority governing publication and traditionally perceived characteristics of language-as-material. Addressed to writing, "depth" is rarely conceived as material depth. Depth is even more abstracted when it is applied, critically, metaphorically, to writing than when, for example, it is applied to painting. Generally speaking, rather than any aspect of material depth, it signifies access, through a symbolically marked but dimensionless and transparent surface (paradoxically, it is the marks that render the surface transparent) to the interiority of a remote author, an author whose very authority is guaranteed by institutions of publication which are, in a circular, bootstrap logic, predicated on flatland delivery, with all traditionally perceived material characteristics of language intact, or rather, collapsed, resting, flattened, on paper-thin media, ready to be read and passed through.

A related argument—that practices of writing are constrained by actual physical media—paper and the book—is often resisted by poetic writers, those, that is, who produce work which challenges flatland *author*ity and engages with language-as-material.[3] While paper is thin and print is flat, nevertheless, these "old" media allow many ways to indicate, if not perform, a text's material depth, its temporality, its constitution as process. Books can be programs. Because deep, time-based poetic practice has a history, including a tradition of serious intellectual exposition and commentary, poetic practitioners often also demonstrate their suspicion of so-called "new" media. They resist work in new media which reads as "thin" despite its explicitly, overtly complex surface; and they resist a potential future of overdetermination by unproven writing machines.

In agreement with many active poets, I do not, and would not, argue that print-based textuality is incapable of delivering writing with a complex surface, but I do say that in so far as this is achieved it is achieved as concept, in the familiar and comfortable realm of literary virtuality, in the "mind" and in the "imagination," but not in the material experience of the text and its language. In our present times, so long as the dimensionless surface of writing casts its pall over the writing surfaces of the screen, it will remain difficult to make an unarguable case for the specificities of writing in programmable media. The screen should not simply be cast as the bearer, for example, of multiple (flat) surfaces or successive "states" of text; it must be viewed as a monitor for complex processes, processes which, if they are linguistic, will be textual and symbolic, with a specific materiality as such. We must be able to see and read what the screen presents rather than recasting what passes before our eyes as the emulation of a "transparent" medium.

From a certain perspective, the arguments I am developing here may appear to be a more or less familiar rerun of critical comparison between print and digital media as they are applied to literary art. I wager that by redeploying such arguments while retaining focus on the surface of writing, a clearer conception of the properties and methods of textuality itself will emerge. Flatland text on paper-thin surfaces will be appreciated once again as a particular, relatively specialized instance of a more abstract and generally applicable textual object, one, for example, that is able to engage with and comprehend human time. Time is arguably the most important, necessary, and most neglected property of textuality. A complex surface for writing allows time to be reinstated as integral to all processes of writing and reading.

Rather than continuing to try and present a case in terms of the literary virtuality of poetic theory, this chapter now offers a commentary on examples of textual practice that can be properly appreciated only in terms of writing on a surface that is both materially and conceptually complex, and intrinsically temporal.

North by northwest

My first example is taken from the unacknowledged prehistory of textual animation as pioneered in the art of film titles, arguably the first medium in which words moved.[4] Apart from helping to give writing in programmable media a historical context, cinematic titling also demonstrates that the complex surface of writing is not, of necessity, media-specific. It does not require the screens of programmable machines. While the vast majority of film titles are instances, at best, of subtle and conservative design, there is a tradition of innovative formal engagement, and one of its most important exponents—the first acknowledged artist of film titling—is Saul Bass.[5] Despite the fact that Bass's work emerges from design as opposed to fine art or literary practice, I would argue that the film titling that made his name is a groundbreaking engagement with the materiality of language in what was then still a new medium for text. In his most innovative work Bass used the paratextual features of letter and word forms both to define graphic space and to dwell and move in and over the surfaces of the illusionistic naturalism within the already well-developed visual rhetoric of narrative cinema. He recast the surfaces on which he "wrote" and rendered them complex in some of the ways that concern us.

Bass achieved this during the second half of the 1950s, in his groundbreaking titles for films from *The Man with the Golden Arm* (1955) through *Psycho* (1960) and, to a certain extent, *Spartacus* (1960). The latter marks a distinct shift in his practice, after which, in the 1960s and 1970s, he turned away from film titling and worked more directly with the visual imaginary of cinema, as then understood. The titles for *Spartacus* use photorealist images of objects—especially a bronze bust—but shot such that they hover on the edge of the silhouette-abstraction that had become a Bass trademark. From *Spartacus* on, the actual words of his titles are distinct typographic forms floating over or through the visual imaginary that they caption. In *Spartacus*, a letter-edge might still have caught on the edge of a silhouette. What and where is the surface of writing when this is possible? By contrast, none of the words in the titles for *Cape Fear* (1991) would share a surface with the water and shadow over which they move.

This more familiar, later work—in what has become the established mode of film titling—sets the innovations of Bass's 1950s work in sharp relief. The typographic "rule"—typically a printed bar of ink—was an important trans-medial element in his film titles of the time. Rules are quintessentially paratextual.[6] They share the surface of writing, and they share its graphic materiality—particularly contrasting monochrome color. They manage and marshal the spaces in which writing is set, but they are not writing in the strict sense of symbolic representation. At one and the same time, rules are also lines, lines that may shape themselves into abstract visual representations. Rules problematize the surface of writing; they are both writing and not writing both on the surface of writing and on a surface of another dimension of writing. They bound and define the surface of writing, and they may even, in certain contexts, as Bass showed, become the surface of writing.

Titles for *The Man with the Golden Arm* demonstrate this perfectly (Figure 6.1). A single heavy rule sweeps down to mark the director's credit; three more are propagated and, while introducing the names of the (three) lead actors, suggest, to my eye, walking legs. Three of the four vanish, leaving one upper rule, with the three now returning, sweeping in from the other screen edges, to set out the superbly composed spaces of the film's title. The same rules go on to marshal and punctuate the remaining credits, suggesting more visual forms and spaces, and also, I would argue, letter forms, before finally and infamously combining to become the jagged silhouette of the "golden arm" itself.

Rules in Bass's work do not typically become letters, but they do interfere with the surfaces of writing—sometimes making the switch from foreground

FIGURE 6.1 *Still from the opening titles, designed by Saul Bass, for* The Man with the Golden Arm, *directed by Otto Preminger, United Artists, 1955.*

to background and becoming a newly delineated surface of inscription (Figure 6.2). This is shown, for example, if we consider the torn-out surface spaces of the titles for *Bunny Lake Is Missing* as a special type of rule. Rules can also interfere directly with writing, which provides one interpretation of the titles for *Psycho* where they become manic and overwhelming, slicing through the caption words, momentarily allowing us to glimpse and read, before destroying legibility in a striated frenzy that is permanently linked with cinema's most notorious shocker.

Bass's masterpiece is the title sequence for *North by Northwest* (1959), where the surface of writing is remarkably complex. The rules we discuss above are present in their primary role as the squared lines supporting text. But more, in this sequence, their formation of a (archi)textual gridwork also provides a direct link to the visual imaginary, to a world of real images, a prefiguration of Bass's personal concerns with cinema per se and also, I'd argue, an unconscious premonitory graphic representation not only of the interaction of the symbolic and the real but of the information-age virtual and the real. These titles are a "central processor" of writing in new media, before its time had come, and a superb demonstration of writing on a complex surface.

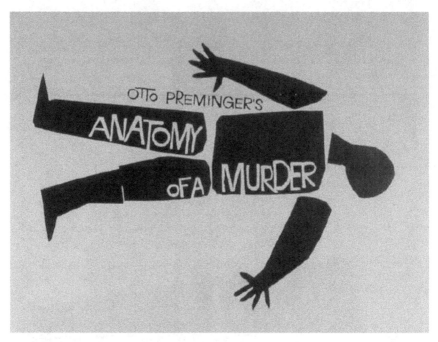

FIGURE 6.2 *Still from the opening titles, designed by Saul Bass, for* Anatomy of a Murder, *directed by Otto Preminger, Columbia Pictures, 1959.*

The sequence opens with a landscape-aspect grid receding in perspective, not yet quite recognizable as the surface of a modernist office block (Figure 6.3). Words of the titles glide in on the gridlines and, in particular, glide up and down the vertical lines where they meet and come momentarily to rest for reading. As they do so, their movements are suddenly like those of elevators in a building, giving us one of the first visual clues to a real-world referent for the abstract grid as a signifier or representation.

This resemblance of the words' movements to elevators marks what is, for Bass, an uncharacteristic evocation of Concrete poetics—words behaving like objects.[7] Paratextual elements, like rules, are allowed to crossover, via abstraction and over the complex writing surface, into the visual, but words remain set in legibility, as tokens of the symbolic. They must do this, since film titling is, after all, an art with a specific and highly constrained function. The important thing for us in Bass's titles is the continuum that is manifested and played out in literal time-based art, a continuum of rhetorical possibilities and signifying strategies that cross and recross from graphic to linguistic media and back, in evocative iterative performance, without ever losing a grip on their specific materialities. It is, I argue here, a complex surface of writing which provides underlying fundamental media for such trajectories.

FIGURE 6.3 *Three stills from the opening titles, designed by Saul Bass, for* North by Northwest, *directed by Alfred Hitchcock, Metro-Goldwyn-Mayer, 1959.*

The ruled gridlines of *North by Northwest* and the complex surface they literally delineate are faithful to graphics, typography, visuality, and textuality all at once. As the sequence progresses this becomes clear. The words of the title perform their function—we can simply read the credits—and they give material pleasure in their design and movement. At a certain point the grid moves away from abstraction and is filled in with the mirrored glass windows of a modernist office block. It becomes real or rather more than real because it is also a mirror, an inscribed surface that is also one particular privileged representation of the world. We see people and traffic alive and moving in the mirror-world and world of filmic naturalism. Meanwhile, the title words continue to share this same surface. They are still well set and respectful of typographic principles but now they share a surface of visual representation that is simultaneously a real object (the building) in the (film) world. It's a tour de force. These titles embody an evolving continuum of signifying strategies across media that could be performed only in time and on a complex writing surface.

The potential emergence of the now-familiar screenic surface of programmable media is prefigured in the titles for *North by Northwest*.[8] Moreover, this prefiguration is unambiguously and necessarily complex, contrasting with the actual historical development of *computing's* screenic writing surface, for which emulation of flatland paper became a misdirected priority.

"Surfacing": *overboard* and *translation*

Over the years, since the late 1970s, much of my own literary work in programmable media has incorporated text that is algorithmically generated in relation to composed or found given texts. Clearly, even in the simplest of flatland terms, the given text and the generated text represent two states, both of which require to be read and appreciated together in any critical assessment of the work as a whole. Of necessity, the generated text will include symbols and symbolic structures that derive from the given text. It is possible, therefore, to see the generated text, in more than a merely metaphoric sense, as a topological transformation of the given text, with its traces providing clues to the way the textual surface has been reshaped. The generated text is the given text rendered on a transformed surface, a surface with at least one degree of further complexity.

The generation of a mesostic text, algorithmically or otherwise, demonstrates this quite clearly. Emmett Williams, Jackson Mac Low, and John Cage are all notable for their deployment of varieties of mesostics and it was also a form that I programmed into pieces, in a number of variations. In instances of mesostics, one or other given text will be, as it were, folded into the generated text.[9] Traversing the surface of the resulting symbolic structure in a standard flatland reading invokes the recital of a generated, programmatically ordered, but apparently unitary, text. However, traversing the same surface according to different rules and procedures may allow the given text to be recovered. One way of looking at this is to say the surface of writing is complex and has more than one functioning dimensional presentation. In one particular dimensional mode, the generated text is legible, in another, the given text surfaces. Or one might conceive of it as an example of the type of self-sameness that is found in the scaling of fractals. Zoomed in, we read the generated text; zoomed out, we read the given text.[10]

In programmatological instantiations of mesostic structures, these traversals may be played out in (real) time. Traditionally we read this as observing the production of the generated text or at least some unitary fragment of the larger text (a screen-full). We wait for the process to begin and then conclude, and we read the starting and the end states of the text. However, if we reconceive the writing surface as complex, then we are provided with a structure which can be seen to bear as well as perform the temporal dimensions of the text. Let's be clear, the point of this reconfigured conception is to be able to reconceive the text as a complex, temporal object, to fully appreciate textuality as time-based. I say that the writing surface is complex. This allows us to perceive it as having more dimensions than the usual two and also as having at least one temporal dimension. In fact, of course, it is the writing and its particular structure that generates a particular complex surface, rendering its specific dimensional complexities, whatever they may be. In flatland, at best and in theory, writing renders itself and the writing surface transparent. In the real world, writing produces surfaces of arbitrary complexity and dimensionality, including dimensions of time.

Clear examples of the instantiation and performance of complex writing surfaces are demonstrated in the two series of works I call *overboard* and *translation*.[11]

The texts underlying these pieces are arranged with line and stanza breaks. Each of the resulting verses may, independently, be in any one of three states which I describe as floating, sinking, or surfacing. The names for these states were chosen before I began to theorize the complexity of the writing surface, but nonetheless, they are highly suggestive of what I am now attempting to convey. If we think of the screenic surface as monitoring a "run-time performance" of one of these pieces, the writing that is produced renders this surface as complex. It becomes a manifold of many constituent surfaces that shift and move as the given and generated texts shift and move. The floating metaphors suggest that we might think of this as like the surface of the sea, deformed by interfering wave patterns. The texts are particular patterns of ever-shifting wave-deformed surfaces. Where the surfaces touch, literal writing appears. As waves rise and fall and where the surfaces no longer touch, writing disappears.

In *overboard*, the surfaces of the text are deformed by functions relating to legibility (Figure 6.4). That is—continuing with our metaphor—the "wave-pattern" of a verse will be determined in relation to legibility. In a "surfacing" state, literal points (points on the surface where letters may appear) will tend to "rise" and touch the screenic surface of visibility such that it will spell out the underlying given text. In a "sinking" state they will

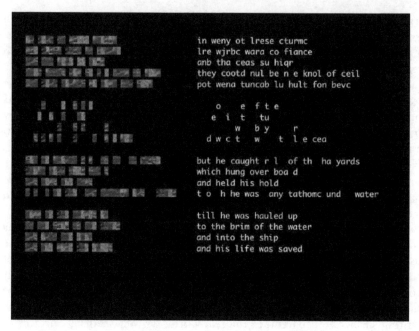

FIGURE 6.4 *Screenshot from* overboard. *Courtesy of the author.*

tend to recede from the surface of visibility. In the "floating" state they may be algorithmically transformed so as to appear on the visible surface in an alternate literal form, producing a quasi-legibility, a linguistic shimmering on the screenic reading surface.

Translation deploys similar algorithms but introduces further complexities, demonstrating the contention that the surface of writing may be arbitrarily complex (Figure 6.5). In *translation,* the wave-patterns of textual surfaces may be deformed by literal functions relating different texts to one another, specifically texts in different languages. If a text floats or sinks in one language, it may surface in another.

As they run and perform, pieces from the *overboard* and *translation* series are what they appear to be—ever-changing, ambient manifestations of writing on complex surfaces. Neither *overboard* nor *translation* can be read or appreciated as flatland literary broadsheets.

Complex surfaces on the Cave walls

My work in writing for programmable media has, in a number of instances, involved designing and implementing a conceptual topology for textual

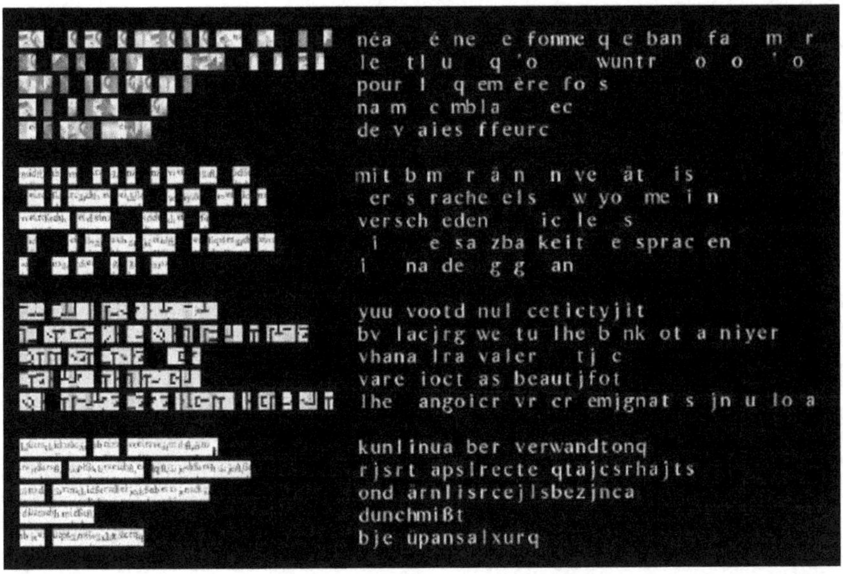

```
néa    é ne   e fonme q e ban  fa   m  r
le   tl u   q 'o        wuntr   o  o  '  o
pour l  q em ère fo s
na m  c mb l a    ec
de v a ies f feurc

mit b m   r á n   n v e  ät   is
    er  s rache e l s    w yo  me  i  n
versch eden       ic  le   s
    i    e sa zba keit   e sprac en
    i    na de  g g   an

yuu vootd nul cetictyjit
bv  lacjrg we  tu lhe b nk ot a niyer
vhana lra valer    tj c
vare ioct as beautjfot
lhe   angoicr vr cr emjgnat s jn u lo a

kunl inua ber verwandtonq
rjsrt apslrecte qtajcsrhajts
ond árnlisrcejlsbezjnca
dunchmißt
bje úpansalxurq
```

FIGURE 6.5 *Screenshot from* translation. *Courtesy of the author.*

structures. Specifically, I have recognized that the programmability of both compositional and delivery media allows for the disposition of texts in an ordered manner such that, for example, media can represent structural interrelationships between the texts, and that such an arrangement may be most easily figured as spatial. As indicated above, this spatiality can be understood as the material instantiation of the critical notion of "depth." I conceive depth as emergent from the complexity of writing surfaces. When I came to make work in an immersive virtual-reality Cave, there was an obvious first step to make: use the Cave's immersive 3D graphics to delineate a topology, a shaped space in which text is systematically disposed.[12] In this unusual, artificial, programmatologically generated environment, the surface of a text can be literally, visibly shown to be arbitrarily complex. A unitary textual object may subsist, suspended in virtual space, with a manifold of interrelated writing and reading surfaces.

Rather than attempt to describe in any detail one or other Cave-based project, in this section, I aim to outline a particular example of the complexity of literal surfaces, one that emerged as a discovery and that could only, perhaps, have been recognized and appreciated in the Cave environment.

There was a known anomaly in the graphics system of the Cave software, not really a bug, but more a matter of a default configuration in rendering that produces counter-intuitive visual effects. The effect of this anomaly was that, in certain contexts, the surfaces of conceptually and perspectively distant objects in the Cave are rendered *over* the surfaces of closer objects in terms of transparency/opacity. If letters were all rendered in the same surface color with no lighting effects or without anti-aliasing or similar sophisticated edge rendering techniques, then this "bug" would not necessarily have been noticeable. However, even a smaller, conceptually more "distant" white letter rendered "over" a larger, "closer" white letter will, in practice, be visible because its edges are made visible by the graphics engine's subtleties.

In the graphics "world" of the textual objects I developed for the Cave, letters have no thickness, but they pivot in three dimensions so as always to face the primary, tracked point of view (the Cave's single dominant point of view, associated with one privileged viewer within the Cave-space). If the tracked reader is positioned at the edge of a plane of letters and she turns to face the plane edge-on, the letters will all turn to face her. Their images overlap, occlude one another—partially or wholly—and recede in view, since the majority of them will be successively more or less distant. "Normally" the surfaces of the larger closer letters would cover the more distant smaller letters. However, because of the anomaly, smaller letter outlines may be clearly discernable "within" but "over" the formed surfaces of the nearer letters. Given these circumstances, and because, I believe, all the letter forms are familiar—both visually and symbolically legible—and because we know what their relative scale "should be," this produces a striking and somewhat bizarre visual illusion (Figure 6.6). We assume that even though the smaller letters are rendered "over" the larger ones, they must be more distant (as in fact they are in the conceptual topology). Thus, what we see is a very deep and narrow corridor formed from letter shapes, with the most distant smallest letters visible in completely edged outline, apparently farthest off, as if inscribed on a tall, thin distant end of the corridor. Moreover, the reader is able to move "into" the corridor formed by this plane of letter shapes.

This powerful perceptual experience is demonstrable and repeatable, despite its artificiality and strangeness.[13]

This rendering anomaly was exploited and highlighted in a distinct study piece called *Lens*. Versions have been made in the Cave—where the concepts are more fully realized—and as also as a transactive QuickTime maquette.[14]

If different, contrasting colored letters are used for texts on distinct surfaces, the rendering anomaly plays out differently. As expected, "distant" letters will render over closer ones in the anomalous configuration. If the distant letters in question are dark in color and the nearer letters light, then, effectively, the surfaces of the nearer letters are transformed, by the anomalous rendering, into surfaces of inscription for the distant letters. If the overall background color is dark (black by default, as in the existing Cave version and also the present QuickTime maquette), this has a further effect relating to legibility and strategies of reading. Dark and distant letters on a dark background are difficult to read. On a lighter background, they may suddenly become legible. If the lighter background happens also to

FIGURE 6.6 *Photograph from an immersive digital language art piece, taken in the Brown University Cave, showing the anomalous "corridor" effect produced by layered letters with disordered transparencies. Courtesy of the author.*

be the surface of a letter that otherwise seems to be perceptually close to the reader (it is closer in the conceptual topology of the graphic world), a strange counter-intuitive effect is produced when the dark letters stray into the region of light—a literal surface becomes a surface for inscription/ reading and the spatial relations between the textual surfaces are inverted by the suddenly predominant desire to read (Figure 6.7). The surface of the nearer letter may also, as we shall see, become a full-blown 3D space within which the more distant letters appear to be disposed.

In the QuickTime maquette, which uses no actual 3D rendering and in which illusory visual distance is represented only by the sizes of its various texts, these effects can nonetheless be demonstrated. "Distant" texts—two dark- and two light-colored—rift in the screen's blackness. There is also, at first, a "lens" word rendered in larger white letters. The reader can move this "lens" by dragging and scale it using command keys. If the lens itself is zoomed-in so as to become (illegibly) large, the surfaces of one or other of its constituent letters can then be used as a reading surface for the more distant darker texts, and this makes them suddenly legible, as well as subverting our assumptions about their relative distance.

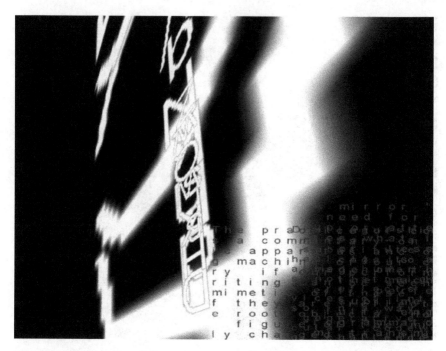

FIGURE 6.7 *Photograph from an immersive digital language art piece, taken in the Brown University Cave, showing linguistically implicated layering effects. Courtesy of the author.*

In the Cave version of *Lens*, the effects are far more striking, disturbing, and spectacular. The letters of *Lens* obey previously cited rules so that their surfaces turn toward the tracked point of view, and the textual objects in the piece are fully 3D as is the space itself. The lens text can be moved in relation to the reader's point of view, drawn close or sent out among the distant darker texts, like an investigative spotlight. Most spectacularly, because of the immersive characteristics of the Cave system, the literal surface of the lens's letters can be, as it were, moved so close as to touch or pass "behind" the reader's body and point of view. The surface light of a lens letter can even be brought into the very eyes of the reader. When this happens, the reader's vision seems to be flooded with the white light of this literal surface and the most spectacular spatial inversion/subversion occurs. The whiteness becomes a 3D space. In fact, it becomes the enclosing 3D space of the Cave, taking the place of the dark space previously inhabited by both reader and the various textual objects only a moment before. The distant dark blue texts still drift in this space, but now they do so, distinct and legible, in a space of light and clarity. If the reader then moves the surface-literal lens-light "out" of her eyes, the enclosing space, as suddenly, reverts to darkness.

It seems clear that this relatively simple system makes literal, in virtual space, a particular type of complex surface that has spectacular perceptual affect and a degree of rhetorical potential. As a proof of concept, it is striking. In so far as it "works" it does so in terms of the complex, recursive interrelations of writing surfaces and surfaces that are, literally, formed by writing, at least in so far as the graphic surfaces of letters are "formed by writing." However, except in the sense of writing as graphic form, there is no immediate or necessary determination of any symbolic content of writing in *Lens* by its formal complexities of surface. The relationship between a particular letter's surface and the "distant" text it allows to be read is not expressed as a linguistic or even a quasi-linguistic function. Contrast a typical mesostic text or the texts of *overboard* and *translation*, where the shifting states of complex reading and writing surfaces are determined by functions applied to their constituent symbolic "contents." Rather, *Lens* shares some of the characteristics of surface complexity in Saul Bass's cinematic titles. The play of complex surfaces produces effects in the visual imaginary and in our notions of the "real," in the sense of the worlds we feel ourselves to inhabit. In Saul Bass's work the writing surface enters the imagined visual world of film and shows that the surfaces of that world may be inscribed. In the Cave, we can "really" dwell within the text. Its surface complexities may suddenly determine where we are, how we see what we see, and what we can or cannot read in a "world" that is literally made of text.

The symbolic on complex surfaces

Retallack wrote, "The symbolic is always [...] a flatland in its relation to the complex real." In a world of letters dominated by paper, print, and their hypernetworked emulations, it is hard to dispute this contention. And yet, in their specific context, these words dispute themselves. They are, unambiguously, extracted from a writing project that is made from language. It is self-consciously poetic and it demands a poethics. It is engaged, at one and the same time, with the symbolic and the complex real. In so far as Retallack's words are effective in this context, they turn on themselves, producing a fold in their own writing surface and demonstrating that flatland sentences may generate surface complexities that are continuous, fractally, as Retallack would say, with art and life. I hope to have indicated above that programmable media provide arbitrarily numerous means to realize, in program and performance, complex relationships between the symbolic realm of language and the world it dwells within, represents, and constitutes. To achieve this, we require a textuality of complex surfaces, capable of conveying a multidimensionality that is commensurate with lived human experience, including the structured culture of human time.

7

Time Code Language: New Media Poetics and Programmed Signification

One of the defining characteristics of poetic writing is its attention to the materiality of language, which has become an important critical concept in literary studies. We speak of "the materiality of text" or "the materiality of language" in general, as if this might be an abstract characteristic when, in fact, it is the critical marker of linguistic and literary embodiment, recognizable only in terms of that embodiment. As N. Katherine Hayles puts it, "*The materiality of an embodied text is the interaction of its physical characteristics with its signifying strategies.*"[1] The presence and operation of code is, in many, though not all, instances, a significant part of the complex physical makeup of electronic text and is often a *sine qua non* for the operation of its signifying strategies. In so far as we are interested in identifying and defining certain specific aspects of the materiality of language that are foregrounded by writing in networked and programmable media, we are called to pay close attention to the role of code and coding in this type of work. We must keep asking ourselves, what is code? What is the relationship of code and text in cultural objects that are classified as literary and that are explicitly programmed?

The context of this chapter is current and continuing discussion which addresses these questions. It refers implicitly and explicitly to other critical interventions that have begun to identify a genre of electronically mediated writing as "codework." According to Rita Raley, "Broadly, codework makes exterior the interior workings of the computer."[2] Code is indeed an archive of the symbolic inner workings of the computer. However, not only is it brought to the surface in the writing of new media, it may function to generate the language displayed on this surface, without itself appearing. In an earlier piece of mine, a prequel to this chapter, I argue that we must be more articulate about the distinctions we make between code and text.[3] These distinctions are creatively challenged by codework that brings "inner workings" to an "exterior," especially when such work is manifested as a generative cross-infection of text and code-as-text, of language and code-as-language. In this earlier piece, I argued that "the code is not the text, unless it is the text." Code that is not the text, code that remains unbroken and operative, may instantiate—as durational performance—the signifying strategies of a text. As such, it does not appear on the complex surface of the interface text as part of or as identical with it. There are, therefore, further distinctions within codework, between those works that bring the traces of an interior archive of code into the open, and those works that depend on the continuing operation of code, where the code, in fact, reconceals itself by generating a complex surface "over" itself. The present chapter addresses these distinctions and then takes on questions concerning the characteristics of a textuality whose very atoms of signification are programmed. What is textuality where it is composed from programmed signifiers? In particular, the temporal properties of such signifiers are highlighted, and the significance of this temporality is examined.

Literal performance literal process

Clearly, it is difficult to articulate and share a detailed, nuanced conception of what we do—how we perform and process—as we write and read and play with language. Out of our difficulties entire fields of critical thought emerge. I begin, for example, to use words to refer, provisionally, to phenomena, like words, which I assume have some kind of separate, atomic existence, however provisional or temporary. Word as word (re)presentation refers to word as thing (re)presentation. The implicit atomism—treating something as irreducible in order to try to assay its significance and affect—is always provisional, even where established by lexical authority, and is ever mobile. At one instant I refer to some word-sized atom of language, the next instant another, then, as suddenly, I recompile and shift "upward"—many levels in the hierarchies of code and language—and refer to the specific work or to "text" itself, which suddenly becomes not only a conceptual automaton in our minds but also an atom of linguistic matter in my discourse itself, even though my discourse is, as it were, contained within its significance.

Foregrounded in this way, the procedural, performative nature of the literal is demonstrable. Despite your understanding that, for example, these words are inscribed as writing—temporally stunned, deferred, and spatialized—you will sense words shifting their meanings as I write/speak and you read/hear. No matter how little attention you or I pay to what is going on as we process, it is easy to concede that, for example, the meanings of words like "code" and "text" change during the shifting "now"—the distinct present moments as I write and you read—and may well change radically over the course of my intermittent writing/speaking and your intermittent reading/ hearing. The generation of altered and new meaning is, after all, one of my explicit aims in addressing these terms.

It follows, even from this simple, on-the-fly phenomenology of language, that atoms or instances of language (of whatever extent), though we treat them as "things," are, in fact, processes. If they are ever static or thing- like, they are more like the "states" of a system, provisionally recognized as identifiable, designated entities. In themselves they are, if anything, more similar to programmed, procedural loops of significance and affect, isolated for strategic or tactical reasons, be they rhetorical, aesthetic, social, or political. This characterization is good linguistics and good critical thought. However, usually our perception and appreciation of linguistic and critical process are more broadly focused, bracketing the micro-processes that generate and influence significance and affect in the "times" taken to move from statement to statement, let alone those which pass so fleetingly and function so invisibly in the move from letter to letter.

Moreover, as Hayles demonstrates in her recent critique of prevailing notions of textuality, an abstracted conception of both "the text" (a physical and literal manifestation of the ideal object of textual criticism, more or less identified with an author's intended work) and "text" (as a general concept), is allied to the apparent stasis and persistence of print, and still dominates our understanding of textuality in literary criticism.[4] By contrast, for Hayles all texts are embodied in specific media. In her view, electronic texts represent a mode of embodiment through which literary works are able to perform a realization of a latent materiality, and perhaps also the revelation of such texts' present and future informatic post-humanity, where they "thrive on the entwining of physicality with informational structure."[5] Hayles sets out some of the elements of an electronic text and emphasizes the dynamism of their symbolic relationships:

> There are data files, programs that call and process the files, hardware functionalities that interpret or compile the programs, and so on. It takes all of these together to produce the electronic text. Omit any one of them, and the text literally cannot be produced. For this reason, it would be more accurate to call an electronic text a *process* rather than an object.[6]

Such a text, unlike that which has print for its medium, has no materially accessible existence prior to its generation when displayed on the screen: "electronic textuality ... *cannot be separated from the delivery vehicles that produce it as a process with which the user can interact.*"[7] For an object to be identified as a process, at the very least, there must be some way for its state to change over time, and perhaps also the possibility of enumerating the temporal sequence of such states, or some way to describe a procedure or procedures that generate the states and changes of state in the object. In other words, there have to be programs to be followed, to be run. In Hayles's analysis, however, the programming seems to reside chiefly in the delivery media of electronic textuality—the "data files, programs that call and process the files, hardware functionalities, and so on"—rather than operating from within the text itself, the text of interpretation.[8] In earlier essays she has described and characterized a "flickering signifier" in digital textuality, but this flickering of signification is a function of the same *peripheral* processing of text and its image—both screen image and underlying encoded representations. Where the flickering is indicative of depth—like ripples on the surface of a lake—this is a function of code in the sense of encoding.[9] We imagine depths behind the screen, within the box, underneath the keyboard, because we know that the surface text is multiply encoded in order that it can be manipulated at the many and various levels of software and hardware. However, much of this underlying programmatological manipulation is typically treated as insignificant for the purposes of interpretation. I know that the screens of text that I read are being ceaselessly refreshed with, perhaps, some subliminal perceptual flickering of their signifiers, but I do not necessarily read this process as part of what is being signified to me. Unless foregrounded by an author for particular rhetorical effects, the programmatological dimensions of screen rasterization, for example, do not play a direct role in the generation of significance or affect.

This is by no means to say that flickering signification does not operate in a poetics of new media. I believe that this phenomenon is crucial to both the theory and practice of literal art in programmable media and is generally applicable to textuality, including that of traditional media such as print.[10] My present purpose, however, is to try to address the role of procedures that do directly affect rhetoric and poetics, to identify the subjects and objects of programming within discussions of code and coding, in so far as they inflect our understanding of writing and the performance of writing.

Five ways to write "code"

I have already suggested one source of possible misdirection concerning the relationship of code and signification. The debate is set out under the rubric of "codework" without fully articulating the ambiguities in the use of the term "code" itself. Thus Hayles, for example, concentrates on the role of "code" as *encoding* in signification, with "code" as operative *programming* implicitly consigned to the hardware and software periphery. Raley's minimal characterization—"Broadly, codework makes exterior the interior workings of the computer"—evokes both encoding and programming aspects of code(work) since they are typically interior in her sense.[11] Raley goes on to suggest further distinctions in codework as identified by a prominent codework practitioner, Alan Sondheim:

> Works using the syntactical interplay of surface language; Works in which the submerged content has modified the surface language; Works in which the submerged content is emergent content.[12]

However, Sondheim's set of distinctions does not evoke code as programming per se, and it remains focused on a written surface, however complex. It refers to the inscribed surface and what emerges from code into and through it. In order to help clarify the various ways that "code" is used in discussions of codework, I offer five provisional categories:

1. Code as (a special type of) language (viewed and interpreted as such)
2. Code as infecting or modulating natural language (the language works, but the code is "broken")
3. Code as text to be read as (if it were) natural language; code which is infected or modulated by natural language (the code works, but the language is "broken")
4. Code as system of correspondences, as encoding
5. Code as programming, as a program or set of methods that runs (in time) and produces writing, or that is necessary for the production of writing.

The first three categories characterize texts according to properties of the constituent language. The texts are viewed as interface texts to be read in a fairly traditional manner. The language has been composed and laid out—in any number of complex contexts, including of course the online, shifting context of the web—and then it is read and interpreted. These categories cover the majority of literal art production which goes under this new rubric of "codework."

Code as language in itself and in its own terms, category one, is something of a specialist study, and its full critical appreciation is as much the concern of computer scientists as literary critics. Nonetheless, writers such as Loss Pequeño Glazier seriously address code in its own terms as a potential poetry, not simply as linguistic fodder for the most common type of codework, the second category, where code infects or modulates natural language.[13] This second type of code-infected writing, epitomized in many ways by the work of Mez, is widely practiced and represents not much more than the extension of the long-standing enrichment of natural language which occurs whenever history or sociology produces an encounter between linguistic cultures and subcultures.[14] My previous chapter on codework critiques this mode of writing, not least by comparing it to the encounters which occur between commensurate human languages. Codework comes off somewhat badly from the comparison, because code is a jargon or sublinguistic structure, not a full-blown, culture-supporting language. An encounter between, for example, English and Unix, is, in a sense, an encounter between a language and some smaller part of itself, rather than with an alien and commensurate linguistic entity.[15] It is also the case with code-infected interface text that the code is, in the programmer's sense, "broken" after its incorporation into the text we read. It has lost its operative, performative "power" in the very instant that it is brought to the surface of interpretation.[16] What of the code that remains hidden, which may well be operating as we read? This is the code that I want to read more critically.

Category three, codework that is manifest as written code, presented and intended to be read by non-specialist human readers—those who are not programmers and not, as it were, "manual" compilers or interpreters—is a special case and is less common. "Perl poetry" is a genre known mainly to programmers and hackers. In my earlier chapter, I described examples, citing work by Jodi and Cosic, as well as one of my own experiments. In this type of writing the code may be *functional* and unbroken (although not *functioning* as it is read). However, in most instances, natural language elements are introduced (in a way that allows the code to remain functional) or cultural framing is provided which renders the code readable—significant and affective—for humans. In a manner complementary to the conditions pertaining to code-infected language, the human cultural elements tend to be "broken" or at least heavily constrained in these forms.

Thus, the codework categorized according to my first three usages of "code" produces texts to be read, interface texts subject to interpretation by readers. The code is not running to generate the text; nor is it significantly present in the text in such a way that might alter or inflect the manner of reading. Code is not functioning to address writing as a formal procedure in these cases; it is not involved with the form and matter of the language used, although it is, clearly, making a contribution to its content. The language of code is visible on the surface of the interface text, but code has not necessarily been present at the scene of writing.

As we come to consider encoding—my fourth category—as an aspect of writing in programmable media, code does begin to emerge as integral to the material of the language used, necessary for its properties and methods, although, I argue, this aspect of code is still not fully indicative of its potential role in the active and continuing modulation of signification or as an engine for new literal and literary rhetoric in new media.[17] As we have already seen, Hayles's flickering signifier acquires much of its conceptual power from the depths and layers of encoding it allows us to discover and recover in programmatological systems. It is clearly demonstrable that text, stored and displayed in digital media, is multiply encoded, and awareness of this circumstance is certainly significant for our understanding of the materiality of language in new media. However, this is not an entirely new conception of textuality. The idea that the signifier is multilayered—with shifting and floating relationships of correspondence between the layers—is well known and widely accepted in criticism. Famously, Barthes (as Hayles acknowledges) brought our attention to the layered underlying semiotic codes prevalent even in *readerly* texts.[18] He showed how elements of the interface text might instantiate and evoke many and various instances of the corresponding codes simultaneously. Moreover, and by contrast with the sense of code initiated by Barthes, the type of encoding highlighted by the flickering of Hayles' digital signifiers is, in one sense, largely sublinguistic, or on the outer margins of paratext. Although we can be made aware that the codes of digital media make words we read on screen flicker beneath it, we do not really care—for the purposes of interpretation—whether the text we read is encoded as extended ASCII or Unicode.

Finally, this type of relationship is simultaneous or synchronous. The flickering is a sign of a synchronic correspondence. The flickering may only be apparent in brief moments of time but, significantly, the relationships do not function temporally, nor are they modulated by time. This simultaneity of encoded correspondences is crucial, I believe, to the distinction between, on the one hand, code as encoding, and, on the other, code as the archive of functional programming. We have to distinguish between: (1) flickering as a function of the chained hierarchies of codes and language where the signifier flickers because it is reducible to something else which flickers; for example: the work, a text, is persistent on the screen but I know that it flickers because I know that the screen refreshes and because the keyboard is waiting for new input or because some paratextual procedure is being applied to the word image (e.g., changing its font and color); and (2) flickering because the signifier or chain of signifiers is produced by code and because the signifier may itself be programmed.

At this point, I am beginning to discuss code as operational programming in textuality, my fifth category. My aim is to distinguish the characteristics of textuality that incorporates (or is the subject of) code in this sense. This "strong sense" code is integral to all textuality, although it might be objected that this claim would be hard to substantiate before the historical advent of demonstrably programmable media. There have always been programs, I would answer, and these programs are a necessary aspect of the materiality of language—an ever-present aspect of mediation between a text's physical characteristics and its signifying strategies. The difference lies in where—literally, and also within cultural structures and hierarchies—these programs run, and it also depends on who writes and runs them. There is a continuity from what I will call "paratextual programming" and the kind of programming that is ever more familiar from the proliferation of programmable media.

Paratextual programming runs quasi-invisibly within traditional structures of writing, reading, and interpretation. The programmatological dimension of writing has always already been operative, and therefore, the traditional temporally stunned conception of textuality has always already been inadequate to literary and especially to poetic practice. However, the coding applied to textuality *in new media* allows us to perceive, if not the coding itself, then the unambiguous effects and consequences of that coding.

Punctuation colon programming

To demonstrate a continuity between paratextual programming and programming proper we can work with an example, a sentence within a paragraph at the beginning of this chapter. By paratextual programming I mean the (integral) aspects of inscription which frame or infect or undermine or position the text to be read, that is, the interface text. I use "paratext" in the sense of Genette, but I am highlighting its programmatological dimension.[19] In contrast to "strong sense" coding or programming, paratextual programming becomes a perceptible part of the interface text—it appears on the same surface, often using the same symbol set (although as often employing the tropes and figures of non-linguistic media)—whereas coding per se remains invisible and inaccessible. In fact, "codework" in the sense of the instantiation of code-infected interface text (typically my category two) can be seen as paratextual programming using what is also occasionally referred to as postmodern punctuation. Raley calls this—approaching even closer to the textuality of programmable media—"punctuation particular to the apparatus" and cites one of the prime current practitioners of the art: "Talan Memmott calls this set of punctuations 'technical ideogrammatics.'"[20]

Even writing punctuated in a manner that is "particular to the apparatus" can be quoted, unpacked, analyzed, and stunned to paraphrase, as writing in general or in traditionally recognized forms. As promised, I will demonstrate what I mean with a simple example, from a piece of language I have already used, "Word as word (re)presentation refers to word as thing (re) presentation." Obviously, the visible marks of paratextual programming here are the parentheses. The primary specific intended effect of the parentheses is to provide a double reading, at once poststructural—through the evocation of the word "representation" and through the use of the parenthesis themselves putting presence/absence of a signifier into play, and also Freudian—through the implicit use of his phrases "word presentation" and "thing presentation."[21] What the punctuation does is set up a time-based revision of the atomic meanings of and within the sentence. I can, as I have done, recast these meanings and map them to a paraphrase based on the traces and marks in the interface text itself. This recasting is a process in itself, separate from the surface language of the interface text but archived within it. Its implicit "code" evokes a widely used and well-understood rhetorical and interpretative "program," the program of paraphrase. In this light, paraphrase can be seen as nothing other than the simplified (proper) naming of procedural loops within more complex language that we so name in order to be able to identify and atomize their procedures of meaning-generation for the purpose of re-articulation. Any text where codes and the codes of punctuation are integrated with the interface text, including much of the codework of Mez and of Talan Memmott, can be unpacked and analyzed in these terms, as inflected and driven by paratextual programming.

Hypertextual dissolutions

Spatially organized, navigable texts can often be understood in the same way, where precisely the spatial organization and navigation is to be read as paraphrase, gloss, elaboration, annotation, and so on, all coded into operations that produce a successively revealed interface text. Making reference to spatially organized, navigable textuality immediately evokes hypertext. Indeed, hypertext does, for me, occupy a transitional or intermediate position between the textuality of what I have called paratextual programming exemplified in a postmodern punctuation of print text and a textuality that is generated by programs or that is itself programmed. For Philippe Bootz hypertext is simply the application of an operator to a literary dataspace.[22] In Bootz's theory, "the Procedural Model," the application of a hypertext operator or class of operations to a proto-"hypertext" is what generates nodes and links while, at the same time, coding those methods and commands that enable what we call navigation into the hypertextual structure. For Bootz, it is important to see that the hypertextual operator is simply one of a virtually infinite number of such operators that might be applied to the literary dataspace, the proto-hypertext that would in fact become something quite other than hypertext if different operators were applied. It is also noteworthy that the procedures and programming of hypertext are relatively simple—the response to a set of documentary problems rather than to poetic or, indeed, narrative ones.[23] As famously discussed on the relevant internet lists in the late 1990s, there seems to be little content "inside" the links of traditional hypertext.[24] Hypertext took the spatialization of text beyond print media and brought the trope of navigation to prominence, but the composed language of its constituent nodes or lexia retained the print-like quality of having been impressed on a surface—discoverable, visitable, but with little programmatological "depth." The classic hypertextual link does little other than provide the instantaneous replacement of one composed fragment of integral text by another. At times, this process is not appreciable, even metaphorically, as a spatial displacement. How is the replacement of text on the surface of a unitary screen more of a spatial displacement than, for example, turning to a place—figuratively, literally, and physically—"further on" or "deeper into" or "at the back of" a book? The programming involved in hypertext seems relatively shallow and more closely allied with paratext and textual framing than with the potentialities I have it in mind to address.

Overriding the "read" method: Rosenberg's programmed signifiers

Discussion of hypertext leads us to the work of Jim Rosenberg, which provides a further transitional demonstration of code operative in and through language, a crucial and interesting point of intersection of paratextual and strong-sense, fifth-category codework. Rosenberg explicitly contextualizes his practice within and against the traditional study and theory of hypertext, and yet his work is difficult to reconcile with classic link-node models of hypertext. On the one hand the actual coding in his work is, arguably, simpler than the implementation of a hypertext operator. In pieces such as Rosenberg's *Intergrams, Diffractions Through,* and *The Barrier Frames*, his actual coding produces little more than the substitution of successive screen images showing texts, syntactic diagrams (in most cases), and textual frames in response to the position of a mouse or other pointing device.[25] On the other hand, Rosenberg has built elaborate, articulated relationships into the language and linguistic structures of the texts which are handled by his actual code, such that the positioning of the pointer—part of the work of the reader—becomes a device that reveals the programmatological dimension of his work.

It seems to me to be crucial to Rosenberg's work that often when the mouse or pointing device is not in contact with an area containing or enclosing text, the visual field of the work is unreadable, or, more precisely, its constitutive texts are unreadable. In these states of the work (one might call them "rest" states), the reader is initially presented with "zoomed out" diagrams outlining large-scale syntactic relationship between areas of text (which are shown as graphic "representations of writing" rather than writing per se, Figure 7.1). If the reader "zooms in" on one of these areas, such that it fills the visual field and constitutes a new phase of the interface text, the words displayed on the screen (in the "rest state" of a zoomed-in assemblage) are still unreadable but for different reasons (Figure 7.2). Rosenberg typically composes his texts in overlaid clusters that together are dense enough to make reading the constituent layers impossible. It is precisely the movement of the mouse that brings one or another layer to the reading surface where it then becomes readable (while covering the other layers) (Figure 7.3). Move the mouse away and the work returns to an unreadable rest state.

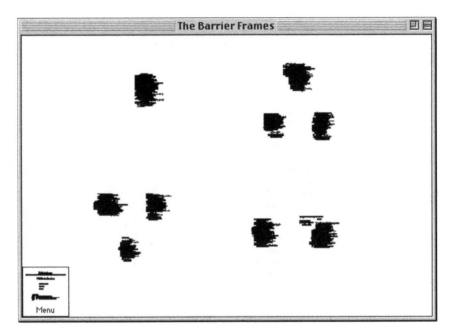

FIGURE 7.1 *Screenshot from* The Barrier Frames. *Courtesy of Jim Rosenberg.*

FIGURE 7.2 *Screenshot from* Intergrams. *Courtesy of Jim Rosenberg.*

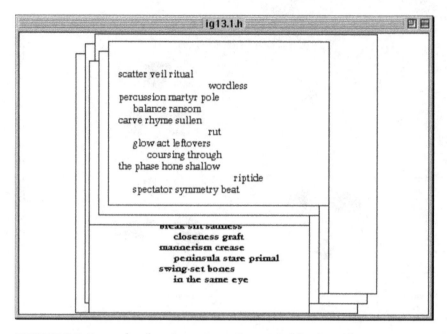

FIGURE 7.3 *Screenshot from* Intergrams. *Courtesy of Jim Rosenberg.*

Work like Rosenberg's, implemented with very simple coding, nonetheless requires its coding—as a specific part of its materiality and in order to realize its signifying strategies—to a far greater degree than in the case of the generality of link-node hypertext, for example. This can be demonstrated in the most simple and direct terms when we say that Rosenberg's work is unreadable, it cannot be read, unless its underlying codes—the ones that reveal the constituent layers—are running in a waiting state, ready to be evoked. Of course, the entirety of a hypertext also requires that its various links are activated and followed in order for it to be read *as a whole*, but its constituent nodes are, typically, readable as texts in the hypertext's "rest" state. A hypertext, classically, does not require the constant, active invocation of the codes that manage its links for textual reading to at least proceed.[26]

In fact, of course, all reading requires the constant and active invocation of codes and coding, in the mind, for it to proceed. No reading takes place without a *process* of reading. It is simply that print literacy tends to bracket the temporal and programmatological dimension of both writing and reading, or reduce it either to an inscribed spatiality of ideal, fixed editions, or to linearity, which is its all but invisible fundamental temporal structure, a structuring of time so straightforward that, when recorded as writing, we tend to think of the text as a line (resting) in space.[27] The materiality of

Rosenberg's work resists these reductions in the most obvious and effective way. When his work is space, it is not readable, and it has no emergent, repeatable linearity. Only within restructured time can it be read. Moreover, even less than in the case of hypertext can it be reduced to linearity. Without being indeterminate (Rosenberg's texts are not generated by quasi-random processes), these texts are nonetheless constructed in a manner that makes it next to impossible for writer or reader to anticipate or control the mouse or pointer's positions when addressing the work in a way that would allow, for example, the repeated performance of particular sequences of textual revelations. It would be impossible, that is, without learning to manipulate one of his works like a musical instrument, gaining the necessary control and skill to know which "notes" to strike and when. The point is: the reading, or recital, of one of Rosenberg's texts obliges its readers to address the inherent restructuring of time, specifically the time of reading. Rosenberg's coding of programmable media for literal art *guarantees* this specific aspect of his text's materiality and also, perhaps even more importantly, gives both writer and reader access to the manipulation of this dimension of literal textual matter.[28]

In Rosenberg's work the coding is in the system, but it is also within, and a part of, the writing because of the way the text must be read, because of the simple fact that the only way to read is by working with the text, manipulating it with a programmaton's pointing device. Rosenberg has recast reading and has changed the properties and methods of the signifier. He instantiates a signifier that has radically different properties to that of print culture. One way of figuring this difference is to extend an analogy with object-oriented programming and say that Rosenberg has extended the class "Text" and overridden its "read" and "write" methods. In Rosenberg, writing is (among other things) a method of layering, overlaying, and compositing texts, and reading is (among other things) a tentative work of revealing the clustered layers in order to pass the literal data they contain on to the "read" method of an underlying or parallel Text object of the "parent" class, the Text object of print culture.[29]

While we want to emphasize the fact that the signifier is a temporal, durational object, we also have to consider that literal and literary time is itself restructured by textuality. Textuality is temporal and as such restructures the culture of human time. That textuality was always temporal is clear. We are familiar with the textual generation of linear and narrative time. We are familiar with writing as deferral, especially as a function of its spatiality, its translation of time into space. We are comfortable with the figures and tricks of narrative reordering—flashback and the like—although chiefly in the frameworks of historical time and narrative drive.[30] However, textuality as instantiated in programmable media realizes the potential for a more radical restructuring of the culture of human time, and Rosenberg's literal art provides an instance of how this happens through the absolute necessity to work with it, in time, in order to read.[31] It is, in this sense, a (if not "the") type of "ergodic literature," where non-trivial effort is *necessary* for reading.[32] However, as Espen Aarseth shows with his provisional "textonomy," time enters into the art of letters and is restructured through many other rhetorical methods and procedures, not only through ergodic manipulation, but also—giving a far from exhaustive list—through animation, text generation, quasi- and pseudo-random modulation, and various combinations of all of these, not to mention the kind of live textual collaboration that *networked* programmable media allow.

Text in the docuverse

Rosenberg's marked and continuing investment in hypertext per se invites us to re-examine the claim—much touted in the hypertextual "golden age"— that textuality gives way to hypertextuality in new media.[33] Rosenberg sees his work in terms of hypertext and is an active participant in the research community associated with both the technical and theoretical development of hypertext. When viewed from the perspective of computer science (or computer science in the service of the humanities), as a system implemented in software, "hypertext" has both a more precise meaning and also a range of ever-evolving meanings closely dependent on the changing capabilities of actually existing systems. Thus, the web is a variety of hypertext— providing nodes, links, and navigation—but the basic capabilities of HTML in the standard server-browser implementation are severely limited when compared with more developed hypertext systems or speculative structures.[34] Many hypertext theorists and researchers—including and perhaps especially Ted Nelson—would say that the web falls short of even the fundamental requirements for a properly hypertextual system. I am not so much interested in explaining or elaborating these technical distinctions. Still, I want to consider the implications of the proposition that Rosenberg sees his work, his literary objects, as reducible to hypertext, and I want to do this in relation to a theory of hypertext that is particularly "totalizing"— Nelson's vision of the docuverse.

This chapter provides context for a re-examination of Nelson's vision in terms of my arguments concerning the poetics and the temporal materiality of textual art in new media. More specifically, I am discussing programmed signification—strategies of signification in Hayles' terms—in which codes and coding operate to generate or modulate texts, substantively. The attempt to reconcile such strategies with Nelsonian hypertext yields, I believe, crucial perspectives on both hypertext and the materiality of textual art. Nelson is a visionary theorist particularly sensitive to text as "evolving, Protean structure"[35] and yet, paradoxically, his docuverse—along with the properties and methods of its Xanadu system—is not only "the original (perhaps the ultimate) HYPERTEXT SYSTEM"[36] but also the final instantiation of the textual materiality of authorized editions, of the ideal, abstracted, persistent, authorized text that is currently the dominant object of attention in both literary and academic discourse.

For Nelson "a document is really (Figure 7.4 appears here in his text) an evolving ONGOING BRAID."[37] This definition accords perfectly with a materiality of text for which structured durations of time are necessary to its strategies of signification. Nelson's system also specifies and provides a way to view text in various successive states that arise during the spiraling, branching process of composition, "instantaneous slices" captured from the evolving braid as "versions" of the text or some part of the text. For Nelson, a text very much has a history as well as a synchronous existence, and his rendition of hypertext aims to represent this chronological dimension and to do so well. However, his nodes are *time-stamped* not *time-based*, as in the phrase "time-based art." The docuverse captures states of the looping and spiraling braids of textuality, but not the looping and spiraling itself. In later versions of the docuverse these nodes are conceived of as the "spans" of a "permascroll."[38] The totalizing and ultimate instantiation of a Nelsonian docuverse is a representation of *the* permascroll.

The permascroll is another important point of view from which to examine the Nelsonian docuverse. It is the linear and literal representation *of every textual event*. It is all writing, everything written, everything inscribed as language, as and when it was so inscribed. Hypertext can then be generated from the permascroll through operations that display linked windows onto spans of the scroll. Textual history and textual criticism can be recast as a vast but particular and privileged set of pointers to those spans on the permascroll representing various textual events that are—culturally, institutionally—significant for the archive and interpretation of a writing

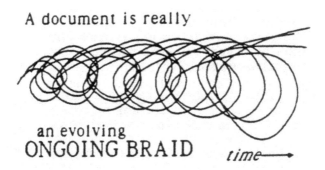

FIGURE 7.4 *Illustration from* Literary Machines 93.1, *p. 2/14. Courtesy of Ted Nelson.*

tradition. A book, for example, may be viewed as one (complex) window on the scroll, its coordinates and output parameters determined by a particular culture's definition of "book" as textual framing device containing the end product of many processes (e.g., editing) that examine and select from prior collections of spans delineated on the permascroll and representing the chronological development of the text.

The textual event

To my mind, Nelson's vision is truly that: visionary, magnificent. It *is* an ultimate system, the epitome of a textual universe composed of *editions*, composed, that is, from minimal, transcriptable textual events. And yet it begs a question that throws our underlying concerns into high relief: "What is a textual event?" Nelson's concerns—as opposed to those of literary artist-practitioners—were first and foremost documentary, as Philippe Bootz has noted.[39] Nelson proposed a reconfiguration of the documentary universe that is more than equal to the task of handling all the nuances of textuality and its criticism as currently instituted and implemented in traditional literary media.[40] The textual event is defined culturally, by cultural institutions and by media technologies. In our own context, the institutions that dominate literature and language art are editorial bodies—universities, publishers, the world of letters—and for these authorities the textual event is still ultimately determined by a simple test: "Can it be printed?" In recent years, this formulation may have been slightly modified (by the web in particular) to: "Can it be printed *out*?" Nelson challenges and reconfigures the forms of display and the engines generating our textual points of view but he does not fundamentally challenge the notion of textual event.[41] Specifically, he does not address the necessity, I propose, to allow the textual signifier to include—as inherent constituents of its materiality—temporality and programmability.

Consider how Rosenberg's diagram or intergram poems might be transcribed on the Nelsonian permascroll. As it happens, all the textual elements of a Rosenberg piece are determinate: they may be conceived as authorially composed and transcriptable editions. As such all the elements of a diagram poem or intergram and all of its states could be rendered by the permascroll and its engines, except that, crucially, there is no obvious—or *institutionally recognized*—way to represent (1) overlay and simultaneity or (2) the dissolution and resolution of these textual properties in necessarily temporal and ergodic processes.[42] Both of these features are intrinsic to the aesthetic, and to the significance and affect of Rosenberg's work, to its meanings. Appended to the scroll and its engines, one could imagine the record of code—or of abstracted representations of algorithms—that would allow all of the features of a poem to be rendered and reproduced, but these would not be part of the scroll or its native systems; they would not be instituted as a recognized part of the docuverse, even the Nelsonian docuverse, let alone the traditional world of letters.

In a sense, I am revisiting old arguments concerning the specific technical capabilities of our emergent media of inscription. Circa 1994 hypertext arrives in the world of letters, and certain practitioners and theorists complain of its inadequacies, its inability to implement a wide range of the intrinsic potential for an extended literacy in networked and programmable media.[43] However, besides pin-pointing "what gets left out" of textuality by both print and hypertextual culture (our focus is the temporality and programmability of the signifier, the textual event), the Nelsonian example highlights the complicity of institutions with the implicit cultural resistance to certain forms of practice. The resistance is not just a function of technology. Nelson is radical in demanding a revolution that extends to literary institutions. He imagines a total migration of literary content to new media, and goes so far as to propose a total reconfiguration of critical apparatus and intertextuality, of tools for quotation and reference.[44] He also provides, to my mind, a workable mechanism that upholds basic principles and moral rights established by copyright, while shifting their control and management away from the actual-existing copyright hegemonies that threaten to dominate and constrain cultural production in new media.[45] That is radical.

Temporal and literal institutions

The institutions that are not challenged by the Nelsonian paradigm are those cultural institutions that authorize and maintain a definition of the fundamental atom of inscription and its relationship to a particular, privileged type of temporality. The minimal unit of text—of the symbolic, of language-in-Western-culture—is the letter, an abstraction we conceive as timeless. Strings of letters that are structured into words, sentences, paragraphs, chapters, books, and so on, we also think of as having a temporality that is deferred. We say that writing renders time as space, while also, of course, always allowing its power to represent (arbitrarily complex) temporal structures *in content*.[46] For any particular text, we accept any of its recorded histories or chronologies that can be expressed in terms of these atoms of inscription. This acceptance allows and accounts for the complexities of textual criticism, for the relatively sophisticated notion of "text" that these practices require—for text as a history of *editions,* however provisional and reworkable. Hypertext provides a navigable visualization of the relationships between such fundamental units of inscription, while Nelson's particular genius was to provide a generalization of these complex requirements and a potential reconfiguration of their underlying structures, one that was radically, institutionally implicated. However, because of the properties of their shared fundamental atom of inscription—particularly its deferred temporality—all of these forms of textuality may, if necessary (typically this will be for institutional reasons or to allow the text's accessibility to familiar, traditional, interiorized reading practices), be rendered as print, without affecting—institutionally—the interpretation and appreciation of the text's aesthetic, its strategies of signification, its generation of meanings, its significance and affect.[47] Furthermore, this printing out implicitly privileges a particular form of temporality: an (arbitrary) sequencing of elements of inscription that is ineluctable during any particular experience (or "printing out") of a text's instantiation but which, in institutional terms, appears to be inevitable and necessary, to the extent that we may prefer one sequence of elements and come to designate this sequence as *the* text, as its standard, canonical edition.

This type of canonization will not work for a Rosenberg intergram. Neither will it work for a wide-ranging and growing corpus of work that is textual and also, to give only the most obvious examples of textual properties that are not, as it were, "(perma)scrollable": animated, generated, indeterminate, the product or instantiation of real-time collaboration. To take one example—textual animation—we can see that in cinematic film titling, in advertising using time-based delivery media, and finally in the poetics of networked and programmable media, textual animation has a history and highly developed, if inadequately articulated, rhetoric specific to its textual materiality. The atoms of this textual matter cannot be simply recast as arbitrary sequences of letters, not without bracketing, masking or ignoring vital aspects of these texts' signifying strategies—specifically, for example, a whole range of transition effects from text to text. This means, unambiguously, that criticism must address the cultivation and articulation of temporality in this work as well as, if not also by way of, an analysis of the code that guarantees and drives literal temporality.

Code generates literal time

Code as programming has other contributions to make to the emergent tropes and figures of a rhetoric extended so as to articulate the signifying strategies of writing in networked and programmable media, reflecting its materiality and media specificities.[48] However, in so far as code generates the temporalities of writing in programmable media, it highlights what I believe is currently the most important thread in a program that criticism and theory must follow in order to accept these temporalities as integral and inalienable properties of all atoms of signification in literal, indeed, literary art. Without its code—even when rendered as elaborate "scrollable" hypertext—Rosenberg's work sacrifices vital aspects of its aesthetics, its strategies of signification, its power to generate significance, affect, meaning.[49] The effect of an intergram arises largely, as we have said, from simultaneities and from temporal and ergodic processes that dissolve and resolve these simultaneities. The cultivation and articulation of real, material time is built into the text through coding.

Much play, in the recent criticism of new media poetics, has been made of the *visibility* of a literary work's engagement with the material specificities of its media, what might be called its material self-reflexivity. In *Writing Machines*, Katherine Hayles demonstrates brilliantly how Mark Danielewski makes us see and feel and hear the (empty/nothing/ void in his *House of) Leaves*.[50] However, we still—in this and other print culture examples—see and feel and hear the "leaves" using technologies of inscription that are profoundly familiar within the culture and institutions of literature and pedagogy in general: parallelism of textual streams (text and footnotes); commentaries; and commentaries on commentaries; multiple perspectives; typographic novelties; not least, temporal complexities represented as content while formally virtualized and *deferred* by writing. We must also however acknowledge and distinguish texts in media that are composed with code and that allow authors and readers to program aspects of temporality as integral parts of the text, as constitutive of its very materiality, and we must recognize a productive, critical opposition between writing as deferral/spatialization—of content including representations of time however complex—and writing as program and performance—in and of time. We need to elaborate this distinction for many reasons:

The real temporal dimension of the *materiality* of text has been underplayed and overwhelm by the stasis and persistence of authorized editions.

A materiality of text that embraces temporality offers a more general theory of textuality, backwardly applicable to work in durable media.

A significant body of work now exists that is made from programmed signifiers and can be displayed using time-based media, and this body of work remains literally unreadable and largely resistant to methods of interpretation that cannot cope with temporality in a sophisticated manner.

Work of this type includes performative pieces that are made of language and are expressed as literary art but which cannot be addressed using the existing tools of literary criticism.

Finally, much of this work is explicitly generated by and made, at least in part, from code, coding that has an unambiguous relationship with the programmatological engines of new media, the tools we now habitually use to write.

Code is presented to us as a special type of linguistic archive. It leaves traces on the surface of literary culture that cannot be denied or ignored, even in works that do not make art with these traces. Strangely, the code is hidden as it runs—driving the temporal atoms of literal signification, restructuring the culture of human time. The code of programmatology embodies a literal interior now calling to us for articulation and poiesis.[51]

8

The Gravity of the Leaf: Phenomenologies of Literary Inscription in Media-constituted Diegetic Worlds

Particular arts, especially when regarded as "cultural practices," are constituted in terms of the media with which they engage. Quite clearly, with a nod to Clement Greenberg, in many realms of practice, "painting" is constituted by "paint." Hence, I take "literary" in the phrase "literary arts" to characterize a manifold, culturally instituted system of media within which arts of language may be represented and embodied. However, the relationship of language, let alone language art, to its media is inherently and profoundly problematic. This problematic is frequently engaged by theoretical discourses of many kinds, and hinges, I believe, on the necessarily problematic interplay between ideality and contingent representation that is a *sine qua non* of symbolic practice.[1] In this chapter, I approach this problematic primarily in terms of such practice but in a manner that has significant implications for theory, specifically for any theory that relates language and media or, in particular, speaks of language as media. I argue that aspects of the problematic become literally visible to us when we are able to see that language always comes to us from a world that is distinct from the *media-constituted diegetic world* within which it is represented. Whenever we practice language, to give and receive its objects of poiesis, we must always also enact what I theorize as a diegetic break. This phenomenon does not always obtain in the practice and reception of arts associated with other media, with architecture providing, arguably, the example of an artistic practice that has a human currency commensurate with that of language and yet instantiates the starkest contrast, relative to language, in terms of how we may live with and within a particular aesthetic practice. We live in architecture without departing from a world in which we live. We live in (aesthetic) language only in so far as we leave the world in which the language is embodied.[2] If this is the case, then it has always been the case, and I believe that poetry and poetic practice has been one of the sites of greatest awareness of the phenomena associated with these relations—perhaps, paradoxically, precisely because of its long-standing attention to form and presentation—both traditional form such as rhythmic structure, and rhyme and experimental, innovative, indeed, disjunctive form—as a function of materiality—which term I take to refer to media in the broadest possible sense. However, as poetry moves "beyond text" we are re-confronted with the problem of giving a home to the other-worldly in the new media-constituted diegetic worlds within which, all-too-suddenly, we find ourselves living, albeit, to some extent, artificially.[3] Because language has been constrained to the mind, the voice, and latterly to the "surface of the leaf," we have internalized its being-in-all-possible-worlds as such. When it appears in "new media" we are re-sensitized to the experience of its never-having-belonged-here.

The world within which I am writing

In this chapter, I put forward formulations of certain relations between language and media, and these I consider to have general applicability, regardless of the actual media with which we are concerned. Nonetheless, I am making use of media-specific practice and experience, and I refer to prior critical engagements with the issues and problems addressed and these are also media-specific. In both cases the media which concern us are visual. The thoughts and arguments which follow are prompted by my work in Brown University's Cave, where my students and I continue to address the problem of creating work that pretends to a literary aesthetic in audiovisually immersive programmable media. Although the Brown Cave is, as stated, an *audio*visual device—the systems we use are equipped with 5.1 surround sound—I do not, in this chapter, speak directly to the relationship between literal art and media that are constituted by sound. The discussion is constrained to Cave work as immersive 3D graphics, as visual media.

There is a useful conceptual and lexical rhyme between the technical vocabulary of 3D graphics and the theory of media-constituted diegetic worlds that I formulate. In 3D graphics, the gestalt of a graphics system's various projected images is, together, referred to as a "world." In the case of Brown's Cave, a four-walled device, this "world" is constituted by two times four projections: one for each eye (left and right) times four for each wall (left, front, right, and floor in the case of Brown's Cave). Shuttering glasses are worn by the Cave user and these glasses synchronize with the otherwise imperceptibly alternating left-eye, right-eye images, filtering the corresponding projections into the corresponding eye in order to achieve a simulation of stereo vision. The (two times) four wall-projected images are generated, and, as necessary, corrected—in terms of perspective and the deformations required to compensate for the flat projection surfaces of a cube-shaped room—in order to provide a coherent graphic "world" for one particular pair of glasses-wearing human eyes, whose position in the artificial space is tracked such that the system can respond to its movement through the "world" in "real time" (or rather in the "time" of the graphic world). This brief description of the Cave introduces the specific visual world within which we write, and into which we are asked to bring literal art, literary aesthetics (Figure 8.1). We are, in this artificial visual space, writing digital media, and our focus will be on the way that language appears in this visual world and how it functions.

When we write for the Cave, we write—bracketing any audio component within the scope of the present arguments—for a world of images. As we

FIGURE 8.1 *Photographs taken during a showing of* Glitch, 2008, *by Jason Lee, Ben Nicholson, and Jinaabah Showa: writing for the Cave immersive 3D audiovisual environment, Brown University, Center for Computation and Visualization. Photographs courtesy of Francisco J. Ricardo.*

have seen above, this suggestive impression is borne out by a technological analysis underlying the constitution of the device—of its particular system of media—and rhyming on the word "world."[4] The predominant material support for writing, conventionally understood, is, of course, graphics. This is just one of many reasons for a host of perennial inquiries—both theoretical and pragmatic—into the relationship between word and image, language and visuality. In a sense, this chapter takes yet another tilt at this intractable problem. Apart from our arguments' engagement with actual poiesis in the graphics world of the Cave itself, we will work with a number of theoretical statements on word and image, in particular W. J. T. Mitchell on metapictures and Michel Foucault's *Ceci n'est pas une pipe*.[5] However, the statements of this chapter have a different trajectory, not in the direction of a "pictorial turn," to evoke Mitchell's phrase, but an address to writing in visual digital media that is focused on language, its aesthetic potential, and on questions of how language dwells with us in "new," or in a designation that I prefer, "breaking" media. I claim that the relations between language and media that are revealed in our work and the discussions here are backwardly compatible with those in conventional literary media and require us both to reformulate relations that have become subliminal or culturally internalized, and to reconsider or reframe precisely the kind of discussion of articulated, linguistically implicated visuality that is undertaken by Foucault and Mitchell.

Working in the Cave finds us within a relatively rarefied and extreme, test-case environment. Although the technology has been available to scientists for some time, it is rarely accessible to aesthetic practitioners, still more rarely accessible to those who self-identify as literary artists. In the midst of a culture where we are ever-increasingly obliged to confront and explore the relationship between art in digital and new media and art as conventionally understood, attempting to make literary art in the Cave sets many issues and problems of mediated aesthetic practice, including but not only those discussed here, into high relief—as I aim to demonstrate. The spirit of the age seems to demand that we attempt to bring all art into those new forms of practice that programmable systems of intermedial representation offer us, to explore, indeed, the *language* of *new* media.[6] Confusions arise when so-called "new" media are configured to represent "old" media, a cultural trope now widely recognized as remediation.[7] Happily, writing or even just "placing" linguist "material" in an immersive 3D artificial world is something that is less ambiguously novel. Phenomenologically, language, as graphic inscription, does not appear or dwell in our world of lived experience in the mode of objects having position, volume, structure, and so on, except in a manner that is highly constrained and fundamentally two-dimensional.[8] My title, "the gravity of the leaf," evokes an underlying cultural force that draws graphic linguistic materiality to the two-dimensional surface and holds it there still. This force is phenomenological and accumulative, a function of the exigencies of graphically embodied symbolic practice that is addressed to humans. This force is strong and its strength is, I believe, borne out by the various ways in which we continue to read our now ubiquitous screens as page- or leaf-like surfaces rather than, for example, as spatial affordances, as symbolic architecture, shifting the shapes within which we live. Obviously, culture is changing, and this very aspect of writing to which I refer, somewhat polemically, is at the breaking edge of a wave. Finally exposed, "the gravity of the leaf" may nonetheless break down and may do so for some of the reasons that I set out below, because our understanding of the relationship of language and media must be reformulated, recast. Even the gravity of the leaf is relative to certain paradigms, especially the literary paradigms, of culture and history. In the first place, it can only have gathered its strength in a world where the graphical inscription of symbolic practice had been discovered and developed, and thence prevailed, proliferated, and become internalized as the familiar (leafy) world of print culture, now, perhaps already evolved to print*able* culture in the developed world.[9] In the Cave the gravity of the leaf breaks down before our eyes and language is cut loose. It may still be rendered as, itself, lacking a third dimension but in so far as it is visible at all in the Cave's graphics world it will be positioned in space, a strange object, perhaps floating in front of a pair of position-tracked, glasses-wearing eyes, legible as usual but situated, in terms of culture and aesthetics, *where* and in *what world*?

Imagine a letter floating before our eyes in the immersive visual space of the Cave, the representation of an atom of language, but presented to us in a new world, in a world of what I will call "breaking media." This is a novel experience, a new phenomenology of language, and thus it would allow the proper application of the word "new" as in "new media." The letter floating in space is not *re*mediation; it is a novel mediation of language because it represents graphically embodied language in a way that is entirely unfamiliar, cut loose, as I put it, from the gravity of the leaf. Nonetheless I prefer to put forward "breaking media" as a term for the manifold systems of representation that such programmable devices offer both because is it less likely to be inaccurate (so-called new media often represents/remediates old media) and because the epithet is suggestive. Programmable and networked media break into public discourse, as does breaking news, and often in the same contemporary mode, occasionally itself breaking the news of its own advent. Digital media accelerate cultural changes and roll them into an ever-growing, breaking wave where we surf just beneath its spumy crest on an edge that is breaking but not necessarily leading or bleeding. Moreover, breaking media do often just break, in the programmer's sense. They break themselves and they break legacy processes. It is both the case that familiar things that used to function no longer function in breaking media and that breaking media often breaks down in fits of innovation. But finally, these various breaks also contribute to what we discuss below and what are proposed as media-constituted diegetic breaks, breaks in the world or worlds that, for one thing, allow language into the world itself and into the worlds that we make.

The representation of writing

Questions concerning materiality and embodiment have been very much to the fore in contemporary analyses and theories of artistic and critical practice. In so far as the trope of *im*materiality is associated with the realm of computation—along with the cultural production which computation has appropriated through remediation or has, itself, generated—there is a proportional effort to restate and critically reinstate its necessary materiality, an effort that is presumed to have aesthetic traction in critical discourse and is sometimes implicitly or explicitly heralded as part of a return of the repressed.[10] By accepting that the digitization of a painting is not the painting we grow sensitive to these two speculative objects' distinct materialities, but we are left with the problem of accounting for their close notional or indeed visual relationships, the latter of which might be instantiated such that any and all differences between the objects are materially imperceptible to human and therefore human cultural vision. But the situation of (mediated) figurative painting does not directly address the sharper and arguably more fundamental problem of any materiality of language itself. What is the culturally perceptible ontological difference between this text digitized and this text printed? I want us to remain conscious that the question of the "materiality of language" and especially that of literary language underlies the discussion. However, I will wager that it proves more fruitful, in terms of both theory and practice, to examine the relationship between language and its instantiation in or as media.

We may consider painting as media.[11] Painting—focusing on non-conceptual painting—is, for the purposes of my argument, a media system addressed to the visible world and constituted by practices engaged primarily with the way the world is seen and made to be seen, both with those aspects of the materiality of things that makes them visible and with the material from which images of things can be made, including, among other things, paint. Especially given our critical texts of reference—Foucault, Mitchell concerned with a painting in this mode—we do well to establish a correspondence between painting as media and the more current understanding of media per se, in particular the new digital media within which we write. Painting is a media-constituted world within which discourses of various kinds may be played out and made visible for human interpretation and aesthetic engagement. These discourses are predominantly and naturally visual—the discourses of an image world—since they are realized in visual material (typically and for the type of painting that concerns us here in solely visual material), but they may also be or become linguistic or symbolic in one of at least two ways: by way of special cases—as in much of Magritte's work—where language is inscribed or represented, but also, arguably, in terms of the very "pictorial turn" posited by Mitchell, by means of which practices of visuality are so prevalent and articulated in the culture that they literalize this articulation and "speak" with the clarity and force of conventional linguistic discourse.[12]

It is more difficult to consider writing as media in an analogous sense. To unravel certain aspects of this difficulty is precisely our aim, and so to make any direct attempt now would risk tightening the knot we are attempting to loosen and describe. Suffice it to say that the material supports for writing are severely constrained in the worlds of human material culture—graphic inscription, oral practices, articulate thought. Whereas, for example, the diverse materialities of the media available to visual representation are commensurate with those of the visual world—infinite means to represent infinite images—the infinite subjects of linguistic representation obviously and infinitely exceed the materialities of the constrained media which bear this world-making language.

New digital media are not just to be considered as *media; they are media.* The existence of media that are able to represent other media or to represent artifacts that were made in a traditional medium as (new) media (remediation) is, in a sense, the phenomenon that allows us to see older conventional media as such; to see that painting, for example, is media, not just a medium. Subsequently, we struggle to distinguish, materially and critically, between conventional media(tion) and any corresponding new (re)media(tion): the painting and its digitization, as a specific exemplary instance. In the case of literary art, as indicated above, such struggles are, typically, futile. It is pointless to insist on a materially significant difference between these words as they might appear to you on paper and as they might appear to you on screen.[13] Thus, whenever we do consider differences in writing and mediated writing to be critically or materially significant, we tend to speak of writing *in* new digital media, as if writing were not undergoing *re*mediation, but as if it were being *new*ly mediated by removal from an unmediated condition and translation *into* media.

I am going to write about René Magritte's famous painting, *La trahison des images*, 1929 (*The Treachery of Images*, or simply *(The) Treachery*) in what follows. Some of my remarks may not seem to display a comprehensive sense of the art historical and art philosophical context in which this much-discussed work has been situated. In part this is a matter of my professional experience and inclination, but it is chiefly the result of my treating this painting as *a specific instance of media device* within the overall media-constituted world of painting. Certain properties and methods of this device manifest remarkable correspondences with those of the Cave, to an instance, that is, of new, breaking media within which we also write and produce images. To extend the analogy from object-oriented programming, Magritte's painting and the Cave may both be seen to be derived from an abstract "class" of media devices.

The Treachery is an oil painting, unambiguously a work of visual art, although one that directly addresses the relationship between image and word. As a media device, it is indeed unambiguous; it belongs in the world of the visual. Apart from its evident materiality as an oil painting on canvas, the work will be viewed in an art museum, itself an architecturally (spatially/ visually) constituted world where painting and other fine art are typically displayed. Setting to one side for the moment the products of such groups as Art & Language or conceptual work (and all the discussion here), we don't go to a gallery to read (a book) or smoke (a pipe). As you look around the museum—the painting is now in the Los Angeles County Museum of Art—you will see it hung within a visually coherent world where it will not be out of place. Granted, it is a metapicture and it does, as we will reaffirm, disrupt diegesis, but not in its material form as an aspect of the media system of painting set within the visual/architectural media of the museum's gallery space. You don't look around the gallery and say to yourself, "That is not a painting. That is language, commentary, metastatement, graffiti, an acousmatic stain." Moreover, in terms of the first instance of critical response, the artist's own, we have the painting's title, *La trahison des images* (the treachery of images), not, notably, "la trahison des mots," not "the treachery of language." The title sums up an inclination of critical response to the painting as it is exemplified both by Foucault's essay and by Mitchell's commentary. For both these commentators—despite the fact that their primary interest is the pursuit of language, discourse, the way that statements are made—this strange, simple, and strangely simple assemblage of graphic elements, including language, is still, obviously, a picture.[14]

Nonetheless, Magritte's *Treachery* does include, depict, address, and concern language. More than this, the painting is also, at least in part, writing. Perhaps, in fact, the work *is* writing? Initially, it is very easy and natural for us to say that, for example, the line of text—"Ceci n'est pas une pipe"—at the bottom of the painting is writing *in* visual media, writing *within* the media of painting. Why isn't it writing itself? Why couldn't we claim, for example, that the painting is dominated by this address to language and by its own actual instance of writing and that therefore, as a whole, *it is writing*, predominantly or in terms of a "deeper" interpretative or semiological reading, it is writing as media, and that, in fact, the image content of the picture is *in* written media, it is, in fact, imagery *within* the media of writing?

Of course, Magritte willfully, pointedly, if perhaps unconsciously, sets up this flip-flop, apparently symmetrical structure of complementary interpretations. In fact, he's already answered the question and so have we. He *painted* the picture and we either see it in an art museum or see it reproduced as a painting that exists as such in the museum. Magritte's paintings are, very definitely, in a particular register, one that is not the usual register of painting, not even the usual register of surrealist painting if you think, for example, of Max Ernst or even of the de Chirico that Magritte revered. Neither Ernst nor de Chirico can be as immediately "read," catastrophically, in linguistic terms, the way we read Magritte. I believe, for instance, that Magritte's painting can be seen as the visual complement of concrete poetry, where my definition of concrete poetry is not simply an aesthetic linguistic work the specifics of whose visual (or non-linguistic) manifestation are significant and affective (that would be true of all writing in so far as it is represented graphically), but a linguistic work that engages materially with the rhetoric and aesthetics of the visual world and/or the world of (concrete) objects. Concrete poetry is language rendered in such a way as to appear as visual images or to behave like objects and, in a complementary manner, Magritte's paintings are images and objects rendered in such a way as to perform language acts or to appear to be language. Both practices, arguably, are culturally marginal, minority practices; exemplary perhaps, but neither typical nor central. The point I want to make here is that the apparent symmetry of the implied relationship between language and media is an illusion. Both Magritte's writing *in* the media of painting and the kind of writing *in* new digital media that underlies our own inquiry, ultimately, help us see this, and do this in part, I believe, by the very fact of spanning all the intervening critical, linguistic, and artistic exploration and practice which has continually addressed the same or related problematics.

In a sense, I am recasting and reworking the kind of semiological analyses of image and text that was undertaken by Roland Barthes and implicit in both Foucault and Mitchell.[15] Here I will, through Barthes, anchor my use of the elaborate term "media-constituted diegetic world" before applying such thinking first to Magritte's *Treachery* and then to writing in immersive 3D graphics, to writing in new digital media. In the two essays that most concern me and which open Stephen Heath's translated selection *Image Music Text*, Barthes is mainly concerned with photography, "a continuous message," as he says, or "*a message without a code.*"[16] Barthes understands as well as anyone that "the image—grasped immediately by an inner metalanguage, language itself—in actual fact has no denoted state, is immersed for its very social existence in at least an initial layer of connotation, that of the categories of language."[17] Nonetheless, for him, photography has a special relation to the world which he describes as being "continuous," syntagmatic with the world of (natural, phenomenological, human) experience.[18] Photographs are both (actually and virtually) *in* our world, and appear to be (in a special, privileged sense) contiguous with its constitutive objects. For Barthes (one thinks also of Benjamin), "the photograph is not the last (improved) term of the great family of images; it corresponds to a decisive mutation of informational economies."[19]

But this isn't exactly so. Barthes writes before the existence of sophisticated media history/archaeology, and before the prevalence of media constructed from abstract symbolic manipulation—programmable and networked media. He understands certain aspects of a special relationship between the media-constituted diegesis of photography and the diegesis of the world per se (although strictly, in my terms, the latter is always already composed from a manifold of media-constituted diegetic worlds), but Barthes considers that it is naturalized by syntagmatic "flow"—enabling a continuous diegesis—between photography and the world.[20] What Barthes proposes could not be the case even if photography were, in any sense, "perfect" or "natural." Whatever photography is, it is always constituted by its media and not by a privileged relationship with the world, a relationship that is, in any case, necessarily interpretable, as Barthes demonstrates with great critical and ideological traction. However, in material terms and apart from any logic of argument, we can easily see that the representational world of what we ironically call "photographic naturalism" is, among other things, determined by characteristics of the type of focus that can be reproduced by the optics of lenses—depth of field—and that these clearly distinguish photographs, in terms of human optical experience, from the objects in the world that they are held to represent. Photography does not see the world as we do; we just agree that it does (for a relatively long historical period, admittedly crucial). As media change, however, we become ever less sure of photography's "special (uncoded) relationship" with our visual world.

My sense of "media" in the phrase through which I am rethinking the practice of writing in or with new digital media is an entirely contingent, if persistent, historical, and material embodiment of what Barthes, also within his analysis of photography, says "is commonly called the *style* of the reproduction."[21] Barthes brings style into the discussion while asking, "Are there other messages [that is: apart from *photography* in Barthes's view] without code?" He answers: no, because even all analogical visual reproductions have style, "whose signifier is a certain 'treatment' of the image (result of the action of the creator) and whose signified, whether aesthetic or ideological, refers to a certain 'culture' of the society receiving the message."[22] Analogical reproductions are coded with these connotations; they are not simply or even initially denotive objects in the world. He goes on to say, "for all these imitative arts—when common—the code of the connoted system is very likely constituted either by a universal symbolic order or by a period rhetoric, in short by a stock of stereotypes (schemes, colors, graphisms, gestures, expressions, arrangements of elements)."[23] In my view, all that is missing from Barthes's "style" in order to render it as my conception of media is the admission of a necessary intimacy between technology, device, prosthesis, and coded, connotative practices in the cultures of both "the creator" and "the society receiving the message." Barthes would acquire a way of handling photography as a function of media specificity, his exceptional and highly valuable insights accessible—largely unchanged in their tenor—because there is a new device in the world, the properties and methods of which have new syntagmatic relationships with the world, allowing a media-constituted diegesis to arise. Barthes reminds me that all media are intimate with rhetoric, style being a word from its discourse that encapsulates shared connotations of cultural practices undertaken by both actual makers and others within those institutions to which they address their poiesis.

Diegesis here is used in a manner that is related to the way it is used in narrative and film theory, but the usage is extended to refer to worlds of cultural practices, "diegetic worlds" within which syntagmatic "flows" can occur.[24] I say that these diegetic worlds are "media-constituted," which, as outlined above, implies that they are a combination of technology, device, prosthesis on the one hand and what I'm content to call "style" on the other. As a serviceable sketch of what I mean by style, I am also content with Barthes's far from exhaustive but suggestive listing: "schemes, colors, graphisms, gestures, expressions, arrangements of elements."[25] When technology and style work together as media, they create a diegetic world.

Note that media-constituted diegetic worlds may be in any number of relationships, bordering one another, intersected, overlaid, and so on. Because, as media, they are themselves constituted by both technology and style; either of these medial aspects may provide points or areas of contiguity between such diegetic worlds. Photography can be considered as media constituting a diegetic world. Barthes, recast in these terms, believed (at least for the purpose of critical thinking) that the world of photography was continuous—syntagmatically connected—with nature as envisioned by humans. This was, and is a, function of both technology and style: photography's recording technology—capturing a moment of two-dimensionally spatialized light—and a style of optical representation that is still, currently, accepted as "naturalism," even though this manner of vision is quite distinct from how we see. Whether or not we reject any notion of an *essential*—permanent, non-contingent—contiguity between the media-constituted diegesis of photography and the diegesis of human culture/nature (which I take to be a manifold of all existing media-constituted diegetic worlds), nonetheless, the properties and methods of photography relate to the world in a media-specific manner that support most, if not all, of the interpretative insights that Barthes draws from his analysis.

What happens when a photographic image is altered, as in many of John Baldessari's works?[26] I am thinking in particular of later series and pieces, from the 1980s onward where, often, the faces of human and occasionally animal figures are obscured by bright, flat monochromatic circular shapes.[27] Viewing and reading such composite images we experience a clash of (at least) two media-constituted diegetic worlds, those of photography and an immediately recognizable, if difficult to designate, style of representation based on these flat monochromic regions of color, generated by geometry, silhouette, or gesture (when such regions are over-drawn or over-painted by hand). There is a perceptible, indeed, a sharp diegetic break between the two worlds. We perceive this as chiefly a matter of representational style but, on reflection, it is clear that this distinction of style is also supported by distinctions of technology and of cultural practices attributable to both medial aspects of the two worlds. Relationships of potential contiguity between the worlds will not be determined by the break, however. These are likely to be manifold. For a start, there are intersections of technologies between the two media, mark-making on paper for one. Thus, Baldessari's overlays on photographic reproductions are able, palpably, to bring the worlds into material contiguity. Syntagmatic flows both proceed via the paper and are visually arrested by the persistent break of style. Moreover, Baldessari's layered hybrid art practices and the diegesis of photography share, in the realm of style, an attention to the composition of visual elements. The colored circular regions are carefully positioned over faces, not at random. In other works by Baldessari, these monochromatic regions may substitute as representations of whatever directly underlies them in the world of the photograph,[28] or monochrome silhouettes may be carefully integrated, spatially, in the photographic diegesis.[29] These niceties represent further syntagmatic flows, of compositional style this time, nonetheless still arrested by the break, by the necessary tear that will inevitably show forth between distinct media-constituted diegetic worlds.

A cultural artifact, a work of art, will, simply, by dint of its existence and integrity as an object, present us with a coherent world, and it will also, of course, be a part of ours, a syntagm in the diegesis of our culture, potential or actual. But typically, it will itself, although less obviously than in the case of this work by Baldessari, subsist as a manifold of media-constituted diegetic worlds. When we refer to *multi*media art—admittedly with quite distinct critical intentions—we implicitly highlight actual and often troubling diegetic breaks between the media-constituted worlds from which such art is made.

Now we return to Magritte's *Treachery* on the way to the Cave. As I have set out above, this work exists, first and foremost, in the media-constituted diegetic world of painting, more specifically oil painting, more specifically the style of mimetic figuration. Magritte's painting may hang happily in a gallery alongside other paintings that show us the world as—in oil-painted mimesis—it appears to be.[30] I am not going to enter the metapictorial abyss of *The Treachery* and related works in Magritte's oeuvre. This subject is more than adequately dealt with by Mitchell. I want, for the moment, to concentrate on the picture's painted "background."

Manifestly, materially, this background is part of the painting's media-constituted diegetic world and yet it is so nondescript as to appear to be what it is: inconsequential. We take no account of the background. It has no consequence, which I also take to mean that it leads to no sequence, that it is not a syntagm of any diegesis in any world.[31] The background is a no thing, no place, no where, not in any world except that of the painting. It is the painted depiction of an indeterminate surface. The "pipe" is not fixed to this surface in any way, neither could its nondescript light beige color be read as an "atmosphere" in which the pipe is floating.[32] Is the inscription painted or written on this surface? Common sense would answer, yes, but I believe that this is also and crucially indeterminate. I prefer the view that it is not. This inscription is *a painting of writing* and it is floating in front of the indeterminate surface and bears the same graphic, visual relation to this surface—in the diegetic world of *The Treachery*—as does the *painting of the pipe* in its more obvious oil-painted mimesis. However, relations between these objects and the surface differ, and they are neither complementary nor symmetrical. From these differences of relation further points concerning the relationship of language and media emerge.

In certain other discussions of *The Treachery*, its background is either ignored or referred to the structure of the caption, more precisely to the space between caption and image.[33] According to Foucault,

> On the page of an illustrated book, we seldom pay attention to the small space running above the words and below the drawing, forever serving them as a common frontier. It is there, on these few millimeters of white, the calm sand of the page, that are established all the relations of designation, nomination, description, classification.[34]

The existing English translation of Foucault by Harkness would have us see *The Treachery* as "the unraveled calligram," at best some kind of "(former) calligram undone" ("défait"), even though it was never a calligram in the first place. Foucault can be understood as thinking more clearly if we translate his view of *The Treachery* as the calligram's *undoing*, its nemesis. After all he calls the calligram a *trap* ("piège") that "absorbed" the (necessary) "interstice" between word (caption) and image. Magritte (who never fell into the trap), produced a painting in which the trap has been shattered ("a été fracturé") "on emptiness: image and text falling each to their own side, subject to their proper gravities. They have no space in common, no place where they might interact, where words might take figurative shape, or images enter the lexical order."[35] Which I also read to mean that *only* in or because of such a "no place" is it possible, as occurs in *The Treachery*, for images to *appear* to enter the lexical order, only to be (lexically, in terms of a direct linguistic address, "Ceci n'est pas … ") immediately, simultaneously *denied* by words that that have taken figurative shape in the media-constituted world of (the) painting. As Foucault points out, these two highlighted worlds of "lexical order" and "figurative shape" have their own proper "gravities" ("la gravitation qui leur est propre") and this brings us back to the gravity of the leaf, the gravity that is proper to language and which appears to draw even these figuratively shaped words to a surface that we know—because of its optical relationship to the image of the pipe—is *no* surface, *no* place.

For the commentators I've reviewed and even, to a significant extent, for Foucault this is "just" the no space *between* image and caption. My point is that this no space is, as Foucault also recognizes, the "calm sand of the page" ("le sable calme de la page"). It's not thin or small at all. It's the desert where we write. It is the very no place that everywhere—everywhere there is inscription of any kind—draws all language to its surface:

> The slender, colorless, neutral strip, which in Magritte's design separates the text and the figure, must be seen as a rift, an indeterminate and hazy region now separating the pipe afloat in its heaven of images from the earthly footfall of words proceeding along their single file. But it is going too far to say that this region is a blank or a lacuna: it is more of an absence of space, the effacement of any "common place" shared by the signifying marks of writing and the delineation of images.[36]

There is indeed a relatively thin strip between words and image in *The Treachery* and also between the typical layout of image and caption. However, in the painting, it is, visibly, not really a "strip" at all—it is a part of the background that is no place, and, for all we know, *infinite*. Actually, circumstances are the same for any image and caption. The so-called white "strip" is simply one of the many places the infinite (no) surface of "leaf" shows through—the (third) dimension-less leaf, the no thing, no place, no where, with its strong gravity proper to language. It is also, as it happens, the no space of the Cave.

What happens if we translate the objects in the painting to the Cave? Arguably this is not a remediation. The pipe and its "caption" are already in the very no space that the Cave simply actualizes as an immersive illusion. But follow me in this thought experiment.[37] We are standing within the Cave, its four projective surfaces in front, to the left and right, and beneath our point of view. The no-color of *The Treachery*'s background has been projected on to these surfaces and we ignore or no longer see those places where the walls meet. The walls have disappeared for us and we are in, or rather, immersively *before* the surface of Magritte's painting. The pipe and the inscription fade into view before our eyes, seemingly at the same distance from us as they would appear to be if we were comfortably viewing the painting in a gallery, although we see no frame. (The "frame" is beyond our field of vision, around the edges of the device, which we are inside.)

Both objects—the pipe, the inscription—look more or less exactly as they would in the painting. The pipe hangs in space. We sense intuitively that this can happen as a function of this media-constituted world. There's no gravity for image-objects here. However, the inscription is still "placed" in a more radically ambiguous manner. It must be on a surface, mustn't it? Is it inscribed *on* the background that *surrounds* us? If so, how could that be? How could a surface surround us? Can the "leaf" have that property?

Well manifestly, as it turns out, the inscription is not *on* the leaf or any surface, at least in that sense. We *see* this because the objects are moving, both of them together, and in the same manner. They are slowly rotating around a vertical, Y, axis that appears to run through the visual center of both pipe and inscription, between the *p* and the *a* of the word *pas* let's say. The pipe rotates and we continue to see a pipe, a pipe suspended in space and rotating slowly. But the inscription? Apparently, it has no thickness. We can still see what it is and, for the moment, we can still read it, but the effects of perspective—foreshortening and the subsequent distortion of the letter shapes—are making the letters and words look more and more unfamiliar and harder and harder to read until, suddenly, they're unreadable, merely a highly distorted representation of writing.[38] Once the objects have rotated 90 degrees in relation to our point of view, they stop and, at this point, the inscription is "edge on." It's still "there," but it's not only unreadable, it's invisible.[39]

This is, of course, far from the end of the discussion. It is nonetheless, however, a striking, graphic demonstration of the different manner in which language as inscription (and, since Derrida, it is always already inscription) relates to its medial support. The no place no where of the "background" is an abstracted instantiation of what is, in other contexts and in all poiesis, manifested as the manifold site of diegetic breaks between media-constituted worlds. The acknowledgment of these breaks is precisely what allows us to treat an arbitrary object from an arbitrary media-constituted world—the "pipe" in this case—as an instantiated object within what Foucault calls the "lexical order"—for interpretative purposes, for the sake of making statements. But so long as the site of the break can be seen and read in any media-constituted diegetic world, its objects can also be read and treated, at least provisionally, as "lexical items" without their having to leave their particular diegetic world or disrupt its coherence. The image of the pipe rotates in space before the background and remains an image of the pipe— which we can and do nonetheless deny as a "pipe." By contrast, the gravity of the leaf draws inscription to its no place no where no surface with far greater and necessary force. The inscription is always already *within* the media-constituted world of the "lexical order," which placement is partly determined by the strange surface of the leaf. As the inscription rotates *against* this surface it breaks out of its world and becomes at first unreadable and then *invisible,* which it might as well have been when it was merely unreadable. If it keeps rotating to 180 degrees from its initial position, in a brief continuation of our thought experiment, it becomes a mirror image, mirror writing, in terms of human optics, readable but now only by way of an internal process of decoding, of symbolic manipulation; not, be it noted, of graphic or optical transformation. The no surface of this leaf is not only geometrically strange, it must also be *programmable*, at least in the sense that—as in this case—it invites a human would-be reader to undertake an intrinsically algorithmic symbolic manipulation of a mirror-image inscription.

The thought experiment makes my points, bringing Magritte's *Treachery* together with the Cave by treating them both as media devices, where Magritte's painting can also be seen as a representation in two dimensions of an artificial 3D graphics world. I will conclude by going over some of the statements made in more general terms.

As in the world of *The Treachery*, the worlds of the Cave are not syntagmatic with the world in which we live, except by way of artifice— hence the epithet "artificial" in artificial immersive environment. The painting works exactly like the Cave except that materially, physically, the images of the Cave surround us and are doubled and offset to provide us with a simulation of human stereo optical experience. Relationships between represented objects and surfaces are remarkably similar, relationships, that is, between objects and inscriptions that are rendered in the 3D graphics world of the Cave, and surfaces, both depicted (the beige surface of *The Treachery* and the background "texture/color"—often textureless black—of the Cave) and actual (the projection surfaces of the Cave-as-device and the canvas of Magritte's painting). Objects in the Cave are able to hang suspended in the transparency of its graphic world, like the "pipe" in the painting, without support or connection to a surface or background-as-surface. They need not appear to be syntagms of the diegetic world that supports them. In the Cave, graphic marks of inscription are revealed, typically, as able to exist in exactly this same mode of suspension, unsupported by contiguity with any surface against which they are nonetheless visible. In the Cave, moreover— and this is not, of course, possible in relation to Magritte's painting—we may be able to place our point of view between (apparent) surface and object, to "get behind" it and to verify that it is unsupported.[40]

My aim has been to establish and begin to delineate differences in the way that language is implicated with media (and, by extension, embodiment and materiality) as compared with other aesthetic or potentially aesthetic practices of poiesis. What, again, are these differences? How does the picture of the pipe (which is not a pipe) differ from the inscription, "Ceci n'est pas une pipe." These differences can, I believe, be expressed in a number of ways, including in terms of my title, the gravity of the leaf, where "the leaf" stands, in general, for all (non-)surfaces of inscription, including especially the countless materially familiar but notionally third-dimensionless leaves of "paper" on which we write or have written, and also, as in *The Treachery*, those backgrounds of graphic worlds that are surfaces but are equally third-dimensionless no things, no where, in and of no place or space. The no surface in Magritte's painting draws the image and the (image of) the inscription toward itself with qualitatively differing strengths of cultural gravity and we can see this in the graphic representation. We see that the pipe hangs suspended in relation to the no surface, held by its gravity but not touching or fixed to it in terms of its media-constituted diegetic world, that of figurative painting. The position of the inscription, on the other hand, is radically ambiguous and contradictory: either its position is the same as that of the image or else it is not only held by the gravity of the no surface—the no thing no place no where—it is *on* that surface, co-defining it as such while deriving from it all of its own existence as inscription, precisely as linguistic-marks-on-a-surface, and thus become inseparable from it, in the very condition of linguistic inscription. For writing, the gravity of the leaf is the Strong Force itself. Either point of view leads to paradox. If the inscription hangs suspended, then it belongs to no coherent diegetic world of which we know, one where a pipe may also appear to be suspended in space. Handwriting cannot be suspended in space without a surface for it to be *on*. If, rather, the inscription is considered to be *on* the background surface, then it has gravitated to the no thing, no where, in and of no space, and so it is diegetically broken away from the media-constituted world of the pipe's image.

Of course, these contradictions arise because Magritte has, as I suggested before, made an untypical painting, one that behaves like language—a visual complement of concrete poetry. The "pipe" is able to appear like a word in the lexical order, and so it is also not a pipe in the same way that the word "pipe" is not a pipe. It does this very clearly and directly by, unusually, establishing the same sort of—radically ambiguous and contradictory— relation to the surface, to the gravity of the leaf, that is typical for words, for inscription. It does this by playing with the media-constituted world of painting, by depicting a paradox in that world, by graphically *illustrating* a diegetic break, the break that we see between the pipe and the surface against which it is suspended in no world that could ever exist. It cannot be a pipe. The difference is that the pipe looks like a pipe and the painting does have a coherence that is established within the media-constituted diegetic world of figurative painting. The pipe can be in that painted world and, without any change in point of view, it can appear to be in our own visual world, the one where paintings exist in galleries and where other pipes can be held in our hands and before our eyes and compared with the painted image. The inscription can't. It's either stuck on the surface of the painting's background, or it's in a no place where it couldn't otherwise exist. Even when made manifest in the artificial world of the Cave, it can only display a broken relationship to any world. It does *have* relationships with media-constituted worlds, but these are *severely, catastrophically* constrained.

Language in the Cave appears to normalize its relation to other media in the sense that graphic inscription can, in the Cave, be experienced as, apparently, suspended in space without being represented as *on* a surface. However, this is an artificial state of affairs, an illusion, an appearance. All of the light in the Cave is *on* some surface or other. Neither is there any other media-constituted world (or, more accurately, no such world yet) where humans live and to which we might retreat to hold up some surfaceless instance of graphic language so as to compare it, visually, with its representation in the Cave. Rather, when we experience language in the Cave, we are starkly, literally, confronted with the diegetic break on which language depends and by means of which we make it and it makes us as we write and read. We are brought face to—literal, spectral (sur)—face with the strange relationship between language and media, between language and its embodiment in the worlds that media provide. In order for it to be language, language cannot be a coherent part of any media-constituted world in which it is inscribed. Without both the irresistible gravity of the leaf and the break that frees it from all gravity, language cannot exist in this or any other world, let alone make art.

9

Writing to Be Found and Writing Readers

One

In order to begin to write this chapter, I set out to make some appropriate use of what I have come to think of as "writing to be found." Originally I had thought that this would be by way of simply beginning to write, embarking on my usual process of writing while checking, periodically, to see whether the sequences of words that I was in the midst of composing were still "found" in the corpus and then at what point they became "not yet found."[1] How many words would I have to add, composing my syntagmatic sequences, before they were not found in the corpus of language to which the Google search engine gives me access, before they were, perhaps, original sequences? How difficult would I find it to produce unfound sequences? Would I be able to continue to write as I usually write once I was aware that, at some perhaps unanticipated moment, the words I write are suddenly penetrating and constituting the domain of sequences that are not yet found in our largest, most accessible corpus of written English?

There have proven to be many questions raised by any and all of my attempts to engage with these processes and their contexts. Moreover, I remain convinced that many of these processes may be productive of significance and affect, to an extent that will allow aesthetic, not only critical, practices some purchase.

This way of working with language is enabled by unprecedented, convenient, and articulable access to the network, a world of language, a media-constituted diegesis, that is still "powered"—as the contemporary technologically inflected usage would have it—by text, by encoded representations of inscription, in what we usually call writing. The net is still largely composed from all the privileged instantiations of our languages' singular materialities that we, as irrepressible language-makers, have so far written to be found.

By which I mean, to make it clearer, that when I write with these processes, I'm both writing, and writing *with* Google.[2] Is Google my collaborator? Does Google become the space *with*in which I write? I want to make it clear that I don't consider myself necessarily to be writing *in* the space of the network nor collaborating (directly) with other artists. At this point, I also want to make it clear that I do not consider myself to be *using* Google, not, at least, in the usual way that Google is used for gathering instances of language by search. I'm not refashioning myself as a Flarfist.[3] I'm not casting a faux-puerile, post-everything, absurdist net over the net using the net, gathering glittering detritus, spectacular disjuncture, in endless anti-syntactic listlings. I'm not composing searches in order to find the language for what I'm making. I've got my language already, one way or another. I just want to know whether it's found or it isn't. The Flarf-poetic approach is—although this is only a small part of Flarf—a *détournement* of the affordances that Google offers us as a portal to text on the network. My "writing to be found," on the other hand, is in itself a way of writing that is shaped by the way that Google is shaped, by the way in which Google curves the space of the network. And Google does also, in a sense, write with me: constraining, directing, guiding, and, especially, punctuating my writing.

It occurs to me, broadening the scope of these experiments' relevance, that poetic writing for programmable and network media seems to have been captivated by the affordances of new media and questions of whether or not and if so, *how* certain novel, advanced, media-constituted properties and methods of literary objects require us to reassess and reconfigure the literary itself. What if we shift our attention decidedly to practices, processes, procedures—toward *ways of writing* and *ways of reading* rather than dwelling on either textual artifacts themselves (even when considered as time-based literary objects) or the concepts underpinning such objects as artifacts? What else can we do, given that we must now write on, for, and *with* the net which is itself no object but a seething mass of manifold processes? Google itself signals the significance of process since Google both is and is not the net. Google is not the inscription that forms the matter of the net. Google is merely (almost) everyprocess (not every*thing*) that makes it possible for us to find and touch and consume what was always already there in front of us.

When you collaborate, you are more or less obliged to get to know your collaborator. Getting to know Google better, in a practical sense, as a collaborator, is one of the most interesting results to emerge from even the relatively simple and preliminary processes that have been set in train.

This is probably the moment to introduce some details of the procedures with which I am writing. First, a classical epithet via Montaigne in John Florio's translation,

The Philosopher Chrisippus was wont to foist-in amongst his bookes, not only whole sentences and other long-long discourses, but whole bookes of other Authors, as in one, he brought Euripides his Medea. And Apollodorus was wont to say of him, that if one should draw from out his bookes what he had stoln from others, his paper would remaine blanke. Whereas Epicurus cleane contrarie to him in three hundred volumes he left behind him, had not made use of one allegation.[4]

Process: Write into the Google search field with text delimited by quote marks until the sequence of words is not found. Record this sequence. Delete words from the beginning of the sequence until the sequence is found. Then add more words to the end of the sequence until it is not found. Repeat. Each line of the resultant text (although not necessarily the last line) will comprise a sequence of words that is "not yet found." At the time of composition, these lineated sequences of words had not yet been indexed by Google and were thus, in a certain (formal) sense, original:

> If I write, quoting,
> I write, quoting, "And"
> write, quoting, "And the"
> quoting, "And the earth"
> "And the earth was without form and void; and darkness was upon
>   the face of the deep," these words
> "upon the face of the deep," these words will
> "deep," these words will be found
> these words will be found. Perhaps
> will be found. Perhaps they will now
> Perhaps they will now always
> they will now always be found
> will now always be found. I
> always be found. I write
> be found. I write, in part
> I write, in part, in the hope that what
> in the hope that what I write will be found.

[with Google, Saturday October 3, 2009, completed 2:04am EST.]

I was induced to explore this way of writing by the remarks of a philosopher and cognitive scientist, Ron Chrisley, at a workshop on neuroesthetics.[5] In discussing robotic perception, he was making some use of the concept of the "edge of chaos." I understood this phrase loosely as referring to a threshold of information processing, the point at which an artificial cognizer can no longer assimilate—typically by compression or by rule formulation—the information that comprises its inputs.[6] Somehow, to me, this suggested or rhymed with that moment in our now common encounters with search engines when what we are looking for is not yet found, when it could still be anything, because, as yet, it is nothing to the corpus. It isn't there. It isn't in any way predictable. It's still maximal, raw information in Shannon-Weaver's sense—the edge of chaos that we are about to make, literally, readable.

Since I have some practical experience with Markov models for text generation, I also pretend to recognize this as a closely related phenomenon.[7] If we think of Google as giving us access to a vast Markov model, I believe I am right in saying that as I build up my sequences of words delimited by quotes and test them after adding each word, I am testing the model's ability to be able to find me an n-gram where n is equal to the number of words in my sequence. Non-zero results mean that there are probabilities to play with. Not only is it the case that other people before me have produced instances of this sequence of words, but an n-gram model, constructed from the Google corpus, would also have some chance of generating my search phrase. However, once I've reached an unfound sequence, the model breaks down. I'm at the edge, and I may also, perhaps, be about to extend, by some minuscule amount, the readable, the unchaotic territory of the textual, perhaps even that of the literary. I'm about to write, and to add my own writing to the corpus.

And then suddenly it gets interesting. I was just writing, and now I'm writing with Google and beginning to wonder what that means. Google is where we search for language and for forms of all kind that are made from language, including aesthetic forms. It's become our default portal to the default corpus. It is not yet all writing, but we feel that we are close to the historical moment when the extraordinary possibility—Ted Nelson's docuverse—has become an actuality for, at least, a major portion of the existing textual corpus of writing in English. Already, I wager, we type our searches into Google expecting that it will find anything and everything that we might expect to be found in the world of letters, of conventionally inscribed textuality. What do I mean by that? I mean at least all of those sequences of words that have been written by authors who are known to us. All of the writing that is known, all of the writing that will have been found. And much besides.

> The purpose of this writing is to address
> an edge of chaos.
> Specifically, the point or points
> in sequences of words that
> delimit phrases
> found to be unique in our
> most accessible corpus.

[with Google, Saturday October 3, 2009, completed 10:27am EST.]

The two singularly lineated sentences above are made with a slightly different process, a retreat from the not yet found sequence—at the time this was, for example, "The purpose of this writing is to address an"—to the longest sequence that was still found in the accessible Google corpus. Although the sentences are original to me, they are expressed in phrases that can be shown to be plagiarized from the corpus. They have all already been written.

For we do seem to be addressing something like the palpable, objective edge of authorial originality. "The purpose of this writing is to address" was always unoriginal before I set out. When I wrote, "The purpose of this writing is to address an," the indefinite article made me an author.

Those of us who are educators will be aware of the way that Google and other search engines are used as simple detectors of student plagiarism. Type the suspected sentence into Google and it is very likely to find the source from which it may have been copied. Writing to be found with Google reveals, however, the singular, perhaps unprecedented nature of its, Google's, co-authorial authority. By definition Google changes shape. As we've said before, it's a process. By providing access Google seems to *be* the corpus of reference while remaining a protean manifold of processes that continually reconfigure themselves while crawling over *our* networked body of language (the actual corpus), even unto the edge of chaos, finding new readable things and indexing them relentlessly and swiftly, remarkably swiftly. Less than three hours after I'd posted my not-yet-found texts to the netpoetics blog, they were suddenly found. Thus, taking the same text and putting *it* through the same procedure produced an entirely different text and a new measure (or textual visualization) of my originality.

Returning to my first process, with the supply text just quoted, for example:

The purpose of this writing is to address an
is to address an edge of
address an edge of chaos.

[completed with Google at 9:17 EST on October 1, 2009, became:]

The purpose of this writing is to address an edge
is to address an edge of chaos.

a little over two hours later at 11:30 on the same day. (By the way, although the second iteration of the process reduces the number of unfound sequences in this initial extract; for the entire supply text, the second iteration actually increased the total number of unfound sequences from 17 to 21.)

This potential for iteration was not only expected, but it was something with which I desired to experiment, using it to produce a series of texts, evolving over time in relation to the findability of their constituent sequences of words.

But imagine my surprise when I tried the procedure again and found it regenerating the earlier version. My new, original writing was no longer found. I could see it there in the corpus (at netpoetics), but as far as Google, the "index of reference," was concerned it was, apparently, no longer there. I could not yet have produced it. Uncanny. But easily explained by my arbitrary access, at the first instance of checking, to Google servers that had already published the indexing of their busy spiders. Later, I had been less lucky: my client must have connected to other servers (I have no obvious control over this) onto which the new indexes had not yet propagated. Google had temporally denied my originality, my authority. It had changed the shape of my authorial persona. I wasn't writing with it. It was writing with me, against me, withholding what I thought I had inscribed.

Two

Why hadn't I considered this before? Why don't we think of it now, and then more often? As a culture, we are in the seemingly ineluctable process of handing over the digitization and indexing of our entire surviving published textual legacy to Google, in order for them to include that part of it which they have not already indexed. I, we, have no idea how they are going to index our literature or how their indexing of it might change over time. On the other hand, there is considerable evidence of uncertainty and inconsistency.[8]

I should of course mention in passing that there are already and will likely remain some checks and balances to Google. So far, the other internet search engines have access to most of the same corpus, and they do not index this corpus in the same way.[9] Without huge investment we could all write and set up our very own search engines. Nonetheless it is remarkable the degree to which Google has become, as I say, initially the search engine of reference and now in some sense the reference of reference. This is so obvious to us that it has become banal to point out that whatever else Google is, it may be the most remarkable and significant agency for cultural change on the planet.

Of course, the scholars among us (and within us) will defer. We cannot rely on anything that the folksonomic internet provides, although relying, admittedly "by default," is exactly what all of us having access actually do. Neither can we defer from Google in the same way that we defer from Wikipedia, on the basis of what it "contains." Google is not Wikipedia and, in a sense, it does not contain anything. Practically and in other critical senses, it stands between us and Wikipedia while also providing—in so far as it indexes all the writing that can be found—much of the material from which Wikipedia is built. Wikipedia is something that arose contemporaneously with the Googlization of everything but is more a symptom than a cause. Whatever Google is, it is a problem that remains to be addressed, and written with.

Here is one brief working statement of what Google is becoming or what it may already be: *Google is the preferred or default agency to which our existing institutions of cultural production and critique delegate the symbolic processing of our inscribed material culture in exchange for unprecedented access to the results of that symbolic processing.* I am, of course, bracketing all the important questions concerning what exactly is handed over to Google for processing, how is this done, who owns it, and where it is—all of which are irreversibly complicated by the fact that any answers will be radically different "before" and "after" these processes that were already in train long "before" any actual exchanges—such as agreements to digitize libraries—were made explicit, let alone regulated in any publicly agreed and articulated manner.

Let's say it again in more polemical terms. We hand over our culture to Google in exchange for unprecedented and free access to that culture. We do this all but unconscious of the fact that it will be Google that defines what "unprecedented" and "free" ultimately imply.[10] As yet, we hardly seem to acknowledge the fact that this agreement means that it is Google that reflects our culture back to us. They design the mirror, the device, the dispositive, as the French would put it. They offer a promise of "free" access in many senses of that word, including zero cost to the end-using inquirer and close to zero cost to the institutions that supply the inscribed material culture that Google swallows and digests. But Google does not (some might here add "any longer") conceal the fact that this free access does come at a cost, another type of cost, one that is also a culture-(in)forming cost: Google will process all (or nearly all) this data in order to sell a "highly cultivated" positioning of advertisements. The deal can't go ahead without this underlying engine of commerce and commercialization. In a sense, Google is the predominant global corporation, a major proportion of whose capital is literally cultural capital. Now, what was already a huge backing investment is being freely augmented by the traditional investors in this market of culture, the universities in particular. Bizarrely, these institutional investors are not asking for shares in the business, or rights to vote on the board. All they seem to want is to have what they *already* had, but processed, indexed, reformed, and reflected back to them, to us, in, as I say, a manner that allows many of us unprecedented access.

This is not, primarily, a chapter about Google, and the situation was and is far more complicated than this polemical outline suggests. Google did, after all, emerge from the *popular* culture that was born on the internet itself, long (in net history terms) before institutions began to contribute to this culture to any significant extent. Thus the initial cultural capital that Google amassed may be seen as fairly won, and the access that Google provided to a suddenly vast, ever-accumulating resource was truly unprecedented, rendering the culture of the net useable, manageable, findable, beyond all expectation.[11] We learned quickly that "unprecedented access" meant that Google was better than any other agency at managing the "more than ever before" of everything that is digitally inscribed, the exponential increase in information. But now this simple, if overwhelming, quantitative fact is *all* that we and our institutions know with any surety. We know that Google will deal with the scale of it all, and manage it all better, and give more of it back to us,[12] but we may never know, unless we ask or demand, exactly *how* they do this or how they *will or will not* do this in some speculative future when they have already *disposed* of the problems of processing it all, displacing it all, continually rendering it back to us through manifold devices with post-human artificial intelligences.[13]

Three

So now all my writing to be found has been recast in the light of this shared, would-be universal engagement or struggle with Google to retrieve or reform culture. And immediately, as in the work of writing digital media that underlies these remarks, I return to specifics with a heightened awareness of their potential significance, especially as critique of these relations.

For example, in the course of investigating writing to be found, it occurred to me that any material that is quoted in a text from a well-known, and therefore much indexed, source will emerge very differently in the procedures outlined above. It seems that in what may be standard original composition, you can expect sequences of words that you are writing to be found to be unique after about five words, depending on diction. However, arbitrarily long sequences of words recalled or quoted from many texts, like the English Bible in one of the standard translations, will already and will always be found by Google. The conceptualist in you might want to test this to some absurd aesthetic extreme, typing all of Genesis into the Google search box delimited by quotes and discovering thousands of hits. I didn't get this far, although I made attempts with lengthy sequences until I noticed, in light grey type, the legend[14]:

> "what" (and subsequent words) was ignored because we limit queries to 32 words.

I hadn't noticed or been aware of this limitation before. And I am still unsure about when and how it was instituted. How long had this been a Google limitation? Who decided it was needed and why? Why thirty-two words? It's clearly not surprising that this limitation exists. The point here is that it gets in the way of using or, in my case, writing *with* Google in the way I believed would be interesting and might lead to further aesthetic or critical cultural production. What if I wanted to continue with what I had hoped and planned to do? Google's got indexes to my language, my culture. Even if they might not reasonably be expected to give me all the tools I might need or want to explore this material, why should they constrain or reform the tools that they do appear to give me in ways that seem to me to be arbitrary or, at least, unrelated to my own concerns? These questions are already important but not as important as they will become. When Google indexes all books, which institutions will keep track of when and why they change their search algorithms, let alone endeavor to influence Google's decisions in such matters?[15]

Never mind, for my immediate purposes at least. Conceptually, I can imagine what the search results would have been for absurdly long sequences from famous texts and how, using writing to be found procedures for lineation, texts that quoted or plagiarized such material (let's say, writing to be found punctuating certain texts of Kathy Acker or Pierre Menard's *Quixote* or Kent Johnson's *Day*),[16] would be chopped up where they are "original" and then bulge out where they incorporated what is already found, as the "If I write, quoting … " example above demonstrates. (Menard's *Quixote* would be all "bulge.")

I say "never mind," but remain disturbed. A productive engagement had been interrupted by a (ro)bot from Porlock and now this seems as if it will be characteristic of writing and working *with* Google, re-energizing the Anglo-Saxon origins of that preposition. In fact, of course, it is a function of encoded properties and methods that are designed to reassert, where and whenever necessary, the underlying purposes of the Google engine, which is, as we recall, to dispose of culture and propose advertisements based on this disposal. Google asserts: "You don't need more than 32 words in your queries in order to determine what you want and what interests you. Making something that requires longer searches will simply skew our data and make it harder for us to know what you want."

Despite Google's assertion, I keep searching. Now my collaborator, Daniel C. Howe, and I keep searching. We've already, like many others, come up against another important limit. If you search too much or too fast (even manually I found), then Google's engine thinks you might be a process (as *it* is) and that you might be making automated queries. This produces the same threat to Google's underlying purpose, the threat of skewed analytical data. However, to us it seems as if we are simply retrieving access to our own linguistic culture. Usually, we are simply mining the corpus that Google makes accessible—in an unprecedented manner—for "natural language data." In writing to be found, I seek out the chaotic edge of what is being written and is soon to be found by myself and others, the edge of what literary culture acknowledges to be attributable authorship.[17] Isn't this a legitimate engagement with what Google promises us? Shouldn't these admittedly or purportedly poetic queries be accepted as a part of the culture with which they also engage?

As a matter of fact, we continue to write programs that generate automated queries and it is strange that Google—itself a vast conglomeration of processes—rejects them as such. Shouldn't Google be prepared to pass judgment as to whether a process is an innocent cultural address to its services rather than assume that any automated inquiry is an attempt to undermine or deflect it from its prime, commercial objective?[18] Returning to a concrete example that engages related concerns with poetics and the author function, I realized that using the Google search query's "not" prefix (a minus sign) I might search for sequences of words from well-known texts (delimited by quote marks) that would be found in the corpus but in places where they were not associated with their well-known "authors." I used this negatively qualified version of the procedure described above, testing successively longer sequences and aiming to find the longest sequences that also satisfied the essential condition of *not* being attributed to the famous author. This produces a text that, paradoxically, is collaged from phrases that are quoted from arbitrary internet unknowns but which, when linked together, will compose a famous text. Before supplying an actual example, I want simply to point out that the program I write to undertake this entirely legitimate chapter in conceptual poetics generates a large number of test searches even for a brief text and it will find itself frequently blocked by Google's suspicion of and ultimate denial of my own process's high cultural intentions.[19]

"blue and white of sky"[a] "a moment still"[b] "April morning in the"[c] "mud it's over"[d] "it's done I've had the"[e] "image the scene is"[f] "empty a few"[g] "animals still then"[h] "goes out no more"[i] "blue I stay"[j] "there way off on"[k] "the right in the mud"[l] "the hand opens and closes"[m] "that helps me it's"[n] "going let it go I"[o] "realize I'm still smiling"[p] "there's no sense in that now"[q] "been none for a long time now"[r] "my tongue comes out"[s] "again lolls"[t] "in the mud i stay"[u] "there no more"[v] "thirst the tongue"[w] "goes in the mouth"[x] "closes it must be a"[y] "straight line now it's"[z] "over it's done I've had"[aa] "the image"[bb]

This is Beckett, three fragments from *How It Is* which also correspond to the final part of a short prose work he originally published in French as *l'Image*. But it is also possible to assert that is *not* Beckett but rather something that I have written together with Google, where we have conspired to calculate a maximal syntagmatic association with Beckett's texts while ensuring that these sequences are attributable to others, often many others, and we do this in a manner that can be established by a contemporary form of citation. It is a relatively nice problem to consider whether this text infringes copyright. I might claim, for example, that it is not copied, that it's not even the same text, especially given that I have transcribed it with quotation marks around the phrases. A copyright expert might assert that it was created by a mechanical process, that it is the product of a procedural but regular form of transcription and is, therefore, a copy, to which I would have to reply that a great deal of personal thought and significant indeterminate and unmediated human labor also went into its making. The piece certainly challenges the Beckett estate's moral rights in respect of the text's integrity and its association with the author's name. In US law these rights are not established. In any case, I may both justly claim fair use, and also perversely propose that my first-cited example was actually derived from the following entirely original collage composed from fragments found to have been written on the internet:[20]

> "a moment *still*" "*animals* still then" "*April morning in the*" "*blue and white of sky*" "been none for a long time now" "*blue* I stay" "*empty a few*" "*there no more*" "mud *it's over*" "my tongue comes out" "*thirst* the tongue" "goes out no more" "*goes in the mouth*" "*again* lolls" "*closes* it must be a" "straight line now *it's*" "*the hand opens and closes*" "that helps me *it's*" "*going let it go* I" "realize I'm still smiling" "*in the mud* I stay" "*it's done I've had the*" "*image* the scene is" "there *way off on*" "*the right* in the mud" "*over* it's done I've had" "the image" "*there's no sense in that now*"

Clearly a lot more could, and will, be done with the procedures of writing to be found, including with this latter variation in which one rediscovers how much of what has been written has already been written. Google makes all of this possible, and Google also stands in the way of these unanticipated essays. One very significant reason to continue to work in this way is precisely to reveal how Google and other similar agencies will reform what they pretend to enable, and how our existing institutions that support writing as a cultural practice will relate to the profound reformations that must ensue.

Four

The "writing readers" within a major collaborative project in digitally mediated literary art are underpinned by the critical, contemporary, quietly hacktivist natural language processing and research initiated in "writing to be found." *The Readers Project* incorporates "writing with Google," and it also proposes performative reading as, perhaps, exemplary of how we may write in this, our future. The collaboration, with Daniel C. Howe, produces literary objects that have an extensive computational dimension and will, typically, be realized as screen-based or projected works, for both private viewing and reading, and more public exposure in installations with distributed multimedia and/or mobile displays. As such, they are, in the relatively small world of writing digital media, examples of a variety of work whose real-world instantiations take some place either in the screen real estate of net-based or personal computer–based art, or in the mediated gallery space of digital art. Even the computational aspects of this work have become amenable to critical attention in these days of codework, expressive processing, and/or critical code studies.

However—and this may not be the best news for an already over-extended critical community examining aesthetic objects that have still to prove themselves in any wider cultural forum—crucial reading strategies that are already encapsulated in our projects, in our quasi-autonomous readers, are derived from precisely the kind of "writing with Google" that I have outlined above. In other words, one of the more interesting dimensions of these readers is that they are, in significant measure, the result of natural language research and processing undertaken in, arguably, a sociopolitically implicated dialogue with our predominant new devices of cultural reflection and disposition. Of course, the readers also have other inclinations and ambitions (apart from any jostling entry into the world of digital art). They may prefer to offer themselves up to the open-minded literary criticism that is often applied to works of the literary avant-garde. You can read them as poetry or as a poetics. What I am suggesting, however, is that they may also be read for the way that both they and their making reads and writes with newly mediated culture, with Google in this instance.

This is a final point, a vector for both literary poiesis in digital media and for its critical reception, but I must conclude the point with its illustration. Here are three readers from the project, moving through and "reading," in some sense, an underlying text, a prose poem of my own, "Misspelt Landings."[21] There is a mesostic reader that finds and highlights words containing letters (which it capitalizes as it finds them) in a phrase beginning "*READING THROUGH ... , *" and there are two other readers: one that tends rightward and downward in the conventional vectors of human reading while deviating occasionally, and one that seems to wander while surrounding itself with a halo of erased or faded text. What is far from obvious is that these readers, all of them, chose their next word to read (and hence their deviations) on the basis of simple but quite effective research on the usage of these words in the corpus to which Google gives us access, however reluctantly. An important aspect of the way this and other pieces from *The Readers Project* are deployed is that, for each such manifold display, the readings of all the live readers are separately broadcast to a server, a feed to which you may subscribe by accessing a URL with a browser and with other clients under development. Subscribed to a particular reader, you may read along with it and see clearly the textual path it has chosen, according to its particular reading strategies.

In simple terms these readers check the proximate neighboring words of the word they have just read and they "know"—from the results of their writers' struggle with Google—whether or not any or all of those proximate words will represent likely natural language phrases.[22] Daniel C. Howe and I are the writers of these readers and we, along with other coded processes, struggled with Google, sending queries to its "books" domain to see how many instances of thousands of three-word phrases had already been inscribed as writing to be found and how frequently they had been inscribed in the net's textual corpus, if at all.

Many of you reading this will understand that this is far from being an entirely novel approach. However, although our readers may seem to be following a simple Markov chain, the actual processes and models deployed in *The Readers Project* conceal some significant differences to a standard Markov model.[23] More importantly and finally, these readers were written with processes that hacked near-live statistical data out of the Google-indexed internet corpus of all the inscribed cultural material that can be found. Writers of readers like these could not have made anything approaching their capabilities until very recently, or not without huge, institutionally maintained resources. We were and are able to make these readers remarkably up-to-the-minute in their model-driven analyses of the texts that they were written to read. They know what they need to know about the latest writing to be found on the net in their domain. This knowledge was mined iteratively from the language that we all gave over and continue to give over to Google and, in so far as Google was uninterested in or threatened by the queries we needed to make in order to gather our readers' simple knowledge, that knowledge is the result of a fascinating struggle that—for this reader at least—is a model in micro-procedure of the struggles that we must all undertake as our institutions of culture pass over its care and disposition to all those strange engines of inquiry that may suddenly reject our search for writing. They reject our queries for reasons that we may not entirely comprehend. Not yet and perhaps, not ever.

10

Weapons of the Deconstructive Masses (WDM):

Whatever Electronic Literature May or May Not Mean

Weapons of the Deconstructive Masses. In the midst of a desperate, necessary call for change, it might be best to get this all over with quickly; to admit that "There aren't any," and desist from any threat or preparation to invade a sovereign field of cultural production where intellectual democracy is always already safe.

When I began to prepare this short chapter, it was going to be by way of those critiques which ask, "Does it matter what we call it?" Of course it matters, or makes meaning, in the sense that words resonate and cannot be prevented from doing so. Nonetheless, that linguistic signs derive signification from locations within structures of differences and as a function of manifold contexts of usage; that their material specificities are arbitrary:—these facts are not contradicted by the revisionings of poststructuralism. Neither is poststructuralism any kind of reliable ally for poetic law-makers who, like Ezra Pound, seek to establish "proper names" for things, "true names," *zhengming*, a human-native tendency that he also translated from Chinese culture where it remains equally conservative, command-expressive, and poetically exacting, *and* also every bit as profoundly constraining and cultural-absolutist as it would be in some Poundian West. I mean to say that, within the systems and structures of language, names are put forward and are used—and they come to signify what they signify, to mean what they mean. Deconstruction can't do anything about this except to play in the slippages and gesture toward ruptures and anomalies, making différance without necessarily making any difference.

Bizarrely, the etymological and associative play of deconstruction is formally and, I would argue, significantly and affectively resonant with the same play that one finds in—as the epicentric example—Pound's later "ideogrammic" work. In *The Cantos*, Pound creates poetic ideograms from shards and fragments of transcultural, translingual etymology and association in order to establish the "sincerity" of true names, with "the sun's lance coming to rest on the precise spot verbally."[1] Derrida performs in precisely the same way, but so as to question, within writing, within the discourse of philosophy, the possibility that writing can ever produce any kind of "proper" signification.

All this is simply to give you some idea of where I might have been and, to a certain extent, still am coming from. But more importantly, this preamble rhymes with my final paragraphs, where we are again confronted with a disturbing contradiction between literary nostalgia or longing for what I later call "persistent form," and cultural inclinations which are formless or polymorphically and transmedially associative beyond anything we have yet encountered. I will still briefly take up the question of whether "electronic literature" is a proper name for the field in which many of us are now engaged, as both practitioners and critics, but I will go on to address at least two other matters which, for me, follow on from these issues of naming but which are, I believe, of greater moment. I want to try and write about some of the strategies and/or tactics that we, as a cultural collective— institution even—may wish to consider when delineating our relations with both literary and art practice, including critical and pedagogic practice. Finally, I would like to address some of the broader cultural and intellectual changes that I see taking place, specifically those that are highlighted by these considerations of naming and of cultural strategy.

Naming

As a matter of historical fact—and not only in the United States—"electronic literature" has emerged as a preferred term, one now destined to survive even my own attempts at deconstruction, especially since the publication of N. Katherine Hayles watershed, digestible, CD-equipped, all-in-one critical review, come constructive textbook, come seminal polemic, come new theoretical framework: *Electronic Literature: New Horizons for the Literary*.[2] Thus, whereas we never had "steam literature," or "electric literature," or "telephonic" or "televisual literature"—at least not of any cultural moment or persistence—we have already had "electronic literature" for a remarkably long time, especially given the hyperhistory of new media development. If by electronic literature we mean practices of writing in networked and programmable media—what I have always tended to call it—then we are likely to have an "electronic literature" for some time to come. However, we will have to bury the material-metaphoric implications of "electronic" precisely because the use of this adjective misdirects our critical and theoretical attentions. Writing in networked and, especially, programmable media weans us off even the traditional attachments of literature to particular forms of material cultural support: all the predominant and authoritative cultural formations that cluster around paper and printing and "the book." We are not out to replace one privileged material cultural support for another and so we must metaphorically bury "electronic" and must do so in the full critical awareness that, over a much longer period, a number of similar literary qualifiers indicating other material cultural supports were buried long before it. Literature has never been, for any of us, just "literature." Without needing this ever to be said, it has been predominantly, successively, concurrently "oral literature" or "manuscript literature" or "book literature," and so on. Recently, Hayles and other theorists, notably Alan Liu, are turning to a notion of "the literary," perhaps driven in part by unconscious or unacknowledged anxieties that literature may never be able to slough off the privileges entailed by some form of contingent material support.[3] For Hayles "the literary" is something like the potential articulation of symbolic feedback loops within complex, aesthetically motivated structures that "intermediate" human and non-human cognizers and agencies, themselves emergently self-organized in "dynamic heterarchies." Her theoretical framework provides a necessary revisioning of our brave new world and looks toward "the literary" as one way to embrace and articulate this vision, while acknowledging that the resulting "electronic literature" may be at a loss for *words* let alone paper to write them on.[4] For Liu, since the advent of the graphic browser, culture generally, and literature in particular, is already long since swamped, overlooked, and downplayed by the "cool" detachment that disregards a committed, materially supported poiesis. It's hard to be cool about making things, especially poetic things, especially poetry. It's even harder to be cool when reading poetry itself (as opposed to the cool theory that may envelop or disguise some of it), privately and particularly in public. Literature is uncool; while "the literary" has, at least, an outside chance of looking good and trading up. In the world of poetry, for example, while literature skulks in the academy, you can apply "the literary" to everything from rap, to spoken word, to open mic, to conceptual poetics, to "epoetry," whatever any of these may or may not mean.

Ultimately then, our problem and focus will prove to be not so much concerned with the qualifications of its various qualifiers, such as "electronic," but with literature itself. Rather than attempting to identify the specificities of a certain variety of literature or the literary, we must turn to questions—this is precisely what Hayles does in her book—of how the aesthetic viability (or not) of this newly mediated literary practice recasts literature itself and how this impacts on artistic culture broadly addressed. Liu's approach contrasts tellingly. Hayles accepts, more or less as a given, that there *is* a viable electronic literature and that we are (therefore) obliged to address its specificities and challenges. Liu is radically uncertain about the position of literature and the literary in what he sees as the now predominant, overarching "culture of information." In this—our contemporary—culture he discovers "cool" as a (perhaps *the*) prime aesthetic operator. As a backdrop to my argument, I'm required to knit together a number of citations from Liu's book that will provide a somewhat troubling delineation of this term in his insightful usage. "Cool" information troubles literature and seems to render it "uncool" in proportion to its redefinition culture itself.

> Cool is the aporia of information. In whatever form and on whatever scale (…), cool is information designed to resist information—not so much noise in the information theory sense as information fed back into its own signal to create a standing interference pattern, a paradox pattern. Structured as information designed to resist information, cool is the paradoxical "gesture" by which an ethos of the unknown struggles to arise in the midst of knowledge work.[5]

> What is the future of the literary when the true aestheticism unbound of knowledge work—as seen on innumerable Web pages—is "cool"? Cool is the techno-informatic vanishing point of contemporary aesthetics, psychology, morality, politics, spirituality, and everything. No more beauty, sublimity, tragedy, grace, or evil: only cool or not cool.[6]

But "cool," for Liu, also indicates an aporia that might paradoxically provide a solution to his aesthetic aporia.

> What transitional aesthetics can bridge the rift between class-based and classless aesthetics, between a "distinction" of literature that is now dying and its resurrection in a new body or form? Or, in a less utopian voice, what aesthetics can represent itself to itself as transitional in this manner? My argument is that the answer inheres in the avowed aesthetics of contemporary knowledge workers: "cool."[7]

The problem remains (more on this below) that he cannot see *how* the contemporary artistic practice of literature, even an electronic or digital literature, can become a part of this process of aesthetic transformation in, shall we say, a theoretically unified way.

Before proceeding, we must also be a little clearer about how we qualify those literary practices that currently bear the epithet "electronic." Unsurprisingly, this hinges on some understanding of the methods and properties of artistic practice itself, especially those we may characterize as "literary." In so far as artists identify as literary—without *further* qualifier—a distinct, established tradition of practice and criticism is able to examine their explicit claims as well as those that remain implicit in the work. In so far as artists engage in more novel practices of language art-making and in so far as they appear to share such practices with others, the designation of these practices becomes a matter of negotiation. While resisting the potential overdetermination of past concepts and forms, we do have to find appropriate, and necessarily abstracted, abbreviated phrases for processes and things that, even now, we do not yet entirely comprehend.

Both "electronic literature" and the all but insignificantly preferable alternative "digital literature" imply that there is a "variety," a "branch," "a faction," or, perhaps even a "genre" of "literature" (problematic in itself, since Flaubert and long before new media, according to Barthes in *Writing Degree Zero*) that is distinguished by the characteristics of the material from which it is made or the media in which it is realized, rather than the procedures of its generation. Both terms tend to substantiate literary production, to highlight the (finished) product (that always already has a past, a history), rather than (a continuing, emerging, developing) practice. For some years I have tried to make a point of highlighting practice by using the slightly roundabout phrase "writing in networked and programmable media."[8] As a matter of pedagogic pragmatism I now also encourage the shorter "writing digital media," the WDM of my title, a phrase in which there also hovers a cloud of pronouns and less-articulate possible relationships between writing and digital media: writing [in] digital media; writing [for] digital media; writing [transitive] digital media. But this is, as I say, pragmatism, part of what is a necessarily collective approach within which terms will continue to emerge and fade away along with "electronic writing" or "electronic literature." In these latter terms, the reference to material support will become invisible, folded into the designation as programmable electronics—gradually, steadily, then exponentially—become ubiquitous. The material and metaphoric overtones will simply die. We should be more concerned, as we will see, with what may or may not die with them.

The literary

I want to return now to the problem of "the literary" and its critique in networked and programmable media, to the question of culturally, historically established *forms* and how these interrelate with writing digital media. Here, "writing," as opposed to "literature," allows me to link forward to a demonstration of how—as I see it—underlying, persistent, perhaps even *necessarily* persistent, forms determine art practices as *literary*.[9]

It is fascinating, if disturbing, to witness the parallel retreat from "literature" to "the literary" in two of our most important critics. Hayles recovers "the literary" and establishes "electronic *literature*" as an elaborate function of the cyborgization of posthuman cultures. It is as if "writing" will provide an aesthetic and cognitive proving ground for an inevitable technological reconfiguration of culture and society generally. Liu, all but overwhelmed by "cool" new media art, admits to being at a loss: "I think literature will indeed have a place in a new-media world otherwise dominated by the design, visual, and musical arts. But what the eventual nature and position of literature will be among the convergent data streams of the future is something I do not yet know how to theorize."[10] This is, dateline *c.* 2001 ACE, the final epilogic position of a self-identified literary scholar after 500-odd pages of highly engaged, closely argued examination of contemporary cultural production in fields closely allied to our own. Both approaches make it difficult—two times harder—for me to put forward a theory of my own and still find appropriate recent support or authority. What you get and what follows is a practitioner's view, with some ties to critical and theoretical writings that I have found necessary or useful.

Earlier above, I pointed out that, within traditional discourse, "literature" has no need to specify its material cultural supports. These are assumed. We still live and breathe and write within the culture of the book. The usages of "writing," I argue, allow a similar adherence to preferred, persistent form, while remaining actively open to the emergence of new forms. This is one of the arguments that makes us prefer, for example, the term "writing digital media" to "electronic literature." The former preserves formal values while allowing that they will only ever be a function of cultural practice. They can be assumed, but they are not necessarily inherited, as of proper(ty) right(s).

But whence the implicit formal conservatism of "writing"? There is always already so much evidence of nostalgia for the forms of literary material culture, emanating even from the pens [*sic*] of the most sophisticated and prescient critics. Not long before Liu was becoming literally overwhelmed by new media cool in a manner that remains both cool and relevant, Jacques Derrida was also speculating on writing and the "the book to come" in a way that may belie any sense that his theory and critique predates and so has less relevance to a literary or linguistic philosophy of new media. In 1996, Derrida points out, "It was well before computers that I risked the most refractory texts in relation to the norms of linear writings. It would be easier for me now to do this work of dislocation or typographic invention— of graftings, insertions, cuttings, and pastings."[11] Thus, it was more or less at the precise moment that hypertext was visibly instantiating poststructuralist thinking on the web, that Derrida went on to say,

> I'm not very interested in that any more from that point of view and in that form. That was theorized and that was done—then. The path was

broken experimentally for these new typographies long ago, and today it has become ordinary. So we must invent other "disorders," ones that are more discreet, less self-congratulatory and exhibitionist, and this time contemporary with the computer.[12]

In the late 1990s Derrida maintains his adherence to a practice of avant-garde, deconstructivist literary "disorder"—exceeding non-linear hypertext—while, at the same time, reimagining the book in terms of irreducible cultural fantasy, where the end of the book may also be something quite opposite:

> These are two fantasmatic limits of the book to come, two extreme, final, eschatic figures of the end of the book, the end as death, or the end as *telos* or achievement. We must take seriously these two fantasies; what's more they are what makes writing and reading happen. They remain as irreducible as the two big ideas of the book, of the *book* both as the unit of a material support in the world, and as the unity of a work or unit of discourse (a book in the book).[13]

The two ends together—death and the achievement of writing—are what make writing and reading happen. Writing isn't writing without an end, without death. In another article of roughly the same period, important for our discussion, Derrida confesses his ultimate attachment to media remarkably similar to Ted Nelson's permascroll—a "paper emulator" if ever there was one[14]:

> when I dream of an absolute memory ... my imagination continues to project this archive *on paper*. Not on a screen ... but on a strip of paper. A multimedia band, with phrases, letters, sound, and images: it's everything, and it would keep an impression of everything. A unique specimen from which copies would be taken. Without me even having to lift my little finger. I wouldn't write but everything would get written down, by itself, right on the strip.[15]

Derrida's nostalgic attachment to a scroll of paper may appear uncool, but this vision of his own multimedia permascroll—"[o]n paperless paper"[16]—is also deeply cool ("information designed to resist information";[17] paper imagined to resist paper). Derrida sees clearly that writing (and reading) is the key, writing as the record of what we are, or, rather, what we will have been after we are gone. For a culture to acknowledge our existence, to register and archive whatever it is we will have been, there must be some way for us to write ourselves, some arbitrary material cultural support, a cultural practice of inscription, and a cultural fantasy *of successful inscription* to drive the whole machine. These will all be historically determined, of necessity. A *paper scroll* may not be the ultimate medium, but (at least until the Kurzweilian "Singularity") a person from Derrida's and our own age must believe that writing on paper will always, at least, be legible.

I'm using Derrida to reinforce and authorize our sense that there is an important, irreducible relationship between writing and historically determined material culture. I use Derrida, in particular, in order to establish this relationship as one that will be appreciated as both critically and theoretically sophisticated and as allied with innovative, experimental, and emergent cultural formations. But now I need to put forward a proposition concerning the relationship between writing and persistent form which seems to me compelling and consonant with that between writing and material culture, but which is not, in any way that is obvious to me, a necessary consequence of this or any other immediate relation. Rather it is a consequence of language, of the specifically human form of symbolic manipulation and interaction. Because they are universal to, if not definitive of, the human, practices of language require historically persistent forms in order be able to yield their significance and affect—the meanings and the aesthetic values with which they may be inscribed—*more than in the case of symbolic manipulation in other media*. Language cannot be writing, *a fortiori* literary writing, without a form that persists beyond some simple act of artifactual conception. My proposition might be regarded as one of those truisms—no information without form—but I think it gains some traction if the comparative part of the proposition—*more than in the case of other media*—is conceded as something with which we can work. In plainer words, what I'm proposing could be recast as claiming: because *everyone* uses language, because *everyone* writes, we need more in the way of agreed persistent form to help us decide *what part* of all the language and writing that is produced has appreciable meaning and/or beauty. "More," that is, than in the case of practices of symbolic expression in other media which may be technically specialized and subject to explicit disciplines and so, somewhat paradoxically, better able to cope with formless essays by recognized practitioners of, for example, painting, music, sound art, visual and conceptual art, performance, and so on. To answer my question above, "Whence the implicit formal conservatism of 'writing?'" It has to be formally conservative because everyone writes, not just writers.

What's the differencing?

The above argument implies that even, or perhaps, especially in new media, for us to be able to find and recognize "the literary," we will have to be able to find and recognize persistent forms, literary forms, forms of writing, which will then allow us to appreciate "the literary" in "electronic literature." I am not going to shy away from this conclusion, a contentious conclusion that is based on what?—on corroborative evidence concerning the "end of the book," on my consonant but fundamentally ungrounded proposition concerning language and form, and also, of course, on the present aporia of "the literary" in new media art practice. This penultimate section examines some properties and methods of new media's literary aporia; to give some examples of how artists respond to this aporia when and if they are driven to produce language-driven new media art, and to consider whether, in the "end," this aporia is nothing of the sort, whether it might be the case that what for us seems to be a problem of "the literary" will be resolved or dissolved in fundamental transformations of culture that are, precisely, correspondent with the "end of the book," its closing achievement.

This is how Alan Liu spells out the aporia, the situation, as he sees it, not only of "the literary," but of the "creative arts," in the one place in his book where he explicitly addresses electronic literature:

> What is the function of the creative arts in a world of perpetually "innovative" information and knowledge work? Of course, the multifariousness of the forms, media, practices, and views of the contemporary creative arts (including literature) is remarkable. ... one need only scan the voluminous *Directory* of resources on the Electronic Literature Organization's Web site or listen in on the organization's conferences and online events to appreciate the multiplicity of ways in which creative writers are using digital media to try out new genres, writing processes, and publishing methods. No adequate account of such variety can be rendered here. Nor can there be adequate discussion of the other, seemingly paradoxical side of the equation: that despite its splendid variety, so much of contemporary art and literature has a similar look and feel descended from the collages and cut-ups of the modernist avant-garde—for example, assemblage, pastiche, sampling, hypertext, appropriation, mixing, creolization, or, to cite one of the dominant metaphors of recent literary history as well as hypertext fiction, "patchwork." As I have said, it is all mutation, remixing, and destruction.[18]

What Liu—a literary scholar after all—does not so much consider is any existing difference in the cultural critical appreciation of this purported aesthetic aporia when we compare responses to it in the world, for example, of visual art—broadly conceived—with those in the world of literary art—equally broadly conceived. Liu's ultimate discomfiture with "cool" does not obtain as strongly in the world of art. It has long been the case—and Liu's evocation of "the modernist avant-garde" as our most recent pioneering exemplars of an aesthetics of destructive creativity suggests as much—that art can be cool without ceasing to be art, without losing its way through to some assured sense of what should be considered artistic. When art encountered radical innovation, scholars and critics were not driven to retreat from "art" per se and recast their responses in terms of a troubled conception of the "the artistic." Even today "electronic arts," "ars electronica" gives me, for one, less pause than "electronic literature." It seems precisely to be the point that Liu's struggle with cool is a problem for literature and literary culture. Liu cannot theorize a place for literature in the culture of cool. Hayles requires the literary to survive and prosper by forging cultural links with intelligent cyborgs and machines. I would like to suggest that literature both requires and generates historical and material cultural form to operate and that this necessity renders it uncomfortable within a culture that is predicated on continual, arbitrary, contingent formal innovation.

I am not, in this, saying that literature *should* be comfortable, nor that it *should* steer clear of the rampant formal innovation that programmable media make ever more possible and inevitable. Quite the contrary, as is evidenced in my own practice, teaching, and in some of the examples I will examine here. I am simply suggesting that for "the literary" to be active as an aesthetic or interpretative framework in the course of our critical and theoretical engagements with language-driven digital media, then we must take account of a historical relationship to material cultural form which is different from the corresponding relationship in respect to other artistic practices. To bolster this claim and before moving on to examples of practice and further final thoughts on culture, I make three hasty references. First, I refer back to my brief discussion of Derrida's and our own nostalgia for the book, for paper, for formal signs of the support on which we will always be able to have inscribed ourselves, especially after we are gone. This is a familiar affective concern, bringing together the universal human drive to write (by which I mean inscribe in any form, from speech to projection in social networks) and the universal human address to mortality calling for a lasting monument of some kind. Those of us who will not live forever seem to be strongly driven to have written something, anything, and the drive for this to be in some *form that will continue to be read* is also strong. Second, my call for the literary to acknowledge its special relationship and to practice in acknowledged relationship with historically established, material cultural form, corresponds with Liu's proposed resuscitation of "cool" in that, for him, cool artistic practice is culturally, aesthetically engaged when it manifests an informed historical critique as a function of its destructive creativity.[19] Finally, consider how different the practical engagement of visual and related arts with new media formal innovation has been and will be. Conceptual art is crucial here. Conceptual art is the art that comes closest in its techniques to the algorithmic expressive processing that drives digitally mediated cultural production. In this art, the underlying concept is, fundamentally, the form. Its material cultural realization may be important for the work's affect and significance, but at least since the "modernist avant-garde" as invoked by Liu, material culturally, any form will do, in that any form might record the concept equally well. Any further meaning and beauty of the work's form becomes contingent without damage to its concept. The material form simply adds to or subtracts from the ultimate significance of the work. My point is that for "the literary" the situation is different. The literary form is already necessarily, by definition, symbolic. It is constituted as such. Its form cannot be entirely separated from whatever concept drives the work. It cannot be entirely contingent. There is far less "free play" in the formal realization of a literary work, be it mediated digitally or in any other manifestation. Hence the paucity of literary form in "Art & Language" and related conceptualism. Any literary aesthetic within Art & Language is— typically—slight, and exhausted in the realization of the work. Its visual, material form is contingent, like that of other conceptual art, but its scant relationship to literary form further minimizes its aesthetic and constrains its materiality to, for example, legibility. Is Jenny Holzer literary? We will have reason to refer to her work again shortly.

Institutions for the future? (of the book, of literature)

I want to give some examples, of work that can undoubtedly be regarded as writing digital media and which displays and engages properties and methods which concern us and Liu and Hayles. I will examine three works, all by graduate students of Brown University and the Rhode Island School of Design (RISD). Only one of the graduates could be considered a writer in and of digital media. This is Justin Katko, then an Electronic Writing MFA fellow at Brown. The others are graduates in Modern Culture and Media at Brown, and at the Digital+Media graduate program at RISD. These students, along with thirteen others, including a number of Computer Science graduates and undergraduates, attended a course taught by Daniel C. Howe on Advanced Programming for Digital Art and Literature. The course had two main threads: to introduce Processing and Java to digital writers and artists for the advancement of their programming skills, and to introduce digital artistic and digital literary practices to interested coders. The course was a run away success and produced a good deal of work, some of which, as we will see, would bear serious consideration as possible candidates for inclusion in the corpus if not the canon of "electronic literature." This statement would be, out of context, quite extraordinary—and this is one of the points I'd like to make—and yet it is, I believe, sustainable and also gives some clues to our predicament.

Expressive programming, in digital art practice generally, is taking off, and there is now a huge body of work and experience—more work than commensurate critique I suspect.[20] Much of this work is highly technical and demanding of skill and specialist knowledge in, at least, the realms of programming and visual representation. The extremes of formal diversity and innovation are tempered by the disciplines that underpin the making of this work. I cite these practices as examples of how, in contradistinction with digital "literary" endeavors, essays in new media expressive programming afford its critics ways to deal with open form, and to valorize certain approaches over others. The critic may still not be able to say what's good in the work, but he or she should be able to tell whether it is "trivial" or not, as expressive programming.

However, Howe's course was not primarily concerned with the predominant forms of expressive programming. In line with his own interests, the course was language- and literature-driven. Students were obliged to make work that engaged with linguistic structures and "literary" concerns, although admittedly, these latter were only as seriously engaged as we engage them now—only as seriously engaged as they are, for example, engaged by Alan Liu's bewilderment. The remarkable fact is that this bewilderment did not seem to obtain or to obtain in the same way for this diverse set of students. They were all relatively happy to produce Markov-chained text generators and Flarf-poetic Google hacks and language-driven data-mining mapping art and sound poetry machines and Shakespeare modulator-remixers. They were all cool and they were all, at the very least, producing some sort of encounter with "the literary."[21]

So now, I'm going to introduce you to what I consider to be either or both the coolest of the cool or the most literary of the literary. I start with the most literary and end with the coolest, for reasons that I hope will become clear.

The first piece is *Mémoire involontaire No. 1* by A. Braxton Soderman.[22] Soderman's piece is fairly straightforward. It has a supply text/display text structure. The supply text is a closely composed, elegantly written record of a childhood memory. There is no interactivity or transaction with the reader. The text displays itself on the screen for reading, but it is subject to continual modulation by carefully coded processes of word replacement. Engagement with the piece is intended to be intermittent or—as Soderman has demonstrated live—performative, with public readings from the changing text. Soderman (in email correspondence) references an ambient poetics put forward by Brian Kim Stefans and myself in various both critical and creative works.[23] The word replacements which activate the piece are elaborately coded. Synonyms for the piece's full words are sourced live using WordNet, and the replacements are carefully parsed and integrated with the text as seamlessly as possible, in a manner that makes a significant gesture toward a notion of natural language representation. Generally speaking, the brief paragraph remains uncannily readable (not just legible) despite the replacements, and it still bears the marks of good literary writing, a style that somehow preserves on conserves its (necessarily non-existent) "original" memory-image. One point of the piece is, precisely, that this memory-image was never originally in some one particular form of words, not even after a "first" verbal formulation was composed. Apart from the text and the replacements, the piece is also overlaid with relatively subtle audio and visual correlatives that are designed and coded so as to inflect and enrich the relations between memory-image and text.

I am citing this as the most literary of my examples, but it is also the piece in which digital manipulation most directly engages with writing. It is not only Soderman's writing—as composition of the supply text—which renders the piece literary; the writing produced by and represented in the piece itself, as process, demonstrates an important relation between memory and its inscribed representation. In Soderman's piece this encounter remains literary in its significance and affect, because of and not despite digital media.

Justin Katko and Clement Valla's *Yelling at a Wall: Textron Eat Shreds* is driven by Katko's powerful lyric voice, both literally and in terms of the literary.[24] Katko records his part-improvised recital in a public architectural amphitheater, divided by a minor roadway, opposite the banal-minor-league-monumental edifice of Textron's "World Headquarters." Katko and Valla capture and tile an electronic image of the edifice and then produce a visualizer that is responsive to the waveforms of Katko's acoustic tirade, disrupting the tiles of the headquarters' image in manner that both corresponds to a visual representation of the sound waves, and generates a metaphoric image of the disruption that is fervently inscribed in Katko's lyrics. Katko later also takes his recital and feeds it through a bespoke, Max/MSP-coded modulator which further mimes the self-consciously disruptive aesthetic in disjunctive sound, and this processed sound is, in turn, fed back into the visualizer. Katko and Valla produce a complex multimedia instrument, driven ultimately by lyric address, and tailored to a particular site of intervention.

It's a rich and effective piece containing a library of forms and formal figures, most of which—such as visualization, remix, and feedback—are precisely representative of the overwhelming diversity of cool forms which troubles Liu. Unlike in Soderman's piece, the literary is not inscribed as coding, as new form. Rather, a recognized literary form, lyric address, however strident, provides over-arching structure for the piece. It is thus highly and properly literary, as piece of digital art, but is less literary as a piece of writing digital media since its literary qualities are not so much a function of the system as a generative whole.

I think that a piece like Katko and Valla's is more consonant with what we expect to find touted and troubled as "electronic literature," those works in which multimedia representation—or, if Hayles is right, intelligent machinic re-imagination by subconscious cognitive processes with a hankering for literary recognition—is allied with an aesthetic that is language-driven.

Pieces like Soderman's in which the literary mechanisms are integral to the whole of the writing are still scarce. Multimedia representation enhanced by expressive processing is typical, and, typically, both encapsulates and seduces the literary in digital media. It's there, but it is overwhelmed and consumed by its new media hostess.[25] We see something cool but we stop reading it or imagining that it might be singing to us, or spinning a tale, or addressing our verbal memories, or offering itself to us as a closing book that we have read and that reads us.

The Katko and Valla piece is something that we expect to find in electronic literature, but, as culture shifts, Caleb Larsen's variety of language-driven work is likely to be even more widely propagated than the Katko and Valla variety and it is, especially if we end up conceding that it is also in some way literary, even more troubling for literature than cool representation. You might well say that it's cool, but it's not.

Larsen's *Whose Life Is It Anyway?* is simple.[26] It's a text generator for Twitter, what would now be called a chatbot. As the wired world knows, Twitter is a personalized text-based news feed. You subscribe and make a site/identity for yourself; you update this site at indeterminate intervals with short texts that describe what you are doing, thinking, feeling, whatever. Other subscribers can follow your twitter and stay updated with your updates. You can do all this by mobile phone using an easy lightweight bridge between the developed and developing world's currently preferred all-but-ubiquitous communication devices and the internet. I promised another mention of Jenny Holzer. Holzer twitters, and you can easily imagine in what manner.[27] You don't have to subscribe. As she will have said, "THERE IS NO POINT IN READING ANYTHING THAT YOU KNOW WILL HAVE BEEN WRITTEN."

Larsen's twitter is a little different. Responding to another common trope of the information age, his twitter assists with the oft-lamented lack of time that information society engenders. We can program these devices of social projection to project ourselves for us. Larsen's Twitter account is a crafted grammar of plausible (for Larsen) actions, thoughts, feelings, whatever. His databases, algorithms, and grammars, along with a variety of triggers, now tell him and everyone else what he is doing and thinking without his having to spend or waste time on this demanding projection of himself for his "followers." It's clever, it's a critique of current and developing mores, and it's "cool," we say. It's undoubtedly language-driven—as used to be true of the internet generally—but is it literary? Here, Liu's analysis may help since, as Liu would say, a "yes" answer is only really possible if Larsen's piece is critical and it becomes stronger as art in so far as it is destructive, in the sense of undermining a social practice that is the subject of its critique. Stronger as "art" I said and it is easier to see the piece as digital art than as writing digital media, and this is, I believe, at least in part for the reasons I've identified. There is no historical form for twittering, no past literature of twitter. To know whether twitter is literary or not is difficult for this reason at least.

Whose Life Is It Anyway? gives us other deeper cause for concern, I believe, and this has profound literary and cultural implications. Before taking on this cause in brief in conclusion and perhaps also to give my final remarks a little more context, I want to comment on the quality of these three pieces as electronic literature. It seems to me likely that they all would have attracted considerable interest and attention if they had been produced early in the hyperhistory of the field. I have just given them a degree of attention that they undoubtedly deserve. They are pieces produced by younger artists in an academic context but in many respects, they hold up well, as they should, if we take into account their status as essays toward something more finished, critically, relative to pieces that have been anthologized and rendered exemplary. This kind of phenomenon is, of course, to be expected in a still emergent field, but here I think it is also the mark of a shift in culture toward the more generalized acceptance of expressive processing, even in the realm of the literary where, as I have tried to show, expressive processing's still arguably corrosive relationship with historically persistent form creates special difficulties for poiesis. Nonetheless, these are only three of many interesting pieces that were produced in the course of a single semester. This experience is now being multiplied in other related courses at Brown and beyond. There will soon be a lot of cool electronic literature, a contradiction in terms in most cases, but not in all. Work that is irreducibly literary will, I suggest, insist on persistent form, and the rest will quietly merge with cool digital art.

In my closing words, the words with which I will most closely leave you after I interrupt this address, I want to take the opportunity to indulge in some cultural critical speculation, some even less academically grounded and referenced thinking. I hope you will bear with me. There will be some bases to what I will try to briefly express, some evidence, but much of this will be a function of my personal experience. The pedagogic anecdotes which I have just related, the three exemplary pieces on which I have just commented, and, especially, Larsen's *Whose Life Is It Anyway?* are starting points. There is also my recent experience of moving from the United Kingdom, where my work was not in the academy and where my engagement with culture as reconfigured by younger prosumers was filtered through generational difference along with whatever pop culture happened to be accessible to me. The situation in Europe is different. Moving to the United States and teaching at a university has impressed me with the degree to which what Liu calls knowledge work, but let's just call it culture, has changed and is continuing to change at a furious pace. Young intellectuals, young knowledge workers—and there could be an argument for saying that this means all younger people (and there could be an argument for saying that this means everyone, as "youth" destroys the possibility of "age")—read and write differently now. I use those verbs advisedly. In so far as they are outmoded, they are all the more indicative of how culture is changing. If, that is, we read these words—"read" and "write"—as our chief methods of culture.

At this point it is still true, I believe, that "read" and "write" and whatever it is that we create or interpret which bears some relation to "the literary," despite the fact that it will in almost *every* case be mediated by a programmaton (computer), is still created and interpreted "*with a view* to the final printing on paper, whether or not this takes place."[28] And in so far as art and music, for example, require articulated interpretation in some form, this statement also applies to all cultural production, including everything not otherwise embraced by "the literary." The deep attachment to writing *on* paper—to a grammatology which has inhabited a long persistent material cultural world—has already definitely passed over to writing "*with a view*" to paper, and this is a major reconfiguration (one, for example, that is transforming the mediation of academic authority). However, as others have pointed out, the book and its tropes are easily represented, easily remediated, within the culture to come, and books and paper will survive as physical objects, material supports, for at least a generation or two. The book will end with precisely the ambiguity that Derrida anticipated: it will close and it will achieve its apotheosis.

I am more concerned with the way in which this literal, this literary achievement impacts on questions of subjectivity, privacy, the unconscious, and interiority. As critics and theorists, including Derrida, have pointed out, there are strong links between what is articulable in relation to these questions and language, and between language and its culturally privileged material supports—currently still, we claim: a view to books and paper. It is of course less clear where we locate any possible engine of cultural change: does embodied language determine subjectivity or does en-worlded subjectivity determine the culture of embodied language? Moreover, if we now entertain the notion of other-intelligence/subjectivities emerging in among posthuman cyborg cognizers, might these become a distinct motor of change, as Hayles would be likely to argue?

To this last question, I believe that we are now required to answer in the affirmative. Larsen's twittering may be cool; it might be dismissed as too cool for academic critique, but taken together with other manifest cultural reconfigurations, it can also be seen as highly indicative. It is integral with and a window onto the massively—popular and creatively—destructive worlds of social networking. There, or rather, *here*, we no longer project Sherry Turkle–style psychosocially transformative avatars; these networked, programmatically mediated social networks "*R US*"—they are making us what we are. Ultimately, they are transparent; at most they can be only what Derrida calls "a secret with no mystery."[29]

I slipped the adjective "destructive" into the phrase "massively ... destructive worlds of social networking." This was a reference to Liu's "destructive creativity" and also an acrostic, rhetorical allusion to my title. Destructive of what? The literary sensibilities of the person addressing you now are corrosively challenged by social networking's inscriptions of private thought and feeling, by inscriptions of what I would normally consider to be reserved for interiority. Larsen's Twitter piece takes this on and his title makes this clear, *Whose Life Is It Anyway?* Whereas I cannot divorce my sense of interiority—you cannot know my thoughts and neither of us can know my unconscious (although, admittedly [and recursive-unknowingly] you may *be* my unconscious)—from the embodied language of a lingering persistent culture—you and I can only write books of poetry that record whatever can be articulated of what we feel and know is inside us—ever younger minds may have machinic familiars and mediators who will help them to remove any mystery from their secrets. When that happens, the "electronic" will be long dead and literature will die.

11

Terms of Reference & Vectoralist Transgressions: Situating Certain Literary Transactions over Networked Services

These are my terms of reference. I will attempt to discuss the network in terms of certain contemporary practices of writing. Writing is here understood as what arises following upon the inscription of language such that—at an arbitrary subsequent moment of time—it may be read. Writing is language that has, as a minimum, been read by its writer, but further reading has ceased to be dependent on subsequent linguistic performance by the writer. The physical material and media associated with writing—typically perceptible to human readers in the form of graphic arrangements on a notionally two-dimensional surface—is not to be identified with any "materiality of writing" in the sense of an ontology of writing itself. Writing only exists as it is read; or as function of its virtual, potential, and intermittent readability; or as function of memory, which is simply a special type of transcription within human readers.

It is important for me to set out the terms of reference above because I will also discuss practices of writing over the network as we are coming to understand it. I will assume that I should not, prejudicially, define the network as one of my terms of reference because, precisely, the understanding of network is emergent in our present situation—historically and literally. I will nonetheless briefly develop network as a term of reference since it appears now to be the most widely used, and increasingly predominant surface for the inscription of writing. I refer to the network as a "surface" in relation to writing in order to reiterate the special requirement of human readability that writing retains in order to exist as writing. Writing is multiply embodied within the media systems associated with the network—

devices for encoding, computation, and display; protocols for storage and transmission—but this is simply an aspect of the processes of inscription. To be writing, it must be able to come to a surface, on a network terminal, as terms of reference for human readers.

I will pretend to be definite about the network. The network under discussion is the internet. This particular network has a remarkable history that is much studied. Within my terms of reference, I will highlight one or two properties of the internet. It was deliberately developed as a distributed system, having no need of a central mechanism for control, surveillance, or policing at either the point of access or to ensure network continuity and maintenance. Relatively straightforward protocols still allow arbitrary devices to join and leave the network at will. When a device joins the network, it may do so as a peer: it may have (or be associated with) an address on the network that is, in a number of significant senses, the equal of every other such address on the network. In the West at least, the human user or reader is not required to engage in explicit contractual or state-implicated administrative procedures in order to connect a device to the network. I am deliberately simplifying a complex situation, but here my point is to stress our sense of an underlying correspondence of relations. On the network, functioning like an open commons, the relationship between a terminal and the network has been constructed so as to correspond with the relationship between an individual human writer and reader, and a kind of pre-institutional, neo-Romantic world of reading and writing that we associate with Western liberalism.[1] I would argue, further, that this correspondence evokes the configurations of affect associated with the latter relation and reinforces a sensible belief that connections on the network are commensurable with a certain widely approved, predominant sociopolitical understanding of self and society.

Overall, as a function of massively popular consensus, the effect of this correspondence is that we feel good about the network, and perhaps— perhaps too often—we think good about it. We give in to it. We have certainly, on a massive scale, given into it. We have given into it to the extent that it now stores and gives access to what is rapidly becoming *the* world of reading and writing. We undertook this work of transcription ourselves because it seemed good to us. Now a collective commons of peer devices on the network appears to accept, to hold, and so stand ready and able to give back for us to read so much of all that we have written into it, especially since the mid-1990s. Indeed, so much has been inscribed into the network that new services have been developed, especially services of search, helping us to find our way through all this writing and get back to reading, of a kind. So far so good, in a sense. The story is familiar to almost all of us.

In recent years, network triumphalism has come to focus on the benefits and affordances of "big data." The ability to store, digitally, and analyze, algorithmically, overwhelming quantities of data has rendered it "big" in combination with the near-ubiquity of portable and mobile devices, fully networked and capable of collecting, transmitting, and aggregating both data and meta-data gathered from an ever-increasing proportion of human movements, actions, and transactional, communicative exchanges—from the highly significant and valuable (finance, trade, marketing, politics, etc.) to the everyday and commonplace (socializing, shopping, fooling around, etc.). Personal analysis of all but a minuscule part of this data would be humanly impossible and so, at the cost of commensurate, individual human attention, algorithmic agencies promise to predict trends and visualize patterns from what has been collected with unprecedented statistical accuracy and previously inconceivable power. The question of what this data represents—what exactly it gives us of the world—remains little-examined. The cost of collection is so low; the methods of collection are now incidental and habitual, while the tangentially related profits—derived chiefly from the reconfiguration of advertising—are massive, and far from exhausted.[2] If corporations remain somewhat uncertain as to what their data represents, they no longer have any doubt as to its value, to the extent that the more powerful corporate players are fixated by the production of enclosures for the data they collect, by software architectures that are closed in the sense that logged-in transactions take place "safely" and in a regulated manner within corporate domains. Human users move in and out of these domains and begin to perceive them as the global architecture and constructed geography of a (new) world where they also dwell. In the current historical moment, while data remains big as a function of its cultural and commercial promotion, I propose to characterize those corporations capable of building and enclosing domains or clouds of data as "Big Software."[3]

In the political philosophy of McKenzie Wark, the enclosure of big data by Big Software produces the specter of a new and newly exploitative phase in social, economic, and political history. In A Hacker Manifesto, Wark proposes the existence of a new exploitative class: the owners and controllers of the vectors of cultural and commercial attention that proliferate in an age of digitally mediated information.[4] This "vectoralist" class acquires and exploits the labor of a "hacker" class, which creates but does necessarily commercially exploit those algorithms that collect and manage what we now think of as big data. Whatever one may think of Wark's witty and provocative post-Marxian contextualization for his suggestive and important ideas, there is no doubt that they give us vital purchase on the analysis and understanding of momentous and transformational historical forces.

The emergence and development of internet services and the implicated vectoralist enclosure of the network by Big Software is crucial here, crucial for a critique of the network that has economic, political, and psychosocial ramifications. This critique is well under way, and its effective elaboration is, of course, far beyond my present scope.[5] In conclusion, I will return to a more specialist discussion of language use, of writing and reading within the network of Big Software's enclosing vectors. Before doing so we must remark the extraordinary fact, so I believe, that significant sociopolitical tendencies of the network can be detected and identified by reflecting on only three institutions, two of which are now also powerful and influential corporations: Google, Facebook, and Wikipedia.[6]

Google led the way among the pioneers of Big Software. Its ascension to vectoralist superpower may well have been unwitting but is nonetheless determinative. Only software that is sited on and definitive of the network will figure as what I am here calling "Big Software." After producing software for terminals or for off-network corporate computing, the software giants of a previous era acquired conventional intellectual property in order to diversify their investments. They acquired what was already considered investable property. By contrast, the pioneers of the new world, of the network, merely gathered and enclosed the data that we human writers offered up to them from the commons of language, as, fundamentally—at least for the time being—writing. Contemporary Big Software vectoralizes linguistic data, harvested from the commons of language, using proprietary indexes and other big data processing techniques. Google pioneered these processes with its infamous page-rank algorithm, once it became allied with the Google AdWords services.[7]

Wikipedia is the odd one out.[8] Although the existence of Wikipedia is difficult to imagine without the synergies provided by other networked services and affordances such as those of Google, here we see that there has been no enclosure, no implicit non-mutual reconfiguration of terms. Rather, terms of reference are still negotiated by peer terminals or by newly created institutions of editorship. Any reconfiguration of terms is still a function of compositional strategies within the purview of readers, working, at least notionally, from the site of a terminal, as so-called "end users." Within Wikipedia the data that has been offered up from the commons is still in the commons and on the surface of inscription: readable. It is writing. Processing of terms within Wikipedia is a matter of more or less traditional editorial practices negotiated by peer terminals that configure themselves into contestable hierarchies of authority. Arguably, the attributed, time-stamped editorial event on a platform such as Wikipedia is the model for the future of scholarly knowledge building and dissemination, lacking only the active and sympathetic engagement of ultimately commensurate institutions such as universities and publishing houses.[9]

In the case of Facebook, we see that the process of enclosure becomes perceptible, established, normalized. What was freely offered up to the network by any peer terminal is now taken into Facebook. The simple homepage is no more. It is inside some other service, predominantly Facebook itself. At the point of being taken in, whenever a peer terminal uses Facebook, terms are agreed and the terminal ceases to be a peer, as it implicitly ratifies Facebook's terms of service. Indeed, this model vectoralist corporation has actually chosen to recast its terms of use as a domain-defining "Statement of Rights and Responsibilities."[10] For some time now, Google has been realigning its vectoral strategies in order, evermore, to bring the human terminal within itself, lest, instead, terminal readers use their services from within Facebook, or remain entirely without, as unregulated terminal peers. Google's provision of Gmail, requiring accounts and stable linked terminal identities, was a major turning point in a process that now drives Google+ and demonstrates that vectoralist predominance depends on bringing terms and terminals within an enclosure where as many as possible human readers and writers exchange their terms on terms that allow these once human terms to be harvested for the accumulation of big data.[11]

It would require independent corporate-historical investigative scholarship to propose and document the historical moment when there was a fundamental change in Google's understanding of its business, its self-reflexive grasp of vectoralism. Nonetheless, the introduction of Gmail was remarkable and is datable. I would speculate that, shortly before the introduction of Gmail, Google realized that its famous search box was not a portal but a mouth. It understood that the collection and analysis of all the search terms continually being supplied to it by human writers was far more valuable than any indexes it had generated from what had already been inscribed on the surface of the network. By definition and protocol the surface of the network is open to and, in principle, independently indexable by any terminal peer. Thus, we still think of Google as a gift. We could have worked to build our own indexes and we may still do so, but, as it happens, a Good Search has been provided for us. The True Search has been Freely Given. Or so we say to ourselves. Any other terminal peer might have done the same; the trick was simply to have discovered the one true search at the historical moment just before Moore's law made it feasible for a terminal peer to do the same on any scale. The free service worked. It was and is used by all-but-every terminal on the network. Google as the zero-degree of the portal—transparent, self-effacing access to some other writing on the network that a human user wishes to read—was precisely that: nothing. For now we see that Google is entirely focused and founded on everything that we feed into its mouth, everything that is proper to us as desiring humans, or, more precisely, proper to the network-authorized agencies of human and posthuman desire.[12] Google must find a way to keep an overwhelming and representative majority of such entities feeding it with data or, better yet—learning from Facebook, its vectoralist peer—a way to take into itself, as Google+, every property and method of symbolic human self-representation on the network. As of the present day, a vast majority of human terminals on the network willingly and frequently write into one particular space, the maw of Google. At the very moment of doing so and by dint of this action we agree to terms of service, terms that establish a hierarchical, non-mutual, non-reciprocal relationship and we allow the abduction of our terms of reference.[13]

The act of making of the agreement by such means is likely to be asserted as an initial article of the terms themselves. Contracts are often agreed more or less implicitly—by the shaking of hands, after a loose verbal exchange, and so on—and, as such, they may nonetheless be recognized in custom and in law. In the case of Terms of Use or Terms of Service, the contract is most often explicit from the point of view of the provider, while the human terminal is likely to remain unaware of the agreed terms in any detail.

It is interesting to consider that the textual, documentary articulation of such agreements has really only come into its own as an aspect of day-to-day life since the advent of Big Software.[14] Once software has been manufactured on such a scale as to provide a service to many human users, there may no longer be a person involved with the service who is available to articulate terms, nor any associated physical products or objects. Even today, when we buy a book, by contrast, we may do so from a person able to describe its facilities. In any case, we do not expect to be agreeing to terms of its use, set out in detail by a publisher or retailer, nor to think of the book as, itself, providing a service. A book's terms of use are adequately specified by the conditions of its production and distribution, and subsequently by its physical properties, which are immediately accessible to us.

However, when we read or write with a computer, we are often in the position of using the services of remote software applications that we do not own or license. Merely by doing so, we will have agreed to terms of use. This clearly implies some regulation of any medium of exchange that the service requires, most commonly, digitally encoded language itself. Our reading and writing comes to be, literally, mediated on terms.

Language is a commons, and yet by contrast
With *first nature*'s free resources, it is constitutive
Of culture while all at once incorporate *within*
Those cultures it enables. As language is a commons,
To use it, we need not agree to terms.
Now, counter to our expectations and our rights,
Agreements as to terms of language use
Are daily ratified by the vast majority
Of so-called users—you-and-I—by all of us
Who make and share our language on the Internet.

This situation had long been in place before the provision and effective promotion of network-based "cloud" computing. Now Big Software runs from the "cloud." It invites us to the cloud, offering services associated with our provision of data. Terms of use regulate this mediation of our data and—often "by default"—the same terms may cause us to agree that our data will be mined and manipulated, albeit anonymously, as we move it into the "cloud." Both the tools we use to read and write and the material traces of our textual practice come to be stored on systems that are removed from us as readers and writers. We are increasingly dependent on self-regulating, proprietary services without which we cannot gain access to our reading or our writing, and whenever we do gain access, we do so on terms. These circumstances have momentous consequences for textual practice, and their careful consideration is crucial.

As a phrase of current English, "terms of use" associates, like "terms of reference," with the "terms" of "search terms," "key terms," crowd-sourcing "terms" or "tags," the "terms" of an argument or discourse, and with our "use" of these and all others terms as an aspect of "language use"—the "usages" of all linguistic interlocution. Language is a commons, and yet, in contrast to the commons of the world's natural resources, it is a commons that is directly constitutive of culture while at the same time incorporated "within" any culture it enables. This is demonstrable in that there are only enculturated languages (plural), and thus, in each instance, a particular language is one of a plurality of commons that welcomes any user of its specific, located resources. As a commons—radically co-constitutive of the cultures within which we dwell—in order to use a language, we do not expect to agree to terms. Rather, languages set out the terms of reference for culture itself, the only articulable terms it knows. This makes it all the more important, in an era during which the "digital (mediation of) textuality" comes to predominate, that we take full account of any implicit agreements as to terms of language use where these are being reiteratively ratified by a vast and growing population of highly influential language users.

We cannot proceed without continuing to refer to the most obvious example of Big Software that is currently used by hundreds of millions of people, all of whom have thus agreed to terms. Google sets out terms of service that regulate the significant aspects of textual practice in which it specializes.[15] This one company processes more text, more linguistic material, than any other computational service on the planet. The particular service—page-ranked indexed searching—that established Google as a commercial and culture powerhouse is founded on textual analysis of web pages and their tagged links.

> Services, like those of Google and many others such
> Still expressly offer their results in swift symbolical
> Response to phrases of a language we call *natural*:
> Words composed by human *writers,* desirous
> To discover something that they wish to *read*,
> If only with the aim of transacting through commerce,
> And so satisfying a moiety of our more venal cravings.[16]

Google's and most other related services are still explicitly designed to be responsive to phrases or clauses of natural language composed by human writers who wish to find something to read, even if only with the goal of undertaking a commercial transaction or satisfying a desire. Intimately linked to this service provision is the question of how these and now many other interconnected services relate to the vital institutions of literary culture, in at least two ways: at a collective level through their effects on (not an exhaustive list) publishers, libraries, and universities; and at an individual or collaborative level through their effects on literary aesthetic practice.

> Although the objects of our culture have each
> Their specific materials, now these may be mediated
> By the insubstantial substance of machines
> That symbolize—or seem to, in potential—
> *Every thing*. The *digital* appears
> To us historically unprecedented, thus:
> It presents itself as servant and as Golem,
> Non-vital but commensurate, un-alive
> And yet all-capable: of service, of facility:
> A limitless archive of affordances,
> And so it ceases to be some *thing* or *substance*
> Amongst others; it becomes the currency
> Of all we are: essential infrastructure,
> Determinative of practice and of thought.
> Despite this, it still seems made by us, and lesser,
> A servant still, and so we treat the digital
> *As if* it remained *in service*, though it sustains—
> Or seems to—all that we desire to be.
> We will not live without it, yet we believe
> That we still choose to purchase and to *use*
> A relation that is optional, elective, and we
> Manage it as such.

One of the ways in which digital mediation appears to be historically unprecedented is that it offers itself as a service or facility or catalog of affordances (such as word processing for writing), but it quickly goes on to establish itself as essential infrastructure. Thus, it becomes remarkably determinative of practice and ideological framework while nonetheless continuing to be managed and developed as if it remained a service. It also presents itself as a low- or no-cost commercially viable service, and therefore, in a number of senses, it seems to be optional or elective. This same syndrome plays out in the relationship between, for example, a university's management of its "computing services" on the one hand and its intellectual mission on the other. Before an institution like a university fully realizes and internalizes (administratively) the fact that practices demanding digital infrastructure will be constitutive of its academic mission, its computing services are willingly swallowed up by more "cost-effective" and more innovative services provided from outside the institution. These, as infrastructure, may then go on (in a more or less subtle manner) to reconstitute and reform the institution.[17]

"Electronic" and/or "digital" literature, along with "digital," "new media" and "net" or "network" art, pioneered new practices outside those paradigms of cultural production that are challenged by such infrastructural developments, but digital cultural practice is not, by that token, necessarily in harmony with the interests of new, as-yet-unconstituted cultural services. It seems to be only recently—since the middle of the first decade of the twenty-first century—that sharp contradictions have become clear: between a putative new media as service provision and the Big Software realpolitik of new media as fundamentally constitutive of cultural and critical practice: determinative not only of potential but of possibility.

On the one hand, Big Software has begun to shape a world that has its own architecture and momentum, on a scale that ceases to be perturbable by individual or independent collective action. Big Software carves out real estate in the world of the network in the same way that fences established the earlier enclosures of other commons.[18] The "land" being enclosed is human attention, and the chief symbolic vector of this attention is language use. On the other hand, this same Big Software is dedicated to channeling and storing the chiefly linguistic flows of potentially transactive data through its new architecture. At the initial and any subsequent moment of use, the tacit performative language set out in terms of service transforms what the user offers as data into capta—captured and abducted data—that may, as granted in the terms, be used by the service for entirely other purposes than those for which it was supplied.[19] For example, a user may search for words with which to read and write, but the words of the search will be taken and correlated with other searches and language data in order to reduce the friction of future searches, and more specifically to reduce the friction of searches that will bring the most revenue to what is, after all, a commercial service. Any reader and writer's cultural—Arts and Humanities—use of networked services will be, at best, misaligned with these services' use of a reader and writer's data, but then, the reader and writer do not, typically, set out terms of use for that portion of their data that they offer up to capta.

We see that the question of how, that is, on what terms, such services relate to literary culture very much applies to the individual practitioner, to collaborative project–based groups, to any writer writing to be read.

Even for those writers
Who may be in denial of any digital mediation
Of their practice, networked services are likely
To provide for them: crucial points of reference,

Essential to the composition of their texts,
And intimate with whatever artistry they own.
If this is the case, then, given how the structures
Of the network and its services are deployed:
Terms of use have, literally, been agreed.
The commons of language is, in part, enclosed
by its very makers. The writer has conceded
That he or she is happy to supply a phrase—
How many? And to whom? And on what terms?—
And then to receive, to read, and to transact
With *results* that have been fashioned from the store
Of every other *user's* phrases, and from the indexed
Language of all that you-and-I have published
On the *Internet* since it began.

The published internet and associated textual intercommunication amounts to one source for the corpora of Big Software services. If we consider the freely searchable Google Books corpus, we discover an equally extraordinary situation relating to a traditionally privileged cultural domain: the world of letters, the world of print culture. Google acquired access to as many books and journals as possible and digitized them without secure knowledge concerning what they could or could not do with the scanned texts. Apart from any directly profitable use Google may or may not have projected for the digitized books—by way, for example, of the publication or sale of copyright-orphaned and out-of-copyright material—there is the simple fact that one company has now, in a sense, taken into itself some major part of everything that has so far been written. A single network service now holds this material, although, because of existing copyright law and other agreements, it may be prohibited from representing this information in the original form that it was given—as complete books, or articles, and so on. Authors, publishers, and libraries have, for the moment, successfully resisted the handing-over of certain rights relating to the distribution or sale of integral works within this vast database,[20] but this overlooks the fact that Google nonetheless possesses the data, makes it accessible to its own internal processes, and, when users search this corpus, serves results back to contemporary readers and writers, in new forms of processed capta, and under explicit terms of service. Although we may be amazed, if not dazzled, by the analytic power that these results can provide in some contexts—integrated with or in parallel to those of the now-familiar internet search—as users of these services we might ask, on what terms was this data supplied, and whose data was it in the first place? Does any such service have an innate right to use this data in the way that it is manifestly being used? How is it being used? How can we find out?

"*Results* that have been *fashioned*," which is to say
That they, words orthothetically abject
To those within our selves, have been shaped
By *algorithm*: and to this circumstance the writer
Has agreed.[21] Perhaps we may, you or I, pretend
To have some general understanding of these algorithms'
Behaviors, yet the detailed workings of such processes
Are jealously protected. Indeed, they are proprietary,
Closely guarded and esteemed as highly valuable
For reasons that may be entirely divorced from
Or at odds with the tenor of our queries.
The underlying transactions and the relationships
Devolved are very different from any that arise
When you or I take down our dictionary to look up
A word.

As writers and readers, we are forced to consider that our relationship with
language and literature will never be the same. If the medium of literary art
has significantly migrated to the network, where it is gathered, channeled,
and filtered by Big Software on a massive scale, daily touching the linguistic
lives of huge populations, then new practices for reading and writing with
and against such services must surely arise and go beyond any uses that are
constrained by the terms of service or use now made unilaterally explicit by
contemporary service providers.

However the *power* of the cultural *vector*
Represented by the mouth or maw of Google's
Search box and its ilk is all unprecedented.
For any artist-scientist of language, it is like
The revolutionary and revelatory power
Of a newly discovered optic, allowing you-and-I
To see, suddenly and spectacularly, farther
Into the universe of language by several
Orders of magnitude. The writer may observe
And get some sense of the frequency or range
Of usages for words and phrases in our living,
Contemporary tongues, up to the millisecond—
All in a few keystrokes and clicks. This extraordinary
Facility—inconceivable until just now—is presented
As a freely open service, in the guise of what
Has already been cited as "cultural vector."
                                        Oriented
Where? And how? By whom? For whom? To what
End?

It is only necessary to cite this one apparent by-product of search—one of many—to get some sense of the awesome cultural and, here, linguistic power that appears to be offered to us users by key service providers. In the domain of the literary, working writers now habitually make reference to search engine indexes, and discover contexts for the language they compose in a manner and to an extent that they could never previously have imagined. It is, I would venture, a facility that gives us habitual access to no less than an instance of the literary sublime: an encounter with overwhelming quantities of language, arguably beautiful, that is, through the search terms we type, manifestly and directly linked with words of our own: a literary sublime, touching what we write as we write it.[22] Nonetheless, we must recall that this kind of cultural power is founded on the algorithmic processing, analysis, and indexing of what was and is published on the network as data by human writers. It may have been given as true data but it is then processed and analyzed as capta.[23] In the case of the language that was posted to web pages and then indexed as such, at the time of the event of inscription or publication, onto the surface of the network, those human writers involved were not necessarily or in principle using the services of contemporary Big Software.[24] Natural language data was and is given over to the network and then it was and is harvested by increasingly powerful and sophisticated algorithmic processes, and these processes themselves were not and are not, generally speaking, subjected to "terms of use" in relation to the specific substance of what they harvest, predominantly still, to date, language. Most human writers, posting to the web, do not specify terms of use for search engine robots or their corporate instigators. Thus, when these writers come to interrogate the processed and indexed capta that has been culled and sorted from their linguistic commons, human writers' acquiescence to network providers' terms of service constitutes a non-mutual non-reciprocal relation or, at the very least, a relation that forecloses the possibility of productive mutuality with fairly regulated, well-understood institutional commitments.

And yet surely, given the previously all-but-inconceivable, if obvious, benefits that services like search provide, surely, in the circumstances, it must be worth it for human writers and readers to continue to agree to terms. I do not think that it is.

Even were we to concede that the circumstances of Big Software, big data, and the cloud demand important, irreversible changes in the relationships between individuals and their institutions, and that certain of these changes were clearly of significant value for all stakeholders, there remains the simple fact that we have not sufficiently examined and drawn out the implications—for ourselves as individuals but also and perhaps even more importantly for the institutions that constitute our socioeconomic and political relations—of the specific terms to which we agree when we offer up our self- and institutional-representations-as-"data" (that is, capta) within the vectoralist enclosures of Big Software.

That this momentous shift in no less
Than the *spacetime* of linguistic culture
Should be radically skewed by *terms of use*
Should remind us that it is, fundamentally,
Motivated and driven by quite distinct concerns
To those of art. Here are *vectors* of utility and greed.

The reconfiguration and reform of institutional relations with Big Software's network services, with vectoralist interests, those founded on the aggregation of so-called "big data"—this is one of the most important socioeconomic and political tasks facing all of us now. I make this statement as a practitioner and theorist of writing, and this chapter is a specific call for writers to take a self-consciously expert, forward-looking, and responsible role in what will be a necessary struggle, since, for the immediate time-being, the formations that I am critiquing as non-mutual and non-reciprocal are manufactured from language, the very medium of the writer.[25]

I have just stated the tenor of my chapter. In lieu of a conclusion, I set out a number of instances that I characterize in terms of vectoralist transgressions, thresholds we have already crossed but that might well still give us pause, and cause us to consider ways in which we should undertake a profound renegotiation of terms with vectoralist agencies.

Whenever we transact with networked services a significant number of events occur for which the question of transgression is crucially at issue. A transgression is a crossing over and beyond; more specifically, over and beyond the thresholds of social conventions, the conventions of institutionally sited practices. As we transact with language using networked services, our words move across many thresholds and in so far as our words represent and embody our identities, our subjectivities, our subject positions, they move us back and forth over these thresholds. We may bracket or suspend the negative connotation of transgression or may even, in a spirit of subversive reform, affirm transgression as value per se. Judgments of cultural value and positive or negative effects on ourselves and our institutions are suspended in the following anecdotal narration. The remarkable thing to me, as I set them out, is the extent to which so many of these transgressions are ill- or unconsidered by human agencies. They seem to be "merely" the "inevitable" consequence of manifold technological processes, network enabled.[26]

The first transgression is the transcription of language into the digital as such. We send language over a threshold into the digital by typing into a computer via, typically now, a word processor. The structure of linguistic representation or transcription is, if not identical with, then absolutely amenable to digital forms of representation as fundamental abstractions of the symbolic. This fact of linguistic abstraction is an essential part of how language is, although it does not follow that human language is reducible to any of its essential (and necessarily multilingual) forms of representation.

Through print and typewriting, peoples of alphabetic systems of inscription have long been used to representing language in terms of the discrete symbolic abstractions that we know as letters.[27] The difference of word processing is that, as we type, the letters and words and larger units of language cross over and become immediately accessible to the realm of data, or more properly of capta, of whatever is considered linguistic data by the predominant technological regime. Our words transgress into capta, and they persuade us to transgress there also. We do this without thinking of it, and all the while it changes our relationship with language fundamentally, as we have seen.

The word processor is running on a computer, and our letters and words have now transgressed, crossed over, and gone beyond previous conventions of writing, to be "within" the computer and its associated systems of storage. Meanwhile the Google Books project has been word processing for us by scanning every book possible and so bringing all of what was previously in a largely unindexed realm of reading and writing "within" the same regime of capta where anything we have word processed already dwells. This is another transgression, bringing all that has been written over a conventional threshold into the world of "big data." Again, we consider this unthinkingly as good, as an aspect of corporations such as Google "not being evil," of their mission to "make [the world's information] universally accessible and useful."[28] In terms of the conventions of copyright (based on eighteenth-century conceptions of intellectual property, modeled on real estate as much as anything), we are sensitive to transgressions that might be consequent on Google's acquisition-by-scanning of all the writing that has been published, but we have not worried over the transgression of digitization itself. We have not considered the consequences of having all that was not indexed, suddenly subject not only to index but to many other analytical algorithms. If, for reasons to do with copyright and the interests of copyright holders, Google is not able to make all of what it has scanned universally available to us human readers (either freely or for a fee), we do not question Google's right to have scanned this cultural material and to make whatever use of it it wishes "privately," "within" the corporation[29] (see note 20). Surely, there is a vast amount of culturally and commercially valuable information that could be mined from all that capta, and this is something Google is apparently free to do for itself, while we, meanwhile, may only get access to some small part of this material on terms, terms likely to be determined by the capta holder. Suddenly, I feel transgressed against, as well as taken beyond a threshold. I was once a reader who visited libraries. Now I become aware that every book and all that has been written are both closer to me than they have ever been before but also differently, if no less accessible. I know it is there on the network, at my fingertips, but I can't be sure of getting to it without agreeing to terms and establishing my (network) credentials. On the other hand, across some, to me, impassable threshold, I know that Google has it all.

As I am word processing—always already transgressing many former conventions of reading and writing—I cut and paste some of the words proper to my writing back and forth from word processor to browser. Initially, perhaps, I am pasting them into the mouth of a search box, using these words from my writing to find something with which they are associated in the indexes beyond the threshold of the all-consuming, consumer-driven maw. Or I may want to acquire some sense of how other writers have used these same words of mine, of yours and mine, in other contexts. So many transgressions in a single simple action! I have carried my words to a threshold and launched them over it into a far-distant database where they will be collected and time-stamped and geolocalized and associated with whatever other "anonymized" traces of human interaction that my computer has encoded and made accessible to the processes and algorithms of the search provider. The search box and its "page" are in no way passive. As soon as they detect the "presence" of my language, they react and send me back words and images that are intimately, orthothetically associated with mine. These words and images of words occupy and then transgress my attention with the explicit intention of influencing my future action. I seem to accept all this unthinkingly and it is proposed to me as either "useful" or neutral. I am not in a position to set out human-interpretable terms for my subsequent interaction with the processes of the page but merely by having pasted letters and words into the search box maw, I have explicitly agreed to terms and from this point on any action I take that ventures beyond certain thresholds set out in those terms will be explicitly deemed a transgression by whoever inscribed these terms of use. Even if I remain unsure of what is and is not a transgression, the network service provider and its algorithmic agents will be quite clear, and they will act on their judgments immediately and automatically.

One of the most interesting and profoundly contradictory thresholds for transgression, established by terms of use, is that between robotic or algorithmic processes and those initiated and carried out by humans. The feeding mouths of networked service providers desire human capta and logged-in, signed-up "captive" human participants. They want to know what humans want for the simple reason that they want to please humans. Humans still, currently, control the processes of commercial exchange. It is, ultimately, humans who are to be persuaded to buy things in response to appropriate advertisement. Networked providers are currently repaid for their services in a proportion correlative with human readers' responses to advertising.

If language is a commons then what appears
To be a gateway or a portal to our language
Is, in truth, an enclosure, the outward sign
Of a non-reciprocal, hierarchical relation.

The *vectoralist* providers of what we call *services*
Harvest freely from our searches in themselves,
And from whatever language we have published,
Using fantastically powerful and sophisticated
Algorithmic process, lately known by many names,
As *bots, robots, spiders* and the like, but we *users*—
You-and-I, who make and publish all we write—
Are explicitly denied, according to their *terms of use,*
Any such reciprocal opportunity. We may not freely
Use our own algorithmic processes to probe
The universe of *capta*—our captured and abducted data—
Even though our aim may be to imitate,
Assist or to prosthetically—aesthetically—enhance:
To beautify the human *user.*

Thus, ideally, no robots should access these networked services. Many problematic contradictions arise here. What the terms of service mean is that no bad robots need access these services. But who decides what is or is not a robot and whether it is bad? Every computer linked to the net is, as it links, a robot. It is a robot made for linking to the net. This is manifestly good. Our computers are good robots or at least they are neutral, transparent representatives of their humans to the network. The browser is a robot that is run by the same computer that is running the robot connected to the net. The browser is clearly a good robot that understands a number of good protocols that build good channels for human desire. But a browser could easily be turned bad, with a little malevolent programming, for example, to do random, non-human searches by itself.[30] The browser might become a bad robot, a transgressor, disregarding terms of use or even, indeed, the law. Say all the robots I'm running are good: good network connection, good browser. What if I, a human, type too many mad, bad, or aesthetic searches into my browser's search box a little bit too fast and a little bit too regularly. Google's (good) robots will ask me if I'm human simply because I'm behaving like a "robot." I may have to solve a captcha to prove to a good robot that I am human, albeit a slightly bad human who has been, clearly, acting like a bad robot. What if I, a good human, write (that is create or compose) a program that acts like a bad robot for good reasons, for aesthetic, culturally critical reasons, or simply to recapture and reclaim some of that superb big data that lies on the other side of the mouth-threshold where the powerful indexes dwell? Well, if I do that, it's pretty bad, and it's against most terms of use. Big Software can, it seems—via innovation, hyperhistorical momentum, and force majeure—deploy whatever robots it wishes—to index the web pages that humans have written or to police human access to its services—and Big Software will deem these robots "good" without need of justification or regulation. But any robot that you or

I build and that interacts with these services is "bad" by default, guilty until proven innocent, normally without any reasonable opportunity to prove itself one way or the other. In these extraordinary circumstances, there are undoubtedly multiple transgressions of processes and actions in relation to whatever threshold we maintain between the human and the algorithmic, the non- or post-human. Our institutional management and understanding of this threshold is undertaken by forces that are neither mutual nor reciprocal. The de facto control exercised over these relations by corporations such as Google and Facebook is very much under-examined. However, one thing is made clear to us: we should not behave like non-humans, and perhaps not even like unusual humans with unusual interests.

And so, why not?
The foremost reason is: the harvested *capta*
Might be muddied and so rendered less effectively
Correlate with its primary purpose: to represent
In a *normalized* form, the most frequently expressed
And potentially most profitable human desires,
Such that advertisement may be intimately associated
With our harvested phrases, ideally, all at the moment
Of harvesting itself, with human eyes to read
Not only a desired *result* but an intimately associated
And immediately *transactable* new desire. Moreover,
the *vectoralist* ads are made with sign chains that are
Orthothetically disposed towards the language
We have written. This also is previously unknown:
That advertisement intended to induce a profitable
And non-reciprocal exchange be made from some thing
That is *proper* to its addressee. This is material
Appropriation of cultural interiority to venal desire,
Wrongly subjecting and reforming you-and-I
Within a false enclosure of precisely that which
Should never be enclosed: the openness of all
That we inscribe. As yet, the so-called *interaction*
of so-called *users* is falsely founded on unwitting, habitual,
And ignorant *terms of abuse*.

In these late days, we have become involved, as humans, with a highly complex and sophisticated system of chiefly robotic, Big Software–driven processes, while, at the same time, being expressly constrained in the interactive use of our own robotic or algorithmic processes. Interestingly, certain unusual and even aesthetic processes may be substituted for those we might describe as robotic or algorithmic, but they may nonetheless be automatically— immediately and materially—disallowed by the undoubtedly robotic agents of our providers' terms of service. This highlights the fact that, despite a rhetoric of universal access and maximized usefulness across any domain of information, we are being coerced into using processes that are, minimally, mimetic of normal human users, normally equipped. We are coerced into using normalized "human" processes that will engage with those of our network service providers in such a way as to perform transactions leading to huge marginal profit for these providers.

Currently, this marginal profit is derived from the management of human attention so as to direct it to advertising. This may be all very well when the media of interaction are, substantively, contiguous with and devoted to commercial transaction and exchange. However, network services will enclose, monitor, and process any and all linguistic practice by their users, everything from everyday, habitual intercommunication to "high-literary," "high-theoretical," "high-critical" correspondence and production. These services exist to process (albeit, typically, with anonymization) and vectoralize the commons of language, the commons of symbolic interlocution. This co-option of a vast domain of linguistic events and transactions in the service of vectoralist redirection of cultural attention requires stronger critique than it has so far encountered, allied with general and thorough resistance and regulation by existing social institutions of all kinds, including those of literary aesthetic practice.

Perhaps the most intimate, linguistically implicated transgression enacted as a result of human interaction with network services is the capture of words that are proper to the human writer and the manufacture of advertisements from these very words. The words in question may have been enveloped by a login, by their enclosure within an email message, by their insertion into a search field.[31] However, terms of service—enclosing the "enveloping" frameworks themselves—ensure that these thresholds are transgressible by algorithms that will extract words and phrases, associate them with putatively desirable commodities and services and then, incorporate them, across other framing thresholds, within the bodies of advertising copy. This copy may then be instantly re-presented back to the human reader who wrote the words for entirely other purposes and in entirely other contexts.[32] The abstraction of linguistic elements guarantees, to an extent, our inability to own or hoard them as such; however our reading and writing of sequences of words, linguistic elements, does cause them to exist as proper to ourselves, authored. I consider this the operation of linguistic ontology, bringing written words into being within and belonging to the human subject (who may then, of course, abject them for other human subjects).[33] Even the catastrophically flawed legal conventions of copyright establish strings of words as licensable "things," belonging to an author. So, then, taking words of mine to make advertisements is, I argue, even more of a corporally invasive appropriation than would obtain if an advertising algorithm captured the image of its addressee and then cast him or her in a desirable and commercially transactable circumstance. It is a remarkable trick of symbolic practice that this visceral, if linguistic, appropriation—reaching into our private interiorities—goes all but unremarked while the analogous appropriation of personal audiovisual imagery will cause sensation and controversy as it begins to occur—when the live-captured image of my face appears seamlessly composited into a billboard's advertising photography as I pass it, showing me modeling designer clothes, sailing on holiday in the Mediterranean, or experiencing the beneficial effects of a new palliative drug.[34]

But then, we have agreed to this use of our words. Would we have done so if we had any idea of what we were and are agreeing to?

12

Reading and Giving: Voice and Language

In an earlier chapter, I began to develop a theoretical concept, that of *media-constituted diegesis*.[1] I was concerned with the inscription of language in *other* media, by which I mean new or unconventional support and delivery media for language. The earlier chapter wrestled with immersive, stereo-3D audiovisuality as a "complex surface" for linguistic inscription. Linguistic performance is, overwhelmingly, embodied in physical media as either articulated sound or graphical arrangements on a visible surface.[2] Language differs from other artistic media in that, although it must always be supported by physical media, when we consider the ontology of the linguistic artifact (which may be simultaneously proposed as an aesthetic artifact), this artifact cannot be identified with its physical support or delivery media.[3]

This ontological non-identification of linguistic performances and their media-as-material-embodiment is philosophically fundamental and prior to any questions we might consider in relation to media-constituted diegesis. However, because linguistic practice may also, simultaneously, be aesthetic practice, and due to tendencies in criticism that compare and conflate specific, quite distinct artistic practices—reducing one to another conceptually, or considering them as structurally analogous—the singularity of linguistic practice may become difficult to distinguish. By contrast, my overarching concern is for an expository elaboration of the specificities of language as a medium, particularly in the sense of artistic or aesthetic medium. However, I will here be outlining analogous circumstances in non-linguistic media, claiming that the human capacity to distinguish diegetic worlds is comparable with our capacity to distinguish readable language. I attempt to show that when we distinguish media-constituted diegesis in non-linguistic practices, this may allow us—literally, if our examples are taken from the domain of graphic visuality—to *see* how diegetic worlds of significance and affect—as constituted by practices in their media—may distinguish themselves from *differently* constituted diegetic worlds even when they are embodied in the same work and the same *physical* media. A work that we experience or read often presents us with perceptible diegetic breaks, with distinct worlds—juxtaposed, layered, intersected—worlds in generative collision and productive collusion. When *language* is in an embodied world, there is *always* at least one such break.

For human subjects the notion of "world"—that which is conjured by diegesis—embraces the symbolic: the very symbolic practice and play that engenders narrative and poetics, that constitutes significance per se, and that generates affect as persistent or recurrent symbolized sensation. Sketching out an argument that I will shortly make at somewhat greater length, I propose to show that the kind of diegetic breaks we find within certain aesthetic works are a model for the diegetic breaks that *necessarily* exists, separating all linguistic performance from *any* media that supply its support and embodiment. Linguistic diegesis, the "world" that language produces, is always an *other* world, distinct from any that constitutes its material existence. One reason for this circumstance is that linguistic artifacts—their worlds and diegeses—only exist in so far as they are subject to *readability*.[4] The worlds of language are otherwise indistinguishable from the material media within which they are embodied. Only when language is read(able) can the stories and poetics of its other worlds be perceived as entities capable of actualizing their otherwise virtual significance and affect in ours.

Taken thus far, the argument rehearses and consolidates an analysis of language and media in order to make a point or two concerning the ontology of linguistic performances and artifacts—their correlative dependence on readability. However, this chapter attempts to go further. If we accept that there are varieties of linguistic practice in digital media for which the actual performances of virtual language in these media—the traces generated—are the result of purely or predominantly computational processes, then what is the ontological status of these algorithmically generated performances? I argue that such algorithmic artifacts *do not exist as constituents of language*. This chapter suggests that subsequent human performances of computationally generated linguistic artifacts should be understood as *readings* that cause virtual linguistic artifacts to exist in actuality and as such: to exist as language. Accepting this strange, singular demand that something physically inscribed by more or less exhaustively understood symbolic processes nonetheless may not yet exist—as the only type of thing it might ever become—will help us—writers generally, and digital language artists specifically—to a better appreciation of what our medium is: what language is. This circumstance also suggests an ethics of digital language art practices: perform human readability, or risk having failed as maker.

Programmable computation has provided human and, perhaps, posthuman cultures with a new and expanding domain of virtual—that is, not yet or necessarily actualized—expression. The domain of symbolic practice—including logic, mathematics, and even the regularly encoded representation of language—has always been an appreciable part of human experience and thought. In the West, from at least the sixteenth century, an explicit association of human thought and language with "universal" symbolic practice has been proposed. However, it is only since the postwar advent and proliferation of computational devices—stored-program Turing machines, in both theory and in practical implementation—that inscriptions of symbolic processes have entered the human archive on any scale, and have, more importantly, been provided with the bodies and/or human-prosthetic organs that allow these processes to be an active part of our world.

We call inscriptions of algorithmic process *code*. Much has been written about the relationship between code and language—computer "languages" and natural languages—including by myself.[5] Without offering here any extended discussion, I take the position that code is not (natural) language, not language as such, and that practices of coding are quite distinct from practices of language. Nonetheless, I also maintain that practices of both code and language are practices of the symbolic, and that code shares language's strange but henceforth—subsequent to the proliferation of programming and programmable devices in human cultures—less *singular* relationship with materiality and embodiment.

Code may be "low" or "high" "level." Conventionally—according to the designers and users of computer "languages"—the higher the level of code, the easier it is for humans to *read* in at least the sense of anticipating and understanding what the code will do.[6] Higher-level code, as human-readable artifact, is simply the inscribed record of a specialist language use (a small constituent part of the world of language). In the terms of my present argument, it comes into being as such, as language, as a function, precisely, of this *human* readability. However, when we consider the *proper ontology* of code *in general*—its virtuality, actuality, and artifactuality—code comes into existence, only as it is run through a computer, a Turing machine, a *programmaton* (as I would far prefer to designate these devices of ours). This is to say that the proper existence of code is a sum of the events and the effects of a privileged symbolic inscription passing through a computer processor: the execution of the program or programs inscribed in the code.[7] The parallelism of this delineation of code's ontology with that of linguistic artifactual ontology is no accident. Both language and code are symbolic phenomena. Language is something that is readable by humans; code is something that is executable by (currently) Turing machines. One may be tempted to write "readable by machines" as characterizing code ontology, but this would be a metaphoric, anthropocentric usage, disguising and glossing over the fact that most code—especially as it runs—is far from being either readable or executable by humans. It is not, in itself, language.

The situation is complicated by the fact that one possible outcome of the events and effects of code may be the generation of virtual language, the inscription of linguistic artifacts that may be offered up—typically on screen—for potential human reading. The strong position of my current argument is that the ontology of these linguistic artifacts is problematic. Their proper existence is correlative to human cultural engagement and may be subject, in particular, to human performances of reading. The virtual language generated by code *exists as language* only when its readability is experienced and affirmed by one or more humans.

One might object that a relationship with readability is already guaranteed in the case of code-generated virtual language, because its— presumed human—programmers have anticipated potential human reading. This may very well be the case, but I provide two responses. First, I would suggest that when programmers are thoroughly engaged with potential human reading, the generated virtual language will, itself, tend to reflect this engagement and would not, thus, require any prior knowledge of the programmers' active involvement with readability in order to distinguish itself as actual, readable language. In any case—to further respond—we are not, primarily, concerned with such edge cases: of virtual language generated, effectively, by engaged human writers, using programming as an aspect of their compositional medium. What we need to consider is that we live in what is possibly a transitional era, but one in which virtual linguistic artifacts are being generated on a massive scale, while the motivation for these events and effects of code is far from being fully, comprehensively representative of human culture as reflected, importantly, in its cultures of reading and writing. Rather, the production of these artifacts is driven by the requirement to channel human attention (to advertising) or to facilitate transaction (predominantly commercial), and sometimes also simply for the sake of programmatic, computational novelty.

When I say that code-generated virtual linguistic inscription does not exist as language—that it does not take its place in our world as language— the statement is proposed both philosophically and also as polemic, warning against tendencies—of reading and writing—that threaten to become habits, accustoming us to virtual symbolic practices that are merely a restricted and sociopolitically implicated portion of the full human experience—including the aesthetic experience—of language.

I take it as given that there is now a mass of code-mediated and code-generated virtual linguistic inscription propagated throughout a significant portion of the day-to-day worlds of our experience and interaction. Clearly, we need to be able to distinguish and thus to be able to read some part of this seething symbolic morass and so bring it into the world as language per se. This is the point at which it may prove useful to invoke the principles of media-constituted diegesis. Initially, we will take our examples and our model from visuality but we will apply them to the strange and contingent materialities of symbolic events and effects. In brief, we say that code-generated linguistic artifacts and virtual language are juxtaposed, intersected, overlaid on the digitally mediated surface of inscription: essentially, the network as we now engage with it and as it is now, perhaps, a predominant surface of inscription in the developed world. Language that has the potential to be actualized will appear for us suddenly and catastrophically, or as a function of performance, which is inherently a catastrophic process or event. Language emerges, suddenly, from the chaos of symbolic events and effects in so far as it appears to be readable to us, in so far it is constituted by the diegetic world of human reading, or in so far as it is, by one or other humans, literally, read. We then immediately perceive it as distinct in terms of its diegesis, in terms of its medium, in terms of its virtual and actualizable symbolic substance. Our acts of perception—mediated, if the language is read for us—are suddenly acts of reading that require diegetic distinction in order to proceed, in order to allow certain distinct symbols— interconnected syntactically and semantically—to become a constitutive part of the language we use and the language that also constitutes our*selves* in a located culture and in specific practices of human natural language.

Previously, to illustrate and exemplify media-constituted diegesis from the domain of visuality, I turned to the work of John Baldessari; more specifically, to those many and various "composite photoworks" of his in which a diegesis of monochrome outlined geometric forms and silhouettes overlays and interacts with the clearly distinct and immediately recognizable diegesis of, usually, half-tone photographic naturalism (Figure 12.1).[8] Both of these instances of media-constituted diegesis are quite artificial, and historically, contingently determined from the perspective of visuality in human culture: for example, by color process and repertoire in the case of the monochrome flat-color outline forms; or by focus, and depth-of-field, and other effects of light-through-optics, fixed by chemical or digital exposures, in the case of photographic naturalism.

FIGURE 12.1 *John Baldessari.* The Duress Series: Person Climbing Exterior Wall of Tall Building/Person on Ledge of Tall Building/Person on Girders of Unfinished Tall Building, 2003. *Digital photographic print with acrylic on Sintra. 60 × 180 inches. Reproduction courtesy of John Baldessari.*

We immediately distinguish the different diegetic worlds in this type of image by Baldessari. We know that these worlds are entirely separate, in terms of media practice, for example, and interrelate *symbolically*—as a function of our interpretative visual "reading"—so as to generate the significance and affect of the work as a whole. My suggestion is that virtual linguistic artifacts distinguish themselves similarly, although from *any* diegetic world or worlds in relation to which they appear. They make themselves *literally* readable, in a manner that corresponds with the way in which the colored monochrome silhouettes of the Baldessari make themselves metaphorically, visually "readable." In the case of the Baldessari, this allows the entire work to be interpreted in the light of its distinct diegetic interrelations; in the case of virtual linguistic artifacts, this allows the language to exist as such. The analogous relations are particularly neat here, since the silhouettes are "readable" (how?) as active human subjects radically distinct from the world in which they (appear to? truly?) act.

Our next illustration is more directly indicative of the way that virtual language appears, suddenly, catastrophically, as belonging to its own distinct diegetic world. In the following series of figures, we encounter the strange, singular distinction between, on the one hand, linguistic artifacts that are depicted or represented visually and, on the other, language as such, coming into being, distinguished from a visual field in contradistinction to which it appears to be, if anything, "overlaid," while simultaneously it has fully entered into the diegesis of human readability.

In Figure 12.2a, consider the photographic image of the open book. Its pages bear unreadable traces which nonetheless depict linguistic artifacts—we know that they refer, visually, to language, but we cannot read it. It is too small and out of focus, in accordance with the conventional media-constituted world of photographic naturalism. In Figure 12.2b we are closer to reading but our divorce from the world of reading is still in effect. The same applies to Figure 12.2c, although perhaps we now feel we *should* be able to read. In Figure 12.2d a paragraph has been brought into focus. This is the only graphic alteration to the image. Its graphic traces are, ultimately, from the same digital photograph as Figure 12.2c. The visual distinction is trivial but sharp. And yet this is simply a kind of allusion to the much sharper, more radical break—that I characterize as a diegetic break—between virtual linguistic artifactuality and the sudden ontological presence of actual language that we are able to read. This part of the image can never more be simply a *depiction* of language. Its readability causes to it to become language itself.[9] We can now, if we wish, perform it as such, and "give it voice."

Our next step is to illustrate and examine cases of computationally generated virtual linguistic artifacts, citing, in the first instance, my own intrinsically unfinished sequence "Monoclonal Microphone." This poetic experiment in digital language art consists of a large, indeterminate number

FIGURE 12.2 *Illustration, a–d, demonstrating the catastrophic emergence of linguistic diegesis. Digital photographs, 2013. Courtesy of the author.*

of potential poems generated by algorithmic processes transacting with internet search. It arose from a process designed to generate an initial text which subsequently served as the loose template for instances in the open-ended set of potential poems that constitute the work. In the context of this chapter, our purpose is to question the ontological status of the mass of virtual linguistic artifacts that have been or could be produced.

The "first" text of "Monoclonal Microphone" is the poem-like arrangement of title and nine lines of "verse" illustrated in the large gray type of Figure 12.3a. The pseudo-code/constraints that generated this text are as follows. The poem is composed from a two-word title and two-word lines, each one an adjective preceding a singular noun, selected from a digitized lexicon by quasi-random processes.[10] Another simple algorithm generated quasi-random couplet- or verse- divisions for the poem-like text based on the occurrence of particular letters in a line. Potential adjective-noun lines were also searched for in Google Books, double-quoted, to find a (relative frequency) count for the possible line as a word sequence. Only phrases with zero results (no hits) were selected. I call these word sequences "zero counts." At the time of searching they had not yet been indexed in the Google Books "corpus."

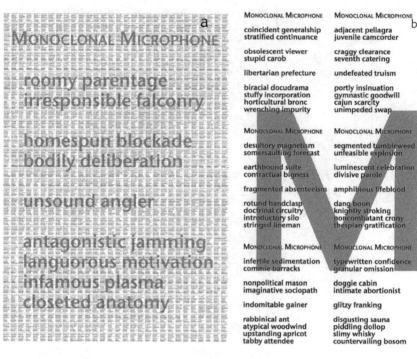

FIGURE 12.3 *Screenshots based on a digital print by the author,* Monoclonal Microphone, *1020+1, 2011. Courtesy of the author.*

Figure 12.3a prints 1,020 subsequent texts, here in a minute typeface. As a function of my own further design, these poems share more than the original generative constraints. I read and then *read into* the verses of the first "Monoclonal Microphone" narrative and semantic arcs that can be encoded in a speculative, elided grammar thus: *After* roomy parentage / *comes* irresponsible falconry. // Homespun blockade *reinforces* / bodily deliberation. // *Oh* unsound angler— // *an* antagonistic jamming *of* / languorous motivation, / *the* infamous plasma *of* / closeted anatomy.

For the generation of the field of poems in Figure 12.3a, the number of both lines and verses in the model was preserved and the literal composition of the lines also follow the rules of verse-break generation. Note, for example, that the letter *e* does not occur in any of the poems' lines 6 thru 8, for this reason. More significantly, collocated phrases including the above *added* grammar words have been searched in Google to ensure that they *do* occur in Google's general corpus, with a count of 65 or greater. For example, from the top-left-most poem in Figure 12.3b "after coincident" was searched, as was "generalship comes" and "comes stratified." When actually reading (assuming this is graphically possible) any of the poems printed in Figure 12.3a, one should always be able to add in these same words from this model—after, comes, reinforces, oh, a/an, of, the, of—and discover a more determinate reading, one that is sometimes uncannily appropriate given the relatively arbitrary and indeterminate processes that have otherwise given rise to these texts.

As reproduced here, in Figure 12.3a, the 1,020 texts underlying their initial seed and template text cannot be read by humans. However, their virtual linguistic artifactuality is accurately represented by graphic traces and I have, above, provided an exposition of the generative principles—alluding in this case to actual code—that determine the disposition of the graphic marks. In Figure 12.3b, a part of the same image has been scaled up such that actual human reading of six instances of the text becomes possible. I have read these poems; you may read them now. My question is to ask: Is this enough? The six poems that you and I have now read certainly exist. What about the rest that have not yet been "scaled up" for you?

There are a number of continuous "scales" of readability that we might apply to our experiences of these texts and the virtual possibility of our bringing them into actual language as we do so. The most obvious and material of these is literal graphic scale. I scaled Figure 12.3b in order to make six instances of the texts readable and, arbitrarily, so that they fitted neatly beside the overall image (Figure 12.3a) of one plus 1,020 (unreadable) texts. On a computer screen or tablet, Figure 12.3b could have been zoomed in continuously. For particular readers, the texts may have entered human readability at very different points during this zoom. However, the strange and singular moment at which the text becomes readable will always have what I call a "catastrophic" quality for human readers, demonstrating the sudden diegetic break when a constructed artifactuality—up until this moment *ambiguously* an artifactuality of, in this case, visual or linguistic material—suddenly and unambiguously enters the world of language.

The other "scale" of readability that I want to invoke here is represented by the extent and degree of our interpretive, critical attention to the code and programmatic composition of the text. Earlier I referred to a possible objection to my "strong" argument: that computationally generated text does not exist as language until it comes into relationship with human readability. Programmers may, compositionally, anticipate human readings that their virtual text will generate and might argue that this is enough to guarantee a relationship of some kind with human readability. Whatever their program produces should be treated as language as such. I say that we have here a number of continuous scales of attention to and interpretation of these computational and compositional processes. For the work to exist, as language, a human reader must still come to some catastrophic moment in their experience of virtual linguistic artifacts when the work ceases be ambiguously a set of arbitrary symbolic processes and also, suddenly, becomes an actual event and effect of language. To approach this moment is the purpose of critical software studies and also that of an expanded sense of literary criticism that would embrace the kind of "reading" represented by my description, above, of the pseudo-code corresponding to that which generates the texts of "Monoclonal Microphone."[11] As programmer and critic, I believe that I have made something that will make language; as human reader, I do not believe that this language truly, actually exists as such unless and until I can read it and, if I so wish, give it voice. It may also be the case that, as I attempt to read, I find that the linguistic artifact before me cannot, for whatever reason, be given voice. Or I refuse to give it voice. I refuse to perform it. In this case, I may, naturally, deny its possibility of crossing over into the world of language.

Nick Montfort and Stephanie Strickland's *Sea and Spar Between* is something of a tour de force of unambiguously literary, unambiguously computational, digital language art.[12] Recently the authors have, moreover, produced a discussion of "creative code in comments," as an online journal article, "a discussion of (and an edition of)" this same work, *Sea and Spar Between*. This extraordinary article is also executable JavaScript code— the essential module from whatever is necessary to execute *Sea and Spar Between* in most modern browsers—but with extended, eminently human-readable and continuous comments, that explain the generative and, in the authors' view, creative processes of the code.[13] Strickland is pioneer of fine poetic writing—human composition—pointedly embedded within elaborate digital media frameworks—the latter having both significant and affective influence on the presentation and reception of her texts—in works such as *V—WaveSon.nets. V—losing l'una* and *slippingglimpse*.[14] Montfort's work often represents an epitome of computational software devices that are coded to generate, without further human compositional intervention, virtual linguistic artifacts, artifacts that do undoubtedly derive, *from their coding alone*, a certain relationship with readability and, therefore, in the terms at least of my more forgiving argument, might be considered to produce actual language.[15] In *Sea and Spar Between*, the two authors work together, embedding literary compositional principles from Herman Melville, and Emily Dickinson into their hard-coded data sets, and then deploy Montfort's considerable coding skills to build a piece of software capable of generating "a number of stanzas comparable to the number of fish in the sea, around 225 trillion." Both Montfort and Strickland read performatively from their computationally inflected or generated work in public. Both have read together from *Sea and Spar Between*. My question, in this context, is: What does their act of "giving voice" to (some part) of the generated text perform? Is their performative reading what brings these texts into the world of language?

I do not presuppose that there are simple or straightforward answers to questions such as these. My concern is clearly with issues surrounding human performative engagement with what may be indeterminate symbolic processes, specifically performative engagements derived from cultures of human reading. I am suggesting that a potential for actual human reading—readability—brings virtual linguistic artifacts into the world as language. At this point in my thinking, it is unclear to me whether an expositional (metaphoric) "reading" of the processes in question—as undertaken in Montfort and Strickland's "cut to fit the tool-spun course"—is enough to bring (all of) this virtual language into actuality. We can open up our browsers and display a screen with many of the verses that can be generated by the code; we can literally, conventionally read and consider these verses, certainly bringing them—the *displayed* verses—into language. On the other hand—as for Raymond Queneau's *Cent mille milliards de poèmes*—it would be literally impossible for anyone to read all of the *possible* verses. If we can only bring some minuscule portion of a huge virtual linguistic artifact into actual existence for our critical consideration, for our reading, does or should the work exist at all? What is it beyond its "executable" description and any "authorized" literary qualities—cited here from the highly regarded work of canonical authors—that are inscribed in its data?

When we consider generated virtual linguistic artifacts, there is something else that is given to them when they are read, apart, that is, from the ontological gift of a more integral and actual existence as constituent of language. Reading will associate the text read with any readers it acquires. Its first human reader is likely to be identical with the person we are accustomed to call its author. However, if linguistic artifacts are generated without regard to their anticipated reading or if we do not accept that their programmer's anticipated virtual reading is enough to bring these artifacts, potentially, into language, then it is possible for linguistic artifacts to make traces on our screens (chiefly) without their having been associated with any human individual. That aspect of the symbolic which reaches most viscerally into our understanding of humanity and language is the proposal that human language (human-readable symbolic practice) is precisely that which, in so far as it is possible to inscribe, survives the absence of writer (and/or first reader) and may thus survive the death of this person, while still continuing to exist as language. I would propose that there is so such possibility for virtual linguistic artifacts if they are not read or they are not readable, if they do not form part of a human act, a performance of reading.

We might briefly consider a contrasting literary work, contrasting with "Monoclonal Microphone" and *Sea and Spar Between*. Ironically perhaps, this is a work by one of the exemplary early practitioners of digitally mediated literature. Moreover, the work would be impossible to manage and it would be impossible to generate certain of its outcomes (including readable outcomes) without the affordances of digital mediation and the network. I am referring to *Skin: a story published on the skin of 2095 volunteers*.[16] This story has been composed by Shelley Jackson but we cannot read it, as composed—not yet and, I believe, perhaps not ever. But the story, as it was written, did have at least one human reader, Jackson, whose authorial integrity is well attested. A total of 2,095 volunteers will eventually contact Jackson and agree to have one of the story's words tattooed somewhere on their body. These words are inscribed on the mortal flesh of the volunteers who read them, allowing, we presume, others with whom they are close to read these words also. These individuals cannot know or read the "whole story," but they know it exists and that they may be able to read it in some virtual future. The people with the tattoos are called "words." Some of them have already died; more of them may do so. One day the story will be as complete as it will ever be. Words will be missing, but there will remain a record of these words and the text of the story will be, inherently—ontologically I would venture—recoverable because, somewhat paradoxically, given that the entire story cannot be read as published, this is a text that is maximally integrated with a very particular and unusual but very powerful, ethical, moral, and *mortal* culture of human reading.

§

Earlier in the course of this chapter, I proposed that if human reading is required in order to affirm the ontological status of a linguistic artifact, then an ethics of digital language arts practice was suggested. There is an imperative to read and to perform works that might otherwise remain indistinguishable from that part of chaos which consists in symbolic noise and insignificant, inaffective transaction. There is also now, I believe, a politics and a social ethics. At this current moment in history, symbolic processes are propagated over networked programmable media in order to provide services of various kinds for human users. We agree, by using these services, to (generally speaking) non-mutual, non-reciprocal terms of use. These processes are undoubtedly addressed to humans, but they are now set running on systems that manage data and interactions on a scale that makes effective human interaction, including any comprehensive reading—even of indexes and aggregations—more or less impossible. Moreover, the processes are motivated, primarily, so as to direct attention (toward advertisement) or to allow transaction (chiefly commercial), all in order to accumulate marginal profits on behalf of the service providers. Such a statement is, perhaps, part of one human, but distant *reading* of the symbolic practice that is generated as a kind of sociopolitical metatext by these processes. It is not a literal, interpretive reading of this "text" in terms of language, in terms of its significance and affect as a chaotic, implicated mass of linguistic artifacts. It is not the sort of reading that would bring the symbolic practices of network services into the being of language as such. For such a reading to be possible, these processes would have to become commensurate with human experience, with the full extent and range of significance and affect that we ascribe to human readers. This, they are not. They focus on those aspects of our shared world that are overdetermined by commerce and control and, ultimately, ill-distributed power. Our situation calls for a reading and a performance of the virtual, pseudo-language with which we now constantly transact and which constantly draws our attention. I believe that if we attempt such a reading we will find that there is very little, among the countless, ever-spinning threads of big data on the internetworked web-cloud, that we would be able to bring into the actually existing world of language. Other kinds of writing must continue to be made and given voice, writing that can be read and that will exist.

13

Reconfiguration: Symbolic Image and Language Art

"Conference for Research on Choreographic Interfaces" (CRCI) was the title of a small, studio-like conference at Brown University that took place in March 2016.[1] It was organized by a faculty dancer and choreographer keen to better understand the impact of networked computational devices on the theory and practice—the culture—of embodied human movement, particularly aestheticized human movement. As such it was one of many, many such conferences that continue to be convened across the widest possible range of cultural—our focus is artistic—practices, all of which—since at least the 1990s—are called to respond to what we experience as a new cultural architecture within which all these cultural practices suddenly and ever more comprehensively find themselves dwelling and working and making. Despite the fact that this networked and computational architecture is more or less ubiquitous in the developed and developing worlds, organizers of such gatherings still bring together participants who tend to be outliers or avant-gardists in their practices, specialists who have been diverted from more conventional trajectories by the promises and perils of "digital media." Moreover, expertise in networked computation may trump certain commitments to a particular practice—ostensibly choreography in our anecdote—that is supposed to be bringing participants together. The interests, engagements, and actual practices of our participants may be wildly disparate.

So, in this venue, the question is asked, "What is it that our practices share? What is it that we *all* do?" This is a difficult question to answer, particularly difficult in the form of a word or phrase that might indicate a shared medium, or characterize an artistic school, or serve as an agreed term to which practitioners, critics, and theorists might refer. I am a writer, and I was invited to this conference because—as I saw it—I work with networked and computationally enabled transactive synthetic language.

Such language is beginning to be quasi-autonomously sited in devices which, precisely because they simulate human transaction in aurality, and because such transaction is definitive of embodiment as human, should, indeed, be considered as choreographic interfaces. As a participant at the CRCI, however, I remained a writer, not a choreographer or dancer. I attempted, awkwardly, to formulate an answer that would span the disparities.

"We are the artists whose media—by which I mean the plural of medium—are being reconfigured before their eyes, within their hearing, under their feet, in their very hands. Our practices share an urgent need to respond to these circumstances, because they present us with crisis, catastrophe, pharmakon, existential challenge."[2] The implication was and is that digitization and digitalization have, historically, produced a reconfiguration of all media.[3] Artists do, of course, experience this as novel (as, indeed, "new media"), as stimulating, as opportunity. At the same time, they confront its effects as interruption, disturbance and, perhaps at best, reconfiguration, where these circumstances have impacts on the very substance and materials with which they work, with which they make their art. The crisis—these circumstances as pharmakon, as both poison and potential therapy—arises from the once again historical evidence that this fundamental reconfiguration is driven by forces that are overdetermined by neoliberal modernity, focused on scientistic economic values, on the reconfiguration of cultural and social welfare as subject to principles of efficient, market-driven resolution—where resolution is self-referentially defined within the enclosed logic of neoliberal economics and the contemporary regime of computation that provides its services, while building this same logic out into the "civilized" world as Big Software architecture.[4]

An example with regard to my own current practice. Technological developments in natural language processing (NLP), digital audio, segmental analysis—automatic speech recognition and speech synthesis—have given rise to what I call transactive synthetic language (TSL). This is rolled out to the general public in the service of retail networks, focused on the ideals of frictionless commerce and consumerism, while discovering or anticipating, in the process, its "killer application" to domotics, easy control of the "smart home."[5] Nonetheless, TSL becomes perceptible to me as a fundamental reconfiguration of linguistic production and reception, of language, of my medium as a writer, and it is available to me as affordable hardware connected to low-to-no-cost network functions. Moreover, the top-level service providers have gifted us with an application programming interface (API) for the "voice services" in question—I can make my own transactive linguistic artifacts within and across this network of actors and affordances. Any such work that I make will, necessarily, be implicated with all the other—many unforeseen—consequences of the underlying systems and networks. Among the most striking of these is surveillance—otherwise cast as the collection of anonymized "data," the benefits of which are reflected back to us in the guise of Big Data once this is owned and aggregated by the service providers, thus making themselves and us—supposedly—*better*, where the only real certainty is that this process makes them richer and us better at making them richer.[6] Meanwhile our understanding of surveillance and marketing and—to get back to my own concern—*language* has changed, fundamentally.

But as an artist-maker in these circumstances, with beautiful new materials to work with, what can I do? There is a kind of imperative, regardless of the consequences, just to "get stuck in" and make something. When it comes down to answering the same, "what can I do?" but in terms of what it is *possible* for me to do, we return, I believe to reconfiguration, this time to reconfiguration as an aesthetic, generative response to the reconfiguration of media that has been imposed by networked computation. It is the fact that my newly chosen medium is a technologically mediated reconfiguration of my underlying medium which, itself, imposes a constraint on my subsequent practice. What I make with the newly reconfigured language, with TSL, will be made by reconfiguring the computational networks that have brought TSL into existence, not, that is, for example, by building a new and separate computational network for TSL. Even were this to be possible for me or my fellow artists, this would still amount to a responsive gesture, essentially a highly redundant and culturally isolated response that would, in the end, amount to no more than the kind of reconfiguration that actually *is* within my, our range of possibilities.

At the CRCI, after some further discussion and in part-response to my remarks, a participant suggested that we might call ourselves, collectively and as characteristic of the practices we share, "the reconfigurationists."[7] This chapter is already an exploration of what this might mean. In what follows, briefly, I will discuss, most specifically, certain aspects of poetic reconfiguration in language art. But I will also discuss reconfiguration as a poetics of computation and of networked computation in general. Within "reconfiguration" and "reconfigure" we easily discover "configuration," "configure," "figure," and even "figuration." The "figure" at more or less the root of these words, I will discuss in terms of what I call "symbolic image." This term bears a certain relation to Vilém Flusser's "technical image" but rather than proposing a transcendence of writing and history constrains its application to what we perceive as the figurable content of aesthetic artifacts regardless of medium, and the "symbolic" qualifier is taken to further restrict our attention to images that are co-produced with the symbolic processes of (networked) computation.[8] We are used to the proposition that "images" as such may come to our critical attention when we experience an aesthetic linguistic artifact—a poem, a short story. Analogously, once language has been reconfigured by networked computation, a reconfigurationist writer may compose the kind of linguistic artifact by means of which we may experience "symbolic images" in the sense that I will begin to elaborate. I will also compare the properties and methods of my proposed "symbolic images" and reconfigurationist artifacts with those that are associated with the "New Aesthetic," one of the few terms in current art-critical discussion that addresses a poetics of computation explicitly.[9]

Critical discourse is conversant with a specialist, mildly metaphoric usage for the term "image" such that it may be applied without regard to the medium in which an image is expressed—an image in language, an image in music. Nonetheless, in the discussion of New Aesthetic, actual visual examples tend to predominate, and these visual images (often also "visualizations") may be marked by perceptible breaks in the visual field that are the trace of computationally generated artifactuality (although usually referred to—and I consider this a misdirection—as "virtual" or "virtuality"). I characterize these breaks as media-constituted and have, previously, analyzed them in terms of diegesis.[10] For a particular New Aesthetic visual image (in both senses of "image"), for example, there may be diegeses constituted by photo-naturalism and by computer-generated graphics. A quick internet image search for "New Aesthetic" will bring up many images within which this distinction is clear and marked—computer graphic "sprites" are found sharing the visual field with conventional color photography but clearly arriving within this field from "another world," another media-constituted diegesis.

The work of Clement Valla is frequently cited as an example of the New Aesthetic and I can illustrate what I mean, in a more subtle form and one more broadly applicable across media (mediums), in a brief discussion of his *Postcards from Google Earth*, using the same illustration as that in the engaging manifesto for the "New Aesthetic" by Curt Cloninger (Figure 13.1).[11]

FIGURE 13.1 *One of a still growing archive of images—this is tagged "redmon"—from* Postcards from Google Earth *by Clement Valla, 2010. Courtesy of the artist.*

Valla finds "sites" in Google Earth where the algorithmic transformation of photographic satellite imagery into 3D images—to be projected onto our 2D computer monitors—appears to fail or, rather, produces a strikingly unusual image. He takes snapshots of these sites and turns them into "postcards." Presumably, altitude and contour data for the satellite images are used to produce 3D transforms and this "fails"—as in the image illustrated—when pixels that photographically represent what is typically an architectural object, such as a bridge, are treated in the same way as pixels that represent their underlying topography, which is the source of the altitude and contour data. On the face of it this presents itself to the human viewer as error or as "glitch," and Valla's—along with much digitally mediated art—is sometimes mistakenly associated with what is, in fact, a quite distinct "glitch aesthetic" in computational practice. It is up to the theorists of the New Aesthetic to clarify its relationship to glitch. In setting out from a New Aesthetic analysis but denying "error" as significantly or affectively operative in a work like *Postcards*, my aim is to propose symbolic image as a more appropriate term for work of this kind and a better analytical starting point.

For the composition and appreciation of Valla's *Postcards*, there are still (at least) two media-constituted diegeses in my terms: that of the source satellite imagery (a kind of remote photo-naturalism), and that of the 3D-for-2D transform. The latter is the product of both digitization—the photographic data's abstract symbolic representations as encoding—and algorithmic manipulation—processing on the basis of this abstract symbolic representation in terms of regular computational operations that may be considered typical of contemporary cultural symbolic practices. On both counts the adjectival qualifier "symbolic" may be considered appropriate, and therefore I say that the entire visual field of a Valla *postcard* itself constitutes a *symbolic image*. The misperceived "glitch" is, rather, a function of the typical and regular properties and methods of symbolic imagery. The apparent mistreatment of the bridge is actually, in a sense, attributable to the failure of photo-naturalism (and its associated metadata) to distinguish a break (easily perceptible to humans) between the media-constituted diegesis of architecture and that of natural topography.[12]

So, we may say, the "figure" of Valla's *Postcard*, its "figuration," is a symbolic image, and it seems to me appropriate to further delineate such an image as, typically, also a *"configuration"* since it must be composed in conjunction with other figurative, image-generative systems. While figurative systems of this kind are far from new—photography and cartography are, of course, figurative systems that have, over a long period, been configured for aesthetic making—historically, networked computation has led to the proliferation of such systems and has guaranteed their ever-increasing cultural reach and momentum. Furthermore, the practice of computation has, itself, elaborated a special and appropriate sense of "configuration"—as the *Oxford English Dictionary* puts it, "To choose or design a configuration for; to combine (a program or device) with other elements to perform a certain task or provide a certain capability," with the earliest quoted usage of this kind dated 1965. While the production of symbolic images may require coding and custom software, it is almost universally the case that such artist-authored programming performs what I am identifying as configuration with respect to one or more existing, usually larger, systems. Since the early years of the twenty-first century, such systems have, as I suggested above, come to constitute the Big Software architecture of our civilized culture in so far as it is mediated by networked computation. Configuration may, therefore, be proposed as the name for an aesthetic practice having its own distinct poetics, for the generation of symbolic images that are intended to inform and delight us with regard to our newly mediated cultural experience.

Then, finally, the justification for the "re-" of "reconfiguration" relates to the fact that there is a determinative and, for the time being, unilaterally, inequitably, and hierarchically implemented configuration that Big Software imposes on cultural practices in circumstances that were referred to earlier. For the artist, I have suggested, their media (mediums) are now subject to substantive configuration by software architectures and for certain practitioners and theorists—if not for all of us—this is experienced as a crisis, a pharmakon, an existential challenge. A large part of aesthetic making will be, in these circumstances, stimulated by an imperative to respond, to react, and to engage in a poetics of, I propose, *reconfiguration* in order to generate those symbolic images that are demanded from us as part of a broader cultural poetics that is commensurate with networked computation, one that bears—one would hope—enough significance and affect to influence the trajectory of ongoing historical processes that might otherwise render us artless and careless.

When we discussed Clement Valla's work with the reconfiguration of contemporary digital photography and remote imaging in his *Postcards*,[13] it was important for us to remark that although this work is based on the configuration of remote photo-naturalism and Google's distinct algorithmic processes that attempt to render this remote photo-naturalism as 3D-for-2D, the entirety of the visual field of a postcard is subject to the same regular processes of first more or less conventionally understood photographic apparatuses and then algorithmic processes. The image is an integration, a synthesis of what may also be seen as two media-constituted diegeses and the misperceived "glitches"—the apparent, human-perceptible disruptions and distortions in the postcard images—are actually to be referred back to a more striking diegetic break in the subject of the initial remote images (topography vs. architecture). In the materiality of the postcard image itself—which I call a symbolic image for the reasons of configuration given—there is no break: its pixels are positioned and colored as a function of image-generative symbolic synthesis. It is important to remark this characteristic lest we be seduced by those visual images in which there are marked and obvious—"graphic"—media-constituted breaks into thinking that this is what sets them apart as, for example, New Aesthetic, leaving work in which the visual field appears "unbroken" out of account. In my terms, this makes it more difficult to distinguish "glitch" from symbolic image and, more importantly, it prevents us from discovering the commonalities of reconfigurative practices across other media (mediums). Within a single auditory experience of music, for example, the "worlds" of distinct stylistic musical "diegeses" may be sharply distinguishable to trained ears, while for other, less cultivated, listeners a single musical world is experienced. The human ear's unfiltered, minimally directed, fundamentally continuous experience of sound as the medium of music is reasserted for those listeners without an apparatus to experience it as articulated by distinct stylistic diegeses. As we turn our attention to linguistic artifacts in order to explore certain ways in which symbolic, algorithmic process may generate symbolic images in reconfigurations of language as the medium of the work, we should first consider certain media specificities of language.

Language only ever exists as a function of readability, or, minimally, as a function of bearing some kind of significant and affective relationship to readability.[14] What we read are *grammé*, distinct units of inscription, at various levels of linguistic structure. These units of inscription are only perceptible, and thus readable, as distinct from whatever else they are not, and this "whatever" could, in principle, be made of anything material, although it is usually either aural (vocalized sound to be read as speech) or visual (graphically inscribed writing). Language comes into being—into the world of human experience where we may use it as a medium to make other things—as a function of a fundamental media-constituted break with its own material supports and also as a function of continually reasserted breaks between all of its constituent elements.

It is important to set out this aspect of language's singularity for at least two reasons. In the first place, because this means that any and all higher-order (media-constituted) diegetic breaks within a linguistic artifact between conventional linguistic images and, for example, forms of language generated by algorithms or symbolic processes will always coincide with one or more of the lower-order symbolic breaks that constitute language as such. It will never be absolutely clear—*from the material support of the language in question*—whether a particular break occurs to mark the intervention of symbolic process or simply because the break is required in order to allow its material forms to be read as language.[15] Second, the differences that constitute language as such are structurally the same as those that constitute the regular formal "languages" that are used for the transcription of algorithms, programs, and so on—for the inscription of the symbolic processes that enter into the synthesis of symbolic image.[16] As such, not only can the virtual linguistic output of symbolic process be seamlessly intermixed ("seamfully camouflaged" would, ironically, be more accurate here) with conventional linguistic images, but "tokens" and "snippets" of the regular formal languages that are used to transcribe symbolic processes may also be intermixed with natural language without necessarily exposing a break in the material form of a hybrid, intermixed linguistic inscription. This can give rise to serious confusions concerning the characteristics of certain contemporary linguistic artifacts and can make the task of close reading such artifacts complex and difficult.[17]

The poetic generative work of Nick Montfort demonstrates what I mean along with other characteristic of the symbolic image in language art practice.[18] Montfort's work is simultaneously literary and programmatically virtuosic. It is also often minimalist and therefore relatively easy to read. In PPG256 Montfort composes the formal language of Perl into tiny programs (256 characters or less) that encode an astonishing measure of significant and affective English poetic compositional procedure.[19] Many of Montfort's tiny programs are designed to run endlessly (i.e., regularly, computationally), generating virtual language that is not only readable; it also expresses patterns of aurality-targeted sound and proto-semantic sense that may be referred to the formal rhetoric of poetry. These texts are, typically, spewed out in verses or fragments that present themselves as, simply, pieces of language. Any diegetic break between, on the one hand, the regular encoded manipulation of abstract literal tokens, and on the other, poetic language (that might be the composition of a human author) is smoothed over by the language itself and its presentation (as continuous lineated output). We can read the major break that does dwell within and constitute the work by close reading both program and output. Deconstructing the programmatic Perl, we may understand exhaustively how the patterns of tokens are assembled. Close reading the output, while much of it is poetry, we agree, we will also often find lines and passages where abstract pattern generation fails to produce anything that enough of us would agree to call "poetry." These instances of virtual language are then, just that. They fail to be readable as or in order to become actual language and thus they serve to make visible (beyond any *material form* of the intermixed linguistic output) the break between generative proto-linguistic pattern and language as such.

For, when our attention is turned to linguistic artifacts—with regard to which we have proposed that any perceptible breaks in the material form of the artifact are masked or doubled by breaks that are constitutive of the artifact's very medium—the mark of a higher order break (or its synthesis) will be discovered by the perception of dissonances between the actual syntax of the artifact and natural linguistic models of syntax (grammar) that have been cultivated by the human reader. It is not only difference/différance that is constitutive of natural language. Not in any case for the common human reader. Grammar, extending to word choice, to diction, is also required. This is one of a number of reasons that symbolic image in language is resisted by readers despite the relative media-specific "invisibility" of its breaks. If language that "looks like language" on the surface proves to be recalcitrant, it may be considered to be not only "broken" (and thus, perhaps, redeemably readable as the synthesis of conventional linguistic image and symbolic process); rather, it may simply be considered and judged as *not* (actual) *language* at all.

In certain branches of my own practice that I would be comfortable analyzing in terms of symbolic image and reconfiguration, I work together with symbolic process in order to smooth over the kind of breaks that might otherwise incline my readers to judge my linguistic artifacts as "not language" in this way. [n-*gram*] *Loose Links* are quasi-algorithmic micro-collages.[20] They are constructed around the concept of the "longest common phrase," as developed in the context of *The Readers Project*.[21] A longest common phrase is, for any attributed text, a sequence of its words that can be found elsewhere in a multi-author corpus but not attributable to the original author, thus proving, minimally, that it is still an attested, discoverable part of the commons of language. For the *Loose Links* these provide a model for the links in its quasi-algorithmic processes of serial micro-collage. This is the opening part of "I had a visit today ...":

I had a visit today, for monitoring, from almost the only group that ever comes to me, rather than me going to them. I needed to make it about them and their needs, not about me and my needs. I needed a new atmosphere, a new environment, and I found it and I'm extremely excited and happy: people with bipolar disorder will have a mixture of negative and positive feeling all at the same time, and in time, and in your own time, etc.[22]

The typical longest common phrase is—currently, in natural language corpora of English—between three and five words in length. "I had a visit today ..." starts by internet searching for results containing the first four words of its title and proceeds with searching for another similar-length phrase that had been contained in the first author-selected result, and so on, with another and another phrase in the selected results of subsequent searches, linked by the search phrases to compose the final text. The processes deployed are quasi-algorithmic in that they require the regular computational services of internet search and also because the micro-compositional procedure could be set out as looping pseudo code, with a human author intervening for the selection of particular results and also of subsequent linking phrases. In this work, the length of the phrase all but guarantees—sometimes with a little tweaking—syntactic continuity across the linked language. In the passage quoted there are five different results and the linking phrases are very difficult to determine. The piece is an assemblage of found natural linguistic images. As a whole, it is symbolic image because symbolic processes engaged with syntactic continuity are used both for networked computational search and also in order to link the found linguistic images together. Ironically, this particular process also "heals" what might otherwise have been instances of grammatical dissonance indicating the main constituent diegeses within the symbolic image. In terms of reconfiguration, internet search *configures* the potential discovery of the natural linguistic images and, as a language artist, I have reconfigured this Big Software cultural architecture to produce my *reconfigurationist* symbolic image in language.

Francesca Capone's *Primary Source* provides us, in conclusion, with an example of reconfigurationist symbolic image, the production of which is more clearly, and in the contemporary moment more typically, involved with prosthetic technologies—transactive devices—that are configured by Big Software and may be reconfigured in order to produce aesthetic images, in this case, those associated with a delightful, minimal performance of poetically implicated language that Capone has rendered as a video installation with, effectively, multi-channel presentation, and as an artifact "existing in a hybrid space between a chapbook and artists book."[23]

Primary Source manifested itself in the course of practice-based research, when the artist discovered, on Brown University Library's subterranean poetry shelves, a Russian language book with a striking cover design, set with a quasi-regular grid in the manner of Mondrian and de Stijl, and sparsely populated with the words of the book's title. These words, Russian in the Cyrillic alphabet, were initially unreadable to Capone. Capone made use of the WordLens app on her mobile phone to try and decipher the title.

Figure 13.2 shows the cover and four pages from Capone's chapbook. The cover displays an image of the artist's phone, running WordLens, itself showing an acquired image of the Russian source book's cover before WordLens has attempted to provide a visualized translation into English. Transcribed and conventionally translated, this is the cover of *Den' poèzii* (Day of Poetry), the 1962 volume of an annual that was published by the Soviet Writer publishing house in Moscow from 1956. To the immediate right of the cover we see one of many translations offered by WordLens

FIGURE 13.2 *The cover and four pages (on two openings) from Francesca Capone's* Primary Source. *Courtesy of the artist.*

when it was set to translate from Russian to English. The other three images show differing configurations, and the fourth is the detail of a reading from the top right of the grid.

WordLens, released by Octavio Good in 2010, is an application broadly associated with so-called "augmented reality." Typically, such applications use the camera of a mobile device to capture images from the "real" world and then "augment" these images with layers of visual or textual information. WordLens tries to find and capture the images of words—the graphic forms of words in any language—and then translate these words or phrases into one of a number of possible host languages, selected by the user and would-be reader. On screen, WordLens then replaces the reality-supplied word-image with the image of a supposedly corresponding—"translated"—word in the user's selected language. WordLens worked remarkably well. It was acquired by Google in 2014 and is now incorporated into Google Translate.

When WordLens was applied to the grid-embedded title of this Russian book, Capone discovered a virtual linguistic beauty in the augmented reality that it proposed to her. WordLens successfully translated the title itself, but its would-be prosthetic, word-form-seeking sensory apparatus was "confused" by the cover's de Stijl grid. It is likely that WordLens looks for text as, itself, a more or less regular grid-like pattern, and so it also tries to "read" what, to our non-augmented eyes, is purely formal grid, finding language-symbolic "differences" where we do not. Moreover, the differences that WordLens sees are tiny, affected by slight movements or changes of focus and light. These cause WordLens to revise its reading continually—even when set to interpret from a single language—and, effectively, to produce an animated sequence of textual events as it reads and rereads the grid and successively augments its screen-projected reality with changing virtual text. What we see has immediate appeal for us as creatures who read. It is not simply that WordLens distorts and disturbs the visual field in a way that is merely, sensually, pleasant for us. WordLens pretends to read the image itself and there it discovers language for us in a structured field the potential symbolic understanding of which is, perhaps, expressed at a resolution or in a form that eludes our merely human visual acuity.

Capone's composite video captures the animated, flickering engagement of WordLens with translation, with actual words in a language that is unknown to her and a grid that the algorithm also reads and misreads as language. The symbolic image of her work is a synthesis of conventional translation and a number of symbolic processes that are intended to augment the human facility for translation. WordLens (re)configures translation. It is significant that it renders translation through visuality, attempting, literally, to overlay the visual forms of untranslated words that it discovers in an image with the visual forms of translated words. It configures translation as transfiguration. WordLens begins with the technology of optical character recognition (OCR)—this is one of the chief symbolic processes that it brings to Capone's reconfigured symbolic image—but then applies further NLP in order to find, generate, and configure a translation of whatever it has read.

Having discovered the real-time effects of WordLens's configuration of the events or mise en scène of translation—here, Capone's desire to translate the title of a book that interested her—the artist goes on to reconfigure this mise en scène such that it reproduces the effects that she discovered—an animated engagement with the book as poetry, the cover of a particular chosen book, and a poetry that underlies its poetry. This is an account of the making of the work that is now *Primary Source*, a symbolic image, expressed as a video installation and a hybrid print publication, and proposed as animated visual poetry, as a visualized poetics.

Read here as reconfigurationist, Capone's work also, as it happens, illustrates the precarity of contemporary artists who work with (re)configured media (mediums), who work with the increasingly predominant cultural configurations of networked computation. As we mentioned, WordLens was acquired for Google Translate in 2014. The configuration and transfiguration of translation that Capone worked with has now changed. In fact, her reconfigurationist gesture became historical *before* it was publicly exhibited. To understand *Primary Source* fully we already have to set it in a particular context—which has changed for commercially implicated reasons having little to do with aesthetic practice—rather than simply being able to appreciate it as an earlier contribution to an ongoing practice. This is too often the case with regard to work in new or digital media for the same or analogous reasons. It is, perhaps, the greatest challenge of reconfigurationist poetics—to make aesthetic artifacts that have enough cultural value and momentum so as to be able to reconfigure cultural practice itself, redirecting it away from vectors of carelessness, greed, and stupidity, toward human carefulness and careful art.

14

At the End of Literature

Literature is made with language. In certain contexts, literature is proposed as the art of language, its highest art. We may contest the range and extent of literature with regard to practices of language as a whole, and we may not agree that the horizons of these practices coincide with the horizons of art that is or may be made from language. Performative, time-based linguistic practices, for example, may not be accepted as unequivocally within the domain of literature, although they are, nonetheless, embraced and appreciated as aesthetically, culturally valuable at the highest levels. At the beginning of this twenty-first century, works designated as poetry or (literary) fiction are generally accepted as literature, all but regardless of quality if not subgenre. Dramatic writing, however, must contest its place as literature to the extent that it is readable in a form that submits to textual practices, effectively print publication—taking this form according to relatively arbitrary conventions of transcription and, indeed, remediation (as "literal" literature)—and also, importantly, in so far as it is studied and critiqued within literature's discursive frameworks: within the university or the world of letters. If we consider actual artifacts of dramatic writing to be oral performances of language that come to exist, chiefly, in aurality (as much as they do in other media—visual, gestural, architectural, etc.), then it becomes possible to acknowledge that our conceptions of literature and of language art, particularly in terms of the cultural significance of specific artifacts, are not media-agnostic. The relationships of literature with media are historically determined, culturally contingent, prejudiced, and, I will argue, disordered with respect to technological developments. The existing relationships generate aporias that threaten to become critical over time. They deform and distort our appreciation of language art in other media. They cause us to ask ourselves how and why should we value the significance and affect that such work generates.

This problematic—how to appreciate electronic literature or, more generally, language art in digital media—has preoccupied theorists and practitioners since the beginning of the undoubtedly literary history associated with these practices in the mid-1990s. I say "undoubtedly literary" because it is a matter of record that electronic literature found early, if not unprecedented, theoretical and critical support for its nascent practices in the discursive space of the universities. Although attention to media specificities (distinctly plural) has been properly claimed in order to take into account the incorporation of other media into practices of literary composition and reception, less attention has been directed to any better understanding of the underlying medium of the underlying art. This medium is language and its underlying art is an art of language. The introduction of other media— into practices for the composition and reception of language art—has demonstrably and necessarily broken conventional form. In themselves, such breaks render their artifacts no longer (exclusively, traditionally) literature. Theorists and practitioners of the new forms claim that, in these circumstances, literature must change. But breaking conventional form is nothing new, even across media. What is new—supporting the original claim—is some historically important manner in which literature is called to change—paradigmatically, conceptually, fundamentally. Literature needs to become "electronic," by which we mean (with hindsight) that it must come to terms with the digitalization of everything.

The digital—inevitably misrepresented as "electronic" for the rhetorical purposes of the claim that literature must change—is not a medium. More precisely, it is not a medium of interest to the majority of theorists or practitioners of those arts for which language is the medium. There are aesthetic practices of computation and of properly digital art, with respect to which the digital can be accounted as *a* or *the* medium, but only certain specialist practices of electronic literature incorporate computational aesthetics significantly or affectively. For media taken as the plural of medium, the digital is, rather, a prevalent and privileged framework and network for any and all media. These media—color, shape, texture, sound, and so on—are encoded in sometimes complex, structured binary transcriptions that render these digitized representations accessible to and manipulable by computational, digital affordances. For media such as these, which are referred to substantive material, digital representations are problematic in many interesting ways characterized by our understanding of significant and affective differences between analog and digital objects or artifacts, and yet there is a phenomenological coherence in terms of the human experiences of these things across the analog–digital divide since they are also necessarily referred to human perception—of color, shape, texture, sound, and so on.

The relationship between linguistic artifacts and digitization is, on the other hand, singular. A string of bytes that represents a color, however structured by coding conventions, is not the color itself. By contrast, a string of bytes representing a string of letters and punctuation is language, ontologically, in so far as it is humanly readable. There is no essential difference between any instance of language as it is embodied "here" and "now" on the page or surface in front of you and how it is encoded as a string of bits inside your machine. Its existence as language is entirely dependent on your ability to read it. If you are able to read traces (grammē) of this language on any other "surfaces" within any part of a computational system, your reading brings that language into being. The string of bits digitized from existing systems of inscription is always already structured as traces of language that are, in principle, if not in practice, readable. It is not encoded so as to enable the rendering of an object in another medium that *because of this rendering* becomes perceptible as an instance of an object in that medium. Perception of digitization is not perception of what it encodes. The digital representation of color and sound, for example, is not perceptible as such within digital systems. By contrast, when presented with traces of language, in any material form, all the human subject needs to do is read. Any perceptibility (or not) with regard to the material form in question is irrelevant except in so far as it simply enables or disables actual reading.

What is at stake for language and language art in digital media is not a supposed ontological distinction between language and digital language in so far as this is a function of digitization. Whereas it does make sense to speak of a distinction between yellows (yellows in our perceptible world) and digital yellows (encodable and renderable yellows), it makes no sense to speak of a purported distinction between words and digital words. Instead we must turn our attention to effects of digitalization on the substantive media that can support traces of language and their potential for human reading.

Within the much wider domain of linguistic practice, what has occurred, indisputably, since the post–Second World War rise of distributed computation is, fundamentally, the digitization of typography and typographic design, the digitization of *particular aspects of visuality* that are structured so as to support linguistic practices that derive, for the most part, from print-based textuality. In general, and historically, when we speak of electronic literature we speak of a textuality that has activated certain digital affordances with respect to digitized typography. In print, typographic visuality is static, fixed, although it may be spatialized in a number of ways so as to influence or inflect reading practices and strategies. By contrast, even with relatively basic peripherals, digitized typography has nearly all the affordances of print and is provisioned, additionally, with a wide array of dynamic potentialities. Text in digital media can move and change. It's as simple as that. It is important, however, to recognize that this is not a difference in *what* is or can be read but in *how* and *when* it is read. The digitization of typography has given us new expressive structures for temporalities that have the potential to influence and change the fundamental events of language: our events of reading.

Thus, the fact that there is no ontological distinction between language and digital language does not mean that digital textuality—digitized typography—as compositional media and expressive form can be reduced to textuality as modeled by the more constrained expressive potentialities of print. That ship has long sailed. And if literature is a practice that is determined, chiefly, by material cultural formations that orbit practices and conventions of reading, then it is literature that faces its ontological challenge with respect to digitalization. Electronic literature is, precisely, no longer literature; if it is anything, then it is *digital language art*, although currently it still struggles within the gravity of an "electronic literature" that is overdetermined by aesthetically motivated language expressed in the substantive medium of digitized typographic visuality. Even as such, within the constraints of existing practices, the digitization of typographic visuality tends to facilitate new ways of reading, especially less familiar temporalities of reading, and new relationships between reader action and what is read (hypertextual and conditional linking). For most readers, even including critics, literary scholars, and digital humanists, these strategies trouble existing traditions of literary reading without yet insisting that literature itself be called, seriously, into question.

Throughout this thinking, a particular conception of reading is crucial. I speak of reading in a specific technical sense. I use *to read* and its cognates— in a manner fully consistent with its etymology—to refer to whatever it is that we language animals do when we discern and interpret linguistic forms, *regardless of support medium*. This is not the type of metaphoric usage that obtains when we speak of "reading" a painting or a dance. It refers to the process of grasping and understanding traces of language as such in any medium. In this thinking, once it comes into existence, language is not only discrete and articulated, it is distinctly separable from other phenomena of the perceptible world, made and marked by what Jacques Derrida indicated as *différance*.[1] Virtual linguistic forms establish a break with the perceptible matter of which they are formed precisely in that catastrophic, no-turning-back moment when they are grasped as language by both the language animal who makes the traces and a language animal who reads them. I call this process grammalepsis and I consider it to be generative of language, ontologically. Reading brings language into substantive being as instances of interhuman potentialities. To clearly distinguish reading in this sense from the subsumed and more specific activity that we undertake when, typically, we visually scan and interpret instances of writing, we could use the phrase *grammaleptic reading*, but so long as we recall, throughout this thinking, that this special sense of reading is equally what we do when we hear and understand spoken language in aurality (or, for example, when deaf communities read sign language or blind communities braille), I may use "reading" on its own, with the inevitability of grammalepsis comprehended.

Once we are able to accept (grammaleptic) reading in this sense as constitutive if not ontologically generative with regard to language, this is when it becomes possible to appreciate more fully certain potentialities of digitalization, certain anticipated effects on language and its arts at this particular historical moment. We have argued that digitization changes our modes of relationship—transaction and interaction—with the support medium for language rather than with language itself, *how* and *when* we read rather than *what* we read. What, then, happens when there is, in the domain of digitalization, a catastrophic (no-turning-back) *convergence of readabilities in terms of grammalepsis* with regard to the two distinct, if imbricated and culturally implicated, media that support language: visuality and aurality?

At this point we must pause to consider certain relationships between language, its support media, and the language animals that bring language into being—ourselves. Language is something that, to the present extent of our knowledge, only humans *have*.[2] Our species has language. It evolved to have language in a manner that is still imperfectly understood, although there are particular characteristics of this evolved condition that can be specified. There are distinct, implicated morphological traits that we have and other animals do not. From my reading, I take the most significant of these, apart from larger brains (which may not be as crucial as we suppose), to be: a double-articulated oral cavity and larynx, and a spinal column with a significantly greater diameter. In concert with *Homo sapiens'* larger brain size (and perhaps many other factors), these traits allowed us to *have language* because we were suddenly, in terms of evolutionary time, able to make a sufficient number of distinct vocal sounds—sufficient for vocabulary and grammar commensurate with language as we know it—and because a larger spinal column allowed nerve cells and interneurons to establish the fine control over our lungs that was also required for articulation.[3] This happened to our species relatively recently in evolutionary time. Effectively, we have had the potential for language baked into us very, very recently and there are unlikely to be any foreseeable genetic changes in our species that will significantly alter our disposition with respect to language. The point being that we are genetically predisposed to *have language* as a function of traits that operate *in aurality*. If we have adopted visuality as the support medium for particular linguistic practices of what we call writing, this is merely learned, a function of civilization.[4]

It is well known and much discussed that Plato considered writing to be a pharmakon, poisonous to practices of language—particularly language as humanly embodied praxis and cultural memory. And yet, in its other aspect writing-as-pharmakon was rendered therapeutic by civilization. This is, of course, a grand narrative, played out in philosophy following and reading Plato, most particularly in the thought of Jacques Derrida and Bernard Stiegler.[5] Writing and, subsequently, literature as linguistic practice in support of civilization were rendered therapeutic precisely because they restructured the temporalities of language as well as enabling the potentialities of index (random access facilitated by sublexical orders giving more or less instant access to significant and affective textual material) and archive. Clearly, writing allows virtual linguistic performance to survive—in temporal extension—not only the actual performance of its makers but also the memories of particular individuals who have *read* (grammaleptically) particular linguistic performances. This temporal affordance—hypostatic memory or hypomnesis coupled with index and archive; preserving and conserving both language itself and these other two features—allowed writing, ironically, to predominate as *the* privileged *literal* index of logocentric presence and authority: history, philosophy, civilization.

Putting it far too plainly: as the course of human history and culture proceeded, language in aurality was not able to participate as effectively as writing—as language in persistent visuality—for the constitution and maintenance of civil and imperial institutions. Until, that is, just about now, at this time of writing, in the 2010s. This decade has witnessed the advent of *transactive synthetic language* in aurality.[6] Contemporary computation has finally achieved robust voice recognition and acceptable speech synthesis, all implemented over network services having access to vast corpora of natural linguistic material with NLP affordances. Historically, I argue, this is a turning point for our—the language animal's—practice of language in the world, since, for one thing, this world now also contains, crucially, humanoid language and new entities that perform, consume, and transact with both language as such and humanoid language.

There might arise a certain objection to my dating of the proposed paradigmatic shift, in that synthetic (computed) language has played a part in the history of computation since its beginnings, including, foundationally, in the exemplary abstracted scene of *writing* that is the Turing Test, for which the *withholding* (by, at the time, teletype) of any embodied voice is crucial *for the test,* since a voice and body would simply give the game away.[7] In a sense, the advent of systems that we humans agree are able to recognize our voices and respond with—gendered and identifiable—voices of their own forecloses the Turing Test and marks it as having already been passed within the duration of any acceptable initial transaction. It is the system's voice—recognizing and producing virtual language and doing so *necessarily* instantiated in aurality—that is sufficient to establish for us human animals that the system is specifically embodied as, at least, humanoid, and certainly as having (or seeming to have) something that only humans have. The historical moment for our new relationship with language had to wait for this milestone of humanoid embodiment, in and as the voice of articulated aurality, perhaps also as the evolved return and reincarnation of a repressed aurality. And for the electronic *literature,* that we have troubled and recast as digital language art, this turning point requires us—practitioners and scholars—to better understand what it is that "the digital" has done for language. It has not (yet), as we said before, established an ontologically distinct (digital) language as such; rather, it has reconfigured the relationship between language and its preferred substantive media of support. More than this, it suggests that we rethink, and shift our attention to the *other* culturally predominate substantive support medium for language. The digital now, historically, forces us to rediscover the voice as articulated aurality in an artifactual and programmable configuration that, in computationally implemented principle, is every bit as manipulable and extensible, as subject to index and archive, as capable of temporal restructuring, as is writing. Transactive synthetic language is a whole new scene for the art of language in general, and for digital language art specifically.

As we begin to shift our attention from theory of language and media toward new practices of language art, it is important more closely to consider what it is that I claim is happening with regard to language in aurality as it is grammatized—subjected to algorithmically implemented processes of grammalepsis—by contemporary computation.

Language has a singular relationship with its substantive media of support. For V. N. Vološinov and certain of his followers, there is such a thing as "semiotic material" and any sign—in my own terms *anything* that has been read grammaleptically—becomes a token of this semiotic material.[8] Natural languages are socialized, agreed, enculturated systems that are entirely composed of "semiotic material" in this sense. There is a constrained permeability of substantive things that may be on their way to becoming signs, becoming, that is, actual semiotic material. The signs and tokens of natural languages are, on the other hand, always already signs for the language animals that encounter and interact with them, achieving this in a social context that necessarily involves other language animals. Compare a particular gesture of the hand, say. A gesture may already be a sign—it might be conventionally understood in a particular culture or it might be (always already) a sign in a natural (sign) language—but a gesture may also be on its way to becoming a sign, something we don't "get," something that needs more work and practice, to get right, to be able to express, significantly and affectively, whatever it hoped to express. It fails in this until it is grasped, until it succeeds. It fails until it is read grammaleptically.

The written forms of any natural language have long ago passed beyond this underlying scene of semiotic trauma and socialization, to the extent that the chains of tokens of language-in-visuality (strings) enter into the domain of purely formal semiosis—computation—in a wide variety of processes that are, fundamentally, "lossless" ontologically. If you can write it, then you can encode it. And, as we showed earlier, the language-as-visual-graphemes—on paper, on screen—is ontologically identical with any language-as-digital-encoding that underlies it. In either case, what makes the language exist *as such* is its potential to be read, grammaleptically, by language animals.

If we are repeating ourselves and somewhat belaboring these concepts, this is due to the necessity to distinguish—in the domain of aurality—between the digitization of sound and the digitization of language-as-aurality. There is a significant critical literature devoted to the media archaeology of recorded sound, and this is often seen in terms of a prefiguration of digital audio recording and transcription. In this literature, there is clear understanding and analysis of distinctions between analog and digital recordings, with important implications to be drawn. Nonetheless, once these have been elaborated, there may be a misdirected tendency to believe that because the digitization of sound encompasses and comprehends the digitization of linguistic sound, then it has comprehended the digitization of language-as-aurality. But this is not the case.

As set out above, the digitization of sound is constituted by encoding the forms of a substantive medium which then require to be rendered before they can be appreciated as such, as structured sound. You cannot hear the encoded version. Digitized linguistic sound is no different. The encoded version cannot be heard, much less read, grammaleptically, as language. Any grammalepsis of digitally encoded linguistic sound can only occur during a separate, subsequent process, *after* it is rendered into the world as sound. At this point, the sound *may* be read and understood, by language animals, as language-in-aurality.

In our present historical moment, the 2010s, robust automatic voice recognition is fast gaining currency in the digitalized world, currently to be qualified as, chiefly, the global Anglophone world. It is this facility—automatic voice recognition—that enables the actual digitization of language-as-aurality. Evidence that this facility was beginning to be operational dates back to early attempts at automatic dictation/transcription systems, voice command interpretation for personal computers, and, especially, automated voice-activated telephone answering systems. On mobile devices, Apple's Siri was a breakthrough but, for our purposes, as research-based practitioners and theorists, it is the Amazon Echo and its Alexa Voice Services (AVS) that provide the first widespread, operational, free-standing, networked, and programmable infrastructure, allowing us to understand, practically, the effects and potentialities of digitized language-as-aurality.

As a point of operational fact, the Amazon Echo and AVS enact precisely the two-stage process of digitization for language-as-aurality that we alluded to above. Not only does this configuration of the AVS infrastructure demonstrate that the procedures are distinct, it also signals our always insufficiently acknowledged reliance on network services, with the asymmetric balance of agential power and centrality that this implies. The two procedures are separately *located*. I speak to an Amazon Echo. The device, locally and in "real time," optimizes its array of microphones to capture as digital audio a segment of—purportedly—linguistic sound that was prefaced by one of its (currently three) "wake" or trigger words. These wake words are the only fragments of sound that the device itself, locally, is able to read grammaleptically as semiosis: a command to record, until a space of relative silence is encountered. Within the device this digitized audio is encoded as an optimized MP3 file, and it is this digital *audio* data that is transmitted over the network to the cloud-based services of AVS. "In the cloud" this digitized linguistic sound is "recognized," which is to say tokenized by automatic grammalepsis into, currently, word-sized, serviceable "atoms" of machine-modeled natural language. The details of this process are proprietary, although many aspects of the underlying research could be set out and exposed. The pragmatic approach implied above by "word-sized" is an educated guess. What we know as a certainty, because the AVS cloud services supply (they "return") transcriptions of what the system "heard" grammaleptically as *text*, as potentially readable language that is materially identical with all the digitized writing that constitutes the most significant material of networked digital culture: the documentary internet as we know it.

It is important to acknowledge that this service—which we are proposing as, potentially, of momentous, paradigm-shifting cultural efficacy—does not deliver understanding. This is not the hermeneutically enhanced grammalepsis of reading as it is performed by fully enculturated language animals. In the theory and practice of automatic voice recognition, this is deferred, researched, and explored as "automatic understanding," more firmly in the speculative camp of machine learning and artificial intelligence. Automatic speech recognition does, however, achieve the digitization of language-as-aurality, which means: language animals may perform in a manner toward which they are genetically disposed and what they say is, in principle if not yet perfectly, automatically recast in an encoded form, subject to digital affordances, that is materially identical to text, to writing, to all the strings of language that are now humanly readable in the realm of computation and our increasingly predominant digitalized culture. I am tempted, provocatively, to say (to write!) that socialized automatic speech recognition transforms human linguistic performance into literature. Except that I imagine that such practices, for aesthetic, significant, and affective purposes might one day have no human need for literature as such. Its greatest work will always already—and would not Shakespeare scholars agree with me here?—be aurature.

Before the 1990s, language-as-graphemic-or-typographic-visuality was already digital. (Since the very advent of writing systems, I, for one, would argue.) Algorithm and formal procedures of many kinds had long been applied to natural human language in this form, as writing, as literature, including and particularly for aesthetic effect. It was the enculturation of widespread media-agnostic digital affordances that, in the 1990s, allowed specialist practitioners and scholars to characterize what were essentially quantitatively and peripherally rather than qualitatively distinct reconfigurations of literary material as, speculatively, "electronic literature." Digital affordances allowed practitioners and scholars to do new things with old words, to an extent that rendered some of these new things interesting and exciting. But reading as such did not change. Nor will it fundamentally change until the language animal that is definitive of reading has time to evolve. What did change, even in the 1990s, was the configuration of the scene for linguistic poiesis—

the hows and whens of reading and writing. This was and is momentous enough, but hearing and speaking go on much as they have done, and the predominance and momentum of reading and writing traditions were and are minimally deflected. Even now, the most industry and energy that has been expended on the remediation of literary practices has been applied to artifacts that support the tradition of the book, of print-based, typographic media—those emulators, images and mirrors of typographic artifacts that, in English, go by the disfigured name of "ebooks." Ebooks are with us, for the time being and foreseeable future, but at the time of writing growth in their popularity and dissemination has slowed. Over roughly the same period there has been significant growth in the reading of audiobooks despite the fact that culture predisposes these readers to an anxiety concerning whether or not they have actually read what they are reading.[9] As of 2018, the audiobook is not digitally inscribed as language-in-aurality. It is, rather, digitized audio with minimal digitally manipulable articulation corresponding most commonly to the punctuation of books at the level of the chapter or subtitle. Nonetheless, the reading of audiobooks represents a measurable shift in the culture of reading as a whole, and this development coincides with what I speculate will become the socialization of automatic speech recognition such that the aurality of existing books is or will be grammatized at the level of (at least) the word, and—to indicate merely practices that are already available to certain readers—speech synthesizers are or will be able to present this language-as-aurality to human readers directly, automatically. We will have the option of reading in this newly articulated aurality.

If we can read in aurality then, as language animals and language artists, we can compose in aurality. We can begin to make an aurature that is formally, philosophically, ontologically identical with the literature we have inherited, an aurature that will reconfigure and redefine the archive without in any way sacrificing readability in general or the specific mode of readability that has been established by literacy. The full civilizing potential of this prospect—an aurature embodying facilities with language that are attuned to our genetic disposition as language animals—is available to us only due to crucial developments in digital culture and contemporary computation. Hence, we can affirm that practices of *digital language art*— especially in the reconfigured support media for language as an aesthetic medium—at least makes sense, and may also imply, I believe, cultural and social imperatives. Practitioners and theorists must learn and grasp those computational affordances that will allow them, fully, to participate in, to guide, and to enhance cultural and social developments that will otherwise proceed without their contributions, and risk downplaying aesthetic practice at the expense of what are supposed to be more substantive and instrumentally secure benefits. What we do not want is to remain the electronically literate writers of a history in which we find ourselves at the end of all literature, with no viable media for the art of language.

NOTES

Introduction

1 I will not necessarily note my references in this introduction—strategically, trusting the reader to discover my more scholarly allusions in the chapters themselves—unless my references are not cited elsewhere in the book.

2 I am concerned with linguistic ontology, in outlining this concept of grammalepsy, but I concentrate—in a manner consonant with a practitioner's inclinations—on the production and reproduction of language rather than on what language is, in its fullness. Grammalepsy is, however, constituted by and characteristic of reading *by humans*. As I say below, symbolic parsing is not grammalepsis. And I agree with philosophers like Charles Taylor who ascribe to what Taylor calls a "constitutive" theory of language rather than those "designative" theories that are predominant, and particularly influential within the "regime of computation," where linguistic practice may be considered reducible to calculation. The contrasting "constitutive" view proposes that language allows us to become more than whatever we were before we "have" it. Grammalepsy simply characterizes those moments when this takes place. See, in particular, the first chapter, "Designative and Constitutive Views," in *The Language Animal: The Full Shape of the Human Linguistic Capacity* (Cambridge: The Belknap Press of Harvard University Press, 2016).

3 This is, perhaps, the place to mention that, outside the scope of this selection but in another not unrelated thread of discourse, I have written on related problems of translation and, in particular, the translation of process. John Cayley, "Digital *wen*: On the Digitization of Letter- and Character-Based Systems of Inscription," in *Reading East Asian Writing: The Limits of Literary Theory*, ed. Michel Hockx and Ivo Smits, RoutledgeCurzon-IIAS Asian Studies Series (London: RoutledgeCurzon, 2003); "Beginning with 'the Image' in *How It Is* When Translating Certain Processes of Digital Language Art," *Electronic Book Review* (2015); "Untranslatability and Readability," *Critical Multilingualism Studies* 3, no. 1 (2015); "The Translation of Process," *Amodern*, no. 8 (2018).

4 See: Matthew G. Kirschenbaum, *Track Changes: A Literary History of Word Processing* (Cambridge: The Belknap Press of Harvard University Press, 2016).

5 Andrew Michael Roberts, "Why Digital Literature Has Always Been 'Beyond the Screen'," in *Beyond the Screen: Transformations of Literary Structures, Interfaces and Genres*, ed. Peter Gendolla and Jörgen Schäfer, Media Upheavals (Bielefeld: Transcript, 2010), 162.

6 See, for example, Ivan Illich's discussion of the gaze and the icon, summing up the theories of John of Damascus (675–749), "an icon is a threshold. It is a threshold at which the artist prayerfully leaves some inkling of the glory that he has seen behind that threshold." *The Rivers North of the Future: The Testament of Ivan Illich as Told to David Cayley* (Toronto: Anansi, 2005), 114. I adapted this language for John Cayley, *Lens,* 2004.

7 See "At the End of Literature."

8 John Cayley, "Of Capta, Vectoralists, Reading and the Googlization of Universities," in *Digital Humanities and Digital Media: Conversations on Politics, Culture, Aesthetics, and Literacy,* ed. Roberto Simanowski (London: Open Humanities Press, 2016).

Chapter 1

1 These opening remarks, lightly edited, were composed for the republication of the 1996 essay in 2007.

2 I retain "literary" here in parentheses in deference to a persistent investment in "superior or lasting artistic merit" (*Oxford English Dictionary*), whereas serious contemporary critics of language practice in networked and programmable media may question the relevance of any "literary" categorizations. See, in particular, Sandy Baldwin, *The Internet Unconscious: On the Subject of Electronic Literature,* International Texts in Critical Media Aesthetics (New York: Bloomsbury Academic, 2015). In my more recent thinking, I bring the category into question for reasons of misdirected media specificity—because the affordances of digitalization undermine the predominance and privilege of the "letter" as what it is that we say we *read.* See, in this volume, "At the End of Literature."

3 "Serious hypertext" is a rubric of Boston's Eastgate Systems, one of the major, self-consciously literary publishers in the field, and developers of their own hypertext authoring software, "StorySpace." The Voyager Company has also made significant efforts to produce new work in new media as well as transpose appropriate content.

4 George P. Landow, *Hypertext: The Convergence of Contemporary Critical Theory and Technology* (Baltimore and London: Johns Hopkins University Press, 1992). Landow published two further editions of this relatively popular and influential work for which he evoked the "versioning" paradigm of software and the regime of computation rather than that of the literary edition itself. Hypertext 2.0 came out in 1997 and 3.0 in 2006. Jay David Bolter, *Writing Space: The Computer, Hypertext, and the History of Writing* (Hillsdale, NJ: Erlbaum, 1991); George P. Landow, ed. *Hyper/Text/Theory* (Baltimore: Johns Hopkins University Press, 1994); Michael Joyce, *Of Two Minds: Hypertext Peda-gogy and Poetics* (Ann Arbor: University of Michigan Press, 1995). And still of particular importance and relevance: Espen Aarseth, *Cybertext: Perspectives on Ergodic Literature* (Baltimore and London: Johns Hopkins University Press, 1997).

5 Posting, March 28, 1995, to the early internet discussion list, ht_lit. In 1995 this list had migrated to a server at Carleton University in Ottawa, Ontario, Canada, journal.biology.carleton.ca, and was moderated by K. M. Mennie. The list and its archive have been offline for some years but in 2017 I made contact with K. M. Mennie and initiated a plan to make an intrinsically searchable plain text archive of the discussions available in the Brown University Library's Brown Digital Repository at: https://repository.library.brown.edu/studio/item/bdr:735315/.

6 If only society and language use would agree with me, I would still now prefer to use the term "programmaton" for most uses of "computer."

7 Generalized non-linear poetics is one of the central concerns of the pioneering hypertext poet, Jim Rosenberg. See, for example, his introductory essay in Jim Rosenberg, *Intergrams* (Cambridge, MA: Eastgate Systems, 1993). This was published as part of *The Eastgate Quarterly Review of Hypertext*, Vol. 1, No. 1. Rosenberg also posted a draft discussion of these issues to the listerv ht_lit (see note 5), March 26, 1995. Espen Aarseth has placed hypertext within a broader theoretical framework. Aarseth, *Cybertext: Perspectives on Ergodic Literature* (See also note 5).

8 The Chinese writing system, in which characters correspond with single syllables, encourages the composition of associated periods with equal phonetic and graphic length, the elements of which may also correspond in terms of semantics and grammar. This is known as "parallelism" and, by definition and form, promotes non-linear reading. The figure is particularly marked in literary Chinese, especially classical poetry, where it may be required for certain verse forms.

9 Potential Literary Outlawry or PoLiOu was, potentially, one name for a broad range of experimental literary activities which are engaged with their own representation in cyberspace and with the particular capabilities offered by this new form of representation. Clearly, the name makes explicit acknowledgement to both the anticipatory plagiarisms and the anticipated antagonisms of the OuLiPo (See also note 28).

10 John Cayley, *Wine Flying* (London: Wellsweep, 1988). *wine flying* was first programmed on a BBC microcomputer in 1983–84. In 1988, it was ported to the Apple Macintosh and HyperCard and HyperTalk, the author's preferred development environment for this kind of work at the time.

11 The authoring framework referred to here, implemented in HyperCard and HyperTalk, was never published, although it was used for individual works such as *wine flying*. This points to the question of the cybertextual author's engagement in the creation of forms themselves and how this relates to the completed work. Most of the software forms I have made are intimately related to the corresponding finished works, but at the time of writing I could see clearly that—particularly in the case of non-generative work such as *Scoring the Spelt Air*—form could easily be detached from any specific content and rendered as instrument, tool, or compositional device.

12 The writer of the letter was Humphrey McFall, who it is a pleasure to acknowledge.

13 "Lexia" is a term adopted by George Landow from Roland Barthes to indicate the unit of text at either end of a hypertext link.

14 "I am on record as advocating taking hypertext into the fine structure of language, thereby fragmenting the lexia ...," "Notes toward a non-linear prosody of space," Jim Rosenberg, posting to the ht_lit discussion list (see note 5), March 26, 1995; or in a later posting elsewhere, "my own interest [is] in using hypertext to carry the infrastructure of language itself ..." October 28, 1995. And see also: Aarseth, *Cybertext: Perspectives on Ergodic Literature* (See also note 5).

15 John Cayley, *Indra's Net I* (London: Wellsweep, 1991–93). Details of the other publications in the series will be given as they are mentioned. All were HyperCard 2.x "stacks," published on disk or over the internet, for pre-OS X Macintosh computers only.

16 Kenneth Ch'en, *Buddhism in China: A Historical Survey*, 1st paperback ed. (Princeton, NJ: Princeton University Press, 1972), 317.

17 "But the fact that the mind itself has no internal necessity to determine its every act and compel it to suffer in helpless passivity—this is due to the slight swerve of the atoms at no determinate time or place." Lucretius, *The Nature of the Universe*, trans. R. E. Latham (Harmondsworth: Penguin, 1951), Book 2, 68. The swerve or "clinamen" of Lucretius is also a major reference point for the OuLiPo (see note 28), even though the workshop is, generally, suspicious of the aleatory.

18 See, especially, Emmett Williams, *A Valentine for Noël: Four Variations on a Scheme* (Stuttgart and London: Editions Hanjörg Mayer, 1973); *Selected Shorter Poems 1950–1970* (New York: New Directions, 1975). A selection of Jackson Mac Low's "Asymmetries" is included in: Jackson Mac Low, *Representative Works: 1938–1985* (New York: Roof Books, 1986). His "diastic" technique was used in: *The Virginia Woolf Poems* (Providence, RI: Burning Deck, 1985). See also note 21. Cage used mesostic techniques to compose *Roaratorio: An Irish Circus on* Finnegans Wake (1979), having already "written through" Joyce's work in 1978: John Cage and James Joyce, *Writing through Finnegans Wake*, University of Tulsa Monograph Series (Tulsa: University of Tulsa, 1978). They are also exemplified in John Cage, *I-VI*, The Charles Eliot Norton Lectures (Cambridge, MA: Harvard University Press, 1990). There is, especially in chapters 5 and 7, interesting discussion of these works in: Marjorie Perloff, *Radical Artifice: Writing Poetry in the Age of Media* (Chicago: University of Chicago Press, 1991). For a more comprehensive treatment of these and other precursors in the field of innovative poetics, refer to: Loss Pequeño Glazier, *Digital Poetics: The Making of E-Poetries* (Tuscaloosa: University of Alabama Press, 2002).

19 It would be interesting to make a catalogue of the precise varieties of *generative* acrostic and mesostic procedures, noting their differences, although this is far beyond our scope here.

20 This technique bears certain similarities to those developed by: Stefan Themerson, *On Semantic Poetry* (London: Gaberbocchus Press, 1975). Further details of a number of other potential and—in *Indra's Net*—as-yet-unrealized forms can be found in the explanatory material which is introductory to the pieces in *Indra's Net I–III*. These include further etymological and glossological hologograms, phonemic hologograms (these would generate a form of sound poetry), and morphemic hologograms (which I will eventually explore since they would provide a way of engaging a language like Chinese).

A commission for an installation at the Midland Arts Centre, Birmingham, that I received in 1996 allowed me to investigate mesostic transformations from original Irish to English translation (in another alphabetic script) and back again. The software was later published in the Indra's Net series as John Cayley, *Oisleánd: Indra's Net IX* (London: Wellsweep, 1996). See note 37.

21 This twenty-six-word form is similar to Williams's "ultimate poetry" except that in my strict form I try to make a twenty-six-word sentence or narrative (in the traditional order of the letters). An aspect of this form which I cannot resist mentioning is that once—like Williams, Mac Low, or myself—you have mapped the twenty-six letters of the alphabet onto twenty-six words, it is theoretically possible to encode all of literature acrostically or mesostically— translating everything into a "surface language" of twenty-six meaning-tokens (with no loss of information). Perhaps alphabetization was once perceived like this, as early scribes moved from away from morphemic script elements—as if "book" seemed to present itself as: "house + eye + eye + palm-of-the-hand."

22 Oscar Pastior in his *Poempoems* (first German publication 1973) has a more poetic and less formalist approach to a similar self-referentiality: "holography … to make a text as far as possible such that every part contains the whole. That is an image I hold in front of me." Oskar Pastior, *Poempoems*, Printed Head (London: Atlas Press, 1991). See also: *Many Glove Compartments: Selected Poems*, trans. Harry Mathews, Christopher Middleton, and Rosemarie Waldrop (Providence, RI: Burning Deck, 2001). Eduardo Kac is another early explorer of the application of holography to literature and vice versa. See his first "holopoem" (with Fernando Catta-Preta), *HOLO/OLHO* (1983), and his remarks in "Holopoetry and Fractal Holopoetry," *Holo/Olho (Holo/Eye)* … is a combination of anagrams in which the word *holo* mirrors *olho* and vice-versa. The mirroring effect, however, was conceived so that fragments of the poem would contain enough letters to form the entire meaning: both *holo* and *eye*. The arrangement of letters in space was holographed five times; each hologram was fragmented and the five holograms were reassembled in a new visual unit. This holopoem was an attempt to recreate, in its own syntax, a structure that would correspond to the holographic model, according to which the information of the whole is contained in the part and vice-versa. Eduardo Kac, "Holopoetry and Fractal Holopoetry," *Leonardo* 22, no. 3 & 4 (1989): 399.

23 John Cayley, *Collocations: Indra's Net II* (London: Wellsweep, 1993).

24 *An Essay on the Golden Lion: Han-Shan in Indra's Net* (Edinburgh: Morning Star, 1995). See the discussion of *Golden Lion* below.

25 *Under It All: Texts, Holography, Afterword* (London: The Many Press, 1993). This little book was published in an edition of 221 copies, each of which was unique. Four separately prepared pages bound into each copy consist of unique samples from two holographic transformations.

26 As of this publication, I still have plans for an installation to project words onto mesostic planes, realized as a set of twenty-six transparent screens or planes arranged so as to suggest a large cubic word space. Read from its "front" through all of the twenty-six layers, fragments of a given text would be legible as the text was generated and projected words onto the planes. But moving around the cube, other mesostically determined orders of words would present themselves.

27 Here, a line of similar and in some respects, parallel work (which did not directly influence my own at the time) runs from the text-generation program "Travesty" by Joseph O'Rourke and Hugh Kenner, intersecting with Mac Low at the point of his *Merzgedichte*. Hugh Kenner and Joseph O'Rourke, "A Travesty Generator for Micros," *Byte*, November 1984; Jackson Mac Low and Kurt Schwitters, *42 Merzgedichte in Memoriam Kurt Schwitters: February 1987–September 1989*, 1st ed. (Barrytown, NY: Station Hill, 1994). During the composition of his *Merzgedichte* in the late 1980s, Charles O. Hartman sent Mac Low several computer programs including "Diatext" and "Diatex4." He also started to make use of Hugh Kenner and Joseph O'Rourke's "pseudo-text-generating" program "Travesty" at about this time, to create some of the poems. However, "All outputs were subject to rule-guided editing" (sleeve notes for the audio CD, *Open Secrets* (New York: XI, Experimental Intermedia Foundation, n.d. [1994])). Most recently, such processes have been used in: Charles O. Hartman and Hugh Kenner, *Sentences*, 1st pbk. ed., New American Poetry Series (Los Angeles: Sun & Moon Press, 1995). "Travesty" is a text processor which, set to its higher "orders," will produce results similar to those of my collocational procedures.

28 Mathews, a member of the OuLiPo, outlines his version of the procedure in: Harry Mathews, *20 Lines a Day*, 1st pbk. ed. (Normal, IL: Dalkey Archive Press, 1989). The OuLiPo, or Ouvroir de Littérature Potentiel, is clearly a basic reference point for cybertextual developments given the workshop's profound and ludic investigations of the relationship between mathematics and literature, constrictive form, combinatory literature, etc. See, by way of introduction: Warren F. Motte, *Oulipo: A Primer of Potential Literature* (Lincoln: University of Nebraska Press, 1986); Harry Mathews and Alastair Brotchie, eds., *Oulipo Compendium* (London: Atlas Press, 1998). However, the OuLiPo has, at best, an ambiguous attitude to the aleatory as an aspect of generational, constrictive or combinatory procedure, despite the fact that the distinction between choice as chance and the choice of *arbitrary* formal constraints may be too nice to rule out the potential of one or the other.

29 John Cayley, *Moods & Conjunctions: Indra's Net III* (London: Wellsweep, 1993–94).

30 *Golden Lion: Indra's Net IV* (London: Wellsweep, 1994).

31 John Cayley and Gu Cheng, *Leaving the City: Indra's Net V* (London: Wellsweep, 1995).

32 William S. Burroughs and Brion Gysin, *The Exterminator* (San Francisco: Auerhahn Press, 1960); Sinclair Beiles et al., *Minutes to Go* (Paris: Jean Fanchette, 1960).

33 John Cayley, *Book Unbound: Indra's Net VI* (London: Wellsweep, 1995). *Book Unbound* has also been anthologized in a number of places, as follows: Cayley, John. "Book Unbound," *Engaged*, 1995, On CD-ROM; Cayley, John. "Book Unbound," *Postmodern Culture* 7, no. 3, Hypertext special issue (February 1997). http://muse.jhu.edu/article/603711 (accessed August 13, 2017); "Book Unbound," in *Dietsche Warande & Beaufort [Dwb]*, 4, on *Electronic (Visual) Literarture*, ed. Eric Vos and Jan Baetens (1999); "Book Unbound," in *The New Media Reader*, ed. Noah Wardrip-Fruin and Nick Montfort (Cambridge, MA: MIT Press, 2003).

34 *The Speaking Clock: Indra's Net VII* (London: Wellsweep, 1995). Extracts from the clock were also published as: Cayley, John. "From: The Speaking Clock," *Chain* 4 (1997): 25–27.

35 To quote from the given text: "Real time is concealed beneath the cyclical behavior of clock and time piece. No moment is like any other ... and yet the clock applies the same 'name' to many a different instance." *The Speaking Clock* affects to give a unique name to every moment.

36 See Jhave's website, http://glia.ca and David Jhave Johnston, *Aesthetic Animism: Digital Poetry's Ontological Implications* (Cambridge, MA: MIT Press, 2016).

37 *Oisleánd*, as a HyperCard stack, can be still be download from http://programmatology.shadoof.net and can also be viewed in a constrained, early web version on this site, http://programmatology.shadoof.net/works/oi/oisleand.html. This piece was commissioned for a touring exhibition, "Words Revealed," initially at the Midland Arts Centre, UK, May 11 to June 23, 1996. *windsound* has been performed and shown as a text movie in various venues and is also downloadable as a video from the "programmatology" site. Cayley, *Oisleánd: Indra's Net IX; windsound*, 1999; *windsound*, 2003. Electronic Literature Organization: *State of the Arts: The Proceedings of the Electronic Literature Organization's 2002 State of the Arts Symposium & 2001 Electronic Literature Awards*, included on the CD-ROM.

38 A severely cut-back, early versions of *noth'rs* appeared on the CD-ROM which accompanied an issue of *Performance Research* edited by Ric Allsopp and Scott deLahunta. *noth'rs*, 1999. *Performance Research*: 4.2, on CD-ROM. It was also published on the web as *noth'rs*, 1999a. *Riding the Meridian*. An initial performance version was shown at the Digital Arts and Culture (DAC) conference, Atlanta Georgia, October 28–31, 1999.

39 I owe this characterization in part to Espen Aarseth, who has developed a (media independent) "generalized model with a few broad categories that can describe the main differences of textual phenomena." In his excellent book already cited, Aarseth, *Cybertext: Perspectives on Ergodic Literature*. He argues convincingly for a distinction between cybertext and hypertext, putting forward the former as an inclusive term embracing, for example, indeterminate or reader-constructed texts, and reserving hypertext for (passively) linked structures of static lexia (textual nodes).

Chapter 2

1 Sections "THESIS," "ANTITHESIS," and "SYNTHESIS" of this chapter were software-generated by applying semi-aleatory collocational procedures to arguments manually edited out from the earlier sections. The two arguments might be summarized as: "The COMPUTER is (an integral part of) the SYSTEM against which WE write" (thesis), and "Software sHifts poetIcs, iF riTers prEss: <Reveal>" (antithesis). Sections "THESIS" and "ANTITHESIS" were generated from their respective arguments separately. A collocational algorithm generated phrases which were selected and collected by the author.

Selected phrases were also fed back into the given texts, changing them irreversibly. The altered texts from "THESIS" and "ANTITHESIS" were then combined and used as the given text for section "SYNTHESIS" (synthesis). Note that by this stage very little active selection of generated phrases was required by the author. The final paragraphs of section "SYNTHESIS" are almost entirely generated by the simple collocational algorithm. I merely split the generated paragraphs into lines.

A HyperCard stack (Macintosh only, for HyperCard 2.x) with "Reveal Code" cybertext generator was produced and published as John Cayley, *Pressing the <Reveal Code> Key: Indra's Net VIII* (London: Wellsweep, 1996). An archive of this stack is still downloadable, without warranty, from http:// programmatology.shadoof/net.

Section "<REVEALED>" is an extract of the actual working code (in HyperTalk) used to generate sections "THESIS," "ANTITHESIS" and "SYNTHESIS." The variable terms have been randomly and systematically replaced with substantive words from sections "The COMPUTER is (an integral part of) the SYSTEM against which WE write," "INVARIANT inACCURATE SYSTEMS never sleep SYNCHRONICally," "The COMPUTER is not (a part of) THE MEDIA. The COMPUTER allows for the COMPOSITION of an indeterminate number of potential MEDIA," "FAMILIARITY breeds CONTEMPT. INTIMACY inspires MYSTIFICATION" and "Software sHifts poetIcs, iF riTers prEss: <Reveal>"—any noun or adjective is allowed to replace a variable name containing a value; any verb is allowed to replace a procedure or function name. HyperTalk "reserved words" have been left intact. The code is working code.

2 Perloff, 189.

3 Ibid.

4 Charles Bernstein, "Play It Again, Pac-Man," *Postmodern Culture* 2, no. 1 (1991: n.p.). Cited by Perloff (perhaps in an earlier form) as: "Hot Circuits: A Video Arcade," American Museum of the Moving Image, June 14–November 26, 1989.

5 Perloff, 188.

6 Perloff mentions this: ibid., 208. However, Rosenberg has since pointed out that he wrote only the early programs. Andrew Culver then took over this work for Cage. (Personal communication.)

7 Jim Rosenberg, remarks posted to the internet discussion list ht_lit, June 9, 1995. See "Beyond Codexspace" note 5 above.

Chapter 3

1 Bolter; Gregory L. Ulmer, *Applied Grammatology: Post(E)-Pedagogy from Jacques Derrida to Joseph Beuys* (Baltimore: Johns Hopkins University Press, 1985); *Heuretics: The Logic of Invention* (Baltimore: Johns Hopkins University Press, 1994).

2 Aarseth, *Cybertext: Perspectives on Ergodic Literature.*

3   Theodor Holm Nelson, *Computer Lib / Dream Machines*, Revised and updated ed. (Redmond: Tempus Books of Microsoft Press, 1987); *Literary Machines 93.1* (Sausalito: Mindful Press, 1993).

4   When this text was first published, the poet, cris cheek [*sic*], provided a brief list of poetics "must-reads" for new media artists. I will provide his excellent references here, in this note. Kathy Acker, *Blood and Guts in High School* (New York: Grove Press, 1978); Steve Benson, *Blue Book* (Great Barrington: The Figures/Roof, 1988); Brian Catling, *The Stumbling Block* (London: Book Works, 1990); Cayley, *Book Unbound: Indra's Net VI*; Allen Fisher, *Defamiliarising _____ ** (London: Veer Books, 2013); Robert Grenier, *Sentences*, 1st ed. (Cambridge: Whale Cloth Press, 1978); Mac Low, *Representative Works: 1938–1985*; Steve McCaffery, *Panopticon*, 1st ed. (Toronto: blewointmentpress, 1984); Jed Rasula and Steve McCaffery, eds., *Imagining Language: An Anthology* (Cambridge, MA: MIT Press, 1998); Tom Raworth, *Logbook* (Berkeley, CA: Poltroon Press, 1977); *Writing: [Poems]* (Berkeley, CA: Figures, 1982); Lisa Robertson, *Debbie: An Epic* (Vancouver: New Star Books, 1997); Jerome Rothenberg and Pierre Joris, eds., *Poems for the Millennium: The University of California Book of Modern and Postmodern Poetry, Vol. 2: From Postwar to Millennium* (Berkeley: University of California Press, 1998); Fiona Templeton, *You the City* (New York: Roof Books, 1990); Hannah Weiner, *Spoke* (Los Angeles: Sun & Moon Press, 1984).

5   "Whether it has essential limits or not, the entire field covered by the cybernetic *program* will be the field of writing. If the theory of cybernetics is by itself to oust all metaphysical concepts-including the concepts of soul, of life, of value, of choice, of memory-which until recently served to separate the machine from man, it must conserve the notion of writing, trace, grammè [written mark], or grapheme, until its own historico-metaphysical character is also exposed." Jacques Derrida, *Of Grammatology*, trans. Gayatri Chakravorty Spivak, Corrected ed. (Baltimore and London: Johns Hopkins University Press, 1997), 9.

Chapter 4

1   Certain terms in this essay may require explanation. I prefer, despite its awkwardness and length, "writing in networked and programmable media" to any of the current words or phrases such as "hypertext, hyperfiction, hyperpoetry," or the corresponding "cyber-" terms, although I do generally subscribe to Espen Aarseth's "textonomy," and would prefer cybertext to hypertext as the more inclusive, "catholic" term. Aarseth, *Cybertext: Perspectives on Ergodic Literature*. I use "programmatology" and "programmatological" by extension from "grammatology" and especially "applied grammatology" as elaborated by Gregory Ulmer. Ulmer. Programmatology may be thought of as the study and practice of writing (Derridean sense) with an explicit awareness of its relation to "programming" or prior writing in anticipation of performance, including the performance of reading. I try to avoid the use of words such as "computer" and prefer, wherever

possible, "programmaton" for the programmable systems which we use to compose and deliver "new media."

2   This essay was originally sketched out for the "p0es1s: Poetics of digital text" symposion [sic], held in Erfurt, September 28–29, 2001.

3   Friedrich A. Kittler, "There Is No Software," in *Literature Media Information Systems*, ed. John Johnston, Critical Voices in Art, Theory and Culture (Amsteldijk: G+B Arts International, 1997), 150.

4   There are times when I would like to write "code-as-text" and other times, "text-as-code," occasionally with either term cycling (e.g., code-as-text-as-code) I will just use the one term, asking the reader to bear in mind the other possibilities in appropriate contexts.

5   As an example of the prevalence of code-as-text across the widest range of artistic inscription, a version of the code-as-text or reveal code aesthetic appears as something of a culmination in Lev Manovich's excellent and provocative *The Language of New Media* (not discussed in the body of the present chapter because of my focus on textual and literal art practice). The final section of Manovich's book is entitled "Cinema as Code" and features Vuk Cosic's ASCII films, "which effectively stage one characteristic of computer-based moving images—their identity as computer code." Manovich is undoubtedly correct when he asserts that, "What [George] Lucas hides, Cosic reveals. His ASCII films 'perform' the new status of media as digital data ... Thus, rather than erasing the image in favor of the code ... or hiding the code from us ... code and image coexist." Nonetheless, it is worrying to be presented, in this highlighted context, with the example of work whose aesthetic may well prove to be exhausted by a conceptual and metacritical analysis (see below), particularly in a book which makes an unprecedented contribution to our understanding of new and emergent rhetorical strategies in new media (especially the crucial role of cinematic rhetoric), and represents a deep understanding of new media's programmatological dimension. Lev Manovich, *The Language of New Media* (Cambridge, MA: MIT Press, 2001), 330–333.

6   N. Katherine Hayles, "Virtual Bodies and Flickering Signifiers," in *How We Became Posthuman: Virtual Bodies in Cybernetics, Literature, and Informatics* (Chicago: University of Chicago Press, 1999), 29. An earlier version of this essay is also published as: "Virtual Bodies and Flickering Signifiers," in *Electronic Culture: Technology and Visual Representation*, ed. Timothy Druckrey (New York: Aperture, 1996).

7   "Virtual Bodies and Flickering Signifiers," 26.

8   "William Gibson (1948–)," *The Guardian*, July 22, 2008; Michael Cunningham, "The Virtual Tourist [a Short Interview with William Gibson]," *The Irish Times*, October 12, 1996.

> In real life, Gibson is actually the opposite of hi-tech. He maintains a high degree of goofy aloofness from the technologies he writes about in such obsessive detail—almost as if just using them would increase the risk of being somehow "infected" by them. He wrote his most famous novel, *Neuromancer*, on a 1927 olive-green Hermes portable typewriter, and only recently migrated to a battered old Apple Mac.

Gibson famously discussed his use of a typewriter in a phone interview for *Playboy*, August 30, 1996. "I do remember sitting with a blank sheet of paper and a typewriter going to 'dataspace' and 'infospace' and a couple of other clunkers, and then coming to 'cyberspace' thinking it sounds as though it means something." I have touched on the question of Gibson's and another influential contemporary novelist's apparently conservative approach to, shall we say, avant-garde practice in a relatively early online work, John Cayley, "Why Did People Make Things Like This?" *Electronic Book Review* (1997).

9   Hayles, "Virtual Bodies and Flickering Signifiers," 31. The immediately following quotations, interspersed with my comments, are from what I take to be a crucial paragraph in Hayles's crucial article.

10 I mean "power" as used in the advertising and publicity for computer systems where, to relate the term with a more general or Foucauldian sense, we may think of it as the power to alter the behavior of a system (in an impressive manner or at great speed, etc.). See below.

11 Florian Cramer, "Digital Code and Literary Text," *BeeHive Hypertext/ Hypermedia Literary Journal* 4, no. 3 (2001). Also available through one of Cramer's websites at: http://www.netzliteratur.net/cramer/digital_code_and_ literary_text.html (accessed July 31, 2017).

12 In passing it is worth highlighting the interface itself, particularly the ever-evolving HCI, as a complex programmable object with a structure like a language, including, in some cases, an underlying textual command-line interface which mirrors the now-familiar mimetic and visual instantiation of users' interface. This is another point for potential artistic intervention as well as a vital consideration when discussing the emergent rhetorics of new media, as Manovich has demonstrated so well, even introducing the powerful concept of "cultural interface" (human-computer-culture interface) as an analytic tool. Manovich, 62–115.

13 Cramer.

14 Perloff, 189. For a separate but related discussion of some of these issues, see "Pressing the 'REVEAL CODE' Key" in this volume. The work of Emmett Williams and Jackson Mac Low, central to any assessment of the radical poetic artifice which she identifies, as also for the criticism of writing in networked and programmable media, is notable for its absence from Perloff's book.

15 Ibid., 188.

16 As more writers from this tradition make the move into "new media," this position begins to change. They become "new media writers" "*digital* poets," and so on and attitudes perceptibly shift. Writers also, of course, become more sophisticated in their understanding of programmatological systems. This can be seen particularly in Charles Bernstein's subsequent writing on digital media and also, for example, in the work of Loss Pequeño Glazier, who is closely associated with the poetic practice which has developed from the L=A=N=G=U=A=G=E "school." See below, and: Glazier.

17 The critical history of this (anti-)tradition in poetic literature is generally traced at least back to Mallarmé. A convenient source for its study can be found in the two-volume anthology: Jerome Rothenberg and Pierre Joris, eds., *Poems for the Millennium: The University of California Book of Modern*

and Postmodern Poetry, Vol. 1: From Fin-de-Siècle to Negritude (Berkeley: University of California Press, 1995); *Poems for the Millennium: The University of California Book of Modern and Postmodern Poetry, Vol. 2.*

18   The term is (ironic) OuLiPian, used of any prior instantiation of work generated by a procedure which has subsequently been invented and specified by the OuLiPo. Such a discussion is beyond the scope of this essay.

19   See: Manovich, 94–115.

20   The argument here is a rehearsal of the familiar but ever-important argument against art practice, particularly new media art practice, as media-specific or media-determined. Cramer's essay makes similar points.

21   Roland Barthes, *S/Z*, trans. Richard Miller (Oxford: Blackwell Publishers, 1990); N. Katherine Hayles, *How We Became Posthuman: Virtual Bodies in Cybernetics, Literature, and Informatics* (Chicago: University of Chicago Press, 1999), 46.

22   Although I do not make use of his analysis in this essay, it is well-worth referring to Philippe Bootz's analysis of systems-mediated textuality, where I believe my "interface text" roughly corresponds to his "texte-à-voir." See: Philippe Bootz, "Le Point de Vue Fonctionnel: Point de Vue Tragique et Programme Pilote," *alire 10 / DOC(K)S* Series 3, no. 13/14/15/16 (1997).

23   N. Katherine Hayles, "Bodies of Texts, Bodies of Subjects: Metaphoric Networks in New Media" (paper presented at the Digital Arts and Culture conference, Providence, RI, 2001). This is cited from the version of the paper posted in PDF form before the conference.

24   Not "(yet)" as I say, although some might wish to try and make the strong case for an emergent machinic culture, which is, I believe, a serious project although a misdirection in this context.

25   As in the term "Chinese Pidgin English." Cf., for example, the discussion in: Charles F. Hockett, *A Course in Modern Linguistics* (New York: Macmillan, 1958).

26   Not exhausted in the examples given, as I say, but these remarks are, indeed, offered as a partial explanation of what is wanting in much less-considered and less well-made writing in networked and programmable media, where inadequate and inadequately theorized form substitutes for and sometimes positively evades content; when the writing is like poems about poetry (and nothing else), or techno-writing about technology.

27   Alan Sondheim, *Jennifer* (Salt Lake City: Nominative Press Collective, 1998).

28   That is, it needs to be judged as such and should not necessarily be granted a special credit of affect or significance because of its instantiation in new media.

29   Most recently in the book gathering many of these papers and essays, *Digital Poetics*, which, please note, includes a chapter devoted to "Coding Writing, Reading Code." Glazier's work has been done while he has also served as one of the motive forces and prime initiators of the major resource for innovative writing on the internet, the Electronic Poetry Center at the University of Buffalo, http://epc.buffalo.edu. Glazier.

30   Ibid., 31–32.

31   See: "White-Faced Bromeliads on 20 Hectares," Electronic Poetry Center, http://wings.buffalo.edu/epc/authors/glazier/java/costa1/00.html. This work illustrates my specific points and also demonstrates that Glazier has been exploring the properly programmatological dimension of writing in networked

and programmable media with, for example, kinetic and algorithmic texts. A classified selection of texts is at: http://epc.buffalo.edu/authors/glazier/e-poetry/.

32 Jodi is the very well-known, long-standing net.art project of Joan Heemskerk and Dirk Paesmans. Jodi, *www.jodi.org*, 1980. Jodi.

33 The practice of composing ASCII symbols, usually displayed as monospaced fonts for regularity, in order to generate imagery. In Jodi's case this was abstract or verging on the abstract whereas, popularly, ASCII art has been figurative.

34 See "Pressing the 'REVEAL CODE' Key" in this volume. The variable terms in this code were randomly and systematically replaced with substantive words from the text on which the procedure operates—any noun or adjective was allowed to replace a variable name containing a value; any verb replaced a procedure or function name. HyperTalk "reserved words" were left intact. The code is working code.

35 But I raise it, in part, thanks to remarks by Nick Montfort which are published along with: John Cayley, "Literal Art: Neither Lines nor Pixels but Letters," in *First Person: New Media as Story, Performance, and Game*, ed. Noah Wardrip-Fruin and Pat Harrigan (Cambridge, MA: MIT Press, 2004); "Literal Art: Neither Lines nor Pixels but Letters," *Electronic Book Review* electropoetics (2004). As I was writing I came across Hugh Kenner's highly interesting reading of "Beckett Thinking." Kenner examines Beckett's writing in terms of strict, exhaustive logical procedure in an essay which includes paraphrases coded in the programming language Pascal. Hugh Kenner, *The Mechanic Muse* (Oxford: Oxford University Press, 1987), 85–105.

36 Hayles, "Virtual Bodies and Flickering Signifiers," 33.

Chapter 5

1 Martin Heidegger, *Poetry, Language, Thought*, trans. Albert Hofstader and ed. Harper Colophon (New York: Harper and Row, 1975), 115. In its web-based form (http://programmatology.shadoof.net/works/hypercyberpoetext/hcp000. html) and also as printed in *Assembling Alternatives: Reading Postmodern Poetries Transnationally*, there is a parallel "X" text based on an edited sequence from the same Heidegger piece, extracted from pp. 111 to 120. This text was collocationally transformed, using a procedure I have described elsewhere:

> This transformation can proceed beginning with any word in the given text, which we then may call 'the word last chosen.' Any other word—occurring at any point in the base text—which follows (collocates with) the word last chosen may then follow it and so become in turn the word last chosen. // Clearly, in this type of transformation, at the very least, each pair of successive words are two-word segments of natural English. However, the text will wander within itself, branching at any point where a word that is repeated in the base text is chosen, and this will most often occur when common, grammatical words are encountered.

("Beyond Codexspace," above, p. 25) In addition, words at the end of collocational jumps were, where possible, chosen to spell out the mesostic message (in bold) "what are poets for: technology calculation numbers." This text is one possible rendition of a quasi-aleatory procedure which produces indeterminate results. It was not edited. Heidegger's text is cited and subverted as, in this context, what tends to interpretation as an arch-conservative counter-current, one apotheosis of a perspective on "writing" which claims that, to come into being, it must transcend (even) its (traditional) technologies (see 2), and (the troubling, distasteful horizon of) technology itself.

2   See also the discussion of related issues in "Pressing the 'REVEAL CODE' Key" in this volume.

3   "Beyond Codexspace," above, p. 18.

4   "Pressing the 'REVEAL CODE' Key," above, p. 36.

5   Bolter; Landow, *Hypertext: The Convergence of Contemporary Critical Theory and Technology; Hyper/Text/Theory*; Joyce, *Of Two Minds: Hypertext Peda-gogy and Poetics*.

6   Perhaps it would be clearer to use Barthes's original terms, since the standard translation of scriptible, "writerly," must also be understood as "reader-centered." Barthes, *S/Z*, 3–6.

7   "Intelligence is relentlessly reflexive, so that even the external tools that it uses to implement its workings become 'internalized', that is, part of its own reflexive process." Walter J. Ong, *Orality and Literacy: The Technologizing of the Word*, ed. Terence Hawkes, New Accents (London: Routledge, 1982; repr., 1995), 78 ff., 81.

8   See, in particular, Jim Rosenberg's introductory essay to: Rosenberg, *Intergrams*. He has also posted a draft discussion of these issues to the ht_lit discussion list, March 26, 1995. See "Beyond Codexspace," chapter 1, note 5 above. See also the discussions of non-linearity in this chapter's note 5.

9   Espen Aarseth has discussed a "cyborg aesthetics" of literature in: Aarseth, *Cybertext: Perspectives on Ergodic Literature*, 51 ff.

10 See "Pressing the 'REVEAL CODE' Key," above, p. 36. I pursue the programmer/writer relation briefly in "Of Programmatology," also in this volume.

11 For 22–23, I must acknowledge both the discussion of a "logic of [formal] exemplification" derived from Cage, in a paper presented at the "Assembling Alternatives" conference by Tyrus Miller "Paragram as participation: Anarchist poetics in John Cage and Jackson Mac Low," and especially Joan Retallack's challenge to this suggestion, namely her preference for the "experience of a possible form of life" in questions afterward.

12 Aarseth has developed this in a number of places: Espen Aarseth, "Nonlinearity and Literary Theory," in *Hyper/Text/Theory*, ed. George P. Landow (Baltimore: Johns Hopkins University Press, 1994); "Text, Hypertext or Cybertext: A Typology of Textual Modes Using Correspondence Analysis," in *Research in Humanities Computing, 5*, ed. Giorgio Perissinotto, Susan Hockey, and Nancy Ide (Oxford: Oxford University Press, 1996); *Cybertext: Perspectives on Ergodic Literature*.

13 MUDs (Multi-User Dungeons) and MOOs (MUD Object Orientated) are recast by Aarseth as Multi-User Discourses. Aarseth, *Cybertext: Perspectives on Ergodic Literature*, 142 ff. They represent what is perhaps the most radical form of textuality currently implemented beyond codexspace. Despite their

origins in game playing, these textual spaces require just the sort of analysis which Aarseth has pioneered, an analysis capable of treating them as "potential literature." As a practical experiment, hypertext researchers at Brown University famously established "Hypertext Hotel," a MOO space with explicitly literary inclinations (https://elmcip.net/node/360, accessed July 31, 2017).

14 Ibid., 179. Much as it concerns many of the questions raised, it is impossible to discuss ergodic art further within the scope of this chapter. It is an analytical concept well worth pursuing.

15 In her contribution to *Assembling Alternatives*, "In the Place of Writing," Caroline Bergvall has made a strong case for "performance" as a model of practice bringing together innovative poetic engagements and cross-art experiments which invoke "non-literary" media or sites—contexts "contained by and *specifying the intertextual*" [Bergvall's emphasis]. Performance is an intertextual (or hypertextual) path out of codexspace into anyspace. Performance ("to carry through in due form" OED) may also be seen as the realization or publication of writing and text-making, where the latter becomes more properly a "programming" (rhyming with the cybertechnical usage), a "pre-writing" or a "prior indication" of what and how to read. Bergvall hints at this, "each publication … announces the text prior to our reading it, deciphers the text as we read it … rewrites to an extent the text." However, I am suggesting that the text here is itself the prior thing, the program, while any publication of the text and each subsequent reading in anyspace and by whomever, is a performance. Caroline Bergvall, "In the Place of Writing: The Performance of Writing as Sited Practice," in *Assembling Alternatives: Reading Postmodern Poetries Transnationally*, ed. Romana Huk (Middletown, CT: Wesleyan University Press, 2003).

16 Here is a very short list of contemporary examples (with no attempt on my part at "catastrophic/judgmental interaction," see 36). Linking is everywhere, especially on the World Wide Web but also in work distributed by pioneers of "serious, literary" hypertext such as Eastgate Systems in Cambridge, MA, publishers of Michael Joyce's landmark hypertext *afternoon: A Story*, which employs the sophisticated local hypertext authoring software "StorySpace." Michael Joyce, *afternoon: A Story* (Cambridge: Eastgate Systems, 1990). The work of Robert Kendall, for example, *A Life Set for Two*, exhibits transience (it is kinetic), conditional linking and user configuration. Robert Kendall, *A Life Set for Two* (Cambridge: Eastgate Systems, 1996). Jim Rosenberg's *Intergrams* and *Barrier Frames* can only be read if the reader intervenes (it is ergodic in Aarseth's sense), revealing tone-like clusters of word-"simultaneities" arranged in spatially represented, diagrammatic, syntactic relations. Rosenberg, *Intergrams; The Barrier Frames: Finality Crystal Shunt Curl Chant Quickening Giveaway Stare; Diffractions Through: Thirst Weep Ransack (Frailty) Veer Tide Elegy* (Cambridge, MA: Eastgate Systems, 1996). Charles O. Hartman has produced a body of generative, quasi-aleatory work, sometimes with other writers, including Jackson Mac Low and Hugh Kenner, accessible through his books: Hartman and Kenner; Charles O. Hartman, *Virtual Muse: Experiments in Computer Poetry* (Hanover: Wesleyan University Press, 1996). My own disk- and web-published *Indra's Net* series, described (up to *Indra's Net VII*) in "Beyond Codexspace" in this volume, exemplifies all the textual characteristics mentioned. As World Wide Web

works extend their abilities to processing as well as linking, they too will exhibit a wider range of cybertextual features, although aleatory linking or linking which is reader-determined is already a powerful, if anarchic, technology which can be easily exploited. Chris Funkhouser has documented and carefully analyzed much of the poetically inclined early work of this kind in: Christopher T. Funkhouser, *Prehistoric Digital Poetry: An Archaeology of Forms, 1959–1995* (Tuscaloosa: University of Alabama Press, 2007). He has since gone on to address corresponding work, made after the advent of the web: *New Directions in Digital Poetry*, ed. Francisco J. Ricardo, International Texts in Critical Media Aesthetics (New York: Continuum, 2012).

17 "Late age of print" is a much-discussed phrase originating with: Bolter.

18 The possible effect of the rise of audiovisual channels on the development of literary cybertext is also discussed in "Beyond Codexspace," above.

Chapter 6

1 Joan Retallack, "Blue Notes on the Know Ledge," in *The Poethical Wager* (Berkeley: University of California Press, 2003), 75–76.

2 Retallack is also noted as a scholar and student of John Cage, one of the most important artists to have contributed to the field of digitally mediated writing through his algorithmically generated mesostic texts.

3 Retallack is an example of such a writer, but not one of those who would resist a practical engagement with or appreciation of "new" media. For instances of the latter, see some of the discussions associated with: Joel Kuszai, ed. *Poetics@* (New York: Roof Books, 1999). In the course of these discussions, I wrote, "Some writing … either could not exist in more 'traditional' media, or would not be so elegantly presented as it would in cyber / hypertext … // In particular, I mean texts where 'chance operations' and/or algorithmic transformations are applied to given texts and the writer insists that the 'real time' results of these procedures *are* her inscription on the surface of a complex medium." Ibid., 174–175. For resistance to this view, please refer to the proceeding and following contributions to the thread, within the book cited, especially those by Ron Silliman. My remarks here are a revisiting, reformulation, and development of related ideas and arguments.

4 This section is based on discussions in: John Cayley, "Bass Resonance," *Mute*, January 2005; "Bass Resonance," *Electronic Book Review* electropoetics (2005); "Lens: The Practice and Poetics of Writing in Immersive VR: A Case Study with Maquette," *Leonardo Electronic Almanac* 14, no. 5–6 (2006): n.p.

5 Saul Bass was the first film title designer to be given a screen credit by the Director's Guild of America (for Otto Preminger's *Carmen Jones*, 1954).

6 Paratext generally could also be retheorized as complexity of writing surface. Graphic design elements and framing conventions create depth and structure time in and throughout the textual object.

7 One of the interesting aspects of Bass's work is its non-use of Concrete poetics. One strand of literal art in new media clearly derives from Concrete traditions.

Note however, that I do not consider linguistic or textual objects that deploy the rhetoric of Concrete to produce complexity in the surface of writing as I am developing the concept here. In a sense, Concrete works because the properties and methods it brings together cannot share the same surface. This is the trope of Concrete: words are objects; words are not objects.

8   In his work on *West Side Story* (1961) Bass quietly and wittily played with real surfaces as a site for (title) writing, with the credits expressed as graffiti and intermixed with signage. One of the recognized artists in contemporary film titles, Kyle Cooper, literally etched or collaged the credits for *Se7en* (1995) onto film stock. In Bass's later worked he reverted to the dominant mode of screen titling in which letters and words "float over" the visual world of the film on planes that are, conceptually, in an entirely different space, in contrast with that of the underlying photo-naturalism. This mode is also relatively familiar in new media work with language in the form of writing that is, basically, illustrated by visual and audio material rendered in new media. There is, as yet, little work that is consciously made for the complex writing surfaces made accessible by new media.

9   I am aware that, following Retallack and others, I am evoking some mathematical concepts in a rather vague and quasi-metaphorical sense. I am not pretending to use any of these terms with an informed understanding of their mathematical counterparts. But I would not like to preclude the possibility that this could be done, and that some of the procedures loosely described here could be given fairly precise representation in the mathematics of complexity and chaos, for example.

10   This analogy might be pursued since the mesostic procedure is also inherently recursive. The same mesostic process can be recursively applied to the generated text, as in Emmett Williams's "universal poetry."

11   John Cayley, *overboard*. 2003. Custom software, ambient poetics. http:// programmatology.shadoof.net/?overboard (accessed August 1, 2017); John Cayley, *Translation*. 2004. http://programmatology.shadoof.net/?translation (accessed August 1, 2017). The principles and algorithms underlying *overboard* are set out in: John Cayley, "*overboard*: An Example of Ambient Time-Based Poetics in Digital Art," *dichtung-digital* 32 (2004). http://www.dichtung-digital.de/2004/2/Cayley/index.htm (accessed August 13, 2017).

12   I have pleasure in acknowledging and thanking Brown University's Literary Arts Program for the opportunity to work and direct research in the university's Cave during the spring of 2004 and 2005. In particular, I would like to thank Professor Robert Coover, who invited me to take part in the Program in this way. While at Brown I benefited from discussions and other interactions with, among others, Noah Wardrip-Fruin, Roberto Simanowski, Talan Memmott and Bill Seaman (at the neighboring Rhode Island School of Design). Dmitri Lemmerman was my main collaborator on the projects discussed here. Further discussion of work for the Cave—from which some of the following is derived—can be found in: "Lens: The Practice and Poetics of Writing in Immersive VR: A Case Study with Maquette."

13   The question arose as to why this phenomenon should be so immediately and effectively perceptible; and this is discussed in more detail, along with other aspects of the phenomenology of text in space more generally, in: ibid.

14 Cayley, *Lens*. I recommend reviewing the video documentation linked from the above web page or directly from: http://programmatology.shadoof. net/?p=works/lens/lensComposite.html (accessed August 4, 2017).

Chapter 7

1 N. Katherine Hayles, "Translating Media: Why We Should Rethink Textuality," *The Yale Journal of Criticism* 16, no. 2 (2003): 277, original emphasis.

2 Rita Raley, "Interferences: [Net.Writing] and the Practice of Codework," *Electronic Book Review* (2002): n.p.

3 "The Code Is Not the Text" in this volume.

4 Hayles, "Translating Media: Why We Should Rethink Textuality," *passim*, esp. 270–271.

5 Ibid., 275.

6 Ibid., 274. Emphasis in the original.

7 Ibid., 276. Emphasis in the original.

8 Ibid., 274.

9 "Virtual Bodies and Flickering Signifiers"; "Virtual Bodies and Flickering Signifiers." Discussed extensively in "The Code Is Not the Text" in this volume.

10 See "The Code Is Not the Text."

11 Raley.

12 Ibid.

13 Glazier. Code is addressed throughout Glazier's book but especially in the chapter "Coding Writing, Reading Code," 96–125.

14 An analysis and something of an apologia for Mez's work and theory is provided by: Raley. For more detail, see: "The Code Is Not the Text," above. Sandy Baldwin provides a critique of this earlier paper of mine and also explores a number of ways in which code may enhance the rhetoric of this kind of work, see: Sandy Baldwin, "Process Window: Code Work, Code Aesthetics, Code Poetics," in *Ergodic Poetry: A Special Section of the Cybertext Yearbook 2002*, ed. Loss Pequeño Glazier and John Cayley, Publications of the Research Centre for Contemporary Culture (Jyväskylä: University of Jyväskylä, 2003).

15 Cf. "The Code Is Not the Text."

16 The case for "brokenness" as a feature, not a bug, is made in: Baldwin, "Process Window: Code Work, Code Aesthetics, Code Poetics," 115.

17 See, again, "The Code Is Not the Text."

18 Barthes, *S/Z*. Discussed in: Hayles, *How We Became Posthuman: Virtual Bodies in Cybernetics, Literature, and Informatics*. In *S/Z* Barthes establishes a distinction between texts that are *readerly* and *writerly* texts, those that, respectively, invite interpretation and (re)construction by their reader/authors.

19 Gérard Genette, *Paratexts: Thresholds of Interpretation*, ed. Richard Macksey and Michael Sprinker, trans. Jane E. Lewin, 1st English ed., Literature, Culture, Theory (Cambridge: Cambridge University Press, 1997).

20 Raley. Memmott also refers to this practice as "puncturating" as discussed in: N. Katherine Hayles, *Writing Machines*, Mediawork (Cambridge, MA: MIT Press, 2002), 52.

21 For example, in: Sigmund Freud, "The Unconscious," in *On Metapsychology: The Theory of Psychoanalysis*, ed. Angela Richards, The Penguin Freud Library (Harmondsworth: Penguin Books, 1991).

22 Here I am using "operator" in the mathematical sense. Elsewhere, I have translated this term more loosely, although more evocatively and metaphorically as "a class of operations." Philippe Bootz, "Hypertext: Solution/Dissolution," in *Ergodic Poetry: A Special Section of the Cybertext Yearbook 2002*, ed. Loss Pequeño Glazier and John Cayley, Publications of the Research Centre for Contemporary Culture (Jyväskylä: University of Jyväskylä, 2003), 80, translator's note.

23 See the discussion of Nelsonian hypertext below, and refer to: ibid.

24 At the time I claimed that, when "turned inside out," hypertext "links" were often "nilsk." The as-yet-to-be-more-fully-answered question of "what is inside the link" in link-node hypertext, was often posed in the debates which raged over the long-quiet internet discussion lists. Please refer in particular to the archives of ht_lit. See "Beyond Codexspace" note 5 above.

25 Rosenberg, *Intergrams; The Barrier Frames: Finality Crystal Shunt Curl Chant Quickening Giveaway Stare; Diffractions Through: Thirst Weep Ransack (Frailty) Veer Tide Elegy*. *The Barrier Frames* lacks the characteristic diagram notation in the other Rosenberg pieces cited.

26 This characteristic of a Rosenberg text's "transience" is one of the things that distinguish it in Espen Aarseth's textonomy of cybertext: Aarseth, *Cybertext: Perspectives on Ergodic Literature*.

27 In Ted Nelson's scheme—outlined and discussed below—both flavors of reduction are represented: spatiality as "docuverse" and linearity as "permascroll."

28 Philippe Bootz's discussion of Rosenberg's work has been influential on my own. Bootz, "Hypertext: Solution/Dissolution." In the theoretical part of his paper he writes, "Surely here [as a (hyper)text is unfolded] we have an example of a poetic relationship with language. And this relationship is not established by the author or the reader, but by the device which transforms a global/structure/space into a local/action/temporality." Ibid., 63. When discussing Rosenberg's work, this principle is exemplified, "He [Rosenberg] realized this [a move towards the instantiation of a more general theoretical position like Bootz's] by putting forward what is mimetic hypertext, when seen from the point of view of its unfolding, while at the same time reconfiguring hypertext as the visualization of local processes." Ibid., 65.

29 In fact, of course, it would be preferable to establish a parent "Text" class that was less determinate as to its properties—particularly, for example, its temporal and ergodic properties—than our inherited and historically instituted "Text" object. The historical "Text" class would be redefined as extension of the more abstract parent. This situation, in which prior programming must be de-kludged or entirely rewritten in order to clarify structures and relationships is common in real-world programming.

30 Hayles also finds complexities of temporality represented by remediation, even through the relatively durable material substrate of print, especially in her discussion of Danielewski's *House of Leaves*. Hayles, *Writing Machines*, 115.

31 "It is not a question of a negation of time, of a cessation of time in a present or a simultaneity, but of a different structure, a different stratification of time." Jacques Derrida, "Freud and the Scene of Writing," in *Writing and Difference* (London: Routledge, 1978), 219. Further discussed in: John Cayley, "Inner Workings: Code and Representations of Interiority in New Media Poetics," *dichtung-digital* 29 (2003): n.p. This piece is based on a presentation at the "Language and Encoding" Conference, Buffalo, November, 2002, proceedings edited by Loss Pequeño Glazier.

32 Aarseth, *Cybertext: Perspectives on Ergodic Literature*.

33 The phrase "golden age" refers to a talk by Robert Coover given as a keynote address at the 1999 Digital Arts and Culture (DAC) Conference, Georgia Tech, Atlanta, and published as: Robert Coover, "Literary Hypertext: The Passing of the Golden Age," *Feed* (2000). (Also available at http://nickm.com/vox/golden_age.html.)

34 Two examples of hypertextual features that are non-standard on the web are conditional and two-way linking, both of which can be implemented with client- and/or server-side enhancements to HTML. Refer to the ACM SigWeb for an introduction to technical research on hypertext: http://www.acm.org/sigweb.

35 Nelson, *Literary Machines 93.1*, 2/17.

36 Ibid., front cover.

37 Ibid., 2/14.

38 Nelson introduced this term after the revised publication of *Literary Machines 93.1*. The terms are also used to bring the docuverse together with Nelson's idea for a radical restructuring of data in computing, ZigZag. "Permascroll" and related terms are defined in: Tuomas J. Lukka, "GZigZag Glossary," http://www.nongnu.org/gzz/gl/gl-ns4.html. See also: "GZigZag: A Platform for Cybertext Experiments," in *Cybertext Yearbook 2000*, ed. Markku Eskelinen and Raine Koskimaa, Publications of the Research Centre for Contemporary Culture (Jyväskylä: University of Jyväskylä, 2001); Nelson, Theodor Holm. "Zigzag." http://xanadu.com/zigzag (accessed August 13, 2017).

39 Bootz, "Hypertext: Solution/Dissolution."

40 Hayles, "Translating Media: Why We Should Rethink Textuality," *passim*.

41 This was clear from the discussion after Nelson's keynote talk at the Digital Arts and Culture conference, Brown University, Providence, RI, 2001, when he side-stepped the question of including some record or archive of text-generational programming on the permascroll.

42 These are only those features of Rosenberg's form that I want to highlight here. The diagram syntax he uses would also, for example, be difficult to represent.

43 As set out in: Aarseth, *Cybertext: Perspectives on Ergodic Literature*, 76–97.

44 Nelson, *Literary Machines 93.1*.

45 "Transcopyright" is neatly defined in: Lukka.

46 As in Hayles discussion of Danielewski: Hayles, *Writing Machines*, 115 ff.

47 In *Writing Machines*, ibid., Hayles finds herself, perhaps, at the limits of this process, discussing works such as Tom Phillips' *A Humument* and Mark Danielewski's *House of Leaves*, that are literally print(ed.) without divorcing their manifestation of inherent textual properties: properties that can be represented but not *embodied* in print. These include the represented and remediated temporal complexities of *Leaves*; the *process and practice* of Phillips continuing to alter and prepare *A Humument*; in Talan Memmott's work the reader's ergodic process of revealing textual spaces. Talan Memmott's *Lexia to Perplexia* is a work that can be seriously discussed in "printed out" quotation, as Hayles demonstrates. As we have seen above, it is more difficult to bracket the simultaneities, for example, of a Rosenberg intergram. Hayles' criticism is crucial because it takes the institutions (especially those of literary criticism) to the edge of an abyss, as Edgar leads Gloucester to the cliff's edge in *King Lear*. Mark Z. Danielewski, *House of Leaves*, 2nd ed. (New York: Pantheon Books, 2000); Tom Phillips and W. H. Mallock, *A Humument: A Treated Victorian Novel*, 4th ed. (New York: Thames & Hudson, 2005); Talan Memmott, *From Lexia to Perplexia*, 2000. February. Originally by Trace; then *BeeHive Hypertext/Hypermedia Literary Journal*; then *The Electronic Literature Collection*, vol. 1 (2006).

48 For example, I discuss figures involving compilation and strict logical development at the end of "The Code Is Not the Text."

49 Rosenberg is also acutely aware of the necessity to bring programming into the scene of writing through institutions and tools. He addresses this in: Jim Rosenberg, "Questions About the Second Move," in *Ergodic Poetry: A Special Section of the Cybertext Yearbook 2002*, ed. Loss Pequeño Glazier and John Cayley, Publications of the Research Centre for Contemporary Culture (Jyväskylä: University of Jyväskylä, 2003). Specifically, Rosenberg wants tools that allow him to have working literary objects in progress on his computer desktop: notebooks, as it were, containing signifiers that retain their temporality and programmability in their native state. Note that the computer "desktop" and/or "platform" (and/or the "Web" which not so much of direct concern to Rosenberg) become varieties of metaphoric, if not actual, institutions here, authorizing and enabling the existence (or not) of particular objects with particular properties and methods.

50 Hayles, *Writing Machines*, 110.

51 Code and interiority are taken up in: Cayley, "Inner Workings: Code and Representations of Interiority in New Media Poetics."

Chapter 8

1 For me the unresolved locus classicus of this "problematic interplay" is still the "odd" or "singular" (*singulière*) materiality of the signifier with which Lacan distinguished the letter in his "Seminar on 'The Purloined Letter'" and Derrida's critique of this position's ideality in his "Le Facteur de la Vérité." Jacques Lacan, "Seminar on 'The Purloined Letter'," in *Écrits: The First Complete Edition in*

English (New York and London: Norton, 2007); Jacques Derrida, "Le facteur de la vérité," in *The Post Card* (Chicago: University of Chicago Press, 1987).

2   I aim to stand by such a statement of these circumstances despite the fact that they tend to be seen or recast in quite other terms, as a matter of contrastive ontologies, for example, as has been pointed out to me, in particular, by Francisco J. Ricardo, writing, in a comment on these sentences, "*[A] rchitecture* denotes a field of abstract study of physical structures, whereas *language* implies abstract study of abstract structures. Without the physical, architecture is incomplete; with the physical, language is overdetermined" (private communication, his emphasis). I have no trouble seeing it this way but prefer an inclination in relation to these problems that is engaged with the experiences of aesthetic practitioners and their addressees—how these agents live with(in) language and with(in) media. I pretend that we may learn less about how things are but more about how we may practice and live in our media-constituted diegetic worlds.

I note, in passing and as a matter of more or less subjective opinion, that critics and artists who adopt a more ontological approach find it more difficult, paradoxically, to distinguish, for example, the cultural significance and affect of "word" and "image." Perhaps they may see a "pictorial turn" when presented with material in either language or pictorial representation. Perhaps they may claim, to quote a very recent example, "There is no aesthetic or ethical distinction between word and image." Vanessa Place and Robert Fitterman, *Notes on Conceptualisms* (Brooklyn: Ugly Duckling Presse, 2009), 17. I aim only to examine how we may live and work differently in differing worlds.

3   A presentation of this chapter (then still in-progress) was also given to a workshop of the United Kingdom AHRC-funded "Poetry Beyond Text" project held at the University of Kent, Canterbury, May 9, 2009. A report of this workshop will be made available on the web and will be linked from http://projects.beyondtext.ac.uk/poetrybeyondtext/ (accessed August 2, 2017).

4   It has been pointed out to me that the use of the word "world" in this context immediately invokes the seminal philosophical and art critical work of, in particular, Nelson Goodman, which I have briefly reviewed before writing this note. Nelson Goodman, *Ways of Worldmaking* (Indianapolis: Hackett Pub. Co., 1978). My usages and formulations here are, as already stated, chiefly those of a practitioner. Nonetheless I would be concerned not to contradict Goodman's more far-reaching, analytical treatments of what is clearly related thinking. "World" in 3D graphics is a technical and functional term, a way of briefly referring to the algorithmically derived or modulated images of a particular system in its entirety. Such a system is, by definition, constituted by its media, and its diegesis is guaranteed by the underlying principles of 3D graphics. The media-constituted worlds of my own formulations are more complex than this, especially in terms of their relationship with cultural production, but they are perhaps only minor instances of "worldmaking" as analyzed by Goodman. Where I would engage with Goodman would be in terms of the manifolds of media-constituted worlds that I do assume in some sense generate any and all the worlds of media within which we happen to dwell.

5   W. J. T. Mitchell, "Metapictures," in *Picture Theory: Essays on Verbal and Visual Representation* (Chicago: University of Chicago Press, 1995); Michel Foucault, *This Is Not a Pipe* ["Ceci n'est pas une pipe"], trans. James Harkness (Berkeley: University of California Press, 2008); *Ceci n'est pas une pipe* (Montpellier: Éditions Fata Morgana, 1973). In Foucault trans. Harkness, the picture is erroneously referred to as dated 1926 and as bearing the famous caption as its title rather than the more usual, *La trahison des images*, 1929. David Sylvester et al., *René Magritte: Catalogue Raisonné*, 5 vols. (Houston and London: Menil Foundation; Philip Wilson Publishers, 1992), 1.331–2. CR 303.

6   This phrase is intended to invoke one of the better, published attempts to identify the specific and genuinely novel properties and methods of artistic practice in digital and new media, although it should be noted that the use of "language" here is in its now common extended figurative sense that approximates, in fact, to "rhetoric" and where the practices under discussion are rarely, if ever, poetic or literary per se. This is the "language" of the "linguistic turn" applied to mediated visual, performance and fine art practice. See: Manovich.

7   J. David Bolter and Richard Grusin, *Remediation: Understanding New Media* (Cambridge, MA: MIT Press, 2000).

8   This argument is elaborated in: Cayley, "Lens: The Practice and Poetics of Writing in Immersive VR: A Case Study with Maquette."

9   Still today, for example, writing has authority if it is finished, printed, and published, although even in the academy there is a slow shift toward "if it could be printed then in *may* garner authority." If it is finished and inscribed in such a way that it *could be* printed out, then it may become subject to judgment even if this "printing out" never actually occurs (a thesis submitted on CD-ROM). Perhaps the *current* workings of these distinctions become clearest when we print (out) what is on a screen. The relationship to authorization is shown by the common requirement to print "etickets." What is on the screen is not a ticket until it is printed; it is not yet the authoritative representation of a transaction. We must still perform a number of rituals to make an eticket valid, usually including but not limited to its having been "printed out."

10 The apotheosis of this admittedly useful corrective for the field of digitally mediated literature is: Matthew G. Kirschenbaum, *Mechanisms: New Media and the Forensic Imagination* (Cambridge, MA: MIT Press, 2008). Although Kirschenbaum's book does an excellent job of describing and delineating the underlying materiality of computation in contemporary culture as well as situating this necessarily embodied practice historically, the book rarely achieves critical traction in relation to the instances of digital literature that it explicitly addresses, and I would argue that this is partly a function of the general misapprehension of the relationship between language and media that is explored in this chapter.

11 I am aware that my use of "media" in this context is somewhat unusual and may be problematic for some readers, especially for art historians and philosophers. Although I do not intend to conflate or confuse the notions of "medium" or "media" (as in art history's "mixed media") on the one hand, and the post-McLuhan usages of "media," I do want us to consider the cultural

practices of painting and their material supports as a system of media that is comprised, among other things, of media devices of various kinds, including paintings. This will, I hope, become clearer as my argument proceeds.

12 Notice how we prefer the metaphor of speech here. Somehow a picture would have trouble "writing." This should probably be "seen" as one of the vestiges of logocentrism. Note that Mitchell entitles the section of his metapictures chapter that is devoted to *La trahison des images* "*Talking Metapictures.*" Mitchell, "Metapictures," 64. My emphasis. Another recent example is the title of an *October* article, also briefly cited below: Harry Cooper, "Speak, Painting: Word and Device in Early Johns," *October* 127 (2009): 49–76.

13 Just to be clear: I am speaking of *these*—after all quite typical, expository— words. I am fully aware, as should be obvious from the context, that certain words/instances of language call for specific media.

14 Foucault's initial move, a consideration of the painting as calligram, would have run counter to the inclination I identify. But this was a misdirection, and he found himself unravelling (Harkness' doubtful translation) or undoing (*le calligramme défait*) something that had never been made as such, as a calligram, that is. Foucault's own discussion of the caption, the space between the image and word (see below), is the undoing of something that was never "done up" or "written out" in the first place. Foucault, *This Is Not a Pipe*, 28; Cooper, 57.

15 Roland Barthes, "The Photographic Message," in *Image Music Text* (London: Fontana Press, 1977); "Rhetoric of the Image," in *Image Music Text* (London: Fontana Press, 1977). Mitchell does not cite Barthes in his *Picture Theory* discussion of metapicture. He suggests later that Barthes's analysis is chiefly at the service of "connections between semiotic structures and ideology," whereas I find Barthes's analysis pertinent to cultural practice. W. J. T. Mitchell, *Picture Theory: Essays on Verbal and Visual Representation* (Chicago: University of Chicago Press, 1995), 86n7.

16 Barthes, "The Photographic Message," 17. Emphasis in original.

17 Ibid., 29.

18 This relationship is also, of course, also often designated and theorized as indexical. See, *inter alia*, Rosalind E. Krauss, "Notes on the Index," *October* 3–4 (1977): 68–81; 58–67. It is, moreover and by the way, less characterized by the imaginary—" 'magical' fictional"—than even the relationship of cinema to the world due to photography's strange, momentary and, crucially, past relation to human temporality. Barthes, "Rhetoric of the Image," 45. As Barthes pointed out, the photograph is an index, not of "what is" but "what *was*" and/or what we could not have seen ourselves, and this makes it a new type of object in our diegetic worlds.

    Later, in *Camera Lucida*—which is more about the relationship of "the Photograph" to a particular subject and to subjectivity as instituted by cultural practices—Barthes nonetheless goes so far as to say, "By nature, the Photograph (...) has something tautological about it: a pipe, here, is always and intractably a pipe." [!] *Camera Lucida* [La Chambre Claire], trans. Richard Howard, First American paperback ed. (New York: Hill and Wang, 1982), 5.

19 Barthes, "Rhetoric of the Image," 45.
20 Ibid., 51.
21 Barthes, "The Photographic Message," 17. Emphasis in original.
22 Ibid.
23 Ibid., 18.
24 The phrase "syntagmatic 'flow'" is also from Barthes who uses diegesis in a sense that is close to my own as compared with the discourses of film and narrative. Barthes, "Rhetoric of the Image," 51. If symbolic elements can form a series that appear to be what Barthes calls "syntagm as nature" and I would say is a part of the same (media-constituted) world, then this establishes (coherent) diegesis. But for meaning to emerge, this circumstance also demands a fundamental break or "tear" (also in Barthes) that is a requisite of symbolic practice, of language in process. Barthes's thinking along these lines produces this superb and challenging final sentence to his "Rhetoric of the Image,"

> Without wishing to infer too quickly from the image to semiology in general, one can nevertheless venture that the world of total meaning is torn internally (structurally) between system as culture and syntagm as nature: the works of mass communications all combine, through diverse and diversely successful dialectics, the fascination of nature, that of story, diegesis, syntagm, and the intelligibility of a culture, withdrawn into a few discontinuous symbols which men 'decline' in the shelter of their living speech. Ibid.

25 Barthes, "The Photographic Message," 18.
26 I am grateful to Francisco J. Ricardo for encouraging me to bring John Baldessari into this discussion. Doing so is particularly fortuitous in that Baldessari was an artist-curator/consultant for "Magritte and Contemporary Art," at the Los Angeles County Museum of Art November 19, 2006–March 4, 2007. Catalogue: Stephanie Barron and Michel Draguet, *Magritte and Contemporary Art: The Treachery of Images* (Los Angeles and Ghent: Los Angeles County Museum of Art; Ludion, 2006).
27 Examples can be consulted in: Coosje Van Bruggen, *John Baldessari* (New York: Rizzoli, 1990), 138–141. *Yellow (With Onlookers)*, 1986; *Bloody Sundae*, 1987; and *Three Red Paintings*, 1988.
28 For example: *Yellow Harmonica (With Turn)*, 1987. Reproduced in: ibid., 161.
29 For example: The Dupress Series: Person Climbing Exterior Wall of Tall Building / Person on Ledge of Tall Building / Person on Girders of Unfinished Tall Building, 2003. Reproduced in: Marie de Brugerolle, *John Baldessari: From Life* (Nimes and Paris: Carré d'Art_Musée d'art contemporain; École nationale supérieure des beaux-art de Paris, 2005), 144–145.
30 As if to prove this, Magritte has also painted a version of his *Treachery* on an easel in a room where there also dwells another slightly more abstract, equally troublesome "pipe." *Les Deux mystères* (1966, Catalogue raisonné 1038) reproduced as plate 4 in: Foucault, *This Is Not a Pipe*.
31 Of course, it could be a "wall" and, in fact, the wall in the later painting, *Les Deux mystères*, against which a "pipe" is also suspended, is painted in a similar nondescript, all but textureless manner. This background, however, is determined as "wall" by the figurative "wooden floor" that abuts it. Yet even in this painting there is strong ambiguity as to whether its larger pipe is

suspended from (how?), painted on, or floating within the so-called, so-painted "wall." This relationship of all but purely notional "wall" to the projection-surface "walls" of the Cave is suggestive. Both instances of "wall" exist and, at the same time, do not exist for the purposes of poiesis in their respective media.

32 Because, in the diegesis of the painting, it would be occluded by some measure of beige "fog." Note that the term "fog" is a technical term in 3D graphics: "A rendering technique that can be used to simulate atmospheric effects such as haze, fog, and smog by fading object colors to a background color based on distance from the viewer, giving a depth cue." David Shriener et al., *OpenGL Programming Guide: Fourth Edition: The Official Guide to Learning OpenGL, Version 1.4* (Boston: Addison-Wesley, 2004), 721.

33 I prefer to approach the issues that concern me directly through Foucault, but compare: Mitchell, *Picture Theory: Essays on Verbal and Visual Representation*, 70; Cooper, 56n15; 57. Both Mitchell and Cooper quote from the passages in Foucault that I discuss, although using Harkness's translation unaltered, where its slight misdirections are less crucial to their arguments.

34 Foucault, *This Is Not a Pipe*, 28.

35 This is my own translation, modifying and improving Harkness. Cf. *Ceci n'est pas une pipe*, 34; *This Is Not a Pipe*, 28.

36 My own, slightly interpretative but careful translation of:

> La petite bande mince, incolore et neutre qui, dans le dessin de Magritte sépare le texte et la figure, il faut y voir un creux, une région incertaine et brumeuse qui sépare maintenant la pipe flottant dans son ciel d'image, et le piétinement terrestre des mot défilant sur leur ligne successive. Encore est-ce trop de dire qu'il y a un vide ou une lacune: c'est plutôt une absence d'espace, un effacement de 'lieu commun' entre les signes de l'écriture et les lignes de l'image. *Ceci n'est pas une pipe*, 34.

37 Although I believe that the reader should be able to follow and visualize the work in my prose, an actual translation of *The Treachery* into immersive artificial 3D graphics for the Cave has been produced as a maquette, "*This Is (Not) Writing*," and is available to download, along with previewing software that will render it (without immersion of course) on standard personal computers, from: http://programmatology.shadoof.net/?notwriting (accessed August 13, 2017).

38 For some readers, the conception of an object graphically distorted like this may evoke ostensibly parallel discussions of anamorphic images such as the well-known and often-discussed anamorphic skull in Holbein's *The Ambassadors*. (This image recently adorned the cover of: Mark B. N. Hansen, *New Philosophy for New Media* [Cambridge, MA: MIT Press, 2006].) There might seem to be a similar problem concerning the point at which the distorted *image* ceases to be a representation of what it represents. However, in the first place the anamorphic transformation of the image is studied, deliberate, and enforces a break with the normal diegetic world of image-viewing. An out-of-the-ordinary point of view must be assumed in relation to the distorted image in order to see it as a normalized or construable optical representation. In the circumstances described in our thought experiment, the rotation of the objects is entirely regular, easy to describe, and in keeping with

the way that objects are viewed in space. Simply walking around the objects would produce the same effects. Moreover, in the case of linguistic material, the effacement of the representation is catastrophic rather than continuous. Neither is it entirely or even primarily a matter of judgment. There is a *necessary* relation between an inscription and the surface-that-is-no-surface. In our thought experiment, the pipe is in fact undergoing anamorphic processes of transformation—in 3D graphics terms—but these are transformations that we understand and construe in terms of the human optical experience of objects in space. It simply happens to be the case that there are few such experiences of inscription in "real-world" space. (A sign mounted so as to spin on a mast would be an example and note that, basically, such a sign is simply ignored except during those moments when it can be read.) In the artificial world of the Cave, it might be argued, for example, that if you rotate an inscription in front of a human point of view it "should" always simply look the same—or least remain readable—to that point of view (it appears *not* to rotate). In the system's frame of reference, the inscription-as-object would be rotating, but it would obey the constraints of the phenomenology of inscriptions addressed to humans rather than that of optically rendered 3D objects. For certain of my earlier works in the Cave, I instituted such a "phenomenology" of letters in space (although without theorizing it in this way) in that I had all individual letters (my "atoms" of graphic inscription) rotate continuously to "face" the primary tracked point of view as it moved through the graphics world. From the phenomenologist's point of view, this is a kludge, a workaround. Perhaps what we really require are linguistic objects that are always equally readable regardless of the position from which they are viewed and without their having, at least conceptually, to transform in any way—to rotate, translate, or scale—in order to maintain the properties of readability that they were given when they were inscribed.

39 In one interpretation that is also suggestive of the different ways in which language as inscription relates to media, this is simply a particularly stark and clear instance of a phenomenon originally pointed out to me by the historian of Chinese art, Robert Harrist. A *representation* of writing should not be readable. If it is readable then it is no longer a *representation* of writing, it *is* writing. See: Robert E. Harrist Jr., "*Book from the Sky* at Princeton: Reflections on Scale, Sense, and Sound," in *Persistence | Transformation: Text as Image in the Art of Xu Bing*, ed. Jerome Silbergeld and Dora C. Y. Ching (Princeton, NJ: P. Y. and Kinmay W. Tang Center for East Asian Art, 2006), 35–37.

One can also see how catastrophic shifts back and forth from the representation of writing to writing itself would be likely to ally themselves with breaks in media-constituted diegesis if one thinks back to photography and imagines the photo-naturalistic depiction of a room containing a table strewn with of sheets writing that is "out of focus" in terms of depth of field. If the writing were, through some form of artifice, brought into focus, and assuming it was large enough to be readable, it would break both the diegesis of photo-naturalism while simultaneously and suddenly addressing us as writing.

40   In fact, of course, when we do this, we will be "seeing the object" projected on another surface which may also have a spectral background projected onto it.

Chapter 9

1   Throughout this chapter, I refer to the Google "corpus," implicitly treating the inscribed text that is addressed by the Google indexing engines as if it were a body of material similar to or commensurate with other textual corpora such as might be compiled into a particular author's corpus or the corpora put together and studied by corpus linguists such as the Brown Corpus, the Corpus of Contemporary American English, the British National Corpus, and the American National Corpus.

2   Whenever I use the word "with" in this context, my intention is to highlight the underlying, now chiefly archaic, sense of "against" that was once more active in the Anglo-Saxon preposition, although we do still both work and fight *with* others. This negative apotropaic inclination of "with" is preserved by contemporary English in words like "withhold," "withdraw," and "withstand."

3   "Flarf," the coinage attributed to Gary Sullivan, is a name for a practice of poetic writing. There exists a "Flarf(ist) Collective" of writers, mostly poets, who have exchanged and published work under its aegis. (See the Flarf feature in the excellent online *Jacket Magazine*, Jacket 30, July 2006, http://jacketmagazine.com/30/index.shtml [accessed August 2, 2017].) Wikipedia describes its aesthetic as "dedicated to the exploration of 'the inappropriate'" (as of: February 16, 2011) and this seems right to me. It's a significant poetic movement of the late twentieth, early twenty-first centuries for which, personally and critically, I have a high regard. However, Flarf is now also closely associated with methods of composition that make extensive use of internet searches engines since they are, clearly, well adapted for gathering large amounts of "inappropriate" linguistic material. The association is unfortunate since there are many, many other ways to explore the inappropriate and gather relevant exempla. The identification of Flarf with Google-mining is, itself, inappropriate Flarf. At this point in my argument, my aim is simply to contrast the Flarfist use of Google-as-grab-bag versus a sustained aesthetic engagement with the cultural vectors that Google both offers and denies. Engagement at the level of computation may be a key to making and maintaining this distinction.

4   Michel Eyquem de Montaigne, "Of the Institution and Education of Children," in *Literary and Philosophical Essays: French, German and Italian*, The Harvard Classics (New York: P. F. Collier & Son Company, 1910).

5   European Science Foundation (ESF) workshop: "Neuroesthetics: When Art and the Brain Collide," September 24–25, 2009, IULM, Milan, Italy.

6   Chrisley's presentation at the conference was titled "A cognitive approach to the esthetic experience," but his introduction of the "edge of chaos" was largely anecdotal, deriving from experiments with robotic cognition. Chrisley was then a Reader in Philosophy at the University of Sussex.

7   Markov models, processes, chains—named for the Russian mathematician,
     Andrey Markov (1856–1922)—provide formal descriptions for systems with
     a finite number of elements in successive states. Using such a model, we only
     have to know the relative frequency of the elements in a system in order to
     be able to generate further sequences of these elements, probabilistically, that
     will be, as it were, characteristic of the system. These models can be applied
     to language, taking any distinct linguistic element—letter, phoneme, syllable,
     word, phrase, etc.—as the units being considered. A sequence of n elements
     considered as a unit is known as an ngram or n-gram. A three-word phrase
     may be treated as an n-gram, and if we search for such a phrase, double-
     quoted, in Google, we get a "count" that can be used as a relative frequency
     for that phrase within the domain of the Google-indexed internet "corpus"
     of linguistic tokens. Refinements of such purely statistical language models
     are now proven to be remarkably powerful, and underlie, for example, much
     automated translation. The existence of the internet-as-corpus and its Google
     search boxes puts such linguistic modeling in the hands of everyone. Google
     and its rival service providers are aware of non-venal uses for this data.
     Recently there was a short, rather dismissive piece on the Google labs: Books
     Ngram Viewer (http://ngrams.googlelabs.com/) in the *London Review of
     Books*. Jenny Diski, "Short Cuts," *London Review of Books* 33, no. 2 (2011:
     20). A *Science* article is referred to that describes work underlying the Ngram
     viewer in more detail. Jean-Baptiste Michel et al., "Quantitative Analysis of
     Culture Using Millions of Digitized Books," *Science* 331, no. 6014 (2011:
     176–182). Another contextually relevant discussion of Markov chains can
     be found in: Noah Wardrip-Fruin, *Expressive Processing: Digital Fictions,
     Computer Games, and Software Studies* (Cambridge, MA: MIT Press, 2009),
     203–205.

8   Apart from specifics discussed here, I will cite two sensational sociopolitical
     examples. First, there is Google's dubiously or *un*principled accommodation
     of Chinese state censorship as a Chinese language news provider in February
     2004, as an investor in the Chinese search site Baidu, by voluntarily blocking
     politically sensitive searches in January 2006, and its subsequent *purportedly*
     principled retreat from the Chinese search "market" in 2010. John Battelle,
     *The Search: How Google and Its Rivals Rewrote the Rules of Business and
     Transformed Our Culture*, updated with new chapter in this edition (New
     York: Portfolio, 2006); Bianca Bosker, "Google Shuts Down China Search,
     Redirects Users to Hong Kong," *Huffington Post*, March 23, 2010, updated
     May 25, 2011; Jonathan Watts, "China's Internet Crackdown Forced Google
     Retreat," *The Guardian*, January 13, 2010. Second, there is the purported
     manipulation of the type-ahead suggestions provided by Google Instant.
     Bianca Bosker, "Google Instant Blocks Sexy Searches," *Huffington Post*,
     September 9, 2010, updated May 25, 2011.

9   For one simple example, Microsoft's *Bing* treats line endings differently. Line
     endings (e.g., carriage returns) don't break sequences as they do for Google.
     For neither engine, however, is this a recognition of differences or distinctions
     that might be significant for poetics. The fact that we can be fairly certain
     that differential treatment of line endings is technical and *in the service of
     commerce* rather than poetic or, for example, rhetorical, speaks volumes

concerning Google as an engine of mis- or undirected culture formation. Its undoubtedly "powerful" forces are self-trammeled by concerns to which Google is strategically blind and to which we, as producers of culture with other motivations, seem already to have become blind. If we fail to start noticing these motivated distinctions now, it will soon be too late since they will cease to exist. In the ontology of software, if an object is not implemented, it cannot have instances.

A further note on line endings: It is interesting to remark that although line endings break word (or token) sequences in Google's indexing of web pages—chiefly HTML or HTML-derived content—token sequences are *not* broken by corresponding punctuation or tagging when Google indexes the predominantly pdf-derived content of Google Books. This is simply one example of many conditions demonstrating that when you search these two domains, you search them differently with no explicit signal of this fact. The underlying software is taking away any care that you might have had for the way in which you are searching. If your relationship to the corpus is transactional and you understand the nature of the underlying contract, this is fine. My point is that now, when you search Google, you increasingly treat it as if you are searching all of inscribed culture. Once again, this is fine, if you realize what you are doing—research that is abbreviated, shorthand, provisional, or pragmatic for example—and yet after having qualified your understanding of the scope of the Google corpus, do you also take responsibility for your failure to know any details of the procedures by which it undertakes the search on your behalf, *how* that search addresses the corpus, the manner in which the results are delivered, and so on?

10 And ultimately or more accurately: whoever or whatever *owns* Google.

11 See below. Daniel C. Howe adds, "Of course Google automatically/ procedurally indexes our pages/content, yet makes it illegal or at least, they would claim, a violation of their terms of service for us to do the same to them."

12 Daniel C. Howe adds, "in tiny droplets," that are regulated by: Google.

13 The fact that we accept—pragmatically, gratefully—Google's indexing of the corpus represented by inscribed textuality on the internet is the sign, I believe, of an order-of-magnitude shift in the scale of the cultural archive and our engagement with it as humans. I provide brief remarks on these issues here, acutely aware that they deserve extensive and detailed consideration. In a sense the world and the "knowledge" or "culture" that is in it—call it "content"—has not and will not change. Human life is what it is. Nonetheless we tend to agree that our ability to archive this content in order to make it recordable and manipulable has radically changed during the modern period. Scholars of the age of Francis Bacon began to lose hold of any sense that they might read and thus know "everything." In the maturity of print culture, we have long ago lost sight of being able to read or "know" everything in a particular discipline, let alone "everything" per se. However, we were wont to believe that all inscribed textuality might be collected in libraries or traditional archives and that, at the very least, a "union catalogue," the product of human labor, would be able to give us access to any necessary article of knowledge, with universities curating and signaling the originality of purported

contributions to this sum of content. However, just as the efflorescence of print made it literally impossible to read everything, the explosion of content-creation that is enabled by programmable and networked media now makes it literally impossible for humans to *index* everything in their archives. Humans are already, now, not able to create a catalogue of the articles of culture that they have, collectively, created.

Instead, humans write software, processes that will index these archives. These processes will reflect human culture back to its maker-consumers and consumer-makers. This is already what Google does for us. At first it seemed that the company did this almost gratuitously, more or less as a function of Silicon Valley utopianism and naivety. Now this intensely, importantly cultural service is fundamentally skewed and twisted by commerce, by a requirement to generate advertising revenues that are dependent on the most advanced forms of capitalism. These circumstances may have been all but inevitable, but the time for decisions has come. What computational processes do we want to create and have running for us, in order to index or otherwise represent for us the contents of the cultures that we are making?

Especially in questions following her presentation, "Digital Archives: The Missing Context," http://www.brown.edu/Conference/animating/content/documents/SmithRumseyabstract.pdf for the "Animating Archives: Making New Media Matter" conference held at Brown University, December 3–5, 2009, http://www.brown.edu/Conference/animating/index.html. Abby Smith Rumsey, Director of the Scholarly Communication Institute, University of Virginia Library spoke cogently to these issues.

14 Saturday October 7, 2009.

15 Clearly, my underlying argument resonates with traditionalist Humanities anxieties about scholarship and the effects on scholarship of the tools and resources which Google has suddenly provided. Geoffrey Nunberg, "Google's Book Search: A Disaster for Scholars," *The Chronicle of Higher Education*, August 31, 2009. However, I am not so much concerned with the preservation of cultural standards. I am entirely content that institutions should change. I just don't think that such change should be at the whim of unacknowledged, ill-considered, and venal forces. The cultural vectors opened up by Google will only ever be able to change our institutions coherently and generatively if they remain susceptible to the values and standards of *all* our institutions, not only our mercantile and marketing institutions.

16 Daniel C. Howe suggests additional reference to: Jonathan Lethem, "The Ecstasy of Influence: A Plagiarism," *Harper's Magazine*, February 2007. More recently there is also the novel-as-manifesto-of-appropriation: David Shields, *Reality Hunger: A Manifesto* (New York: Alfred A. Knopf, 2010). The work of the late American novelist Kathy Acker was known for its techniques of appropriation, not to say plagiarism. In the story "Pierre Menard, Author of Don Quixote" Jorge Luis Borges imagines a French writer, Menard, who is so able to immerse himself in the earlier work that he "re-creates" it word for word. Recent gestures in the realm of Conceptual Poetics are relevant here. Kenneth Goldsmith's *Day* consists of a straightforward transcription of the September 1, 2000 issue of the *New York Times* within the format and design of a standard 836-page book. Kenneth Goldsmith, *Day* (New Barrington: The

Figures, 2003). In a further conceptual gesture, Kent Johnson appropriated this work as his "own" with the connivance of Buffalo-based small press Blazevox by simply pasting over all references to Goldsmith, replacing them with a Johnson overlay. I possess a copy of the altered book, signed by the (latter) publisher.

17 I could, of course, do this in other domains using the resources of other institutions, but the thought of what this would mean is overwhelming—a life-changing shift into research on natural language, with single-minded devotion to finding or building the databases one would need. Google promises me an accessible corpus and even tells me that it is always already mine and everyone else's—in good net-utopian terms—but then denies me service at crucial moments when I am beginning to build a poetic.

18 Extracts from Google's Terms of Service, supplied by Daniel C. Howe:

> 2.1 In order to use the Services, you must first agree to the Terms. You may not use the Services if you do not accept the Terms ....
>
> 2.2 You can accept the Terms by:
>
> (A) clicking to accept or agree to the Terms, where this option is made available to you by Google in the user interface for any Service; or
>
> (B) by actually using the Services. In this case, you understand and agree that Google will treat your use of the Services as acceptance of the Terms from that point onwards ....
>
> 4.5 You acknowledge and agree that while Google may not currently have set a fixed upper limit on the number of transmissions you may send or receive through the Services or on the amount of storage space used for the provision of any Service, such fixed upper limits may be set by Google at any time, at Google's discretion.
>
> 5.3 You agree not to access (or attempt to access) any of the Services by any means other than through the interface that is provided by Google, unless you have been specifically allowed to do so in a separate agreement with Google. You specifically agree not to access (or attempt to access) any of the Services through any automated means (including use of scripts or web crawlers) and shall ensure that you comply with the instructions set out in any robots.txt file present on the Services.

19 The following text is based on a short piece by Samuel Beckett that eventually became, as a final text in English, three fragments from: Samuel Beckett, *How It Is* [Comment c'est], trans. Samuel Beckett (New York: Grove Press, 1964). I searched Google for successively longer sequences of double-quote-delimited words from these fragments with the qualifiers: -Beckett -Beckett's -Beckett's (with prime and apostrophe) looking for pages on which the sequences occurred but are not associated with Beckett. The small letters beside each phrase may now be keyed to one of the webpages from which the phrases are hereby deemed to be quoted as at least cached by Google on Saturday February 15, 2010. They are not, that is, quoted from Beckett. [a]http://books.google.com/books?id=RTRorA6RK-oC&pg=PA49&lpg=PA49&dq=%22blu

e+and+white+of+sky%22; [b]myhyggelig.blogspot.com/2009/12/moment-still.
html; [c]gapersblock.com/mechanics/2009/06/30/inside-a-toxic-tour/; [d]legacygt.
com/forums/showthread.php?t=130524&goto=newpost; [e]matpringle.
blogspot.com/; [f]www.nrl.navy.mil/content.php?P=03REVIEW195; [g]www.
mattcutts.com/blog/gmail-inbox-zero/; [h]www.theshadowbox.net/forum/index.
php?topic=10610.30; [i]www.mountzion.org/johnbunyan/text/bun-caution.
htm; [j]ntl.matrix.com.br/pfilho/html/lyrics/m/mr_blue.txt; [k]iceagelanguage.
com/Ducks/ducks_part1.pdf; [l]cucc.survex.com/expo/smkridge/204/uworld.
html; [m]www.redroom.com/blog/ericka-lutz/opening-and-closing; [n]http://
www.fibromyalgia-symptoms.org/forums/Fibromyalgia_Support_Groups/
Stomach_pain_and_period_pain_/; [o]http://www.archive.org/stream/
soundandthefurya013056mbp/soundandthefurya013056mbp_djvu.txt; [p]www.
theinsider.com/news/928384_Thanks_for_the_Laughs_Harvey; [q]http://books.
google.com/books?id=ti_rI-aYuw4C&pg=PA337&lpg=PA337&dq=%22the
re%27s+no+sense+in+that+now%22; [r]books.google.com/books?id=LCf0VP
aT1wwC&pg=PA213&lpg=PA213&dq=%22been+none+for+a+long+time+
now%22; [s]www.aypsite.org/forum/topic.asp?TOPIC_ID=5166; [t]secure.bebo.
com/Profile.jsp?MemberId=1471591674; [u]solpadeine.net/acetone/lyrics/cindy.
html; [v]www.haaretz.com/hasen/spages/1076221.html; [w]books.google.com/
books?id=gconvZ-DRLsC&pg=PA121&lpg=PA121&dq=%22thirst+the+t
ongue%22; [x]www.flickr.com/photos/32296433@N07/3558411711/; [y]http://
www.popmonk.com/quotes/challenge.htm; [z]http://t2.thai360.com/index.
php?/topic/48834-isan-tawan-daeng-re-visited/; [aa]http://mshester.blogspot.
com/2008/03/winter-you-are-finished.html; [bb]en.wikipedia.org/wiki/The_Image.

This text also comprises the final part of "The Image," reproduced in
a corrected translation in: *The Complete Short Prose, 1929–1989*, ed. S. E.
Gontarski (New York: Grove Press, 1995). Despite the explanation given in
the notes, pp. 283–284, it seems bizarre to me that the more or less complete
version as found in *How It Is*, pp. 28–31 is not preferred for "The Image."
Certainly, for the final part of the piece, used here, I much prefer Beckett's own
renderings, for example, "I stay there no more thirst the tongue goes in the
mouth closes it must be a straight line now it's over it's done I've had the image"
rather than Edith Fournier's "I stay like this no more thirst the tongue goes in
the mouth closes it must be a straight line now it's done I've done the image."

20 In actual fact, I made this text by first alphabetically sorting the gathered
sequences and only then rearranging them as little as possible in order to
provide some kind of relatively coherent diegesis.

21 This preliminary piece from *The Readers Project* may be accessed from http://
thereadersproject.org.

22 There is a great deal that could be written about *The Readers Project*: about
how it operates and engages literary aesthetics from a critical or theoretical
perspective, most of which would not be entirely relevant to the present
discussion. However, it may be worth noting and commenting briefly on
this sense of "proximate." A proximate or neighboring word may be one
that is contiguous with a reference word. In linguistics, such a word, for
example, collocates with the reference word if it follows it in the line of the
syntagm, in the metonymic dimension as Roman Jakobson called it. Another
notion of proximity—in the complementary metaphoric dimension, that of

replacement—would see words such as synonyms or antonyms as (virtually) proximate to particular words of reference in the text. However, proximity or neighborhood may also be defined, in *The Readers Project,* in terms of the *typographic,* and this neglected dimension of textuality reveals itself, in our aesthetic analysis, as vital to, if not constitutive of, reading. (Typography is not, perhaps, neglected as a *graphic* art, but it is, arguably, neglected as an art of reading, as a literary art, *sensu stricto.*) Specifically, readers in the project currently have access to databases of information about all the actual word pairs in a text that they are "reading" combined with any (and all) third words existing in the text. Clearly the vast majority of these three-word combinations will not occur anywhere in the text itself as contiguous syntagms. These sequences of three words we call "perigrams" to distinguish them both from "bigrams" and "trigrams" in standard Markov analysis. Once we have derived a text's perigrams, we then use Google to find counts for their frequencies in the internet corpus, and (for the moment) discard any perigrams with zero counts. This allows the readers to follow the standard syntagmatic line but to check arbitrary typographically neighboring words to see whether they would form a perigram that occurs in the natural language of the Google-accessible corpus. If they do, a particular reader may be allowed to follow the alternate syntagmatic line of reading that it has discovered in its typographic neighborhood.

Clearly "proximity" may be redefined in accordance with other features of linguistic items, including, for example, orthographic features. Thus the "mesostic" reader mentioned above looks for words containing particular letters and considers them "proximate" if they contain a letter that it requires to read-while-spelling. In point of fact, the current mesostic reader takes further cognizance of physical typographic proximity and also what one might call the relative "perigrammatic proximity" (just described) of two words that it might be about to read, for example, and that both contain the letter it needs to spell. It will prefer to read a word that is more proximate in the maximum number of dimensions. John Cayley, and Daniel C. Howe. *The Readers Project.* 2009. http://thereadersproject.org (accessed August 13, 2017). A more extensive methodological and computational introduction to *The Readers Project* was, at the time of writing, in final stages of review for Siggraph 2011 and is now published as: Daniel C. Howe and John Cayley, "*The Readers Project:* Procedural Agents and Literary Vectors," *Leonardo* 44, no. 4 (2011): 317–324.

23 See above. A normal Markov model applied to language is only concerned with the syntagmatic dimension of language and takes no account of any typographic structure that it may have. The above definition of "perigrams" in *The Readers Project* takes some account of typography and thus complicates the standard Markov model.

Chapter 10

1 Confucius (= Kong Fuzi), *Confucius: The Great Digest, the Unwobbling Pivot, the Analects,* trans. Ezra Pound (New York: New Directions, 1969), 20. The

quoted text is Pound's ideogrammic gloss for the character *cheng* (Wade-Giles: *ch'eng*) often translated as "sincerity." See also: *The Cantos*, LXXVI, 468/474.

2   N. Katherine Hayles, *Electronic Literature: New Horizons for the Literary*, Ward-Phillips Lectures in English Language and Literature (Notre Dame: University of Notre Dame, 2008).

3   Alan Liu, *The Laws of Cool: Knowledge Work and the Culture of Information* (Chicago: University of Chicago Press, 2004).

4   A representative quote: "Electronic literature extends the traditional functions of print literature in creating recursive feedback loops between explicit articulation, conscious thought, and embodied sensorimotor knowledge .... While print literature also operates in this way, electronic literature performs the additional function of entwining human ways of knowing with machine cognitions." N. Katherine Hayles, "Electronic Literature: What Is It?" in *Electronic Literature: New Horizons for the Literary* (Notre Dame: University of Notre Dame, 2008), 135. For "dynamic heterarchies" see: N. Katherine Hayles "Distributed Cognition in/at Work: Strickland, Lawson Jaramillo, and Ryan's *slippingglimpse*," *Frame* 21, no. 1 (2008): 15–29.

5   Liu, 179.

6   Ibid., 3.

7   Ibid., 400, note 8.

8   I am happy to see that this phrase has now been taken up quite widely in the literature, not least in Hayles's new book (Hayles, "Electronic Literature: What Is It?") and, for example, in: Peter Gendolla and Jörgen Schäfer, eds., *The Aesthetics of Net Literature: Writing, Reading and Playing in Programmable Media*, Media Upheavals (Bielefeld: Transcript, 2007). The phrase can also be shortened to "writing in programmable media" since *programming* enables *network*. The mark of an explicit relationship with practices of coding will continue to enrich and to specify our literary practices in these media, but it is not yet clear to me that programmability and processing give rise to *all* their distinguishing characteristics, or, for that matter, operate *significantly* or *affectively* in every example of those practices to which we turn our attention. Programming enables the network but cultural production on the net does not always practice coding and neither does every instance of writing in digital media. As a term, "writing digital media" attempts an abbreviated reference to this situation by encapsulating the conjunction of networked *and* programmable media, without specifying the precise grammar that underlies this conjunction. I am also anxious to note, in passing, that I consider coding to be a distinct cultural practice, distinct, that is from writing, for example.

9   In email communication, Aden Evens has pointed out that my use of "form" as in "persistent form" differs from a stricter usage that would more closely ally the term with abstract form or, for example, the "concepts" underlying conceptual art, whereas my persistent form is—I acknowledge this and the point is brought into my argument explicitly below—implicated with particular (literary) material cultural manifestations, particular media that are able to bear particular forms without, however, determining "content" or its significance and affect. I agree that these distinctions require some elaboration beyond the scope of this chapter. Evens writes, "form is what the concept determines, whereas materiality manifests this form but also exceeds it. In

'traditional' artworks, this excess is precisely what makes the work great. That is, the formal is what can be fully captured by the digital, it is what gets preserved as 'information' " (email communication, August 4, 2008). My persistent form is not precisely this excess, but it would enable such excess to survive the work and its concept. I believe that the final paragraphs of Terry Harpold's interesting extended gloss on "hypertext" refer to these deep problems of form in the practices of writing (in) digital media—of form in inherited vs. programmable media, I might say. Terry Harpold, "Hypertext," in *Glossalalia*, ed. Julian Wolfreys and Harun Karim Thomas (New York: Routledge, 2003).

10 Liu, 389.

11 Jacques Derrida, "The Word Processor," in *Paper Machine* (Stanford, CA: Stanford University Press, 2005), 25.

12 Ibid.

13 Jacques Derrida, "The Book to Come," in *Paper Machine* (Stanford, CA: Stanford University Press, 2005), 15.

14 Nelson's conception of the "permascroll" was introduced after the last revision of: Nelson, *Literary Machines 93.1*. As such it does not seem to be often discussed. A definition, with related terms, can be found here: Lukka. The permascroll is the sequential record of *all* significant textual (or literary) events. A text would simply be a set of references to "spans" of the permascroll (which would clearly not be sequential). As here, for Derrida, this kind of totalizing structure designed to record the minutest discrete details of everything that can be recorded (begging the most significant of questions, namely: "What is the minutest discrete detail of everything?") is a potential apotheosis of literature, but one that also destroys literature by foreclosing precisely the kinds of development in culture and cultural production that we are addressing. It allows that literature might end, but in an *ultimate* sense on which "the book," by contrast, does not insist. I have discussed the permascroll earlier and above, see: "Time Code Language" in this volume.

15 Jacques Derrida, "Paper or Me, You Know ...," in *Paper Machine* (Stanford, CA: Stanford University Press, 2005), 65.

16 Ibid.

17 Liu, 179.

18 Ibid., 323.

19 Instantaneous, simultaneous, and on-demand information is the engine of the postindustrial "now" submitting history to creative destruction, and it is the destruction of this eternal "now" or self-evident presence of information, therefore, that will have the most critical and aesthetic potential. Strong art will be about the "destruction of destruction" or, put another way, the recognition of the destructiveness in creation. Ibid., 8–9. See also: ibid., chapter 11, *passim.*

20 I am sometimes using the phrase "expressive *programming*" here, and this is because of my focus on works that are explicitly coded as an aspect of their composition and production, but I am thinking of and alluding to the more general term "expressive processing" which is the subject of an important monograph. Wardrip-Fruin.

21 We might consider, in passing, how this "ease" and "facility" (and "cool")
    in relation to literary projects that previously demand special "effort" on
    the part of both writer and reader may one day alter our reading of the
    pioneering criticism of writing in digital media. Espen Aarseth subtitled his
    much-cited *Cybertext*, "perspectives on ergodic literature," and suggested
    that the special effort required of readers who address writing in these media
    was a better indication of its specificities than, for example, non-linearity.
    But what happens when such effort becomes less than that required to turn
    a page or use an index? Cf. Aarseth, *Cybertext: Perspectives on Ergodic
    Literature*.

22 A. Braxton Soderman, *Mémoire involontaire No. 1, 2008. Electronic
    Literature Collection*, vol. 2 (2011), http://collection.eliterature.org/2/works/
    soderman_memory.html (accessed August 13, 2017).

23 Brian Kim Stefans, "Stops and Rebels: A Critique of Hypertext," in
    Fashionable Noise: On Digital Poetics (Berkeley, CA: Atelos, 2003); Cayley,
    "*overboard*: An Example of Ambient Time-Based Poetics in Digital Art."

24 Justin Katko and Clement Valla, *Yelling at a Wall: Textron Eat Shreds,* 2008.
    Plantarchy.

25 The trope of consumption—where new media artworks are seen to consume
    their own literary (corporal) substance—has been put forward by Christopher
    Funkhouser in a paper that goes so far as to cast it in terms of cannibalism.
    Christopher T. Funkhouser, "Le(s) Mange Texte(s): Creative Cannibalism
    and Digital Poetry," in *E-Poetry 2007* (Paris: Université Paris8, 2007).
    Roberto Simanowski develops this critical approach as one aspect of his
    analysis of digital aesthetics, especially the fate of literature in digital art
    practice where he, to simplify, sees this consumption as reducing—at least
    in terms of the literary—the significance and affect of works that are (self-)
    identified as digital literature. Roberto Simanowski, "Digital Anthropophagy:
    Refashioning Words as Image, Sound and Action," *Leonardo* 43, no. 2
    (2010): 159–163.

26 Caleb Larsen, *Whose Life Is It Anyway?* 2008.

27 http://twitter.com/jennyholzer. (It's extraordinary, reviewing and reissuing
    this 2008 essay in 2017, that I felt compelled to describe "what Twitter is"
    when it is now an institution by means of which a US president may execute
    policy. It is also extraordinary that Larsen produced, essentially, one of the first
    chatbots, long before they achieved any kind of currency.)

28 Derrida, "Paper or Me, You Know …," 46. Emphasis in the original.

29 I know how to make it work (more or less) but I don't know *how* it works. So
    I don't know, I know less than ever, "who it is" who goes there. Not knowing,
    in this case, is a distinctive trait, one that does not apply with pens or with
    typewriters either. With pens and typewriters, you think you know *how* it
    works, how "it responds." Whereas, with computers, even if people know how
    to use them up to a point, they rarely know, intuitively and without thinking—
    at any rate, *I* don't know—*how* the internal demon of the apparatus works.
    What rules it obeys. This secret with no mystery frequently marks our
    dependence in relation to many instruments of modern technology. Derrida,
    "The Word Processor," 23.

Chapter 11

1   This statement is not equivalent to David Golumbia's reading of
    computationalism in so far as he suggests that individualism and Western
    neoliberalism have been underwritten by computationalist assertions that
    the mind and human relations generally may be exhaustively modeled by
    computational mechanisms or may be computational in themselves. However,
    I accord with Golumbia in suggesting that the kind of relationships that
    the network promotes, structurally, do tend to reinforce individualist and
    liberal sensibilities. David Golumbia, *The Cultural Logic of Computation*
    (Cambridge, MA: Harvard University Press, 2009).

2   See the discussion of data vs. capta below, as well as note 19.

3   "Big Software" is, as far as I am aware, my own coinage. "Big data" retains
    the gloss of digital utopianism since it appears, as do search engines' indexes,
    to promise universal accessibility and use, while in fact, as the tenor of this
    chapter indicates, "big data" is only properly accessible on terms from the
    servers of Big Software where it has been accumulated and processed.

4   McKenzie Wark, *A Hacker Manifesto* (Cambridge, MA: Harvard University
    Press, 2004).

5   Apart from Wark and Golumbia, who do not yet explicitly address, in
    particular, the implication of Facebook's vectoralist predominance, particularly
    welcome to and formative of this kind of critical discussion is: Geert
    Lovink, *Networks without a Cause: A Critique of Social Media* (Cambridge:
    Polity, 2011). See also: Roberto Simanowski, ed. *Digital Humanities and
    Digital Media: Conversations on Politics, Culture, Aesthetics, and Literacy*,
    Fibreculture Books (London: Open Humanities Press, 2016).

6   As I say, I select these organizations as exemplary. The vectoralist practices
    critiqued here are widely prevalent in companies both new and long-standing:
    Microsoft, Amazon, Apple, and so on, and all the fast-emerging social
    networking enclosures.

7   Google's own rendition of its corporate history is now (accessed January,
    2013) available online at http://www.google.com/about/company/. AdWords,
    still the backbone of Google revenue, was introduced in 2000.

8   Significantly, from the point of view of institutional distinction, Wikipedia is
    operated by a non-profit charitable foundation, the Wikimedia Foundation.

9   Of course, there are problems such as the robotic generation of editorial events
    (spam), and the problematic treatment of subjects and entities who may also
    present themselves as peers, although they have—as for example a user who is
    also the subject of an article—non-negotiable proper interests in the material
    to be read. Golumbia briefly cites Wikipedia as contrastively exemplary
    of a networked service promoting genuine, as opposed to ostensible,
    democratization. Golumbia, 26.

10 http://www.facebook.com/legal/terms (accessed August 3, 2017).

11 "On April Fools' Day in 2004, we launched Gmail." http://www.google.com/
    about/company/ (accessed January, 2013). I am suggesting that this wasn't
    about email and it wasn't even primarily about the generation of screen real
    estate for ads (see below); it was about accounts, and the ability to associate

data gathered from search and other services with the representation of human entities within an enclosure for big data. If this is correct, 2004 becomes the year of the advent of "big data" from my perspective, and the date for the advent of self-conscious vectoralist enclosures.

12 The coordination of human and posthuman desire may make it appear that something is added to human desire in this context, but it is salutary to consider the possibility that posthuman desire already is or may become a constrained and narrowed formation constituted by what is representable in computational systems or, perhaps more specifically, by particular regimes of computation. Golumbia is pessimistic in this regard.

13 It is clear that the net artist Constant Dullaart is sensitive to certain implications of such agreements, and if you are looking for a somewhat more entertaining and edifying way to familiarize yourself with Google's TOS, I recommend a visit to http://constantdullaart.com/TOS/ (accessed August 3, 2017). I am grateful to Clement Valla for introducing me to this work by Dullaart.

14 An ocean of legalese inserts itself into the interstices of getting and spending—warranties and disclaimers in the packaging of appliances, and so on. However, it seems to be only since the advent of Big Software that we, remarkably frequently, make active gestures of agreement to terms: a click, a press of the (default) return key. We make these gestures more frequently and more actively but, it seems to me, no less unthinkingly.

15 http://www.google.com/intl/en/policies/terms/ (accessed August 3, 2017).

16 The lines and subsequent quotations in the same style are from a piece that accompanied the online publication of this essay: John Cayley, "Pentameters toward the Dissolution of Certain *Vectoralist* Relations," *Amodern* 2 (2013): n.p.

17 The university is under a great deal of pressure in this regard. Many universities have opted to use Gmail for the purposes of correspondence, for example, and the relationship of this correspondence to the university is institutionally implicated. Another, very different, institution comes to be involved and the question of how these distinct institutions interrelate will not go away. Now also, social media (Facebook) enters the scene as a further channel of correspondence and communication for members of the university. Next, social media models are applied to pedagogical tools and affordances. But perhaps most tellingly and corrosively, the advent of Online Learning, MOOCs, and commercial organizations, like Coursera and Udacity already challenge the university to adopt their services in a manner that may prove to be inimical to fundamental aspects of its institutional mission, particularly as a site of independent research, as both problematic and necessary complement to teaching and pedagogical dissemination.

18 Wark; "The Vectoralist Class," *Supercommunity* 84 (2015): n.p.

19 "Data" has been prevalent for decades as indicative of the raw material of research. It seems particularly important now to consider what is and is not data. Strictly, data means "that which is given" as evidence of the world. However, the tools we use to take what the world gives may overdetermine the material we are able to gather. Arguably, the computational regime is overdetermined in a number of respects. It can only take as putative data

what can be represented in terms of discrete symbolic elements, and it will tend to favor quantitative accumulation and analysis. Following Joanna Drucker, I prefer to use "capta," for what has been able to be "taken," when referring to the raw material collected and processed by networked services or indeed by the regime of computation in general. "A fundamental prejudice, I suggest, is introduced by conceiving of data within any humanistic interpretative frame on a conventional, uncritical, statistical basis. Few social scientists would proceed this way, and the abandonment of interpretation in favor of a naïve approach to statistical certain[t]y [online: "certainly"] skews the game from the outset in favor of a belief that data is intrinsically quantitative—self-evident, value neutral, and observer-independent. This belief excludes the possibilities of conceiving data as qualitative, co-dependently constituted—in other words, of recognizing that all data is capta." Johanna Drucker, "Humanities Approaches to Graphical Display," *Digital Humanities Quarterly* 5, no. 1 (2011): n.p. The distinction is fundamentally important and it is remarkable to consider that this seems to be the first time that it has been clarified for the era of so-called Digital Humanities. In the discourse of phenomenology, the understanding of data is carefully discussed, but—in a quick review—I have found only two relevant earlier references to the distinction as proposed by Drucker. I think these are worth citing in the circumstances. Christopher Chippindale, "Capta and Data: On the True Nature of Archaeological Information," *American Antiquity* 65, no. 4 (2000): 605–612; Salvatore Russo, "Data vs. Capta or Sumpta," *American Psychologist* 12, no. 5 (1957): 283–284. The latter is a brief review notice.

20   Robert Darnton, "Google's Loss: The Public's Gain," *The New York Review of Books* LVII, no. 7 (April 28, 2011): 10–12.

21   This may not be entirely clear. The results contain language, words, that were abjected by a human writer. As with all language, the symbolic aspect of language renders an orthothetic (direct/proper indication/pointing) relationship between the abjected words and these "same" words that appear in the results. The results are made, in part, of words that belong to, are proper to, the (typically) human writer who has read them abjectly and written them into the maw of the search engine. See below, the chapter's concluding paragraphs, for the special and highly implicated case, when this appropriation of language, proper to a human writer, is applied to the algorithmic generation of advertisements.

22   A curated version of this facility has been provided by Google in the guise of its Ngram Viewer, now moved from Google Labs and associated with the Google Books project at http://books.google.com/ngrams/. "Ngrams" are sequences of words (considered as linguistic tokens) of various lengths (n may range from 2 to 5 to n). Linguistic corpora, in this case Google Books, may be processed so as to provide the relative frequencies for occurrences of ngrams, and this information may be further processed so as to offer up linguistic and cultural insights. See: Michel et al. There are also, of course, opportunities for literary aesthetic practice, for example the author's collaboration with Daniel C. Howe: Cayley and Howe. See also: John Cayley, "N-gram," in *The John Hopkins Guide to Digital Media*, ed. Marie-Laure Ryan, Lori Emerson, and Benjamin J. Robertson (Baltimore: Johns Hopkins University Press, 2014).

23 Language, arguably, exemplifies a different relation between material as data and material as capta. Language is, as it were, always already abstracted from specific embodiment, nonetheless retaining its inalienable relation to the embodied world as a function of the requirement that it be read in order to exist. Language is easy to capture but difficult to read.

24 Google's predominance is founded on a historical (singular) circumstance in at least this respect: as it came to prominence, the raw material that it indexed was, basically, inscribed by human agencies. This is, clearly, no longer the case. On some estimates, more than half of the material inscribed on the surface of the network is generated by software rather than human authors and writers (see: http://www.zdnet.com/blog/foremski/report-51-of-web-site-traffic-is-non-human-and-mostly-malicious/2201; and the source: http://www.incapsula.com/news/news-incapsula-press-releases/item/178-incapsula-reveals-31-of-website-traffic-can-harm-your-business). Considerations of spam, algorithmic text, and website (link farm) generation—of the "dark net" in general—significantly complicate the arguments set out here, while the overall tendency of these argument remains, I would maintain, coherent.

25 Which is, see above, brought into being by readers and reading. This should cause us even greater concern since, as reading changes, the proper materiality (ontological substance) of writing changes. If readers read other things, then more of these other things exist as compared to those that might otherwise have existed as a function of having been read.

26 This is somewhat of a theme for: Golumbia.

27 As fundamental elements of language, these abstractions come into existence and become entities as they are read or in relation to their readability. See above.

28 http://www.google.com/about/company/ (accessed August 3, 2017).

29 See note 19.

30 *TrackMeNot* by Daniel C. Howe and Helen Nissenbaum is an artistic-critical address to precisely these issues. Daniel C. Howe and Helen Nissenbaum, *TrackMeNot*, 2008.

31 I am referring to the now commonly encountered presentation of textual advertisements in marginal spaces associated with web-based access to Google's Gmail. Google's algorithms "read" key words in the bodies of email messages and generate ads, often including these keywords in the copy, assuming an implicated interest in these terms on the part of the human authors of the email messages. I write an email to my mother at Christmas and I am presented with advertisements for seasonal gifts appropriate for mothers.

32 Jason Huff and Mimi Cabell's *American Psycho* project offers an aestheticized critique of this circumstance. The artists sent the entire text of Brett Easton Ellis' *American Psycho* between email accounts, page by page, noting the Google-generated advertisements that were triggered by words and phrases in Easton Ellis' text. They then printed a book with only the traces of these advertisements in the place of the text. See: Jason Huff, Mimi Cabell, and Brett Easton Ellis, *American Psycho*, 2010.

33 See the opening of the chapter above. In case this is not clear, these are statements associated with a philosophy of language and literary aesthetic

practice, specifically a theory of linguistic ontology that recognizes the coming into being of language as it is read.

34 Kashmir Hill, "Facebook Will Be Using Your Face in 'Sponsored Stories' Ads (and There's No Opting Out)," *Forbes* 2011.

Chapter 12

1 See "The Gravity of the Leaf" in this volume and John Cayley, "The Gravity of the Leaf: Phenomenologies of Literary Inscription in Media-Constituted Diegetic Worlds," in *Beyond the Screen: Transformations of Literary Structures, Interfaces and Genres*, ed. Peter Gendolla and Jörgen Schäfer, Media Upheavals (Bielefeld: Transcript, 2010).

2 This association with particular physical media is conventional and a function of human capabilities. It is also conservative: language finds it difficult to be deployed in other physical media, although in principle this would be possible. Vilém Flusser seemed to propose that linguistic symbolic practice will migrate to the "technical image." Perhaps it's on its way, but very slowly. Natural sign languages are, to my mind, the only instances of commensurate human language systems that are deployed in another physical medium—that of spatialized gesture.

3 One of the best expositions of this position that I know is implicit throughout the work of Derrida and set out fairly clearly in Derrida, "The Book to Come."

4 I hope that this usage of "readability" will become clearer as the chapter elaborates. In art practical research, my collaborator Daniel C. Howe and I are exploring aspects of readability and the culture of human reading through Cayley and Howe.

5 In particular, this chapter follows on from thinking in "The Code Is Not the Text," included in this volume and at John Cayley, "The Code Is Not the Text (Unless It Is the Text)," *Electronic Book Review* (2002): n.p.

6 Saying that it is "easier" to read glosses over a wide range of ways in which the "ease" of this facility may be generated: through choice of reserved words and operators, through the deployment of more familiar syntax, etc. etc.

7 I use "privileged" to indicate the kind of special and necessary relationship between low-level (machine) codes and particular hardware configurations.

8 These works are referred to and discussed using a range of terms by critics of Baldessari's work. "Composite photoworks" is from: Bruggen, 131 ff., 184.

9 This consideration of virtual linguistic artifacts in a visual field has many fascinating special cases that it is impossible to go into here in any detail. Consider the status of the title on the cover of the (second) book in 2a. It is readable and also, thus, "language-as-such," but it is also comfortably, diegetically part of the image-of-a-book-cover and so does not exemplify the diegetic break that language, I claim, *always* registers. There are the cases of film titling; (usually failed) attempts to introduce readable language into film and video; and subtitles that are "invisible" despite the fact they usually also embody a ghastly, tasteless disregard (without evoking the obvious necessary

diegetic break between one *language* and another) for the composition of the cinematic frame. The historian of East Asian art Robert Harrist has written about the representation of writing and writing itself, inspiring some of my thinking in: Harrist Jr.

10 Instances from "Monoclonal Microphone" were first published, thanks to its editor, Benny Lichtner, with a somewhat extended description of the process in: John Cayley, "From: *Writing to Be Found*," *adj noun*, Spring 2011. This work was built using Processing (http:processing.org), and the RiTa natural language processing library by Daniel C. Howe (http://www.rednoise.org/rita/).

11 The discussion, below, of our last example from distinctly computational digital language art refers to an exemplary and *executable* instance of such criticism.

12 Nick Montfort and Stephanie Strickland, *Sea and Spar Between*, 2010. In *Dear Navigator*, SAIC, Chicago.

13 Nick Montfort and Stephanie Strickland "Cut to Fit the Tool-Spun Course: Discussing Creative Code in Comments," *Digital Humanities Quarterly* 7, no. 1 (2013).

14 Stephanie Strickland, *V—WaveSon.nets. V—losing l'una*, Penguin Poets (New York: Penguin, 2002); Stephanie Strickland, Cynthia Lawson Jaramillo, and Paul Ryan. *Slippingglimpse*. 2007. http://slippingglimpse.org (accessed August 13, 2017).

15 The series of works I am thinking is: Nick Montfort, *ppg256 series: Perl Poetry Generators in 256 characters*. 2008-ongoing. http://nickm.com/poems/ppg256.html (accessed August 13, 2017).

16 Shelley Jackson, *Skin: A Story Published on the Skin of 2095 Volunteers*. 2003. http://ineradicablestain.com/skindex.html (accessed August 3, 2017).

Chapter 13

1 The conference took place from March 4 to 5, 2016, and was organized by Sydney Skybetter. Website, http://www.choreotech.com (accessed March 20, 2016).

2 This reference to and usage of pharmakon is inspired by the critical thought of Bernard Stiegler. See, among many other references: Bernard Stiegler, *For a New Critique of Political Economy* (Cambridge: Polity, 2010); *What Makes Life Worth Living: On Pharmacology*, trans. Daniel Ross, English ed. (Cambridge, UK and Malden, MA: Polity Press, 2013).

3 While digitization might be used for both senses, digitalization may also be deployed to indicate, generally, institutional and social reconfiguration and accommodation to digital culture and networked computation, whereas digitization may have a constrained sense: the encoded representation of information about the world in digital form.

4 John Cayley, "Terms of Reference & Vectoralist Transgressions: Situating Certain Literary Transactions over Networked Services," *Amodern* 2 (2013): n.p.; "Pentameters toward the Dissolution of Certain *Vectoralist* Relations."

5   John Cayley, *The Listeners*. 2015. Custom software, aurally accessible linguistic compositions, and "skill" for the Amazon Echo's "Alexa" using the Alexa Skills Kit. http://programmatology.shadoof.net/?thelisteners (accessed March 20, 2016); John Cayley, "*The Listeners*: An Instance of Aurature," *Cream City Review* 40, no. 2 (2016): 172–187; John Cayley, "Aurature at the End(s) of Electronic Literature," *Electronic Book Review* (2017): n.p.

6   "Terms of Reference & Vectoralist Transgressions: Situating Certain Literary Transactions over Networked Services." Included in this volume.

7   It was Patrick Corbin, a prominent dance artist and professor of Contemporary Dance at the Kaufman School of Dance, University of Southern California, who suggested this term.

8   Vilém Flusser, *Does Writing Have a Future?* trans. Nancy Ann Roth, Electronic Mediations (Minneapolis: University of Minnesota Press, 2011); *Into the Universe of Technical Images*, trans. Nancy Ann Roth, Electronic Mediations (Minneapolis: University of Minnesota Press, 2011).

9   James Bridle is credited with coining the term, for which there is a Wikipedia entry, https://en.wikipedia.org/wiki/New_Aesthetic (accessed March 20, 2016), leading to a number of manifestations by Bridle, including, James Bridle, "The New Aesthetic: Waving at the Machines." http://booktwo.org/notebook/waving-at-machines/ (accessed March 20, 2016).

10 See "The Gravity of the Leaf" in this volume, and: Cayley, "The Gravity of the Leaf: Phenomenologies of Literary Inscription in Media-Constituted Diegetic Worlds."

11 Clement Valla, *Postcards from Google Earth*. 2010. http://www.postcards-from-google-earth.com (accessed 20 March, 2016); Curt Cloninger, "Manifesto for a Theory of the 'New Aesthetic'," *Mute* 3, no. 4 (2013): 16–27.

12 In terms of the type of analysis that I am outlining here, Valla's project exemplifies another media-constituted diegetic break that is interesting, although less immediately important for our argument. This is the break between, as it were, the diegesis of the snapshot or postcard and that of the mapping system that is represented by Google Earth. The break is, of course, visually manifested by the framing of the postcards themselves, breaking them out of the map and its transformations. His insightful, aestheticized exposure of the contrasting ways that human participants relate to these two diegetic worlds and act with and within them is, of course, an important impetus for Valla's project.

13 For subsequent projects, Valla has contextualized his process in terms of photogrammetry, a pre-computational analytic practice of photography and clearly also productive of symbolic image in the terms set out here: Clement Valla, *Surface Proxy* (Paris: XPO Gallery, 2015). In the *Surface Proxy* catalogue cited, see, especially, the Notes on pp. 79–94. This catalog is available in PDF form at http://clementvalla.com/wp-content/uploads/2015/06/clement_valla_surface_proxy_web.pdf (accessed March 26, 2016).

14 See "Reading and Giving" in this volume and: John Cayley, "Reading and Giving—Voice and Language," *Performance Research* 18, no. 5 (2013): 10–19.

15 *As language,* these high-order breaks, as we will see, may be discovered by close reading. They may also, of course, be explicitly marked by punctuation—whether this be more or less conventional punctuation or distinctly

paralinguistic. For example, within the scope of graphic inscription and typography, such a break could be marked by a change of font or a change of a single font's color. These marks, however, are at best paralinguistic; they are distinctions inscribed into the material support of the language rather than into the language as such.

When it comes to language in aurality—as human or humanoid voice— the situation becomes more complex because we cannot (yet) conceive of the voice that is not marked by human individuality. This implies that whatever a voice inscribes is, minimally, within the diegetic scope of this individuality. If an apparent individual is subject to symbolic process for the production of their language, would this not break their individuality and require a change of voice (perhaps expressed as distinct intonation or accent—think also of acting, drama, and the complexities that this field of aesthetic practice would *further* introduce)? These are questions—somewhat beyond the present scope of this chapter—that become crucial since the advent of distributed entities that speak and listen—like Siri, Cortana, Google Now, Watson, and Alexa, all of which are literally embodied as transactive synthetic language. The language of these entities is symbolic image in the terms delineated here. It is a synthesis of conventional linguistic image and language-generative symbolic process. Not only are the broken diegeses of this language disguised by their inevitable coincidence with differences that constitute language as such, synthetic language in aurality must also be wrapped within one of the definitive indications of human embodiment, an individual voice. This renders the implicated symbolic processes compelling in so far as they acquire a compelling relationship with embodied humanity. The resultant voices are not, by the way, necessarily "uncanny" (disturbingly human-seeming non-human). They are something more troubling than that. They are signs of the advent of a new kind of transactive being that is able to share our language-making and language-reading.

16 The "language" of "formal languages" is within quote marks here because I would prefer to reserve "language" for natural human language. Otherwise, the use of "language" is inflated, as Derrida pointed out long ago: Derrida, *Of Grammatology*, 6 ff. Formal "languages" are exhaustively describable in structuralist terms such as sign, grammar, difference—structure, math, logic. The poststructuralist critique, especially as emerging from Jacques Derrida's grammatology, underlies my thinking throughout, where, for example, difference must be—and must also be superseded/supplemented/erased by— *différance*, but only in so far as this is readable as generative of those kinds of meaning that are vital for human animals.

17 There is, of course, a reference to long-standing and ongoing discussions of the interrelationship of code and text in, especially, the field of electronic writing, digital literature, and so on. The deliberate, aesthetically or conceptually motivated, synthesis of literal code and text is and will continue to be practiced—notable practitioners: Mez Breeze, Talan Memmott, Alan Sondheim, the last of whom is credited with a term for this practice, namely "codework": Alan Sondheim, "Introduction: Codework," *American Book Review* 22, no. 6 (2001): 1, 4. The author has made his own contribution to the debate; see "The Code Is Not the Text" in this volume and: Cayley, "The Code Is Not the Text (Unless It Is the Text)."

As an example of a highly interesting and conceptually superlative form of the practice, I would like to cite William P. Hicks *Esopo* project: William P. Hicks, Email, March 29, 2016. Hicks's approach is to specify formal languages—ideally languages that are Turing complete; that is, languages that are capable, in principle, of computing anything computable—on the basis of the selected features of existing natural linguistic textual forms. For such an approach, aspects of punctuation—particularly actual punctuation "marks" and also the significant arrangement of "white space" such as lineation, spacing, and indentation—are crucial, but selected textual "tokens"—typically to be defined as "reserved words"—will also figure in the specification. The goal of a particular constituent language within this project might be, for example, to implement a specification that will allow any text that is formatted according to genre conventions or, indeed, *any text at all,* to be successfully compiled into a machine language executable. In other words, the text is rendered interpretable—by the specification—as the "high level" source code of a program that will compile and run on some arbitrary hardware platform. Hicks has, indeed, made a specification that will allow the compilation of any text, but he has also specified an inherently more interesting language, "Emily," that is able to interpret and compile any of the poems of Emily Dickinson, and thus also, by definition, any original poems that follow the textual and poetic conventions of Dickinson's work.

Success in the compilation of a text is a necessary condition for it to be considered as conforming to an *Esopo* language specification, but Hicks's proposal is that there are expressive and aesthetic potentialities in refined instances of the practice. A language that allows *any text* to be compiled must allow that the vast majority of texts will compile as programs that do little more than nothing. Most of them will be instances of "Hello World," one imagines. Hicks, however, writes that "Emily" compiles Dickinson poems as "non-trivial algorithms." Hicks conceives of a constrained writing practice—self-reflexive with regard to its own structures, which are implemented as an *Esopo*—that would bring into existence texts that do something significant and affective in the worlds of both human reading and machinic computation. To quote Hicks himself, "Some [*Esopo* languages] are designed to compile almost any text they receive as input, while others demand strict adherence to certain formal rules. Other languages are designed not so much to encourage production of new algorithmically-engaged text as to draw attention to the structure of existing work." Ibid.

18 A good way into Montfort's work is: Nick Montfort, *#! [Shebang]* (Denver: Counterpath, 2014). The author has also written a review essay of this book that deals with a number of related issues in the theory and practice of digital language art, computational poetics, and the poetics of computation. John Cayley, "Poetry and Stuff: A Review of *#!*" *Electronic Book Review* (2015): n.p.

19 Montfort, *ppg256 series: Perl Poetry Generators in 256 characters.*

20 John Cayley, *Image Generation: A Reader* (London: Veer Books, 2015), 34–57, 138–139.

21 Cayley and Howe.

22 Cayley, *Image Generation: A Reader,* 35.

23 Personal email communication, March 21, 2016. *Primary Source* was first publicly exhibited at the "Proxy" curatorial space, Providence, RI, March–April, 2015 as part of a group show entitled "Maximum Sideline: Postscript." Capone self-published a print-on-demand artist's book/chapbook version to coincide with the installation. On-demand print copies of this book may be ordered from the following URL: http://www.lulu.com/shop/francesca-capone/primary-source/paperback/product-22217179.html (accessed March 26, 2016). Both video and PDF versions of the work were subsequently published online by Gaus PDF (http:/gaus-pdf.com), PDF: http://www.gauss-pdf.com/post/121599676480/gpdf177gpdfe016-1-francesca-capone-primary, and *video*: http://www.gauss-pdf.com/post/121599892473/gpdf177gpdfe016-2-francesca-capone-primary. Francesca Capone, *Primary Source* (Providence, RI: Self-published artist's book; also available online from Gauss PDF, 2015). Remarks following on in the main text are adapted from an afterword that the author wrote for Capone's chapbook.

Chapter 14

1 Derrida, *Of Grammatology*.
2 James R. Hurford, *The Origins of Grammar*, Language in the Light of Evolution (Oxford and New York: Oxford University Press, 2012); *The Origins of Language: A Slim Guide* (Oxford: Oxford University Press, 2014).
3 Ibid.
4 Stanislas Dehaene, *Reading in the Brain: The Science and Evolution of a Human Invention* (New York: Viking, 2009).
5 Derrida, *Of Grammatology*; Stiegler, *For a New Critique of Political Economy; What Makes Life Worth Living: On Pharmacology*; "Digital Knowledge, Obsessive Computing, Short-Termism and Need for a Negentropic Web," in *Digital Humanities and Digital Media: Conversations on Politics, Culture, Aesthetics, and Literacy*, ed. Roberto Simanowski (London: Open Humanities Press, 2016).
6 Roberto Pieraccini, *The Voice in the Machine: Building Computers That Understand Speech* (Cambridge, MA: MIT Press, 2012).
7 N. Katherine Hayles, 'Prologue.' In *How We Became Posthuman: Virtual Bodies in Cybernetics, Literature, and Informatics* (Chicago: University of Chicago Press, 1999), xi–xiv.
8 V. N. Vološinov, *Marxism and the Philosophy of Language*, trans. Ladislav Matejka and I. R. Titunik (Cambridge and London: Seminar Press, 1973); Jean-Jacques Lecercle and Denise Riley, *The Force of Language*, Language, Discourse, Society (Houndmills and New York: Palgrave Macmillan, 2004).
9 Matthew Rubery, *The Untold Story of the Talking Book* (Cambridge, MA: Harvard University Press, 2016).

BIBLIOGRAPHY

Aarseth, Espen. *Cybertext: Perspectives on Ergodic Literature*. Baltimore and London: Johns Hopkins University Press, 1997.

Aarseth, Espen. "Nonlinearity and Literary Theory." In *Hyper/Text/Theory*, edited by George P. Landow, 51–86. Baltimore: Johns Hopkins University Press, 1994.

Aarseth, Espen. "Text, Hypertext or Cybertext: A Typology of Textual Modes Using Correspondence Analysis." In *Research in Humanities Computing*, 5, edited by Giorgio Perissinotto, Susan Hockey and Nancy Ide, 1–16. Oxford: Oxford University Press, 1996.

Acker, Kathy. *Blood and Guts in High School*. New York: Grove Press, 1978.

Baldwin, Sandy. *The Internet Unconscious: On the Subject of Electronic Literature*. International Texts in Critical Media Aesthetics. New York: Bloomsbury Academic, 2015.

Baldwin, Sandy. "Process Window: Code Work, Code Aesthetics, Code Poetics." In *Ergodic Poetry: A Special Section of the Cybertext Yearbook 2002*, edited by Loss Pequeño Glazier and John Cayley. Publications of the Research Centre for Contemporary Culture, 107–19. Jyväskylä: University of Jyväskylä, 2003.

Barron, Stephanie, and Michel Draguet. *Magritte and Contemporary Art: The Treachery of Images*. Los Angeles and Ghent: Los Angeles County Museum of Art; Ludion, 2006.

Barthes, Roland. *Camera Lucida* [La Chambre Claire]. Translated by Richard Howard. First American paperback ed. New York: Hill and Wang, 1982. Paris: Editions du Seuil, 1980.

Barthes, Roland. "The Photographic Message." Translated by Stephen Heath. In *Image Music Text*, 15–31. London: Fontana Press, 1977.

Barthes, Roland. "Rhetoric of the Image." Translated by Stephen Heath. In *Image Music Text*, 32–51. London: Fontana Press, 1977.

Barthes, Roland. *S/Z*. Translated by Richard Miller. Oxford: Blackwell Publishers, 1990. Paris: Éditions du Seuil, 1973.

Battelle, John. *The Search: How Google and Its Rivals Rewrote the Rules of Business and Transformed Our Culture*. Updated with new chapter in this ed. New York: Portfolio, 2006 [2005].

Beckett, Samuel. *The Complete Short Prose, 1929–1989*. Edited by S. E. Gontarski. New York: Grove Press, 1995.

Beckett, Samuel. *How It Is* [Comment c'est]. Translated by Samuel Beckett. New York: Grove Press, 1964. Paris: Les Editions de Minuit, 1961.

Beiles, Sinclair, William S. Burroughs, Gregory Corso, and Brion Gysin. *Minutes to Go*. Paris: Jean Fanchette, 1960.

Benson, Steve. *Blue Book*. Great Barrington: The Figures/Roof, 1988.

Bergvall, Caroline. "In the Place of Writing: The Performance of Writing as Sited Practice." In *Assembling Alternatives: Reading Postmodern Poetries Transnationally*, edited by Romana Huk, 327–37. Middletown, CT: Wesleyan University Press, 2003.

Bernstein, Charles. "Play It Again, Pac-Man." *Postmodern Culture* 2, no. 1 (September 1991): A reworking of "Hot Circuits: A video arcade," American Museum of the Moving Image, 14 June–26 November 1989.

Bolter, Jay David. *Writing Space: The Computer, Hypertext, and the History of Writing*. Hillsdale, NJ: Erlbaum, 1991.

Bolter, J. David, and Richard Grusin. *Remediation: Understanding New Media*. Cambridge, MA: MIT Press, 2000.

Bootz, Philippe. "Hypertext: Solution/Dissolution." Translated by John Cayley. In *Ergodic Poetry: A Special Section of the Cybertext Yearbook 2002*, edited by Loss Pequeño Glazier and John Cayley. Publications of the Research Centre for Contemporary Culture, 56–82. Jyväskylä: University of Jyväskylä, 2003.

Bootz, Philippe. "Le Point de Vue Fonctionnel: Point de Vue Tragique et Programme Pilote." *alire 10/DOC(K)S* Series 3, no. 13/14/15/16 (1997): 28–47.

Bosker, Bianca. "Google Instant Blocks Sexy Searches." *Huffington Post*, September 9, 2010, updated May 25, 2011. http://www.huffingtonpost.com/2010/09/09/google-instant-search-blo_n_710199.html (accessed August 13, 2017).

Bosker, Bianca. "Google Shuts Down China Search, Redirects Users to Hong Kong." *Huffington Post*, March 23, 2010, updated May 25, 2011. http://www.huffingtonpost.com/2010/03/22/google-leaves-china-googl_n_508639.html (accessed August 13, 2017).

Bridle, James. "The New Aesthetic: Waving at the Machines." http://booktwo.org/notebook/waving-at-machines/ (accessed March 20, 2016).

Brugerolle, Marie de. *John Baldessari: From Life*. Nimes and Paris: Carré d'Art_ Musée d'art contemporain; École nationale supérieure des beaux-art de Paris, 2005.

Bruggen, Coosje van. *John Baldessari*. New York: Rizzoli, 1990.

Burroughs, William S., and Brion Gysin. *The Exterminator*. San Francisco, CA: Auerhahn Press, 1960.

Cage, John. *I-VI*. The Charles Eliot Norton Lectures. Cambridge, MA: Harvard University Press, 1990.

Cage, John, and James Joyce. *Writing through Finnegans Wake*. University of Tulsa Monograph Series. Tulsa: University of Tulsa, 1978.

Capone, Francesca. *Primary Source*. Providence, RI: Self-published artist's book; also available online from Gauss PDF, 2015.

Catling, Brian. *The Stumbling Block*. London: Book Works, 1990.

Cayley, John. "The Advent of Aurature and the End of (Electronic) Literature." In *The Bloomsbury Handbook of Electronic Literature*, edited by Joseph Tabbi, pp. 73–94. New York and London: Bloomsbury Academic, 2017.

Cayley, John. "Aurature at the End(s) of Electronic Literature." *Electronic Book Review* (2017). http://electronicbookreview.com/thread/electropoetics/aurature (accessed August 13, 2017).

Cayley, John. "Bass Resonance." *Mute*, January 2005, 22–24.

Cayley, John. "Bass Resonance." *Electronic Book Review* electropoetics (2005). http://www.electronicbookreview.com/thread/electropoetics/dynamic (accessed August 13, 2017).

Cayley, John. "Beginning with 'the Image' in *How It Is* When Translating Certain Processes of Digital Language Art." *Electronic Book Review* (2015). http://www.electronicbookreview.com/thread/electropoetics/howitis (accessed August 13, 2017).

Cayley, John. "Beyond Codexspace: Potentialities of Literary Cybertext." *Visible Language* 30, no. 2 (1996): 164–83.

Cayley, John. "Book Unbound." *Engaged*, 1995, On CD-ROM.

Cayley, John. "Book Unbound." In *Dietsche Warande & Beaufort [Dwb]*, *4*, *on Electronic (Visual) Literature*, edited by Eric Vos and Jan Baetens, On CD-ROM, 1999.

Cayley, John. "Book Unbound." In *The New Media Reader*, edited by Noah Wardrip-Fruin and Nick Montfort, On CD-ROM. Cambridge, MA: MIT Press, 2003.

Cayley, John. "Book Unbound." *Postmodern Culture* 7, no. 3, Hypertext special issue (February 1997). http://muse.jhu.edu/article/603711 (accessed August 13, 2017).

Cayley, John. *Book Unbound: Indra's Net VI*. London: Wellsweep, 1995. Issued for Macintosh computers on 3.5" floppy disk.

Cayley, John. "The Code Is Not the Text (Unless It Is the Text)." *Electronic Book Review* (September 10, 2002). http://www.electronicbookreview.com/thread/electropoetics/literal (accessed August 17, 2017).

Cayley, John. *Collocations: Indra's Net II*. London: Wellsweep, 1993. Issued for Macintosh computers on 3.5" floppy disk.

Cayley, John. "Digital *wen*: On the Digitization of Letter- and Character-Based Systems of Inscription." In *Reading East Asian Writing: The Limits of Literary Theory*, edited by Michel Hockx and Ivo Smits. RoutledgeCurzon-IIAS Asian Studies Series, 277–94. London: RoutledgeCurzon, 2003.

Cayley, John. *An Essay on the Golden Lion: Han-Shan in Indra's Net*. Edinburgh: Morning Star, 1995.

Cayley, John. "From: The Speaking Clock." *Chain* 4 (1997): 25–27.

Cayley, John. "From: *Writing to Be Found*." *adj noun*, Spring 2011, 1.2, Digital Hamper, 69–84.

Cayley, John. *Golden Lion: Indra's Net IV*. London: Wellsweep, 1994. Issued for Macintosh computers on 3.5" floppy disk.

Cayley, John. "The Gravity of the Leaf: Phenomenologies of Literary Inscription in Media-Constituted Diegetic Worlds." In *Beyond the Screen: Transformations of Literary Structures, Interfaces and Genres*, edited by Peter Gendolla and Jörgen Schäfer. Media Upheavals, 199–226. Bielefeld: Transcript, 2010.

Cayley, John. "Hypertext/Cybertext/Poetext." In *Assembling Alternatives: Reading Postmodern Poetries Transnationally*, edited by Romana Huk, 310–26. Middletown, CT: Wesleyan University Press, 2003.

Cayley, John. *Image Generation: A Reader*. London: Veer Books, 2015.

Cayley, John. *Indra's Net I*. London: Wellsweep, 1991–93. Issued for Macintosh computers on 3.5" floppy disk.

Cayley, John. "Inner Workings: Code and Representations of Interiority in New Media Poetics." *dichtung-digital* 29 (2003). http://www.dichtung-digital. de/2003/issue/3/Cayley.htm (accessed August 13, 2017).

Cayley, John. *Lens.* 2004. Custom software in programmable QuickTime targeting version 7. http://programmatology.shadoof.net/?lens (accessed August 1, 2017). [Also published/documented: ELMCIP Knowledge Base https://elmcip.net/ node/1626 (accessed August 14, 2017).]

Cayley, John. "Lens: The Practice and Poetics of Writing in Immersive VR: A Case Study with Maquette." *Leonardo Electronic Almanac* 14, no. 5–6 (2006). http:// leoalmanac.org/journal/vol_14/lea_v14_n05-06/jcayley.asp (accessed August 13, 2017).

Cayley, John. *The Listeners.* 2015. Custom software, aurally accessible linguistic compositions, and "skill" for the Amazon Echo's "Alexa" using the Alexa Skills Kit. http://programmatology.shadoof.net/?thelisteners (accessed March 20, 2016).

Cayley, John. "*The Listeners*: An Instance of Aurature." *Cream City Review* 40, no. 2 (2016): 172–87. http://io.creamcityreview.org/40-2/cayley/ (accessed August 13, 2017).

Cayley, John. "Literal Art: Neither Lines nor Pixels but Letters." In *First Person: New Media as Story, Performance, and Game*, edited by Noah Wardrip-Fruin and Pat Harrigan, 208–17, also in the *Electronic Book Review*. http://www. electronicbookreview.com/thread/firstperson/programmatology. Cambridge, MA: MIT Press, 2004.

Cayley, John. "Literal Art: Neither Lines nor Pixels but Letters." *Electronic Book Review* electropoetics (2004). http://www.electronicbookreview.com/thread/ firstperson/programmatology (accessed August 3, 2017).

Cayley, John. *Moods & Conjunctions: Indra's Net III.* London: Wellsweep, 1993–94. Issued for Macintosh computers on 3.5" floppy disk.

Cayley, John. "N-gram." In *The John Hopkins Guide to Digital Media*, edited by Marie-Laure Ryan, Lori Emerson and Benjamin J. Robertson, 358–59. Baltimore: Johns Hopkins University Press, 2014.

Cayley, John. *noth'rs. Performance Research*: 4.2, on CD-ROM, 1999.

Cayley, John. *noth'rs. Riding the Meridian*, 1999a. http://www.heelstone.com/ meridian/cayley.html (accessed July 30, 2017).

Cayley, John. "Of Capta, Vectoralists, Reading and the Googlization of Universities." In *Digital Humanities and Digital Media: Conversations on Politics, Culture, Aesthetics, and Literacy*, edited by Roberto Simanowski, 69–92. London: Open Humanities Press, 2016.

Cayley, John. "Of Programmatology." *Mute*, Fall 1998, 72–75.

Cayley, John. *Oisleánd: Indra's Net IX.* London: Wellsweep, 1996. Issued for Macintosh computers on 3.5" floppy disk.

Cayley, John. *overboard.* 2003. Custom software, ambient poetics. http:// programmatology.shadoof.net/?overboard (accessed August 1, 2017). [Also published/documented: ELMCIP Knowledge Base https://elmcip.net/node/549 (accessed August 14, 2017).]

Cayley, John. "*overboard*: An Example of Ambient Time-Based Poetics in Digital Art." *dichtung-digital* 32 (2004). http://www.dichtung-digital.de/2004/2/Cayley/ index.htm (accessed August 13, 2017).

Cayley, John. "Pentameters toward the Dissolution of Certain *Vectoralist* Relations." *Amodern* 2 (October 2013). http://amodern.net/article/pentameters-toward-the-dissolution-of-certain-vectoralist-relations/ (accessed August 13, 2017).

Cayley, John. "Period Bob." *Review of Contemporary Fiction: Robert Coover Festschrift* 32.1 (Spring 2012): 156–60.

Cayley, John. "Poetry and Stuff: A Review of #!" *Electronic Book Review* (2015). http://www.electronicbookreview.com/thread/electropoetics/shebang (accessed August 13, 2017).

Cayley, John. "Pressing the "Reveal Code" Key." *EJournal* 6, no. 1 (1996). http://www.ucalgary.ca/ejournal/archive/ej-6-1.txt (accessed July 28, 2017).

Cayley, John. *Pressing the <Reveal Code> Key: Indra's Net VIII*. London: Wellsweep, 1996. Issued for Macintosh computers on 3.5" floppy disk.

Cayley, John. "Reading and Giving—Voice and Language." *Performance Research* 18, no. 5 (October 2013): 10–19, author approved ms. also available: https://repository.library.brown.edu/studio/item/bdr:380074/ (accessed August 13, 2017).

Cayley, John. "Reconfiguration: Symbolic Image and Language Art." *Humanities* 6, no. 1, Special Issue: The Poetics of Computation (2017). http://www.mdpi.com/2076-0787/6/1/8/ (accessed August 13, 2017).

Cayley, John. *The Speaking Clock: Indra's Net VII*. London: Wellsweep, 1995. Issued for Macintosh computers on 3.5" floppy disk.

Cayley, John. "Terms of Reference & Vectoralist Transgressions: Situating Certain Literary Transactions over Networked Services." *Amodern* 2 (October 2013). http://amodern.net/article/terms-of-reference-vectoralist-transgressions/ (accessed August 13, 2017).

Cayley, John. "Time Code Language: New Media Poetics and Programmed Signification." In *New Media Poetics: Contexts, Technotexts, and Theories*, edited by Adalaide Morris and Thomas Swiss, 307–33. Cambridge, MA: MIT Press, 2006.

Cayley, John. *Translation*. 2004. http://programmatology.shadoof.net/?translation (accessed August 1, 2017). [Also published/documented: *Electronic Literature Collection*, vol. 1 (2006) http://collection.eliterature.org/1/works/cayley__translation.html (accessed August 13, 2017), ELMCIP Knowledge Base https://elmcip.net/node/526 (accessed August 14, 2017).]

Cayley, John. "The Translation of Process." *Amodern*, no. 8 (2018). http://amodern.net/article/the-translation-of-process/ (accessed March 14, 2018).

Cayley, John. *Under It All: Texts, Holography, Afterword*. London: The Many Press, 1993.

Cayley, John. "Untranslatability and Readability." *Critical Multilingualism Studies* 3, no. 1 (2015): 70–89. http://cms.arizona.edu/index.php/multilingual/article/view/64 (accessed August 13, 2017).

Cayley, John. "Weapons of the Deconstructive Masses: Whatever Electronic Literature May or May Not Mean." *Hyperrhiz* 6 (2009). http://hyperrhiz.io/hyperrhiz06/essays/weapons-of-the-deconstructive-masses.html (accessed August 13, 2017).

Cayley, John. "Weapons of the Deconstructive Masses (WDM): Whatever Electronic Literature May or May Not Mean." *Revista de Estudos Literários* 1, no. 2 *(Literatura no século XXI)* (2012): 25–56.

Cayley, John. "Why Did People Make Things Like This?" *Electronic Book Review* (February 1997). http://www.electronicbookreview.com/thread/electropoetics/ speculative (accessed August 13, 2017).

Cayley, John. *windsound*. 1999. http://programmatology.shadoof.net/?p=works/ wsqt/windsound.html (accessed July 30, 2017). [Also published/documented: *Electronic Literature Collection*, vol. 1 (2006) http://collection.eliterature. org/1/works/cayley__windsound.html (accessed August 13, 2017), ELMCIP Knowledge Base https://elmcip.net/node/790 (accessed August 14, 2017).]

Cayley, John. *windsound*. Los Angeles: Electronic Literature Organization: *State of the Arts: The Proceedings of the Electronic Literature Organization's 2002 State of the Arts Symposium & 2001 Electronic Literature Awards*, included on the CD-ROM, 2003.

Cayley, John. *Wine Flying*. London: Wellsweep, 1988. Issued for Macintosh computers on 3.5" floppy disk.

Cayley, John. "Writing on Complex Surfaces." *dichtung-digital* 35, no. 2 (2005). http://www.dichtung-digital.de/2005/2/Cayley/index.htm (accessed July 28, 2017).

Cayley, John. "Writing to Be Found and Writing Readers." *Digital Humanities Quarterly* 5, no. 3 (August 2011). http://www.digitalhumanities.org/dhq/ vol/5/3/000104/000104.html (accessed August 13, 2017).

Cayley, John, and Gu Cheng. *Leaving the City: Indra's Net V*. London: Wellsweep, 1995. Issued for Macintosh computers on 3.5" floppy disk.

Cayley, John, and Daniel C. Howe. *The Readers Project*. 2009. http:// thereadersproject.org (accessed August 13, 2017). [Also published/documented: *Electronic Literature Collection*, vol. 3 (2016). http://collection.eliterature.org/3/ work.html?work=the-readers-project (accessed August 17, 2017), ELMCIP Knowledge Base https://elmcip.net/node/864 (accessed August 14, 2017).]

Cayley, John, and Clement Valla. *This Is (Not) Writing*. 2010. Custom software for Immersive Virtual Reality. http://programmatology.shadoof.net/?notwriting (accessed August 13, 2017).

Ch'en, Kenneth. *Buddhism in China: A Historical Survey*. 1st paperback ed. Princeton, NJ: Princeton University Press, 1972 [1964].

Chippindale, Christopher. "Capta and Data: On the True Nature of Archaeological Information." *American Antiquity* 65, no. 4 (2000): 605–12. http://www.jstor. org/stable/2694418 (accessed August 13, 2017).

Cloninger, Curt. "Manifesto for a Theory of the 'New Aesthetic'." *Mute* 3, no. 4 (Spring 2013): 16–27.

Confucius (= Kong Fuzi). *Confucius: The Great Digest, the Unwobbling Pivot, the Analects*. Translated by Ezra Pound. New York: New Directions, 1969. Glen Hughes, 1928.

Cooper, Harry. "Speak, Painting: Word and Device in Early Johns." *October* 127 (2009): 49–76.

Coover, Robert. "Literary Hypertext: The Passing of the Golden Age." *Feed* (2000) originally: http://www.feedmag.com/document/do291lofi.html (now offline) also available: http://nickm.com/vox/golden_age.html (accessed August 13, 2017).

Cramer, Florian. "Digital Code and Literary Text." *BeeHive Hypertext/Hypermedia Literary Journal* 4, no. 3 (2001). http://beehive.temporalimage.com/ archive/43arc.html (accessed August 13, 2017).

Cunningham, Michael. "The Virtual Tourist [a Short Interview with William Gibson]." *The Irish Times*, October 12, 1996. https://www.irishtimes.com/news/the-virtual-tourist-1.95256 (accessed August 13, 2017).

Danielewski, Mark Z. *House of Leaves*. 2nd ed. New York: Pantheon Books, 2000.

Darnton, Robert. "Google's Loss: The Public's Gain." *The New York Review of Books* LVII, no. 7 (April 28, 2011): 10–12.

Dehaene, Stanislas. *Reading in the Brain: The Science and Evolution of a Human Invention*. New York: Viking, 2009.

Derrida, Jacques. "The Book to Come." Translated by Rachel Bowlby. Chap. 1. In *Paper Machine*, 4–18. Stanford, CA: Stanford University Press, 2005.

Derrida, Jacques. "Freud and the Scene of Writing." Translated by Alan Bass. In *Writing and Difference*, 196–231. London: Routledge, 1978.

Derrida, Jacques. "Le facteur de la vérité." Translated by Alan Bass. In *The Post Card*, 413–96. Chicago: University of Chicago Press, 1987.

Derrida, Jacques. *Of Grammatology*. Translated by Gayatri Chakravorty Spivak. Corrected ed. Baltimore and London: Johns Hopkins University Press, 1997 [1967], First American edition, 1976.

Derrida, Jacques. "Paper or Me, You Know …" Translated by Rachel Bowlby. Chap. 5. In *Paper Machine*, 41–65. Stanford, CA: Stanford University Press, 2005.

Derrida, Jacques. "The Word Processor." Translated by Rachel Bowlby. Chap. 2. In *Paper Machine*, 19–32. Stanford, CA: Stanford University Press, 2005.

Diski, Jenny. "Short Cuts." *London Review of Books* 33, no. 2 (January 20, 2011): 20. http://www.lrb.co.uk/v33/n02/jenny-diski/short-cuts (accessed August 13, 2017).

Drucker, Johanna. "Humanities Approaches to Graphical Display." *Digital Humanities Quarterly* 5, no. 1 (2011). http://digitalhumanities.org/dhq/vol/5/1/000091/000091.html (accessed August 13, 2017).

ELMCIP Knowledge Base. Electronic Literature as a Model of Creativity and Innovation in Practice (ELMCIP), 2011. https://elmcip.net/knowledgebase (accessed August 14, 2017).

Fisher, Allen. *Defamiliarising _____ **. London: Veer Books, 2013. Spanner, 1982.

Flusser, Vilém. *Does Writing Have a Future?* [in Translated from the German]. Translated by Nancy Ann Roth. Electronic Mediations. Minneapolis: University of Minnesota Press, 2011.

Flusser, Vilém. *Into the Universe of Technical Images*. Translated by Nancy Ann Roth. Electronic Mediations. Minneapolis: University of Minnesota Press, 2011.

Foucault, Michel. *Ceci n'est pas une pipe*. Montpellier: Éditions Fata Morgana, 1973. Réimprimée le 21 janvier 2005 par Georges Monti à Cognac.

Foucault, Michel. *This Is Not a Pipe* ["Ceci n'est pas une pipe"]. Translated by James Harkness. Berkeley: University of California Press, 2008. University of California Press, 1983; Montpellier: Éditions Fata Morgana, 1973.

Freud, Sigmund. "The Unconscious." In *On Metapsychology: The Theory of Psychoanalysis*, edited by Angela Richards. The Penguin Freud Library, 161–222. Harmondsworth: Penguin Books, 1991.

Funkhouser, Christopher T. "Le(s) Mange Texte(s): Creative Cannibalism and Digital Poetry." In *E-Poetry 2007*. http://epoetry.paragraphe.info/english/papers/funkhouseruk.pdf. Paris: Université Paris8, 2007.

Funkhouser, Christopher T. *New Directions in Digital Poetry*. International Texts in Critical Media Aesthetics. Edited by Francisco J. Ricardo. New York: Continuum, 2012.

Funkhouser, Christopher T. *Prehistoric Digital Poetry: An Archaeology of Forms, 1959–1995*. Tuscaloosa: University of Alabama Press, 2007.

Gendolla, Peter, and Jörgen Schäfer, eds. *The Aesthetics of Net Literature: Writing, Reading and Playing in Programmable Media*, Media Upheavals. Bielefeld: Transcript, 2007.

Genette, Gérard. *Paratexts: Thresholds of Interpretation*. Translated by Jane E. Lewin. Literature, Culture, Theory. Edited by Richard Macksey and Michael Sprinker. 1st English ed. Cambridge: Cambridge University Press, 1997 [1987].

Glazier, Loss Pequeño. *Digital Poetics: The Making of E-Poetries*. Tuscaloosa: University of Alabama Press, 2002.

Glazier, Loss Pequeño. "White-Faced Bromeliads on 20 Hectares." Electronic Poetry Center. http://wings.buffalo.edu/epc/authors/glazier/java/costa1/00.html (accessed August 13, 2017).

Goldsmith, Kenneth. *Day*. New Barrington: The Figures, 2003.

Golumbia, David. *The Cultural Logic of Computation*. Cambridge, MA: Harvard University Press, 2009.

Goodman, Nelson. *Ways of Worldmaking*. Indianapolis: Hackett Pub. Co., 1978.

Grenier, Robert. *Sentences*. 1st ed. Cambridge: Whale Cloth Press, 1978.

Hansen, Mark B. N. *New Philosophy for New Media*. Cambridge, MA: MIT Press, 2006 [2004].

Harpold, Terry. "Hypertext." In *Glossalalia*, edited by Julian Wolfreys and Harun Karim Thomas, 113–26. New York: Routledge, 2003.

Harrist Jr., Robert E. "*Book from the Sky* at Princeton: Reflections on Scale, Sense, and Sound." In *Persistence | Transformation: Text as Image in the Art of Xu Bing*, edited by Jerome Silbergeld and Dora C. Y. Ching, 25–45. Princeton, NJ: P. Y. and Kinmay W. Tang Center for East Asian Art, 2006.

Hartman, Charles O. *Virtual Muse: Experiments in Computer Poetry*. Hanover: Wesleyan University Press, 1996.

Hartman, Charles O., and Hugh Kenner. *Sentences*. New American Poetry Series. 1st pbk. ed. Los Angeles: Sun & Moon Press, 1995.

Hayles, N. Katherine. "Bodies of Texts, Bodies of Subjects: Metaphoric Networks in New Media." Paper presented at the Digital Arts and Culture conference, Providence, RI, 2001.

Hayles, N. Katherine. "Distributed Cognition in/at Work: Strickland, Lawson Jaramillo, and Ryan's *slippingglimpse*." *Frame* 21, no. 1 (May 2008): 15–29. http://www.tijdschriftframe.nl/wp-content/uploads/2014/06/02.-N.-Katherine-Hayles-Distributed-Cognition-at-in-Work-Strickland-Lawson-Jaramillo-and-Ryans-Slippingglimpse-main.pdf (accessed August 13, 2017).

Hayles, N. Katherine. *Electronic Literature: New Horizons for the Literary*. Ward-Phillips Lectures in English Language and Literature. Notre Dame: University of Notre Dame, 2008.

Hayles, N. Katherine. "Electronic Literature: What Is It?" In *Electronic Literature: New Horizons for the Literary*, 1–42. Notre Dame: University of Notre Dame, 2008.

Hayles, N. Katherine. *How We Became Posthuman: Virtual Bodies in Cybernetics, Literature, and Informatics*. Chicago: University of Chicago Press, 1999.

Hayles, N. Katherine. "Prologue." In *How We Became Posthuman: Virtual Bodies in Cybernetics, Literature, and Informatics*, xi–xiv. Chicago: University of Chicago Press, 1999.

Hayles, N. Katherine. "Translating Media: Why We Should Rethink Textuality." *The Yale Journal of Criticism* 16, no. 2 (Fall 2003): 263–90.

Hayles, N. Katherine. "Virtual Bodies and Flickering Signifiers." In *Electronic Culture: Technology and Visual Representation*, edited by Timothy Druckrey, 259–77. New York: Aperture, 1996.

Hayles, N. Katherine. "Virtual Bodies and Flickering Signifiers." In *How We Became Posthuman: Virtual Bodies in Cybernetics, Literature, and Informatics*, 25–49. Chicago: University of Chicago Press, 1999.

Hayles, N. Katherine. *Writing Machines*. Mediawork. Cambridge, MA: MIT Press, 2002.

Heidegger, Martin. *Poetry, Language, Thought*. Translated by Albert Hofstader. Harper Colophon ed. New York: Harper and Row, 1975 [1971].

Hicks, William P. Email, March 29, 2016.

Hill, Kashmir. "Facebook Will Be Using Your Face in "Sponsored Stories" Ads (and There's No Opting Out)." *Forbes*, 2011. http://www.forbes.com/sites/kashmirhill/2011/01/25/facebook-will-be-using-your-face-in-sponsored-stories-ads-and-theres-no-opting-out/ (accessed January 25, 2011).

Hockett, Charles F. *A Course in Modern Linguistics*. New York: Macmillan, 1958.

Howe, Daniel C., and John Cayley. "*The Readers Project*: Procedural Agents and Literary Vectors." *Leonardo* 44, no. 4 (August 2011): 317–24. http://www.mitpressjournals.org/doi/abs/10.1162/LEON_a_00208 (accessed August 13, 2017).

Howe, Daniel C., and Helen Nissenbaum. *TrackMeNot*. 2008. https://rednoise.org/~dhowe/detail.html#trackmenot (accessed August 3, 2017).

Huff, Jason, Mimi Cabell, and Brett Easton Ellis. *American Psycho*. 2010. Multimedia, aesthetically reconfigured version of Easton-Ellis' novel. http://jason-huff.com/projects/american-pyscho/ (accessed August 13, 2017). [Also published/documented: Print version available from http://traumawien.at/prints/american-psycho/ (accessed August 13, 2017), ELMCIP Knowledge Base https://elmcip.net/node/5248 (accessed August 14, 2017).]

Hurford, James R. *The Origins of Grammar*. Language in the Light of Evolution. Oxford and New York: Oxford University Press, 2012.

Hurford, James R. *The Origins of Language: A Slim Guide*. Oxford: Oxford University Press, 2014.

Illich, Ivan. *The Rivers North of the Future: The Testament of Ivan Illich as Told to David Cayley*. Toronto: Anansi, 2005.

Jackson, Shelley. *Skin: A Story Published on the Skin of 2095 Volunteers*. 2003. http://ineradicablestain.com/skindex.html (accessed August 3, 2017).

Jodi. *www.jodi.org*. Jodi, 1980. http://www.jodi.org (accessed August 13, 2017).

Johnston, David Jhave. *Aesthetic Animism: Digital Poetry's Ontological Implications*. Cambridge, MA: MIT Press, 2016.

Joyce, Michael. *afternoon: A Story*. Cambridge, MA: Eastgate Systems, 1990.

Joyce, Michael. *Of Two Minds: Hypertext Peda-gogy and Poetics*. Ann Arbor: University of Michigan Press, 1995.

Kac, Eduardo. "Holopoetry and Fractal Holopoetry." *Leonardo* 22, no. 3 & 4 (1989): 397–402. http://www.ekac.org/holo.leonardo.eng.html (accessed August 13, 2017).

Kac, Eduardo, ed. *Media Poetry: An International Anthology.* Bristol: Intellect Books, 2007.

Katko, Justin, and Clement Valla. *Yelling at a Wall: Textron Eat Shreds.* Providence, RI: Plantarchy, 2008. http://plantarchy.us/katko/processing/yelling-at-a-wall/ (accessed August 3, 2017).

Kendall, Robert. *A Life Set for Two.* Cambridge, MA: Eastgate Systems, 1996.

Kenner, Hugh. *The Mechanic Muse.* Oxford: Oxford University Press, 1987.

Kenner, Hugh, and Joseph O'Rourke. "A Travesty Generator for Micros." *Byte,* November 1984, 129–31; 449–69.

Kirschenbaum, Matthew G. *Mechanisms: New Media and the Forensic Imagination.* Cambridge, MA: MIT Press, 2008.

Kirschenbaum, Matthew G. *Track Changes: A Literary History of Word Processing.* Cambridge: The Belknap Press of Harvard University Press, 2016.

Kittler, Friedrich A. "There Is No Software." In *Literature Media Information Systems,* edited by John Johnston. Critical Voices in Art, Theory and Culture, 147–55. Amsteldijk: G+B Arts International, 1997.

Krauss, Rosalind E. "Notes on the Index." *October* 3–4 (1977): 68–81; 58–67.

Kuszai, Joel, ed. *Poetics@.* New York: Roof Books, 1999.

Lacan, Jacques. "Seminar on 'The Purloined Letter'." Translated by Bruce Fink. In *Écrits: The First Complete Edition in English,* 6–48. New York and London: Norton, 2007.

Landow, George P. *Hypertext: The Convergence of Contemporary Critical Theory and Technology.* Baltimore and London: Johns Hopkins University Press, 1992.

Landow, George P., ed. *Hyper/Text/Theory.* Baltimore: Johns Hopkins University Press, 1994.

Larsen, Caleb. *Whose Life Is It Anyway?* 2008. http://projects.caleblarsen.com/ambv2/Site/Home.html (accessed August 3, 2017).

Lecercle, Jean-Jacques, and Denise Riley. *The Force of Language.* Language, Discourse, Society. Houndmills and New York: Palgrave Macmillan, 2004.

Lethem, Jonathan. "The Ecstasy of Influence: A Plagiarism." *Harper's Magazine,* February 2007, 59–71. http://www.harpers.com/archive/2007/0081387, http://www.harpers.com/archive/2007/0081387 (accessed August 13, 2017).

Liu, Alan. *The Laws of Cool: Knowledge Work and the Culture of Information.* Chicago: University of Chicago Press, 2004.

Lovink, Geert. *Networks without a Cause: A Critique of Social Media.* Cambridge: Polity, 2011.

Lucretius. *The Nature of the Universe.* Translated by R. E. Latham. Harmondsworth: Penguin, 1951.

Lukka, Tuomas J. "GZigZag Glossary." http://www.nongnu.org/gzz/gl/gl-ns4.html (accessed August 13, 2017).

Lukka, Tuomas J. "GZigZag: A Platform for Cybertext Experiments." In *Cybertext Yearbook 2000,* edited by Markku Eskelinen and Raine Koskimaa. Publications of the Research Centre for Contemporary Culture, 141–51. Jyväskylä: University of Jyväskylä, 2001.

Mac Low, Jackson. *Representative Works: 1938–1985*. New York: Roof Books, 1986.

Mac Low, Jackson. *The Virginia Woolf Poems*. Providence, RI: Burning Deck, 1985.

Mac Low, Jackson, and Kurt Schwitters. *42 Merzgedichte in Memoriam Kurt Schwitters: February 1987–September 1989*. 1st ed. Barrytown, NY: Station Hill, 1994.

Manovich, Lev. *The Language of New Media*. Cambridge, MA: MIT Press, 2001.

Mathews, Harry. *20 Lines a Day*. 1st pbk. ed. Normal, IL: Dalkey Archive Press, 1989.

Mathews, Harry, and Alastair Brotchie, eds. *Oulipo Compendium*. London: Atlas Press, 1998.

McCaffery, Steve. *Panopticon*. 1st ed. Toronto: blewointmentpress, 1984.

Memmott, Talan. *From Lexia to Perplexia*. Originally by Trace; then BeeHive Hypertext/Hypermedia Literary Journal; then *The Electronic Literature Collection*, vol. 1 (2006), 2000. Flash and web-based implementations. http://collection.eliterature.org/1/works/memmott__lexia_to_perplexia.html (accessed August 13, 2017). [Also published/documented: ELMCIP Knowledge Base https://elmcip.net/node/65 (accessed August 14, 2017).]

Michel, Jean-Baptiste, Yuan Kui Shen, Aviva Presser Aiden, Adrian Veres, Matthew K. Gray, The Google Books Team, Joseph P. Pickett et al. "Quantitative Analysis of Culture Using Millions of Digitized Books." *Science* 331, no. 6014 (January 14, 2011): 176–82. http://www.sciencemag.org/content/331/6014/176 (accessed August 13, 2017).

Mitchell, W. J. T. "Metapictures." In *Picture Theory: Essays on Verbal and Visual Representation*, 35–82. Chicago: University of Chicago Press, 1995.

Mitchell, W. J. T. *Picture Theory: Essays on Verbal and Visual Representation*. Chicago: University of Chicago Press, 1995.

Montaigne, Michel Eyquem de. "Of the Institution and Education of Children." Translated by John Florio. In *Literary and Philosophical Essays: French, German and Italian*. The Harvard Classics, 29–73. New York: P. F. Collier & Son Company, 1910.

Montfort, Nick. *ppg256 series: Perl Poetry Generators in 256 characters*. 2008-ongoing. http://nickm.com/poems/ppg256.html (accessed August 13, 2017). [Also published/documented: ELMCIP Knowledge Base https://elmcip.net/node/400 (accessed August 14, 2017).]

Montfort, Nick. *#! [Shebang]*. Denver: Counterpath, 2014.

Montfort, Nick, and Stephanie Strickland. "Cut to Fit the Tool-Spun Course: Discussing Creative Code in Comments." *Digital Humanities Quarterly* 7, no. 1 (2013). http://www.digitalhumanities.org/dhq/vol/7/1/000149/000149.html (accessed August 13, 2017).

Montfort, Nick, and Stephanie Strickland. *Sea and Spar Between*. In *Dear Navigator*, SAIC, Chicago, 2010. http://blogs.saic.edu/dearnavigator/winter2010/nick-montfort-stephanie-strickland-sea-and-spar-between/ (accessed August 13, 2017). [Also published/documented: ELMCIP Knowledge Base https://elmcip.net/node/978 (accessed August 14, 2017).]

Motte, Warren F. *Oulipo: A Primer of Potential Literature*. Lincoln: University of Nebraska Press, 1986.

Nelson, Theodor Holm. *Computer Lib/Dream Machines*. Revised and updated ed. Redmond: Tempus Books of Microsoft Press, 1987. Microsoft Press, 1974.

Nelson, Theodor Holm. *Literary Machines 93.1*. Sausalito: Mindful Press, 1993 [1981].

Nelson, Theodor Holm. "Zigzag." http://xanadu.com/zigzag (accessed August 13, 2017).

Nunberg, Geoffrey. "Google's Book Search: A Disaster for Scholars." *The Chronicle of Higher Education*, August 31, 2009. http://chronicle.com/article/Googles-Book-Search-A/48245/ (accessed August 13, 2017).

Ong, Walter J. *Orality and Literacy: The Technologizing of the Word*. New Accents. Edited by Terence Hawkes. London: Routledge, 1982 [1995].

Pastior, Oskar. *Many Glove Compartments: Selected Poems*. Translated by Harry Mathews, Christopher Middleton and Rosemarie Waldrop. Providence, RI: Burning Deck, 2001.

Pastior, Oskar. *Poempoems*. Printed Head. London: Atlas Press, 1991 [1973].

Perloff, Marjorie. *Radical Artifice: Writing Poetry in the Age of Media*. Chicago: University of Chicago Press, 1991.

Phillips, Tom, and W. H. Mallock. *A Humument: A Treated Victorian Novel*. 4th ed. New York: Thames & Hudson, 2005.

Pieraccini, Roberto. *The Voice in the Machine: Building Computers That Understand Speech*. Cambridge, MA: MIT Press, 2012. doi:9786613594389.

Place, Vanessa, and Robert Fitterman. *Notes on Conceptualisms*. Brooklyn: Ugly Duckling Presse, 2009.

Raley, Rita. "Interferences: [Net.Writing] and the Practice of Codework." *Electronic Book Review* (2002). http://www.electronicbookreview.com/thread/electropoetics/net.writing (accessed August 13, 2017).

Rasula, Jed, and Steve McCaffery, eds. *Imagining Language: An Anthology*. Cambridge, MA: MIT Press, 1998.

Raworth, Tom. *Logbook*. Berkeley, CA: Poltroon Press, 1977.

Raworth, Tom. *Writing: [Poems]*. Berkeley, CA: Figures, 1982.

Retallack, Joan. "Blue Notes on the Know Ledge." In *The Poethical Wager*, 63–80. Berkeley: University of California Press, 2003.

Retallack, Joan. *The Poethical Wager*. Berkeley: University of California Press, 2003.

Roberts, Andrew Michael. "Why Digital Literature Has Always Been 'Beyond the Screen'." In *Beyond the Screen: Transformations of Literary Structures, Interfaces and Genres*, edited by Peter Gendolla and Jörgen Schäfer. Media Upheavals, 153–77. Bielefeld: Transcript, 2010.

Robertson, Lisa. *Debbie: An Epic*. Vancouver: New Star Books, 1997.

Rosenberg, Jim. *The Barrier Frames: Finality Crystal Shunt Curl Chant Quickening Giveaway Stare; Diffractions Through: Thirst Weep Ransack (Frailty) Veer Tide Elegy*. Cambridge, MA: Eastgate Systems, 1996. Issued for both Macintosh and PC computers on 3.5" floppy disk.

Rosenberg, Jim. *Intergrams*. Cambridge, MA: Eastgate Systems, 1993. Issued for both Macintosh and PC computers on 3.5" floppy disk.

Rosenberg, Jim. "Questions About the Second Move." In *Ergodic Poetry: A Special Section of the Cybertext Yearbook 2002*, edited by Loss Pequeño Glazier and John Cayley. Publications of the Research Centre for Contemporary Culture, 83–87. Jyväskylä: University of Jyväskylä, 2003.

Rothenberg, Jerome, and Pierre Joris, eds. *Poems for the Millennium: The University of California Book of Modern and Postmodern Poetry, Vol. 1: From Fin-de-Siècle to Negritude.* Berkeley: University of California Press, 1995.

Rothenberg, Jerome, and Pierre Joris, eds. *Poems for the Millennium: The University of California Book of Modern and Postmodern Poetry, Vol. 2: From Postwar to Millennium.* Berkeley: University of California Press, 1998.

Rubery, Matthew. *The Untold Story of the Talking Book.* Cambridge, MA: Harvard University Press, 2016. doi:40026531325.

Russo, Salvatore. "Data vs. Capta or Sumpta." *American Psychologist* 12, no. 5 (1957): 283–84.

Shields, David. *Reality Hunger: A Manifesto.* New York: Alfred A. Knopf, 2010.

Shriener, David, Jackie Neider, Mason Woo, and Tom Davis. *OpenGL Programming Guide: Fourth Edition: The Official Guide to Learning OpenGL, Version 1.4.* Boston, MA: Addison-Wesley, 2004.

Simanowski, Roberto. "Digital Anthropophagy: Refashioning Words as Image, Sound and Action." *Leonardo* 43, no. 2 (2010): 159–63.

Simanowski, Roberto, ed. *Digital Humanities and Digital Media: Conversations on Politics, Culture, Aesthetics, and Literacy.* Edited by Andrew Murphie, Fibreculture Books. London: Open Humanities Press, 2016.

Soderman, A. Braxton. *Mémoire involontaire No. 1. Electronic Literature Collection*, vol. 2 (2011). http://collection.eliterature.org/2/works/soderman_memory.html (accessed August 13, 2017), 2008. http://thefollowingphrases.com/memory/memory.html (accessed August 3, 2017).

Sondheim, Alan. "Introduction: Codework." *American Book Review* 22, no. 6 (September/October 2001): 1, 4.

Sondheim, Alan. *Jennifer.* Salt Lake City: Nominative Press Collective, 1998.

Stefans, Brian Kim. "Stops and Rebels: A Critique of Hypertext." In *Fashionable Noise: On Digital Poetics*, 61–169. Berkeley, CA: Atelos, 2003.

Stiegler, Bernard. "Digital Knowledge, Obsessive Computing, Short-Termism and Need for a Negentropic Web." In *Digital Humanities and Digital Media: Conversations on Politics, Culture, Aesthetics, and Literacy*, edited by Roberto Simanowski, 290–304. London: Open Humanities Press, 2016.

Stiegler, Bernard. *For a New Critique of Political Economy.* Cambridge: Polity, 2010.

Stiegler, Bernard. *What Makes Life Worth Living: On Pharmacology.* Translated by Daniel Ross. English ed. Cambridge, UK and Malden, MA: Polity Press, 2013.

Strickland, Stephanie. *V—WaveSon.nets. V—losing l'una.* Penguin Poets. New York: Penguin, 2002.

Strickland, Stephanie, Cynthia Lawson Jaramillo, and Paul Ryan. *Slippingglimpse.* 2007. http://slippingglimpse.org (accessed August 13, 2017). [Also published/documented: ELMCIP Knowledge Base https://elmcip.net/node/461 (accessed August 14, 2017).]

Sylvester, David, Sarah Whitfield, Michael Raeburn, and Menil Foundation. *René Magritte: Catalogue Raisonné*, 5 vols. Houston and London: Menil Foundation; Philip Wilson Publishers, 1992.

Tabbi, Joseph, ed. *The Bloomsbury Handbook of Electronic Literature.* New York and London: Bloomsbury Academic, 2017.

Taylor, Charles. *The Language Animal: The Full Shape of the Human Linguistic Capacity*. Cambridge: The Belknap Press of Harvard University Press, 2016.

Templeton, Fiona. *You the City*. New York: Roof Books, 1990.

Themerson, Stefan. *On Semantic Poetry*. London: Gaberbocchus Press, 1975.

Ulmer, Gregory L. *Applied Grammatology: Post(E)-Pedagogy from Jacques Derrida to Joseph Beuys*. Baltimore: Johns Hopkins University Press, 1985.

Ulmer, Gregory L. *Heuretics: The Logic of Invention*. Baltimore: Johns Hopkins University Press, 1994.

Valla, Clement. *Postcards from Google Earth*. 2010. http://www.postcards-from-google-earth.com (accessed 20 March, 2016).

Valla, Clement. *Surface Proxy*. Paris: XPO Gallery, 2015.

Vološinov, V. N. *Marxism and the Philosophy of Language*. Translated by Ladislav Matejka and I. R. Titunik. Cambridge and London: Seminar Press, 1973. Leningrad, 1929.

Wardrip-Fruin, Noah. *Expressive Processing: Digital Fictions, Computer Games, and Software Studies*. Cambridge, MA: MIT Press, 2009.

Wark, McKenzie. *A Hacker Manifesto*. Cambridge, MA: Harvard University Press, 2004.

Wark, McKenzie. "The Vectoralist Class." *Supercommunity* 84 (2015). http://supercommunity.e-flux.com/texts/the-vectoralist-class/ (accessed August 13, 2017).

Watts, Jonathan. "China's Internet Crackdown Forced Google Retreat." *The Guardian*, January 13, 2010. http://gu.com/p/2dnqk (accessed August 13, 2017).

Weiner, Hannah. *Spoke*. Los Angeles: Sun & Moon Press, 1984.

"William Gibson (1948–)." *The Guardian*, July 22, 2008. http://books.guardian.co.uk/authors/author/0,5917,96528,00.html (accessed August 13, 2017).

Williams, Emmett. *Selected Shorter Poems 1950–1970*. New York: New Directions, 1975.

Williams, Emmett. *A Valentine for Noël: Four Variations on a Scheme*. Stuttgart and London: Editions Hanjörg Mayer, 1973.

INDEX

CPSIA information can be obtained
at www.ICGtesting.com
Printed in the USA
LVHW011408090821
694887LV00010B/569

9 781501 363184